CW00673273

Faith&Fate

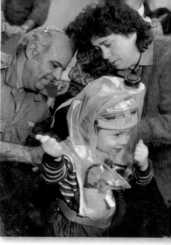

Faith

THE STORY OF THE JEWISH PEOPLE

A SHAAR PRESS PUBLICATION

&Fate

IN THE TWENTIETH CENTURY

BEREL WEIN

Published by SHAAR PRESS
and Distributed by MESORAH PUBLICATIONS, LTD.
4401 Second Avenue / Brooklyn, NY 11232 / (718) 921-9000 / www.artscroll.com

Distributed in Israel by SIFRIATI / A. GITLER
6 Hayarkon Street / Bnei Brak 51127 / Israel

Distributed in Europe by LEHMANNS
Unit E, Viking Industrial Park, Rolling Mill Road / Jarrow, Tyne and Wear, NE32 3DP / England

Distributed in Australia and New Zealand by GOLDS WORLD OF JUDAICA
3-13 William Street / Balaclava, Melbourne 3183, Victoria / Australia

Distributed in South Africa by KOLLEL BOOKSHOP
Shop 8A Norwood Hypermarket/ Norwood 2196 / Johannesburg, South Africa

ISBN: 1-57819-593-4

Printed in the United States of America by Noble Book Press
Custom bound by Sefercraft, Inc. / 4401 Second Avenue / Brooklyn NY 11232

Table of Contents

Faith & Fate

Introduction

EASURING THE PASSAGE OF TIME IN HUMAN AFFAIRS IS DONE BY arbitrary means. There are numerous calendars that exist in human society, and the units of time measured by them — years, centuries, millennia — all have different points of departure and ending. Today, one measure of time has come to dominate world civilization. That measure, Christian in origin but today secular in practice, records that we have recently ended the twentieth century and are now embarking on our journey of life in the twenty-first century. For convenience and historical understanding therefore, our time is measured in the one-hundred-year spans that mark the passage of centuries according to that general secular calendar. This book will deal with the events and occurrences of the recently completed twentieth century with a specific focus on to how those events and occurrences impacted on the Jewish people. But since the Jewish people do not live in a vacuum of time or space, the general story of mankind during this century will necessarily serve as the backdrop and frame for the particular Jewish story.

Perhaps no century in human existence has witnessed the terrible contrasts of the twentieth century. War, plague and organized governmental murder during that century snuffed out the lives of at least 150 million people: equivalent to the entire population of the world at the time of Julius Caesar. The terrible technology of war created fiendish new ways to maim and kill. But as a counterpart, the medical technology of war saved millions of wounded and pioneered breakthroughs in the use of new drugs, surgical procedures and breathtaking diagnostic and therapeutic technology. Agriculture became ever more productive as the world's population tripled in the century and therefore, in theory, there was enough food for all. But the reality was that a third of the world suffered from problems of obesity while the rest of mankind teetered on the brink of malnutrition. Monarchies and empires disappeared from the political scene but totalitarian regimes and cruel dictators persisted in the Balkans, the Middle East, South America and Asia. Humans walked on the moon and airplanes linked the world's countries, but ancient quarrels and ethnic tensions remained seemingly as strong as ever.

It was a century of enormous human progress in knowledge and communication. Scientific discovery and research helped to unravel many of the mysteries of nature and of the human body. Physicists discovered new ways of seeing the unseen and understanding the previously unknown. At the end of the century, the computer had revolutionized world commerce as well as individual behavior and work habits. Television became the most influential social tool in the world, for better or for worse. Psychology and psychiatry began to unravel the workings of the human mind, and the stresses causing imperfect mental health were revealed and categorized. It is no wonder then that the great advances in all these areas began to force a reassessment of long-held verities, beliefs and societal norms. But the basic nature of human beings had not changed and it is that basic nature, more than anything else, which is the determining catalyst of human history — certainly of the history of the twentieth century.

No nation or religious community in the world was more affected by the events of the twentieth century than was world Jewry. The bitter conflict between the forces of secularism and modernism on one hand and tradition and ritual observance on the other hand — a struggle that began in the eighteenth century and shows no sign of abatement even now in the twenty-first century — would govern much of the twentieth century Jewish story. But this internal struggle, persistent and important as it may be, was dwarfed by the external events that shaped the Jewish people in the 1900's. Every period of that century — pre-World War I Europe and America, the Great War, the time between the wars, the Great Depression, the rise of Hitler and Stalin, World War II, the Holocaust, the creation of the State of Israel, the Cold War, the continuing Arab-Israeli wars, the social revolutions of the 1960's, '70's and '80's, the globalization of commerce, the collapse of the Soviet Union, the Gulf War — all intimately involved the Jewish people.

It is no exaggeration to state that the twentieth century changed the makeup, direction and face of world Jewry as no other century had done for nineteen hundred years. It must also be said that no century in world civilization changed the way that civilizations and societies viewed themselves. All of the verities and long-held beliefs of all world societies and beliefs were called into question by the events of the twentieth century. It is for these reasons that it deserves the attention and study of all human beings and especially of contemporary Jews living at the cusp of the next century. For there is no substitute for knowing the past: it serves the vital purpose of assessing the present intelligently and accurately.

Most of the events revolved about the major wars — hot and cold — that bloodied these past hundred years. Though war is a constant in all human history, no century saw war conducted on such a global and ferocious scale as did the twentieth century. Though Jews were involved in all of the wars, it would not be wrong to state, as did the historian Lucy Davidowicz, that the Second World War in Europe, initiated by Germany, was a war *against* the Jews. That such a war could and did take place in the heartland of twentieth century Christian Europe came as a major and surprising shock to world Jewry, which was completely unprepared for even the possibility of such an eventuality. The shadow of the Holocaust hovers over all other events of the last five decades of the century, and not only as far as Jews are concerned. Because of the "success" of the Holocaust, mass murder and genocide became publicly acceptable methods of settling ancient scores — real or imagined — and yet so reprehensible that war criminals were apprehended and actually subjected to prosecution and punishment.

The twentieth century, therefore, was a century of ambivalence and mixed messages. Terrorism on a global scale was clandestinely justified by governments and religious groups while at the same time it was officially and piously condemned by almost all world leaders. Nationalism remained strong, virulent and dangerous, and yet for the first time an effective supra-nationalist international organization was created and operated with some effectiveness and influence. Formal religion weakened in much of the developed world while making great strides among the masses of the less developed areas of the globe. Women, racial and ethnic minorities and workers the world over gained rights and opportunities denied them in previous centuries, and yet bigotry, chauvinism and economic exploitation continued to ravage much of the world. The twentieth century was heroic and terrible, progressive and reactionary, forward-looking and frighteningly regressive. It is this confusion and contradiction, both in general and Jewish world terms, that more than anything else defines this century.

In a dramatic, almost tragic way, the twentieth century would serve to unite the two main societal streams of the Jewish people — the Sephardim and the Ashkenazim. By 1900, the Ashkenazim far outnumbered the Sephardim in population by a ratio of at least three to one. The Ashkenazim had undergone great changes, even revolutions, in the preceding centuries: These changes, and the ideas and ideals they represented, were both internal and external to the Ashkenazic Jewish world. That world was rocked by the movements of *Chasidus, Haskalah*, Reform, Emancipation, Zionism, Marxism, secularism and mass emigration. All of the events of the eighteenth and nineteenth centuries in Europe had little influence on the Sephardim who lived around the Mediterranean basin and in the Middle East. In the main, the Sephardim escaped these seismic events and thus entered the twentieth century with a completely different culture and worldview than their Ashkenzic brothers.

Ultimately, the horrific and sometimes heroic events of Jewish life in the twentieth century would smash the old Sephardic world order just as it had destroyed the European Jewish world forever. The Sephardim would be forced to confront the challenges of modernity, rapid change, societal dislocation, violence and rebirth.

I have chosen to record the events of this century in a loosely chronological order, approximately decade by decade. Though I have not followed any general theme of categorization by geography, economic theory, political, social and religious movements, or theory of history in the book, an overlapping of the dates and decades in the book will necessarily have occurred in order to render the story in a clearer and more logical fashion (even though history always defies logic). I have concentrated on describing in some detail Orthodox Jewish life in this century as part of the overall story. This is due to my personal bias that Orthodoxy remains the most vital and creative element in the Jewish world and also because of my belief in the divinity of Torah, the authenticity of the Orthodox tradition and its unique role in ensuring the survival of the Jewish people throughout the ages. Nevertheless, I have attempted not to ignore other movements and groupings in the Jewish story of this last century and to accord them their fair due. This work is meant as a history book and not as a religious polemic.

My sincerest appreciation is extended to the executives and staff of Shaar Press who have published this book, as they have my previous books. I treasure their personal friendship and professional advice. Rabbi Nosson Scherman has contributed greatly to this book by reading the entire draft and commenting upon it. His insights, knowledge and good sense have saved me from many an error in fact and judgment in this writing. I am grateful for his interest, time and effort in this book, as well as being rewarded by his good cheer and warm friendship. I especially wish to thank Charlotte Friedland for her superb editing skills and her devotion to improving the original draft of this book. I am indebted to her for her insights, comments and tenacity in persuading a recalcitrant author to review his work, clarify his opinions and refine his language and style.

Many thanks are due to the talented people who have assisted me in this project and contributed their outstanding skills to its success. My appreciation goes to Art Director Eli Kroen, Hershy Feuerwerker, the designer of the book and its cover, Avrohom Kay for his work on maps and pictures, as well as to Tzini Hanover and Frady Vorhand for their work. Shmuel Blitz is thanked for his expertise and for his help in procuring photographs in Israel. Proofreader Tova Ovits labored with dedication and admirable precision over the entire book.

My wife and family have extended me their vital support and understanding during the long years of research and months of writing. May they be blessed for their kindness and patience. I have no words to truly express my love and gratitude to them. And above all, I am thankful to the God of Israel who has preserved me in life and health and allowed me to be a participant in the story of my people over the last century.

Berel Wein
Jerusalem, 5761/2001

Chapter One

At the Dawn of the Century

1901-1910

ALL NEW BEGINNINGS ARE VIEWED WITH GREAT HOPE. THE NEW YEAR is always represented in the popular mind and media as a newborn infant, symbolizing the hope for the future and for better times. In Jewish tradition, we are taught to say at the conclusion of the old year and the beginning of the new year: "May the misfortunes of the [old] year be ended; may the blessings of the [new] year begin." Although Jews do not count their years or centuries according to the secular calendar, nonetheless the end of the nineteenth century and the beginning of the twentieth century did raise hopes within the Jewish world for a better tomorrow. The nineteenth century, and especially its later decades, had brought major changes to the Jewish world. New movements and ideas arose to challenge the old ways and much of Jewry subscribed to truly revolutionary programs that promised to improve the dismal lot of the Jews. Any change was perceived as being beneficial. Zionism, socialism, trade and labor unionism, great waves of emigration, and the spirit of restless change undermined the hegemony of traditional Jewish life and behavior. What was certain at the beginning of the twentieth century was that vast numbers of Jews were convinced that the old ways were no longer viable and that a new Jew, if not even a new Judaism, had to be created in order to ensure Jewish survival and vitality. In fact, much of the Jewish story of the twentieth century will focus on the illusory pursuit of creating that new Jew and new Judaism.

The general world also labored under false illusions at the beginning of the century. England was engaged in the Boer War in South Africa and there were other military actions being pursued around the world by major and minor powers. At that time, war still was seen as having romance and adventure to it, and it was conducted mostly by relatively small, professional armies. Total war, absorbing all of the population of the nations into its chasm, was to be a twentieth century phenomenon.

In 1900 the British Empire was the sole superpower. It had rivals in Europe, as the United States today has one rival in the European Union, another in Russia and still others in Asia. But the conventional belief a century ago was expressed by Norman Angell in a globally best-selling book in 1910, "The Great Illusion," which held that the common interests of the great powers, and above all their economies, were so closely interlinked and interdependent that war no longer made sense. The existence of empires and the gold standard made the world's economies and international finance more "globalized" than they are today. The destructive forces that were to dominate most of the twentieth century were without influence in 1900 or did not yet exist. Marxism as a political movement was a marginal affair. Lenin was 30 years old and in 1900 was concluding a period of political internment and about to go into exile. Hitler was eleven years old, Mussolini was seventeen, a budding pacifist and socialist. Fascism and Nazism did not exist. The European empires dominated Asia and Africa; the United States was putting together its own empire from the Spanish possessions it had just seized in the Caribbean and the Far East. The Habsburg system was troubled by nationalism in the Balkans and the Ottoman Empire was in decline, but all that seemed manageable ... The twentieth century began in circumstances of apparent security more reassuring than those of today.[1]

In 1900, the vast majority of Jews lived in Eastern Europe. There were close to five million Jews who lived under the autocracy of the czar in Russia, Poland and Lithuania.[2] There were another nearly two million Jews who were subjects of Emperor Franz Josef in the Austro-Hungarian Empire or of the kaiser in Germany.[3] Smaller Jewish communities existed in England, Ireland, Belgium and France. A large

---

1. William Pfaff, article in *International Herald Tribune,* January 6, 2000.

2. Milton Meltzer, *A History of Jewish Life from Eastern Europe to America,* Northvale, N.J. 1996, p.46.

3. Ibid.

Jewish community of over one and a half million also resided in the United States, mainly in New York, composed primarily of recent immigrants from Russia and Central Europe.

The condition of the Jews in Eastern Europe was deplorable. Pogroms, high unemployment, a severe rate of infant mortality, social upheaval due to the pace of urbanization and governmental anti-Semitic decrees were the parameters of everyday life for most Russian Jews. But, above all else, it was the grinding poverty of the Eastern European *shtetl* (small village) that colored Jewish life. An English nobleman, Sir Moses Montefiore, who visited Russia in 1846, reported that in the village of Vilkomir, near Vilna, one-quarter of the town's Jews had died of hunger in the previous year. The situation was not that much improved a half-century later in 1900.

Samuel Schwartz, who came from Nagyzollos in Hungary, described his world:

The poverty of the shtetl fostered yearning for social and economic solutions.

> *When I say poverty I mean a situation which is hardly thinkable in our land of plenty [America]. It was nothing unusual to have been occasionally without bread in the house. To obtain it, we either had to borrow a slice from a neighbor or buy a loaf on credit. It often happened that there was not a match in the house to kindle a stove or light the petroleum lamp, if there was wood in the stove or kerosene in the lamp ... Most of the time our home consisted of one or one and a half rooms and a kitchen. The latter was shared most of the time with another tenant. If you ask how we managed — well, we just managed. Even if I told you, you would not understand ... Our food was sparse and simple ... We often did not have enough wooden spoons with which to consume it when we were all together. Our bread was made of coarse corn meal, not the fancy corn bread we know here as a delicacy, but a huge coarse loaf ... A piece of white bread was a rare treat. Potatoes, beans and other vegetables furnished the diet. Milk was a rarity, as were eggs. Meat was only for Shabbos...*[4]

---

4. Samuel Schwartz, *Tell the Children*, New York, 1959.

Nevertheless, Jewish life in Eastern Europe was still vibrant and varied. The Chasidic *rebbeim* were yet very powerful and influential, especially in Poland, Galicia, Hungary and the Ukraine. The Lithuanian yeshivos, now almost universally under the guidance and direction of the *Mussar* movement (a movement that searched for an ethical and spiritual renewal in Lithuanian Jewry in the late 1800's and early 1900's), continued to grow in numbers, leadership and influence. The main yeshivos in Lithuania were located in the towns and villages of Mir, Telshe, Slobodka, Kelm, Radin, Slonim and Navaradok. After years of closure, the yeshivah in Volozhin reopened at the beginning of the century, though it never was able to regain its former preeminent position in the Torah world. Yeshivos were not limited to Lithuania. In the Austro-Hungarian Empire there were tens of such institutions. The leading yeshivah was in Pressburg (present day Bratislava) and there were other major schools in Chust, Selish (Szollos), Eisenstadt, Matasdorf, Kosice (Kashoy), Eiger (Erloy), Kalov, Munkacz as well as tens of other smaller schools. In Germany, there were also a number of yeshivos, though not necessarily in the form and manner of Lithuania and Hungary.

In Poland, there were almost no formal yeshivos per se, but Torah studies were conducted in the small *shtieblach* (prayer houses) of the Chasidim throughout the country on a daily and intensive basis. Many thousands participated in Torah study in this way. However, in 1909, under the aegis of Rabbi Eliyahu Chaim Meisels, the rabbi of the community, a major yeshivah was founded in Lodz.[5] The great Rabbi Shimon Shkop headed the famous yeshivah Shaar HaTorah, located in Grodno, Poland, which was founded in the early decades of the century. The growth of the yeshivos was great, yet in 1900 there were more Jewish students attending Russian universities than there were yeshivah students.[6]

The yeshivos themselves, especially in Lithuania, were not immune to criticism from the ruling Orthodox establishment. They were seen as advocating a departure from the accepted method of Torah study that had prevailed in Eastern Europe for centuries. The heads of the yeshivos were often seen as undermining the authority and stature of the local rabbis and thus conflicts arose. In most cases, both in Lithuania and in Austria-Hungary, this difficulty was ameliorated by appointing the same person as both community rabbi and head of the local yeshivah. However, this was an imperfect solution for it was quickly recognized that the duties (and the personalities required) of the two positions — com-

Rabbi Shimon Shkop

5. The head of that yeshivah at its founding was Rabbi Shraga Feivel Hindes, the son-in-law of Rabbi Shimon Shkop.
6. Shaul Stampfer, *The Lithuanian Yeshiva*, Jerusalem, 1995, p.224

munal rabbi and academic head of a school – did not often coincide. Tension between the community rabbis and the yeshivos would continue in varying intensities and forms throughout the century.

Change and Turmoil

THE YESHIVOS WERE THE CONDUITS FOR INNOVATIONS IN THE traditional approach to Torah study and normative Jewish life. The *Mussar* movement, which its founder, Rabbi Yisrael Lipkin of Salant, hoped would become a mass movement in Lithuanian Jewish life, instead became almost the exclusive province of the Lithuanian yeshivos. Opponents of the *Mussar* movement attempted to create non-*mussar* yeshivos to counter the influence of the *mussar* yeshivos. For example, the family and confidants of Rabbi Yitzchak Elchanan Spektor, the late rabbi of Kovno (Kaunas) and the halachic authority of his day, founded a competing non-*mussar* yeshivah (named Knesses Bais Yitzchak, for Rabbi Spektor), near the famous school Knesses Bais Yisrael (named for Rabbi Yisrael Lipkin) in Slobodka, a small suburb of Kovno.[7] Nevertheless, the strength and number of the *mussar* yeshivos eventually prevailed. They purposely separated themselves from the organized Jewish communities in which they were located and became not only independent of the local and even general community, but in essence cloistered from them as well. They saw themselves as being spiritual "cities of refuge," "a Noah's Ark against the flood tide of their times," "a citadel in the time of siege."[8] At the same time, however, their presence and their independence contributed to the further erosion of the power and influence of the established rabbinate and Orthodox leaders of the communities, who were then already under severe attack from the forces of secularism then gaining strength in Eastern European Jewry.

Yeshivah Knesses Yisrael in Slobodka

---

7. For a full description of the controversy regarding *mussar,* yeshivos and *kollelim* at the end of the nineteenth century and the beginning of the twentieth century, see *Pulmus HaMussar* by Rabbi Dov Katz, Jerusalem, 1972, chapters seven and eight. Rabbi Boruch Ber Leibowitz, the foremost disciple of Rabbi Chaim Soloveitchik, himself not an adherent of the *Mussar* movement, was the head of the non-*mussar* yeshivah in Slobodka.

8. Mordecai Breuer in *Chinuch V'Historya*, Mercaz Zalman Shazar, Jerusalem, 1975, p.192.

Rabbi Chaim Soloveitchik

It was not only the innovation of *mussar* that brought criticism and opposition to the yeshivos at the beginning of the century. By 1900, most of the Lithuanian yeshivos had adopted the methodology of Talmudic study pioneered by Rabbi Chaim Soloveitchik when he was the assistant head of the yeshivah in Volozhin. "Rabbi Chaim's way" was a radical departure from previous study methods in teaching Talmud. Rabbi Chaim analyzed, dissected and categorized Talmudic concepts and rulings in a detailed and intensive fashion. He also created a new vocabulary to define halachic terms. His explanations were not addressed to interpreting the text as much as they were the method of finding the explanation within the text itself. There was no room for convoluted explanations, no matter how brilliant, in his "way" of learning. The emphasis on pure textual analysis and categorization of ideas was new and soon gained almost universal acceptance and imitation in the Lithuanian yeshivos.[9] Initially, this new method also raised fierce opposition. Perhaps the strongest words uttered against the new method were those of Rabbi Yaakov David Willovsky of Slutzk, (known as *Ridvaz*, later of Chicago and Safed):

> *In this present time, the study of Torah has changed completely ... Instead of the traditional way of learning, a rabbi [meaning Rabbi Chaim Soloveitchik] has invented a way of "chemical analysis" and many have adopted this type of analysis and this has harmed us [the religious Jewish world] greatly. For it is a strange and foreign wind that has entered the study of Talmud, a wind from the outside world, and it is not the method of Torah study that Moses transmitted to us from Sinai. This new method of study has spread amongst the yeshivah students, many of whom know little actual Talmud. By studying Torah in this fashion, the student will never achieve true purity [of thought] and since the day that this new type of study has spread, the Torah has lost its ability to protect its students [from foreign influences]. The few wise men who understand this situation weep in isolation over this.[10]*

The complaint against both *mussar* and "Rabbi Chaim's way" was that they were departures from the previously established norms. The

---

9. See Rabbi S.Y. Zevin's classic *Ishim V'Shittos*, Tel Aviv, 1958, beginning on page 48, for the definitive elucidation of "Rabbi Chaim's way" of Talmudic studies.

10. *Responsa of Bais Ridvaz*, Jerusalem, 1905, in the introduction to the book. Also see the introduction of Rabbi Chanoch Henich Aigus of Vilna to his great work, *Marcheshes*. While his criticism of the new method of study is much more muted than Rabbi Willovsky's, it is nonetheless clearly present. The dispute about "Rabbi Chaim's way" would continue throughout much of the twentieth century. Rabbi Avrohom Yeshaya Karelitz (*Chazon Ish*) was a critic of "Rabbi Chaim's way" and the limited learning curriculum of the Lithuanian yeshivos generally. Rabbi Yaakov Yechiel Weinberg (*Seridei Aish*) wrote: " ... one gets the impression [from the words of Rabbi Joseph B.

entire Eastern European Jewish world was swept up in the turmoil of change as the twentieth century began. The forces of "Enlightenment" (*Haskalah*) had swept east from Germany and invaded Eastern and Central European Jewish societies. The Orthodox establishment, suffering from external pressures to reform placed on it by the anti-Semitic governments of Russia and Austria-Hungary, as well as from internal pressures of the *Haskalah* and the secularists to abandon Jewish tradition, fiercely resisted any changes or innovations. It felt that modifying anything, even if only a custom or teaching method, would eventually lead to abandoning everything that was authentic to Judaism. Therefore it is not surprising that there developed a tension between the yeshivos and the organized Jewish communities, for the innovations of the yeshivos — *mussar* and "Rabbi Chaim's way" — were suspected of being of foreign, almost *Haskalah*, origin. The yeshivos, on the other hand, claimed that *mussar* and the new method of Talmud study were weapons against the spread of *Haskalah* in their communities and in the Jewish world generally.[11]

The primary challenge to the yeshivos and its way of life came paradoxically from within the student bodies of the schools. The ideas of anarchy, political democracy, socialism, Marxism, Zionism and secularism were to be found among some of the students at all yeshivos. There were active cells of students in all of the yeshivos that fostered these attractive utopian ideas. Upon discovery by the authorities that governed the school, these cells would be disbanded forcibly and the ringleaders expelled. Many of these former yeshivah students later became leading socialists, Zionists, Marxists and secularists. There were revolutions within the yeshivos themselves.[12] But the moral and educational fiber and inner spiritual strength of the yeshivos were so strong that the institutions were able to grow and prosper spiritually despite all of the opposition and troubles that they suffered.

Soloveitchik, Rabbi Chaim's grandson] that the Torah was not given through Moses, God forbid, but rather through Reb Chaim. It is true that Reb Chaim brought a new type of logical *pilpul* into the yeshivos. Anyone can have a grasp of logic, and therefore all yeshivah students can come up with novel insights in this fashion. This is not so with regard to the approach of the *Shach* (Rabbi Shabtai HaKohen, 1621-62) and Rabbi Akiva Eiger (1761-1837), concerning which one needs to have great erudition in order to be a little sharp-witted (*charif*). Therefore, since all yeshivah students want to be 'creators' [of such analytic insights] they prefer Reb Chaim to all the sages that preceded him." Quoted in *Between the Yeshiva World and Modern Orthodoxy* by Marc B. Shapiro, Portland, Oregon, 1999, p.195.

11. See Rabbi I.Y.Unterman's article in a *Sefer Hyovel L'Rabi Shimon Shkop*, Vilna, 1936, p.20.

12. The most famous of which took place in Telshe Yeshiva, first in 1898 and again in 1905.

Class Differences Foment Cultural Revolution

THERE WAS A SERIOUS FAULT LINE RUNNING THROUGH JEWISH SOCIETY in Eastern and Central Europe at this time. Originally, this division was social, economic and educational in nature. It was not yet an argument about religion and ritual observance, but it would soon become that as well. It pitted the educated Jews, the scholars and rabbis, the ritual slaughterers and cantors, the very thin upper crust of Jews who were wealthy, the factory owners and bankers — the privileged few — against the tenant farmers, small merchants, artisans, factory workers, teamsters, day laborers and the unemployed, of whom there were many. The first group disdained work with their hands and viewed their lower class fellow Jews as little better than the loutish Russian peasants who were scorned by all Jews because of their illiteracy, alcoholism and violence. The second group viewed this upper class as being lazy, exploitative, insensitive to the true social conditions of the Jewish masses and uncaring as to their future and improvement. Of course, both views were stereotypes and not really very accurate. But for millions of Jews, these stereotypes were believed and formed the basis of the great splits in the Jewish world that the events of the twentieth century would deepen and emphasize. The terrible decrees of the Russian authorities against the Jews, most of whom were declared "useless" by the czar, took an awful toll from the faith and strength of the Jewish community. But it was especially the lower classes, restive and resentful, that suffered under their terrible burdens.

The pace of industrialization and urbanization in Russia at the turn of the century was fast and oppressive. Russia industrialized itself more rapidly than any other European nation during the last decades of the nineteenth century. New industries and factories sprung up throughout Russia proper and in Russian-controlled Poland and Ukraine. Jews were prominent in this burgeoning process of industrialization, particularly in Russian Poland. Their presence was concentrated especially in the textile, tobacco, meatpacking and liquor industries. The city of Lodz, which had a one-third Jewish population, came to be known as the "Manchester of Poland."[13] Jews were not only the owners of these types of factories and enterprises, but also comprised the overwhelming majority of workers. A small number of Jews also became very wealthy in railroads, banking, tea import and timber export. Most of this wealthy class soon assimilated into the Russian upper class, shedding their Jewishness in the process. They eventually became willing allies of the czar and his anti-Semitic political ministers in the attempt to "modernize" their Jewish brethren.

---

13. Manchester was the center of textile production in the British Empire – and the world – in the nineteenth century.

But the real industrialization of Russia took place in the large factories, which now employed hundreds of thousands of workers. The conditions under which factory workers the world over toiled were appalling, including factories owned by Jews in Poland, Lithuania and Russia. Sixteen-hour work days, child labor, fire hazards, choking dust and smoke, no safety guards on machinery, poor wages, the tyranny of the boss and the foreman, and the terrible filth of the shop floor and air all were the norm in these workplaces. The fact that it was a Jewish owner who treated his fellow Jews who worked for him so shabbily only intensified the Jewish workers' antipathy towards "the boss." It was natural, therefore, that some of these suffering Jewish workers should become the leaders and prime catalysts for the growth of the labor unions, both in Eastern Europe and the United States in the early 1900's. The sense of the injustice done to them by factory owners burned deeply within the psyche of the exploited Jewish workers, contributing mightily to their alienation from traditional Jewish life with which they identified their bosses.

The Jewish labor movement in Europe was concentrated in local organizations called Workman's Circles and ultimately united nationally in a major labor union called the General Jewish Workers Union. It was more commonly known by its Yiddish nickname – the Bund. By 1900, the new Jewish proletariat in Russia, Poland and Lithuania consisted of over 500,000 artisans and skilled laborers, 100,000 day and unskilled laborers and more than 50,000 factory workers. The Bund drew its strength and popularity from this large pool of workers and their families. Though its original goals and purpose were mainly economic — shorter working days, higher wages, a safer and more healthful working environment and recognition of the union's right to collective bargaining — the Bund soon became an ideological movement. The Bund championed Jewish culture and scorned religion and ritual. It was ardently secular and even atheistic, holding its banquets and festivities on the night of Yom Kippur to demonstrate publicly its rejection of Jewish tradition and ritual observances. The extreme example of the Bund served to raise anti-religious and public desecration of Jewish tradition among even the more moderate secularists. The Bund's newspaper, *The Voice of the Worker*, was published in Yiddish and had a wide underground circulation. The Bund adopted Yiddish as its language of Jewish culture. It organized a widespread and popular school system in which the language of instruction was Yiddish, with a curriculum that was militantly secular and exclusively socialist.

Postcard depicting the "Capitalist System Pyramid." Captions from the top down read: "We rule you;" "We fool you;" "We shoot you;" "We eat you;" "We work for everyone, we feed everyone."

As part of its revolutionary stance towards the replacement of the Jewish religion by Jewish culture, the Bund contributed morally and financially to the burgeoning growth of Yiddish literature. It opposed the use of the Hebrew language in promoting Jewish culture and was in the main non-supportive of Zionism. It was originally attached to the general Russian Social-Democratic Party, but because the Bund insisted on Yiddish language and particularly Jewish culture as part of its overall program, it was attacked bitterly by the Russian socialists. The Marxists, especially Trotsky, condemned the Bund for being too narrow (i.e., too Jewish) in its outlook and aims. Moreover, he charged that the Bund did not follow the banner of the universal workers' revolution, which according to Marx, would alone solve all of the economic and social problems of all workers, Jew and non-Jew alike. The Marxists opposed any negotiations or the acceptance of any economic concessions from the capitalist owners of the means of production. They belittled and even ridiculed the achievements of the Bund in improving the lot of the Jewish workers, and labeled its heads as counterrevolutionaries. Indeed, when the Bolsheviks came to power, first in Russia and later in Poland (in 1939-40), almost all of the leaders of the Bund were eliminated and the organization crushed.

Tradition Dissolves in the American "Melting Pot"

WITH THE GREAT JEWISH IMMIGRATION TO AMERICA IN THE 1890's and 1900's, the divisions and arguments of Eastern Europe were transported to the shores of the New World. The great culture shock which Jewish immigrants experienced in America seriously challenged their traditional way of life. This was especially true for the young. Their main goal was to become Americanized quickly and completely. The younger generation was ashamed of their elders and revolted by their old-country ways. Here is a representative sample of this attitude from a sixteen-year-old child of immigrant parents living in a California town:

> I don't like to bring my American friends around. They were born here and so were their parents. My mother speaks "English" to them, and they make fun of her. When I ask her to leave them alone she says, "They are only goyim (non-Jews); ain't I good enough to entertain them?" Sure, she entertains them — at my expense. My father won't allow us to play ball on the lot. He says it's a waste of time and a disgrace to make such a lot of noise about nothing. He was raised in Poland. But then he don't believe in sweatshops either, but has never been anything but a cutter in a sweatshop. It's awfully embarrassing to bring any American friends to the house … My parents don't believe in beaches and never go swimming. I don't like to stay home, and my parents don't understand what boys need, and they expect me to be old-fashioned and go to shul.

Orchard Street, turn of the century

I have never taken very much stock in religion. I don't see any sense in it. Our Sabbath begins Friday at sunset, but my father works in the shop all day Saturday. Oh, he sighs and hopes to be in the land of the "faithful" before he dies, but that don't help him any. I don't see why a faithful people should suffer and be laughed at like we are. My parents nag me to go to *shul* on holidays. They make many sacrifices to keep their traditions, but they don't mean anything much in my life … That's why I just don't like to stay home. I don't want to hurt my parents [but] I can't follow their advice."[14]

This poignant, tragic description of the estrangement of the generations of immigrant Jews is representative of the trauma of adjustment to American life at the onset of the twentieth century. In just one generation of American life, the centuries-old connection to traditional Jewish life was broken for many Eastern European immigrant Jewish families in America. The almost impossible working conditions of the six-day work week that destroyed Sabbath observance; continuing and almost endemic corruption and scandal in the kosher meat industry;[15] the old folkways that were Eastern European in origin, but had no bearing to true Jewish ritual requirements;[16] the continuing use of Yiddish as the exclusive spoken language in teaching and sermons; the lack of meaningful Jewish education for the young generation — all combined to cause widespread abandonment of the

אַ נייַע תְּחִנָה פֿון ליכט בֶּענְשְׁן:
(סְפֶּעצְיֶעל פֿאַר אַמֶעריקאַ.)

"A new prayer (to be added) after candlelighting, special for America" In this Yiddish prayer, published in 1916, a wife pleads that her husband and children will not have to desecrate the Shabbath and holidays in order to make a living.

14. Lucy Davidowicz, *From That Place and Time*, New York, 1989, p. 115.

15. Meltzer, p.277.

16. I still recall, as a child (and this was in the 1940's), how ashamed I was that in the main sanctuary of the synagogue where my father was rabbi, men publicly blew their noses and spat into open spittoons. The main drawback to the Orthodox synagogue, however, was its insistence on the use of Yiddish as the language of speech and sermons and the persistence of Eastern European social customs to dominate the life and operation of the synagogue.

traditional Jewish way of life among the children of the immigrant generation. Intermarriage, however, was still practically unknown in the early decades of the century. But, seemingly, the handwriting was on the wall for the future of traditional Judaism in America.

America in the early 1900's was a place of open and often violent bigotry. Blacks were hardly considered human beings; lynchings of Blacks were commonplace in the South and were not unknown even in the North. Jews were also subjected to open intolerance. "Kikes" and "Yids" were the common terms used to describe Jewish immigrants. Oftentimes, pitched battles raged between Jewish youth and their non-Jewish tormentors, most of whom were themselves immigrants or of immigrant families. The police in New York had a reputation for anti-Semitism, wielding their truncheons against the Jews at every opportunity. In 1902, as the funeral procession of Rabbi Jacob Joseph, the Chief Rabbi of New York, wound its way past the R. Hoe and Co. printing plant, non-Jewish workers hurled stones, pieces of metal and garbage at the mourners' heads. In the ensuing melee, the police concentrated their blows on the Jews, many of whom were severely injured. A public denouncement of police behavior on this occasion by leading American politicians later began the process of redressing the problem as far as the Jews of New York were concerned. But there were many Jews who felt that the problem of anti-Semitism in America could be solved only in the general context of promoting tolerance for all in American society. The American Jewish Committee, the American Jewish Congress, B'nai B'rith and its Anti-Defamation League, all grew out of this Jewish struggle begun in the early 1900's to defend Jewish rights worldwide and to make America a place of tolerance for all.

First generation immigrants usually tried to hold fast to traditions, no matter where they lived. As Jews in New York said Tashlich in 1907 (left), their brethren in Minot, North Dakota (right) did the same.

The Bund had its counterpart in the American Jewish community as well. The Workman's Circle organized Yiddish-speaking, Jewish-culture schools in America. These schools, as was the fate of the traditional *cheder*/afternoon Hebrew schools, did not have much of a lasting effect upon the lives of their students. Just as Orthodoxy was to suffer grievously from the process of Jews becoming Americanized, so too would the Bund, the Jewish socialist and communist groups, and those who advocated Jewish or Yiddish culture as the salvation of Jewry. The children of the immigrant generation were unwilling to preserve Yiddish culture for their children, for they viewed both secular Judaism and ritually observant Judaism to be equal hindrances to the process of Americanization. The immigrant generation viewed the "old home" and its ways and culture with sad nostalgia. Their children viewed it with disdain. The immigrants' grandchildren, in the main, were unaware that it ever existed. The powerful medium of American culture would overwhelm all efforts at preserving the old ethos of the *shtetl* in the United States for most American Jews.

American Religious Movements Take Root

THERE WERE, HOWEVER, STUBBORN JEWS WHO WERE DETERMINED somehow to plant the seeds of traditional Jewish life, the study of Torah and the observance of Jewish ritual in the inhospitable ground of American Jewish life. A small school, Etz Chaim, founded in 1896, eventually began to grow and after many transmutations emerged as the parent of today's Rabbi Isaac Elchanan Theological Seminary/Yeshiva University. Yeshivas Rabbi Jacob Joseph was also established early in the 1900's. Named after the first and only chief rabbi of New York, the school became a pioneer of the "day school movement" which would not truly gain strength for another half-century. The establishment and growth of other American yeshivos would also have to wait for a later time. Lacking at that time in the American Orthodox community were the scholarly teaching manpower, the critical mass of potential students and the financial resources to establish schools of higher Torah studies. As this was the case in New York, the heartland of American Jewry, the problems of Jewish education were even more severe in other American cities.

In 1902, the Union of Orthodox Rabbis of the United States and Canada — Agudas HaRabanim — was established. This organization would prove to be influential, almost powerful, for decades until its decline towards the latter third of the century. Rabbis Bernard Levinthal of Philadelphia and Moses Zevulun Margolies (known as the *Ramaz*) were the initial leaders of this rabbinical group. Comprised almost exclusively of Yiddish-speaking Eastern European rabbis, the organization attempted to address the religious and social problems of the new immigrants to America and to strengthen their faith and observance of tradition. A number of great European rabbis came to America (for example, Rabbi Jacob Joseph in New York and Rabbi Yaakov David Willovsky [Ridvaz] in Chicago) but the chaos and corruption of *kashrus* supervision[17] and the alienation of the American-born children of the immigrants rendered them largely ineffective on the American scene. The problems of Americanization were so overwhelming that Orthodoxy was restricted to fighting what amounted to a purely defensive holding action, soon undermined by a defeatist attitude towards the future of Judaism and the Jewish community in America.

This attitude of defeatism, coupled with the harsh reality that the vast majority of Jewish immigrants in America rapidly ceased to be strictly observant of Jewish ritual within a short time of their arrival in America, led the rabbis and Chasidic *rebbeim* of Eastern Europe to almost universally condemn immigration to America. The antipathy of these religious leaders towards America remained unabated until World War II. Jews who left Europe to live in America were always defensive and apologetic for having done so when they returned to the "old home" to visit their relatives and once again make contact with their Eastern European rabbis and leaders. This attitude of negativism towards America and American Jewry was also present among the leaders of the small Jewish community then living in Palestine, and is present there even a century later, in spite of the enormous accomplishments of the American Jewish community over the past century.

Under these circumstances, it was almost inevitable that American Jewry would form new structures and organizations to attempt to meet its needs. The infrastructure of American Jewry had been established by the leaders of Reform who had immigrated to America in the middle third of the nineteenth century. In the latter third of that century, under the strong leadership of Isaac Mayer Wise (1819-1900), the Union of American Hebrew Congregations, the Central Conference of American Rabbis and Hebrew Union College in Cincinnati were established. These Reform institutions came to represent American Jewry to the general non-Jewish American public, a perception that persisted throughout much of the twentieth century as well. The purpose of Reform in America, much as it had been in Germany in the nineteenth century, was to assimilate the Jew totally into the general Protestant religious environment of the country. Therefore, Reform Sabbath services, such as they

---

17. The control of the kosher slaughtering houses and butcher shops lay in the hands of thugs, gangsters and charlatans. The strict standards for employing and certifying *shochtim* – ritual slaughterers – were in the main ignored and pseudo-rabbis could always be found to grant "rabbinic certification." There was no strong kosher supervision in American Jewish life until much later in the century.

were, were transferred to Sunday from Saturday,[18] the entire service was conducted in English and all Hebrew language was removed from the prayer services, as was any mention of Zion, the Land of Israel and Jerusalem. Clergy dressed in the black robes of the then dominant Protestant denominations of America, organ music was the background noise for all prayer services, Jewish divorce was deemed unnecessary, dietary laws were denounced and requirements of Jewish ritual were eliminated from Reform Jewish life. As such, Reform held very little attraction for the immigrant generation of Eastern European Jews arriving in America, raised as they were in the synagogues of Eastern Europe. However, for their grandchildren, Reform became the symbol of Americanization, acceptance into American society and a stepping-stone to achieving upward social mobility. Thus, the Reform movement in America would become strong and powerful due to the influx of the descendants of Orthodox Jews into its ranks.

Intermarriage was not yet a vexing problem for American Jewry at the early part of the century. There were isolated cases of intermarriage, primarily among the wealthy and "German" Jews who rose to social prominence in spite of their Jewishness. On the whole, Jews in America still only married Jews during the first half of the twentieth century. This may not have been so much a matter of Jewish loyalty and pride as it was a matter of strong and stubborn non-Jewish resistance to marrying Jews. In the first decade of the century, Jews were openly discriminated against in employment, hotel and resort lodgings, higher education and entry into various professions. If a Jew was not welcome even in one's hotel, that same Jew's son or daughter would hardly be welcome as a member of one's own immediate family. The challenge to Jewish life in the early part of the century was not intermarriage; it was acculturation.

As the European-type Orthodox synagogue and way of life was deemed impractical for survival in America and Reform was far too radical and foreign for the immigrants, a vacuum automatically appeared in early twentieth century American Jewish life. In Orthodox Jewish life, a new, "modern," English-oriented, yet halachically correct communal type of synagogue service emerged. It was appropriately named Young Israel, for it attempted to speak to the children of the immigrants and appease their quest for Americanization through changes in form, sermon-language and folkways, along with more melodious prayer services, but with no intention of changing content or ritual obligations and tradition. Youth groups, outings, social gatherings and informative lectures on var-

---

18. I recall from my younger years that the largest and most prestigious Reform Temple in Chicago conducted its weekly Sabbath prayer service on Sunday morning, as late as the 1950's!

1915 — *Talmud Torah class — Seattle, Washington*

1913 — *Yeshiva Etz Chaim class — Denver, Colorado*

1909 — *Talmud Torah in New Britain, Connecticut*

ied subjects, including classes in English and Americanization, were part of the Young Israel program. Its influence and positive accomplishments saved many families for Orthodoxy.

Despite these efforts, early generations of American Jewish immigrants were lost to Jewish life and observance due to the lack of a Jewish educational school system that could compete with the American public school system. The afternoon *talmud Torah*/Hebrew school system was doomed to failure. Though many an individual student profited from attendance at these schools, it was unreasonable to expect that the majority of the children of Jewish immigrants would enjoy attending school for an additional number of hours a day after a full day in public school. Many of the teachers in these Hebrew schools were unqualified. Corporal punishment, which was the norm in Eastern European Jewish schools, was frowned upon by many American Jews. Sadly, it still survived in the afternoon Jewish schools well into the twentieth century. The afternoon schools rapidly transformed into institutions devoted to preparing boys for their bar mitzvah ceremony. Most American Jews of that generation did not give Judaism a serious second thought after their thirteenth birthday passed. It would be yet many decades before the American Jewish community would undertake the basic task of providing a comprehensive Jewish education for its young.

A college of higher Jewish learning, in the spirit of the *Haskalah* and "scientific Judaism," was founded in 1893 in Philadelphia. Originally called Gratz College, it came to be known as Dropsie College, after the name of its first president, a prominent Philadelphia lawyer. It was a place of ivory-tower scholarship on matters relating to Judaism and the Jewish people and made many academic contributions to Jewish culture and knowledge. Nevertheless, its impact on American Jewry was hardly noticed and it certainly was unable to pioneer a direction by which mass assimilation of American Jews could be avoided. Moreover it had no relevance to the masses of immigrant Eastern European Jews then pouring into America, the vast majority of whom were unaware of its existence.

One of America's Jewish visionaries, Rabbi Dr. Henry Pereira Mendes, came to the United States from England in 1877. He was the spiritual leader of the Spanish-Portuguese Congregation, the patrician Orthodox synagogue in New York founded in the 1600's. A man of action and daring, he attempted to give American Orthodoxy a framework and infrastructure. Many of his grand plans did not come to fruition, but his efforts and presence served as a rallying point for many Orthodox Jewish leaders. In 1886, together with Rabbi Dr. Sabato Morais of Philadelphia, he helped found the Jewish Theological Seminary of America. At its founding, it was an Orthodox institution dedicated to the advancement of Jewish scholarship and the training of English-speaking rabbis and teachers. The institution did not meet with great success and was on the verge of closing in 1901, due to a lack of students and funds. However, a new group of directors assumed responsibility for the institution and in 1902 the noted Wall Street financier and philanthropist, Jacob H. Schiff, contributed $500,000 to the Seminary. Under the influence of the new "Americanized" lay leadership, the Seminary now took a different tack from the one envisioned by its Orthodox founders. Dr. Solomon Schechter of Cambridge University was invited to become the head of the school. He proposed that Judaism was not God-given nor based on revelation, but that it is an evolving religion of customs, folkways and values that could and would change from time to time. Judaism was whatever the Jewish people as a whole would decide it was. Mendes resigned from the Seminary when Schiff's group became dominant; under Schechter's leadership and impetus, the Seminary then became the flagship of a new and particularly American Jewish grouping called Conservative Judaism.

Conservative Judaism in practice, as opposed to ideology, hardly differed from its Orthodox origins at the onset.[19] True, its students attended university classes in secular subjects, were trained English-speakers, studied Jewish history and philosophy as well as Semitic languages, were exposed to the pseudo-science of Biblical Criticism and were less versed in the Talmud than their counterparts in Orthodox yeshivos, but in the

---

19. Funk & Wagnall's monumental *Jewish Encyclopedia*, published in 1912, contained no reference as yet to Conservative Judaism.

Seminary itself, the synagogue's physical form (including the separation of the sexes during prayer, the absence of musical instruments in the service and a central *bimah* reading table) and contents of the prayer services did not deviate from the Orthodox norm. However, the Seminary soon produced rabbis who would countenance a "little Reform" in their congregations. Originally, this deviation usually meant mixed seating of the sexes during prayers and the relaxation of the observance of certain halachic customs. Many of the early graduates of the Seminary, in fact, held Orthodox pulpits and were recognized as legitimate Jewish religious leaders even by the Orthodox group.[20] In addition, the faculty of the Seminary itself included many Orthodox scholars of note as teachers and counselors. But by the end of the opening decade of the twentieth century, it was clear that Conservative Judaism was going its own non-Orthodox way. It meant to "conserve" Judaism in America and prevent the domination of assimilation and Reform. It felt that only through adjusting Jewish practice to American life and norms, being lenient in matters of ritual and observance, could it accomplish its goal of "conserving" the core of Judaism for its American constituents. By 1913, Rabbi Dr. Mendes sadly concluded: "The word 'Conservative' ... in its meaning as demonstrated in the history of American Jewry, means gradual but sure alienation from traditional, Orthodox Judaism."[21]

The Varied Faces of Zionism ... and its Vehement Opponents

AT THE END OF THE NINETEENTH CENTURY, THE ZIONIST MOVEMENT emerged.[22] An enigmatic, proud, almost vain, cultured Viennese journalist and playwright named Theodore Herzl was a visionary who brought the issue of Jewish settlement in the Land of Israel to the fore in both the Jewish and non-Jewish world. He was a handsome, charismatic person whose personal integrity was unquestioned in all matters.[23] Ironically, Herzl's attachment and identification with Jews and Judaism in his early years was peripheral, at best. His apathetic attitude towards his fellow Jews changed when he witnessed the virulent anti-Semitism that

---

20. Meyer Waxman was Professor of Jewish History and Jewish Thought for many decades at Hebrew Theological College in Chicago, an Orthodox yeshivah. Jacob H. Hertz was rabbi of the Orach Chaim Congregation, one of the leading Orthodox congregations in New York and later served with great distinction as the Chief Rabbi of the British Empire. Herbert S. Goldstein became a major Orthodox rabbi and founded the West Side Hebrew Institute in New York City.

21. Saul Bernstein, *The Orthodox Union Story*, Northvale, NJ, 1997, p.52.

22. The term "Zionism" was coined in 1890 by Nathan Birnbaum, then a Jewish socialist and free-thinker. Later in life, Birnbaum became a strictly observant Orthodox Jew and was one of the early thinkers and philosophers of the Agudath Israel movement, which was staunchly anti-Zionist.

23. Herzl never took any salary or even expense money from the Zionist movement during all of his years of service. Yosef Ptai, *Herzl*, Tel Aviv, 1936, p.213.

Theodor Herzl with a Zionist delegation in the Old City of Jerusalem in 1898

the Dreyfus trial generated in France and throughout Europe. Herzl saw the solution of the "Jewish problem" and of anti-Semitism in the "normalization" of the Jewish people. That "normalization," in his opinion, was dependent on Jews having a country of their own. Though Herzl himself would countenance the establishment of that country in Africa or any other area of the world, the vast majority of the masses who supported the Zionist movement (mostly Eastern European Jews) took the word "Zionist" literally and looked towards the establishment of a Jewish state in Zion, the Land of Israel.

Herzl traveled the world to enlist the interest and agreement of the Great Powers in achieving the Zionist goal. He wrote to Bismarck, met Kaiser Wilhelm II twice, traveled to London to meet with the leaders of England's political parties, visited Constantinople and the sultan of the Ottoman Empire, came to France for an interview with Baron Edmond James de Rothschild and visited Jewish communities in Russia. All of his travels netted great popular fervor amongst the masses of the Jews, but very little tangible results. There yet remained open hostility of many Jews and non-Jews to his seemingly utopian dreams. As we shall soon see, Herzl was not in any way fazed by this opposition and he continued his efforts of promoting the Zionist idea among his people.

Herzl's Jewish opponents were varied in personality and motive. Reform and assimilated Jews saw him and Zionism as a great danger to their newly won minimal acceptance in the non-Jewish societies of the time. In their minds and fears, the Zionist movement and its support by Jews in many different countries would confirm the anti-Semitic accusation that Jews are inherently disloyal to the country of their dwelling. But even the Orthodox Jewish rabbinic leaders in the countries of the West opposed Herzl and his ideas. In Vienna, Herzl believed that he had convinced its Chief Rabbi, Dr. Moritz Guedemann, a disciple of Zecharia Frankel and a graduate of the Jewish Theological Seminary of Breslau, to support him and Zionism. In fact, Guedemann had helped Herzl formulate his thoughts in his famous pamphlet *The Jewish State*. But Guedemann rapidly became disenchanted with Herzl and his idea. Herzl responded furiously in his "Diaries:"

> *Dr. Guedemann has published a malicious attack [on Zionism] in a pamphlet entitled* Jewish Nationalism. *Obviously at the behest of the local "upper-class" Jews. He confines himself to vague, cowardly ambiguities ... I shall answer him — and following the Machiavellian formula, it will be a crusher.*[24]

---

24. Marvin Lowenthal, ed., *The Diaries of Theodore Herzl*, 1958, p.208.

Herzl was also rebuffed by the Chief Rabbi of Belgium, Armond Bloch.[25] The Hirschian *kehillah* in Frankfurt-am-Main was vociferously opposed to the idea of Zionism, though there were Orthodox communities in Berlin and other German cities who supported Herzl's ideas, with varying degrees of enthusiasm. However, the most prestigious and influential opponent to Herzl's Zionist movement among the Orthodox rabbis of Western Europe was Hermann Adler, the Chief Rabbi of the British Empire. On April 23, 1909, he was quoted by the *Manchester Daily Dispatch* saying:

> *Since the destruction of the Temple and our dispersion we no longer constitute a nation; we are a religious communion. We are bound together with our brethren throughout the world primarily by the ideas of a common faith. But in regard to all other matters we consider ourselves Englishmen and we hold that in virtue of being Jews it is our duty and privilege to work as zealously as possible for the welfare of England.[26]*

The Orthodox Jewish community in Eastern Europe was badly split in its reaction to the Zionist movement. Most of the Chasidic *rebbeim*, prominent rabbinical figures and heads of yeshivos in Eastern Europe were opposed to Zionism. They could not imagine that anything truly worthwhile and beneficial for the people of Israel could emanate from an organization dominated and run by secular, semi-assimilated Jews. They were afraid of the incipient secular messianism that lay at the heart of the Zionist dream. In addition, many of them felt that the Jewish people had no right to force God's Hand, so to speak, on the matter of Redemption from the Exile and the establishment of a Jewish homeland in the Land of Israel. But the main reason for the opposition to Zionism by many of the leaders of Orthodoxy in Eastern and Central Europe was the realization that Zionism and Jewish nationalism would become a substitute "Torah" and religion, replacing the traditional Jewish faith and lifestyle of many Jews. This last fear was actualized in the progress of the century.

Yet many Orthodox leaders did support Zionism, sharing Herzl's dream and participating in his organization. These "religious Zionists" eventually formed the Mizrachi section within the Zionist movement. They were headed by a brilliant student of the great yeshivah in Volozhin, Rabbi Yitzchak Yaakov Reines, the rabbi of Lida, Lithuania. Also very active in the promotion of religious Zionism were Rabbi Yehuda Leib Fishman (later Maimon) and Rabbi Meir Berlin (later Bar-Ilan), the youngest son of the famed saintly scholar of Volozhin, Rabbi Naftali Zvi Yehuda Berlin

---

25. Immanuel Jakobovits, *If Only My People...*, London, 1984, p.239, note 17.
26. Ibid. p.217

Early Mizrachi leaders –
Rabbi Reines wears a top
hat, Rabbi Fishman is
seated at right.

(*Netziv*). Mizrachi was widely popular and made deep inroads into the rabbinate and masses of Orthodox Eastern European Jews. It also gained support from a number of Chasidic *rebbeim* and from the fledgling Union of Orthodox Rabbis of the United States and Canada. Rabbi Meir Berlin arrived in America before World War I and created a very strong base and infrastructure for the organization. It would not be an exaggeration to say that Mizrachi dominated much of Orthodox Jewish life in America and *Eretz Yisrael* for the first half of the twentieth century, also proving very strong in Eastern Europe until the onset of World War II. Mizrachi had the tacit support of many great rabbis who, though not officially members of the movement, nevertheless lent quiet prestige to it and its ideals.

Zionism itself faced many internal struggles at the beginning of the century. Though Herzl was encouraged by the strong popular response that the concept of a Jewish state inspired among the masses of Eastern European Jewry, he was anguished by the opposite stream of anti-Zionism prevalent among many Orthodox leaders. He was even more surprised and disappointed by the reaction of some of the leading Jewish secular leaders to the Zionist idea. Ludwig Geiger and Hermann Cohen, the leading Jewish intellectuals of Germany, issued a statement warning that Zionism was a movement "fully as dangerous to the German spirit as are social democracy and ultramontanism."[27] Aside from the opposition of Reform as outlined above, "official" Jewry in Austria, England and France opposed, or at best ignored, the Zionist movement. Herzl's attempts to convince the sultan of Turkey and the kaiser of Germany had also met failure. A firm believer in his dream, Herzl still searched for alternative methods to actualize it.

Early on in his role as the Zionist leader, Herzl considered other localities besides Palestine as the place for the Jewish State. Cyprus, South America, and even empty parts of the vast, but rapidly receding, American frontier were recorded by him in his diary as possibilities. But

27. Howard M. Sachar, *A History of Israel*, 2nd Edition, New York, 1998, p.52.

as long as he saw some hope for achieving Palestine, he did not pursue these other locations.

By the beginning of 1902, however, he began to have doubts about ever establishing a Jewish political base in Palestine, as long as it was controlled by the Ottoman Empire. On July 7, 1902, Herzl testified before a parliamentary committee in London that was examining legislation to prevent the further influx of Eastern European Jews into England. At the conclusion of his testimony, Herzl added the following suggestion: "If you find that they [the Eastern European Jews] are not wanted here [in England], then some place must be found to which they can migrate without raising the problems that confront them here. These problems will not arise if a home be found for them which will be legally recognized as Jewish."[28]

1903 was the year of the dreadful Kishinev pogrom in Russia. Forty-five Jews were killed, eighty-six more were wounded (many of these were maimed for life), synagogues despoiled, Jewish women ravished and hundreds of Jewish homes and shops burned and destroyed by the raging mob. The czarist police took no action to protect the Jews and some of them even participated in the massacre. The entire civilized world protested to the Russian government, but to no avail, for encouragement of pogroms was an integral part of the Russian government's policy towards the Jews.

Herzl was now driven to act. He consulted with the leading British political figure Joseph Chamberlain and was assured that England would favor a Jewish colony in East African Uganda. When the Sixth Zionist Congress convened in Basle in August, 1903, Uganda was the dominant issue. Though Herzl portrayed the Uganda proposal as being only a way station on the road to Jewish colonization of Palestine, the Uganda proposal provoked a firestorm of protest. Though the proposal to investigate the Uganda offer passed the Congress (295-177, with 100 abstentions), the vehemence of the protest — mainly led by the Eastern European Zionist leaders such as Chaim Weizmann and Menachem Ussishkin — prevented any positive action to be taken on the scheme. By 1904, it was apparent that Zionism stood for the Jewish people's return to the Land of Israel, and no place else.

Herzl was also bedeviled by the "cultural Zionists," a group headed by Asher Ginzberg, better known by his pen name, Achad Ha'am. Ginzberg was born to an observant Chasidic family, but became secularized soon after his marriage. He moved to Odessa, then a gathering place

---

28. Ibid. p.53.

for *maskilim* ("Enlightened Ones"), where he served as an employee of the famed Wissotzky Tea Company. Ginzberg saw the revival of the Jewish people in spiritual and cultural terms (secular *Haskalah* culture, devoid of ritual observance) solely. He mistrusted Herzl, as well as his motives and policies, because Herzl had no real Jewish knowledge or understanding of Jewish life and culture. Achad Ha'Am opposed founding more Jewish agricultural colonies in the Land of Israel, believing that the Jews could not be ready for a national state until they first underwent a cultural revolution: i.e. they must first shake off the dust of exile and the ghetto.

According to his plan, language, literature, Jewish universities and scientific erudition were the foundation stones of any Jewish revival. Jewish faith and halachic rituals were to be replaced by this new humanistic and progressive culture. Jewish nationalism and state-building were useless and counter-productive to Jewish revival without a new Jewish culture at its core, said Ginzberg. Jerusalem was meant to be a capital of the spirit more than the home of a Jewish government. In 1902, the Fifth Zionist Congress merged Achad Ha'Am's "culture" with Herzl's political nationalism. This decision had a profound effect on many Orthodox leaders who previously had been sympathetic to Herzl's ideas and plans. Rabbi Reines, head of Mizrachi, retired from active Zionist participation due to the officially sanctioned "culture" domination of Zionism and the Jewish future envisioned by the secularists. Both Herzl and Achad Ha'Am regarded each other as wild-eyed dreamers pursuing an illusory fantasy. Nevertheless, political expediency often makes for strange bedfellows.

Another version of the Zionist dream in the first decade of the 1900's was that of Labor Zionism.[29] Just as the "cultural Zionists" wedded Achad Ha'Am's philosophy to the political organization that he had railed against, so too did Jewish radicals and socialists combine their proletarian dreams with the rapidly growing movement of Zionism. A movement arose in the 1880's among the Jewish people that glorified physical, unskilled labor as the longed-for vehicle of Jewish self-redemption. Such radicals as Michah Joseph Berditchevsky, and later Yosef Chaim Brenner, emphasized the "holiness of physical agricultural labor," arguing that agricultural labor alone would suffice to redeem Israel from its difficulties and degradation. Only by the sweat of the Jewish brow, and not by the cerebral ingenuity of Jewish brains, would Zion be redeemed. The foremost prophet of this physical labor movement was Aharon David Gordon. He immigrated to Palestine in

---

29. A movement of socialism attached to the idea of Zionism. It was formed by Ber Borochov, a devoted Marxist at the beginning of the twentieth century. Yitzchak Ben-Zvi, the second president of the State of Israel, and later David Ben-Gurion, emerged as the leaders of Poalei Zion in Palestine. They became the guiding lights of the Second Aliyah and were eventually of the group of founding fathers of the State of Israel.

1903 to devote himself to the popularization of the goal of Jewish labor. Building upon the growing Jewish labor movement of the Bund and of Poalei Zion — the Labor Zionists — in Eastern Europe, Gordon became their spiritual mentor and created a religion of manual labor. In one of his essays, he wrote:

> *A living people always possesses a great majority to whom labor is its second nature. Not so among us. We despise labor ... There is only one path that can lead to our renaissance — the path of manual labor, of mobilizing all of our national energies, of absolute and sacrificial devotion to our ideal and tasks ... Our people can be rejuvenated only if each one of us recreates himself through labor and a life close to nature.*[30]

Gordon's philosophy, though non-Marxist, fit perfectly with the utopian socialist ideals of the early secular settlers of Palestine. The organization of Marxist communal communities — kibbutzim — had begun in this decade and rapidly gained momentum. The kibbutz was the home of utopian idealism and idealists. The slogan of the kibbutzim, which abhorred the notion of private property, was: "Each will contribute according to his abilities. Each will take according to his needs." Even though this Marxist utopian scheme ran against basic human nature, the kibbutzim were successful and popular in the early twentieth century. The fierce idealism of the kibbutz founders overcame the fact that in the early years many of their members died from malaria, work accidents, marauding Arabs and physical exhaustion. Their firm belief that they were rebuilding themselves, the Jewish people, the Land of Israel, the world as a whole, through this actualization of the Marxist dream, carried the kibbutzim for a number of generations.

The early kibbutzim cast away any semblance of Jewish tradition from their midst. There was no synagogue, no kosher food, even no marriage or divorce procedures. Marxism, collectivism and physical labor combined to create the new faith of the Jewish Left. The Jewish holidays were celebrated as agricultural feasts and the Passover *Haggadah* was rewritten to commemorate the thrust for Marxist freedom on behalf of the workers of the world. The kibbutz movement, though relatively small in numbers, wielded great influence in the Jewish world and stamped an unmistakably secular image on the emerging Jewish community in the Land of Israel.

Herzl died in 1904, at the age of forty-four. His death sent a shock wave through much of the Jewish world, where he was mourned by the masses of simple Jews, especially in Eastern Europe.[31] Max Nordau, a

---

30. Sachar, p.76.

31. Menachem Begin's grandfather, an Orthodox Jew, who was the leader of the Jewish *kehillah* (community organization) in Brisk (later, Brest-Litovsk) Lithuanian Russia in 1904, allowed the memorial service for Herzl to be conducted in the main synagogue of the city, over the unavailing objection of Rabbi Chaim Soloveitchik, the rabbi of the community.

Nachum Sokolow

French/German confidant of Herzl's — and like him, Westernized and assimilated — replaced him as head of the Zionist movement. It would not be long, however, before the Eastern European Jews would take control. By the end of the decade, Chaim Weizmann and Nachum Sokolow emerged as the new leaders of Zionism. Weizmann was an ex-yeshivah student from the town of Motele, deep in the heart of the Jewish Pale of Settlement in czarist Russia. He left Russia and Jewish observance,[32] attending a university in Germany where he emerged with a doctorate in chemistry. Chemistry and science were really only his avocation. His life's work was the cause of Zionism and the establishment of a Jewish state in the Land of Israel. He was single-minded, indefatigable and shrewdly capable in pursuit of his goal. Sir Ronald Storrs, who would serve as a British High Commissioner for Palestine in the 1920's, described Weizmann (with the usual British upper class sarcasm of the time) as, "a brilliant talker with an unrivaled gift for lucid exposition … As a speaker almost frighteningly convincing, even in English … In Hebrew, and even more in Russian, overwhelming, with all that dynamic persuasiveness which Slavs usually devote to love and Jews to business, nourished, trained, and concentrated upon the accomplishment of Zion."[33]

By 1905, those in the Orthodox camp opposed to Zionism had organized themselves. Convening in Katowicz (now Poland, then Austria-Hungary) in 1912, they established Agudath Israel. Most of the great Chasidic *rebbeim* of Poland, White Russia and the Ukraine, numerous leaders of Lithuanian Jewry, such as the sainted Rabbi Yisrael Meir Kagan (commonly known as the Chafetz Chaim after the title of one of his famous works) and the scrupulously Orthodox, yet Westernized German Jews were active in the new organization. Agudath Israel remained staunchly opposed to Zionism throughout the first half of the century, but somehow also supported the idea of Jewish settlement and development in the Land of Israel. It was largely successful in negotiating this ideological tightrope safely and positively. Zionism was to become one of the most divisive issues within the Orthodox Jewish camp in the twentieth century, and groups within Orthodoxy would henceforth define themselves relative to their attitude towards Zionism.

Revolutionary Fervor Sweeps Through Russia

MOMENTOUS EVENTS IN RUSSIA IN 1904 AND 1905 QUICKLY overtook the Jewish world. Nicholas II, Czar of Russia and the

---

32. At the end of his life, he returned to Jewish observance. A High Holiday prayer book was found open on his bed's reading table when he expired.

33. Sachar, p.98.

last of the Romanovs, was a weak, overly proud, insecure, wife-dominated monarch. His wife, Alexandra, a granddaughter of Queen Victoria of England, constantly prodded him to play the autocratic dictator. "Show them the knout!" was her advice on how to deal with the political and social unrest in Russia that was already a half-century old.

In 1886, Nicholas' father, Alexander III, had begun to build the Trans-Siberian railroad line, the longest in the world, which would stretch from Moscow to Vladivostok on the Pacific Ocean. Through this monumental feat of railroad building, Russia hoped to become a major Pacific power, encouraged in this desire by Kaiser Wilhelm II of Germany, Nicholas' cousin and another grandson of Queen Victoria. The kaiser wanted Russia's expansionist nature directed eastward rather than competing with German ambitions in Western Europe, Africa, Asia and the Middle East. In 1896, Russia shortened the length of the Trans-Siberian line then being built by extracting from China the right to build the final section of the railroad across Chinese territory in Manchuria. Even though Manchuria was under Chinese sovereignty, which Russia had agreed to respect, Russia soon garrisoned Manchuria with sizeable numbers of Russian troops. In 1898, Russia forced China to grant it a lease over the port and naval base at Port Arthur.

Another major power interested in establishing a foothold in China was Japan. It had modernized and industrialized rapidly in the last half of the nineteenth century and now stood poised to launch the aggressive adventurism that characterized its military behavior in the first half of the twentieth century. Japan therefore felt its interests threatened by the appearance of Russian troops in Manchuria and the Russian navy so close to its shores. Japan offered Russia an arrangement by which Russia could control Manchuria, providing Japan would be allowed to control the Korean peninsula. The Russian czar, offended by even having to negotiate with the "monkeys who play Europeans,"[34] procrastinated and toyed with the Japanese diplomats. Furious and determined, Japan opened hostilities without an official declaration of war against Russia in February, 1904.[35] It bottled up the Russian fleet at Port Arthur and invaded Korea with a large army. Russia invaded Korea to oust the Japanese. But the Japanese generals proved to be a strong foe and they outfought the Russians, forcing them out of Korea. Japan then invaded Manchuria, driving the Russian army back into the defenses of Port Arthur, which the Japanese then laid under siege.

---

34. Czar Alexander III's infelicitous description of the Japanese. It represented an attitude that his son, Nicholas II, absorbed.

35. In the nineteenth century, such "sneak attacks" were unheard of and were considered to be outside the realm of "civilized" warfare. Japan would repeat such behavior in its attack on Pearl Harbor, Hawaii, in 1941.

On January 1, 1905, Port Arthur surrendered. The Russians, in a last desperate attempt to win the war, dispatched their Baltic Sea Fleet on a round-the-world trip to confront the Japanese navy. In less than an hour on May 27, 1905, the Japanese navy crushed Russia's hopes of becoming a dominant Pacific power in the Battle of Tsushima Strait. Of the 36 Russian warships that entered the battle, only two made it to the safety of the Russian naval base at Vladivostok. Twenty-two Russian ships were sunk, six were captured and six interned in neutral ports. In the peace treaty negotiated through the offices of American President Theodore Roosevelt, Japan was granted control of Korea and of Port Arthur, Manchuria was returned to China and Russia ceded the southern half of Sakhalin Island to Japan. The war left Russia with 120,000 soldiers killed, its naval power destroyed and its international humiliation complete. The czar had failed miserably in diplomacy and war — and the masses of Russia, led by the revolutionary anarchists, socialists, communists and Social Democrats would now make him accountable for that dismal failure.

Even before the crushing defeats of Port Arthur and Tsushima Strait, the spirit of revolution was in the air. In January 1905, more than 80,000 workers went on strike in St. Petersburg. The city was effectively paralyzed. On January 9, the workers and their supporters staged a peaceful demonstration. They attempted to send their representatives to the Winter Palace to present their demands for better social and economic conditions to the czar. The czar responded by unloosing his Cossack cavalry on the defenseless mob. More than two hundred demonstrators were slaughtered that day. The general strike spread throughout Russian cities and especially in Russian Poland. The czar's uncle, Grand Duke Serge, was assassinated.

For the next six months, Russia was in turmoil. The Russian army was unable to control the rampaging mobs and the country spun out of control. In desperation, the czar agreed to create a parliamentary body to represent the Russian people — the *Duma*. He announced that, "while preserving the fundamental law regarding autocratic power," he had decided "to summon elected representatives from the whole of Russia to take a constant and active part in the elaboration of laws."[36] But this statement was too little, too late. By December, full-scale revolution, led by anarchists and Marxists, broke out in Moscow. Pitched battles were fought for ten days between the revolutionaries, the police and the army for control of government offices and the railway stations. Slowly, the czar's forces gained the upper hand. Throughout Russia, thousands died in the unrest and other thousands were captured and exiled to Siberia.

---

36. Martin Gilbert, *A History of the Twentieth Century*, Vol. 1, New York, 1997, p.112.

On May 10, 1906, the first session of the elected *duma* was called into session and addressed by the czar. The members of the new parliament were optimistic that Russia was finally on the way to democratic rule. They chose to ignore the czar's words in his speech when he expressly stated that the *duma* would have to operate within the constraints of royal autocracy. The *duma* was led by the representatives of the Kadets (Social Democrats) and the Peasant Party. The right-wing supporters of autocracy and a policy of no-change were very much in the minority, yet as the police and the army slowly subdued all of the revolutionaries, the czar took heart and the *duma* was "temporarily" suspended, less then a year after its formation. Autocracy had won the battle, but it had lost the war.

Richard Pipes, a noted expert of Russian history, succinctly summed up the situation:

> It is fair to say ... that the 1905 Revolution not only failed to resolve Russia's outstanding problem — estrangement between rulers and ruled — but aggravated it. And to the extent that attitudes rather than institutions or "objective" economic and social realities determine the course of politics, only unbounded optimists could look to the future with any confidence. In fact, Russia had gained only a breathing spell.[37]

Calculated Persecution, Inevitable Migration

A SCAPEGOAT FOR ALL OF THESE MILITARY AND GOVERNMENTAL DISASTERS had to be found in order to divert the wrath of the masses (especially the peasants who suffered most in the army and due to the poor economy) away from the czar and his cruel, inept government ministers. The most convenient scapegoat was the Jews: the Jewish capitalists of Wall Street, especially Jacob H. Schiff, stood accused of helping to finance the Japanese war machine in its war against Russia. In 1905-6, numerous pogroms broke out all over Russia. The government's policy originally had been to repress these violent outbreaks. In stopping anti-Jewish pogroms the government was acting in its own best interests, for it was thereby also protecting the wealth of the landed estate noblemen whose palaces would be next on the list of the raging mobs. But late in 1906, the government changed its policy towards pogroms. Instead of resisting the anti-Jewish violence, it now actively promoted them, printing and distributing leaflets openly inciting mob violence against the Jews. When such violence took place, the police stood by and did nothing or, in many cases, joined the mob and took part in the killing and looting. The czar

---

37. Richard Pipes, *The Russian Revolution*, New York, 1991, p.48.

justified the pogroms by saying that "nine-tenths of the revolutionaries were Yids (*Zhids*)."[38] In simple fact, many of the revolutionaries were Jewish, but nine-tenths of the Jews in Russia certainly were not revolutionaries. But the dirt thrown at the Jewish community stuck, and Jews would henceforth be viewed by most Russians as Russia's most revolutionary and anti-government population. The czar himself accepted the insignia of The Union of Russian People (The Black Hundreds), a virulently anti-Semitic group that supported his autocracy. The Jewish communities in Russia would now suffer from a further decade-long reign of terror, encouraged by the government and perpetrated by the frustrated and embittered peasant masses of Russia.

The reactions of the Jews in Russia to this sustained government-sponsored violence against them were varied. A large number of Jews, over a million, picked up and left during this decade. They'd had enough. As noted previously, most of them went to North America, though many immigrated to England, Germany, Belgium, France and South Africa as well. In the half-century between the 1870's and the 1920's, over three million Jews left Eastern Europe.

Of this number, a small group made their way to the Land of Israel. Many of them were revolutionaries who gave up on their dream of reforming Russia and looked for a new arena in which to practice their utopian schemes. All of them were idealists who were determined to create a new social and national entity for the Jewish people. The concept of *chalutziut* – pioneering – fired the imaginations of young Russian Jews. Their cause was eloquently recorded by Yosef Vitkin, a schoolteacher in the Galilee, who wrote:

> *The major causes of our blundering are our search for a shortcut, and our belief that the attainment of our goal is close at hand. Out of this belief we have built castles in the air ... and have turned aside with contempt from the longer and harder road, which is perhaps the surest, and in the end, the shortest ... Awake, O youth of Israel! Come to the aid of your people. Your people lies in agony. Rush to its side. Band together, discipline yourself for life or death; forget all the precious bonds of your childhood; leave them behind forever without a shadow of regret and answer to the call of your people ...* [39]

More than 30,000 Eastern European Jews came to Israel between 1905 and the beginning of World War I in 1914. Most of them died there of malaria, malnutrition and marauding Arabs, or returned home, crushed by the experience. These arriving Jews were greeted with fear and enmity

---

38. Ibid. p.51.
39. Sachar, p.72.

by those Jews already established in the country. Since most of the new Jews were socialists and atheists, the entrenched religious community (the *yishuv hayashan* — the previous settlers who had come in the early 1800's) and the representatives of the Jewish colonies (funded by the French Jewish capitalist, Baron Rothschild) found the ideals and behavior of the newly-arrived Jews hostile to their traditions and economic welfare.

Only about 2,000 of these pioneers survived the decade, but they were the ones who laid the foundation of the agricultural kibbutzim and moshav settlements (a farming cooperative less communistic in structure than the kibbutz), formed a Jewish self-defense group that curtailed Arab depredations and set the stage for a militantly socialist, secular Jewish society in Palestine. They combined the ideas of Marx, revolution, holiness of Jewish labor

A Poalei Zion group in Plonsk, Poland. David Ben-Gurion is seated second from the right.

and the creation of a new secular Jewish society and culture into a new, godless striving for the messianic era. Under the leadership of Eliezer ben Yehuda, they recreated and modernized the Hebrew language and made it the official language of the new *yishuv*. Later, many thousands more would come from Eastern Europe to join them under their red banner of Labor Zionism.

Most Eastern European Jews, however, whether out of choice or no choice, bowed their heads and stayed in "the old home." Their economic and social situation continued to deteriorate, but they accepted their lot stoically. The rabbinic leaders and Chasidic *rebbeim* did not soften their stand against Zionism or immigration to America, even after the pogroms of the decade. Although there were now an enormous number of defections from Orthodox Jewish life in Eastern Europe, paradoxically, the yeshivos continued to grow and the Chasidic courts remained full on the holidays. Yet the groundswell of change in the Jewish world of Eastern Europe was unstoppable: a product of the crumbling of the czar's government and of the terrible conditions that imprisoned its millions of Jews.

Not only Russia was in chaos. The Austro-Hungarian Empire, peopled by dozens of nationalities and ethnic groupings, was also beginning to crack at the seams. There were two Balkan Wars before World War I and constant minor rebellions against the rule of the Hapsburgs. The

Ottoman Empire, which bordered the Austro-Hungarian Empire and competed with it for dominance in the Balkan and Aegean areas, also faced constant turmoil and violence. Greece, Macedonia, Kosovo, Bosnia, Albania, Serbia, Croatia, Slovakia and Galician Poland all had centers of rebellion against the Austrians or the Turks, or against both, as the case might be. Jewish communities, both Sephardic and Ashkenazic, some of them quite sizable and ancient, existed in all of these troubled areas. Unlike Russia, there was no large Jewish presence in the revolutionary ranks attempting to destroy these formerly powerful, but by now obsolescent, empires. Nevertheless, as was always the case in times of political unrest and instability, Jews suffered from violence and hatred directed against them from both sides of the conflict. Because of this persecution during the early 1900's, there was sizable Jewish emigration from Austro-Hungary and other parts of Central Europe as well.

Zionism also penetrated the Jewish areas of the Hapsburg Empire, but the Jews of Hungary and Austria were much more assimilated than their Russian brethren. There was a sizable rate of Jewish intermarriage and even conversion to Christianity (especially among the academics, artists, musicians and wealthy businessmen) throughout Central Europe. Despite all of the unrest, most Jews in the Austro-Hungarian Empire found the rule of Emperor Franz Josef relatively benign, and willingly said prayers on his behalf, whereas in Russia their co-religionists had to be coerced to do the same on behalf of the czar.

Tensions Sizzle in Palestine

THE WEAKNESS OF THE OTTOMAN EMPIRE AT THE BEGINNING OF THE century would prove to be an important factor in the Jewish story that would unfold. Known as "the sick man of Europe," the Ottoman Empire was drowning in corruption, inefficiency and mismanagement. All of its subjects, the many different tribes of the Arabs, Jews, Turks, Greeks, Armenians and other nationalities, were restive under its rule. Backward in terms of the standards of European Christian civilization,[40] the sultan bravely attempted to hold together the disparate parts of his kingdom. Failing tyrants generally thought that war could save their thrones from toppling. But the major European powers forced a peace settlement on the Ottoman Empire, ending the Balkan Wars. Its neighbors looked hungrily at the vast expanse of land that was yet under the weak control of the Turks.

The Jews in Palestine, whose population had risen from 24,000 in 1881 to close to 85,000 by 1914, were unhappy subjects of Ottoman

---

40. It was not until 1909 that the institution of the Ottoman sultan's harem was officially brought to a close. (J.M. Roberts, *The Twentieth Century*, New York, 1999, p.13.)

rule. The Turks ruled the inhabitants of Palestine, Arab and Jew alike, with cruelty and corruption. The Jews, being non-Moslem, were discriminated against and abused in myriad ways in everyday life. In 1908, a revolution of the "Young Turks" occurred in Turkey and a representative parliament was to be chosen to help govern the empire. In spite of the attempt at reform and fairness, the area of Palestine continued to be governed by two local governors, one in Beirut and the other in Jerusalem. These governors were apparently accountable to no one and ruled tyrannically and arbitrarily. The head of the Jewish community was the *Chacham Bashi* — the Sephardic Chief Rabbi of Jerusalem. He was a leader in title alone, with little influence on the Turkish governors or on his Jewish constituents. The Ashkenazic community in Palestine did not recognize his authority, for relations between the Ashkenazim and Sephardim were strained in general. As the number of Ashkenazic East European Jews grew substantially in this time preceding World War I, the Sephardim soon found themselves outnumbered and shunted aside by the new immigrants. The social and religious background of the Sephardim, based on Moslem societal norms, rendered them completely unprepared for the ideas of socialism, "holiness" of manual and agricultural labor, denial of tradition and ritual, and the fierce nationalism that now characterized the majority of the Ashkenazim in Palestine.

Most of the Ashkenazic residents of Palestine were under the "protection" of the consuls of their countries of origin who were stationed in Jerusalem. The Austrian and Russian consuls were especially active on behalf of the Jews from their countries. Their zealousness was not so much due to humane concern for their Jewish countrymen (such concern was hardly noticeable in Russia and the Austro-Hungarian Empire themselves) as it was an expression of hostility to the Ottoman Empire. In the elections for the new Turkish parliament, almost no Jews in Palestine were allowed to participate in the voting and they waited to see how the rule of the Ottoman Empire might change. They hoped, naively and unrealistically, that the government would take a benign view of Jewish attempts to intensively settle and develop the land. In fact, one of the traits of Zionism, and later of the State of Israel, was to underestimate the intensity of Moslem opposition to Jewish settlement in the Land of Israel.

More than 300,000 Sephardic Jews were living in the Middle East and the Balkans under the Ottoman Empire at this time. There were additional large Sephardic Jewish communities in Algeria, Morocco, Tunisia, Egypt and Libya. These communities were already under the influence of England, France, Italy and the other colonial powers of Europe who held sway, and sometimes direct power, in these lands. There was also an ancient Jewish community in Yemen, though the Yemenite Jews never identified themselves as Sephardim. In addition, there were "Western" Sephardic communities in England, France, Holland and the United States. These communities accounted for an additional 200,000-300,000 Jews.

The Western Sephardim, especially in England, had undergone a rapid assimilation into English society. Publicly loyally traditional Jews, such as Sir Moses Montefiore, were rare in British life in the nineteenth century. And these genteel, assimilated Sephardic grandees looked askance, if not with horror, at the wave of Ashkenazic immigrants who migrated to the West. Nevertheless, the Sephardic community in London, centered around Bevis Marks Synagogue and the Spanish-Portuguese Congregation, attempted to aid their fellow Jews gain freedom from discrimination and achieve economic and social equality.

In the United States, the great Sephardic congregation of the Spanish-Portuguese Synagogue in New York City represented the Sephardic community, which was well rooted and highly successful in American society. There were smaller Sephardic communities in all of the major American cities, but they were soon overwhelmed in American Jewish life, first by the Reform German Jews and then by the mass immigration of the Ashkenazim from Eastern Europe. New Sephardic immigration from the Middle East during the rest of the century, especially after both World Wars, would revitalize the Sephardic Jewish communities in America, but for many decades the Sephardic communities would play a secondary role in American Jewish life.

At the beginning of the century, French was the dominant cultural international language. The French saw themselves as being the dominant political and cultural influence in the Middle East and the Mediterranean basin. It was therefore natural that French Jewry would attempt to "modernize" the Jews of the Levant. The instrument for this modernization was the Alliance Israelite Universelle (Kol Yisrael Chaverim, was its Hebrew name.) This organization opened schools in the major Jewish communities in the Middle East, North Africa and the Balkans. By the end of the first decade, close to 50,000 Jewish children were studying in the Alliance school network. The Sephardic rabbis, who were rapidly losing their previously iron hold on the masses, bitterly opposed the Alliance schools. To traditional eyes, the secular nature of the schools and the absence of ritually observant teachers made the entire Alliance project suspect. Yet, even without the appearance of Alliance schools, the newly emerging Sephardic bourgeoisie was drifting away from the old ways. Many of them sent their children to Christian schools to obtain a Western education. The debate then was whether the Alliance schools, which at least taught a minimum of Jewish subjects, were really the lesser of two evils. Sephardic Jews began to send their sons to France to obtain a higher education. The old order was gradually eroding. Leon Sciaky, in *Farewell to Salonica*, (London, 1946) describes the westernization of traditional Sephrdic Jews during this era:

> *The [nineteenth] century was drawing to a close. Stealthily the West was creeping in, trying to lure the East with her wonders. She dangled before our dazzled eyes the witchery of her science and the miracle of her inventions. We caught a glimpse of her brilliance, and timidly listened to the song of the siren.* (Quoted by Howard Sachar in *Farewell Espana*, New York, 1994.)

The Sephardim were not the only group swamped by a tidal wave of secularization. The *yishuv hayashan* in Palestine (known today as the Chareidi or by the unfortunate designation of "ultra-Orthodox" community) was also overwhelmed by secular, earthy and ambitious newcomers from Eastern Europe. Though the children of the *yishuv hayashan* also pioneered new settlements outside of Jerusalem and Safed,[41] the nature and programs of the anti-religious kibbutzim and the substitution of Jewish culture for Torah study and observance by the Zionist movement horrified the leaders of the almost century-old Orthodox community centered in Jerusalem. They reacted by banning any innovations in their own community system, mode of dress or lifestyle, refusing to adopt Hebrew as a spoken language, or changing in any way the curriculum or pedagogical methods of their schools. Forced on the defensive by the secular onslaught loosed upon them, they refused to accommodate their rivals in any fashion and were determined to preserve their way of life and traditions at all costs and with all means possible.

The "Wailing"/Western Wall in Jerusalem in 1910.

Rabbi Avraham Yitzchak HaKohen Kook arrived in Jaffa from Bolsk, Lithuania, at the turn of the century to become the rabbi in that dusty, derelict port city. The Jewish population there then numbered about 6,000 souls. Rabbi Kook also served as the rabbi of the agricultural "colonies" (about 30 in number) near Jaffa. Most of these colonies were founded through the wealth and efforts of the aforementioned Baron Rothschild of Paris.[42] Unlike the new kibbutzim and moshav settlements, the "colonies" were officially observant of Jewish tradition — but they were rapidly falling under the secular influences of the Labor

---

41. Petach Tikva and Rosh Pina are two examples, among others.

42. Known as the *nadiv hayadua* – the "famous philanthropist."

Rabbi Avraham Yitzchak HaKohen Kook

Zionists. Rabbi Kook developed a relationship with the "colonists" and attempted to arrest the spread of secularism among them and their children. The lack of an organized religious school system to meet the needs of this group hampered Rabbi Kook's efforts greatly. By the end of the decade, however, Mizrachi attempted to found schools that would preserve Torah studies and tradition and yet be in tune with the new Zionist cultural reality that was taking form in the Land of Israel. Its schools were roundly condemned by the secular as being too religious and by the *yishuv hayashan* for being too cultural and non-traditional. Nevertheless, the new schools, though never satisfying the criticism of its opponents, gradually gained students and adherents and became the basis for a general religious school system that would survive and even prosper during the century.

In 1909, Rabbi Kook published a scholarly book, *Shabbat HaAretz*,[43] defending the *heter mechirah*[44] that allowed Jews in the Land of Israel to do certain work on the land during the *shemittah* (sabbatical) year when the Torah commands that the land lie fallow. Even though this brought him into open disagreement with the leaders of the *yishuv hayashan* who opposed the *heter mechirah*, Rabbi Kook never felt isolated from the *yishuv hayashan* and would identify himself with its cause and goals many times during his stormy public career. Rabbi Kook was a many-faceted personality: scholar, dreamer, political leader, organizer and executive, mystic and teacher. In the first decade of the twentieth century, he was a person of influence and power in many different areas of the Jewish world.

Facing the second decade of the new century, it was obvious that it would be a period of great change, but no one could imagine how meaningful it would be. The cataclysmic change about to unfold — the disappearance of the old, stable world of empires and monarchs, of accept-

---

43. *Shabbat HaAretz* is an exhaustive halachic treatise regarding the laws of *shemittah* and was highly regarded even by those who disagreed with and opposed its halachic conclusions.

44. The question of the practical observance of *shemittah* on a large scale was first raised by Baron Rothschild concerning his "colonies" in the 1880's. Rabbi Yitzchak Elchanan Spektor of Kovno, Rabbi David Friedman of Karlin and Rabbi Shmuel Mohilever, among others, issued rabbinic responsa permitting certain agricultural labor by Jews in the Land of Israel if the land was first "sold" to a Moslem. This *heter* was based on the exigencies of Jewish food production in the Land of Israel being a matter of life-saving importance. The proponents, including Rabbi Kook, ruled that the *heter mechirah* was an expedient that should be re-examined every *shemittah* and could be utilized only as an emergency measure. Naturally, authorities would differ regarding whether or not the current circumstance necessitated reliance on the *heter*. The *heter* was controversial from the start and was opposed by the rabbis of the *yishuv hayashan* as well as by Rabbi Naftali Zvi Yehuda Berlin of Volozhin and other Eastern European scholars. Nevertheless, the *heter* was renewed by Rabbi Spektor for later *shemittos* and was widely accepted by most of the religious farmers in the Land of Israel at the beginning of the century. Rabbi Kook's book strengthened this acceptance of the *heter mechirah*.

Leaving from Danzig, bound for new worlds. Most Jews went to America; some joined the yishuv *in Palestine.*

ed culture and small professional armies, of limited wars and European domination of peoples of color — would impact on the entire world, including all of Jewish society.

No one in 1910 could predict that the destruction of the old order was almost upon the world. But death grinned hideously just around the corner.

Chapter Two

Implosion of the Old Order

1911-1920

THE STREAM OF JEWISH IMMIGRATION INTO AMERICA CONTINUED IN the years just before World War I. The continued worsening of the Jewish condition in Russia and the encouragement of relatives who had already settled in America to come join them generated the desire for change and movement. The economic situation of the Jewish immigrants in America was far from attractive. A very large percentage of Jews worked in the textile and needle trades. Garment workers were working an average 60-hour workweek. At this time, $800.00 a year was considered the minimum income for a family to live decently. Economic data gathered at the beginning of this decade indicate that the average annual wage of Jewish women employed in the garment industry was $240.00 while that of Jewish men was $450.00.[1] Yet the values of the Jewish immigrants provided integrity and an admirable framework. An American reporter writing about their plight noted: *...ideas of Americans and East European Jews on minimum necessities are* not *the same. The poor are not on charity, except for hospitalization; they save money, and they send great sums to relatives in Europe each year.*[2]

---

1. Meltzer, pp.236-7.
2. Ibid.

The Eastern European Jews lived in self-created ghettoes such as the famous "Lower East Side" of New York City. These ghettoes existed in every American city in which Jews lived. Living conditions in the overcrowded, unsanitary and unsafe tenement houses were dreary and difficult. Almost every family was forced to rent out rooms to boarders in order to make ends meet, further reducing privacy and sanitation. Communal bathrooms, one on each floor of the apartment building, sometimes serving as many as six or eight families, were the norm. There was no running water in the apartments; tenants had to manage with a central water spigot located in the common hall. The situation was aptly described by a former tenant:

> *Twenty-four families occupied our tenement, six families on each floor.*
> *The halls were very busy places, mostly because the toilets and running*

In a coal cellar dwelling,
Ludlow St.,
New York City

A tenement on the Lower East Side

water were community services in the halls. If you went to the sink to fetch water, you were bound to meet a neighbor or two. Someone would have a pitcher to fill with drinking water. Someone else would have a cooking pot to fill. And usually a mother would be waiting to fill a tub for her youngsters' bath.

You walk along the street ... The flies and mosquitoes add to the discomfort. The smells from the uncollected garbage are nauseating. The rivulets in the gutter, sweeping along the slops from the wash-pail water dumped by the storekeepers, are black and the smells are putrid. Little boys, unabashed, urinate into the flow of bilge and add to the stench.[3]

Conditions were even worse in the workplace. It was not only that the workers were underpaid and overworked that embittered their lives. It was the fact that their lives were in constant danger due to the unsafe conditions in the garment factories. Workers were literally locked into these poorly lit and barely ventilated firetraps. A twelve to fourteen hour workday was the norm, and all of the factories (even the Jewish-owned ones) had a six-day workweek. The slogan of the employer was, "If you don't come in on Saturday, don't bother to come on Monday." Some shops and factories required a seven-day week.[4] The practical effect of these policies was the destruction of Sabbath observance, even among well-meaning religious Jews.

Labor Becomes a Potent Social Force

As THE JEWISH WORKERS GROANED UNDER THEIR BURDEN OF SERVITUDE, bold people took steps to improve the situation. Abraham Cahan,[5] Morris Hillquit, Joseph Barondess and others organized the laborers

3. Ibid. pp.202-3.

4. Ibid. p.299

5. Founder and editor of the *Jewish Daily Forward*, a socialist, Yiddish, New York-based daily (including Saturday) newspaper that for decades was the most popular and influential of the Jewish newspapers in America. Its circulation peaked at about 250,000 in the 1920's. It was anti-Zionist, anti-religious and preached complete Jewish assimilation into American society, though it itself always remained militantly non-American socialist. Its masthead contained the slogan: "Workers of the world, unite!" It survives only in name today as an English language weekly.

forming The United Hebrew Trades. The International Ladies' Garment Workers' Union, the largest trade union of its kind, was almost completely Jewish in its membership and leadership. By 1910, the union had close to 100,000 members. Its leadership was intimidated and hesitant to use the weapon of the general strike, but its hand was forced by a mass meeting of women workers and organizers held at Cooper Union hall on November 22, 1909.[6] Ida Tarbell,[7] Lillian Wald[8] and Clara Lemlich[9] led the meeting, demanding a general strike of all women workers in the New York garment district. For the next few months, the strike raged,[10] closing down hundreds of shops and factories. The results of the strike were mixed, but a critical point had been proven: workers could and would strike. Later in 1910 a larger strike, involving more than 60,000 workers, occurred. Prominent Americanized Jews including Louis Marshall, Jacob Schiff and Louis Brandeis formed a committee to settle the strike and meet the workers' just demands. Samuel Gompers, a Jew who headed the American Federation of Labor, negotiated the labor agreement[11] on behalf of the garment workers, and wages and working conditions slowly began to improve.

After the aborted Russian revolution of 1905, many Jewish radicals of the Left came to America. One of them, Sidney Hillman,[12] arrived in Chicago in 1907 and eventually became the leader of the Amalgamated Clothing Workers of America, the male equivalent of the International Ladies' Garment Workers' Union. These two Jewish labor unions spearheaded militant union activity in America and succeeded in having their demands — union shop, collective bargaining, minimum wage, government-supervised working conditions — accepted as the norm for American factories under Franklin Roosevelt's New Deal. The Amalgamated Clothing Workers of America founded its own bank, built low-cost housing for its members, provided old-age facilities for its retirees and successfully lobbied for the introduction of unemployment compensation for workers who temporarily lost their jobs.

---

6. The site of Abraham Lincoln's famous "house divided" speech.

7. A well-known muckraker and journalist – the female Lincoln Steffens of her day.

8. A settlement-house leader and activist on behalf of the rights of the Jewish immigrants.

9. A very militant unionist and feminist, famous for her violent confrontations with the New York Police Department, evidence of which were present in the bruises she proudly carried on her body.

10. The strike was immortalized in American labor history as the "Uprising of the Twenty Thousand."

11. The agreement was given the pompous title the "Protocol of Peace."

12. This talented and dynamic person was a student of the Slobodka yeshivah in Lithuania. He was radicalized, as were many other yeshivah students of that period, during the 1905 revolution against the czar. He abandoned his Talmud studies and his traditional beliefs and substituted the ideas of moderate socialism and militant trade unionism for his former faith.

Unfortunately, it took a tragedy to give the garment workers and their unions their greatest boost. On March 25, 1911, the Triangle Shirtwaist Company's factory on the Lower East Side of Manhattan went up in flames, trapping hundreds of workers in a fiery prison. One hundred forty-one young women met their deaths suffocating or burning, or by jumping desperately from the roof or windows of the flaming building. Fifty thousand people gathered for the mass funeral of the victims, vowing that such inhumane labor conditions would no longer be tolerated.

Interior of a sweatshop, 1904

By the end of the second decade of the century, over a quarter of a million Jews were members of labor unions affiliated with the United Hebrew Trades. Over later decades, the Jewish trade unions would lose much of their original militancy and settle for pragmatic cooperation with the employers. But their major contribution, that of organizing workers to fight for their rights, left a deep impression on American economic life.

A key factor in the success of the Jewish labor unions was the attraction to socialism that many Jews felt at the beginning of the century. The socialists, more than anyone else, organized Jewish labor and made the Jewish population in the United States a consistent supporter of liberal causes. In the words of historian Milton Meltzer:

Their [the socialists] great achievement was that they transformed these degraded Jewish immigrants into a social force that not only altered the course of Jewish history in the United States but left its mark on the country's entire labor movement. The remarkable thing was that these beaten-down laborers, who worked under such abominable conditions, who were not part of a tradition of independent trade union action, who were perhaps in their majority Orthodox in religion, founded the first trade unions as socialist organizations. The socialist ideology of the leaders found a warm response in the sense of social justice that lived in the heart of the ordinary Jew — a sense that derived from a combination of the prophetic vision and his unjust treatment at the hands of the non-Jewish world.[13]

Workman's Circle 14th Annual Convention, New Haven, Connecticut 1914

Not only were there Jewish socialists in America at the beginning of the century, there were also Jewish communists. In fact, there were only 17,000 members of the Communist Party (by 1920), and Jews made up about 10% of that number. The vast majority of these Jewish communists were Yiddish-speaking immigrant radicals, though there were a few

---

13. Meltzer, p.308

hundred English-speaking Jewish communists as well, some American-born. Small in number, they were nonetheless highly vocal and publicly prominent, something which would contribute to later anti-Semitism in American society. The communist Yiddish newspaper, *Freiheit* (Freedom) was published daily and had a readership far wider than those Jews who were actual communist sympathizers. The Jewish affinity for the political Left, both in America and the Land of Israel, was quite apparent in the first half of the twentieth century.

The Ultimate "Foreigners"

BETWEEN 1870 AND 1910, MORE THAN 200,000 JEWS ARRIVED AND settled in England and Ireland (then still part of Great Britain). Many of these Jews believed that they had arrived in the United States, their intended destination. They were soon disabused of this notion and settled down willingly in the cities and towns of England. Most lived in London, and especially in London's East End district, which soon appeared as the English equivalent of Manhattan's Lower East Side. Jews in England generally kept a very low profile. Harry Austryn Wolfson, famed professor of Hebrew Literature and Philosophy at Harvard University, observed in 1915:

> *In England it is quite fashionable to admit Judaism into the parlor. Parlor Judaism, to be sure, is not more vital a force nor more creative than kitchen Judaism, but it seems to be more vital than the Judaism restricted to the Temple. At least it is voluntary and personal and what is more important, it is engaging. So engrossed in the subject of his discussion was once my [English] host at tea, that while administering the sugar, he asked me quite absent-mindedly: "Would you have one or two lumps with your Judaism?"*
>
> *"Thank you, none at all," was my reply. "But I am wont to take my Judaism somewhat stronger, if you please."[14]*

England was coolly hospitable to the new arrivals, though whenever unemployment rose, Jews were used as the scapegoat. Numerous immigration restrictions were proposed to keep the Jews out. In August 1911, a full-blown pogrom (though without fatalities) took place in Tredegar, a town of 20,000 in South Wales. Even though there were only 30 Jewish families in the town, and only one family derived its income from rents, the wrath of the unemployed miners was turned against the "Jewish landlords." The *Jewish Chronicle* newspaper reported:

> *Happily, up until the time of going to press, no lives have been lost, so far as is known, but hundreds of Jews have been ruined [throughout*

---

14. *Menorah Journal*, Vol. 1 No.1, (July,1915) p.27.

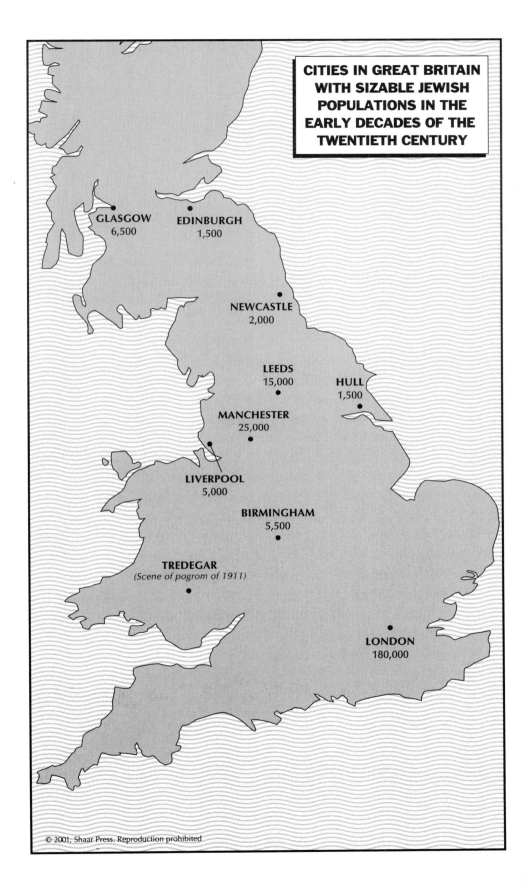

CITIES IN GREAT BRITAIN
WITH SIZABLE JEWISH
POPULATIONS IN THE
EARLY DECADES OF THE
TWENTIETH CENTURY

GLASGOW
6,500

EDINBURGH
1,500

NEWCASTLE
2,000

LEEDS
15,000

HULL
1,500

MANCHESTER
25,000

LIVERPOOL
5,000

BIRMINGHAM
5,500

TREDEGAR
(Scene of pogrom of 1911)

LONDON
180,000

© 2001, Shaar Press. Reproduction prohibited

South Wales], having been robbed of their all, and many who were in good positions are now left destitute. Indeed, the happenings of the last few days in South Wales read of nothing so much as the pogroms we have deplored in Russia.

At Ebbow Vale on Monday, rioters armed with crowbars, sticks, stones and bottles, broke into a tobacconist's shop and entered the living quarters, so that the inhabitants — [Jewish] men, women and children — who were unarmed, had to secrete themselves in an attic, and were rescued only by the arrival of the military. Upon being released from their hiding-place, they found the shop totally wrecked and the goods stolen. Gas fittings had been wrenched off and the boardings of the floor torn up. On all hands there was one cry — that the Jews must be forced out of South Wales. Many of the Jews hastily departed from Tredegar and the neighboring towns, leaving their homes untended, fearing to remain because of their lives.[15]

There was also much anti-Semitic agitation in the United States. Reacting to to the flood of new immigrants, a nativistic and populist upsurge took hold of Americans. "Foreigners" were portrayed as the cause of all problems in American life from unemployment and crime, to the pressures of urbanization and industrialization. Racist organizations such as the Ku Klux Klan printed and distributed anti-Semitic tracts and crude anti-Jewish cartoons, fanning anti-Jewish fears and hatred. Crackpot theories about the inferiority of race and nationality that ominously presaged Hitler and his "Aryan superiority" theories were popularly accepted.[16]

A vicious Southern populist, Tom Watson, long known for his diatribes against Blacks and Catholics, now targeted the Jews. In 1915, a white woman working in an Atlanta, Georgia factory was murdered. A Jewish worker by the name of Leo Frank was unjustly accused of the crime, convicted on the weakest of circumstantial evidence and sentenced to death. However, the governor of Georgia commuted Frank's sentence because of the obvious injustice done. Watson goaded his followers to take the law into their own murderous hands. Frank was removed from his jail cell by the wild mob and lynched.

Less dramatically, Jews were quietly and conspiratorially excluded from many hotels, organizations, commercial enterprises and educational institutions in America. Even those schools and universities that did admit Jews did so on a numerical quota basis. After World War I ended, the sit-

---

15. Quoted by Martin Gilbert, *A History of the Twentieth Century*, Vol. 1, New York, 1997, p.234.
16. Madison Grant in the United States and Houston Stewart Chamberlain in England were the chief proponents of these "scientific" theories. Meltzer, p.311.

uation would become even more cloudy for American Jews. It would not be until well after World War II that most social, professional and business restrictions against Jews would nearly disappear.

Author Arthur Herzberg writes in *The Jews in America*:

In 1919, A. Mitchell Palmer, the redbaiting attorney general of the United States, went looking for Bolsheviks in America ... Palmer had no particular bias against Jews but his campaign against Communism lent itself to such uses. Jews were prominent among Communists, both in Russia and in the United States. A forgery of a generation earlier, "The Protocols of the Elders of Zion," was published in the United States ... In 1919, Henry Ford, the most famous industrialist in America, financed a daily newspaper in his hometown of Dearborn, Michigan, The Dearborn Independent, *which had this fantasy reprinted in hundreds of thousands of copies ... On the basis of this forgery Ford's paper became the chief trumpet of anti-Semitism in the 1920's.[17]*

The "Golden Land" was not quite glittering as of yet, though most Jews felt that America would eventually grant them the equality of opportunity that no other country ever before had afforded them.

Harbingers of War

HOWEVER TURBULENT THE JEWISH SITUATION IN NORTH AMERICA and England, the main stage of the Jewish drama in this era would be in Europe. In 1911, a crisis erupted between Britain and France on one side, and Germany on the other, over the control of the tiny port of Agadir on the Atlantic coast of Morocco. The crisis however soon dissipated by itself when the German gunboats in the harbor withdrew. The world seemed confident that war between the major powers was becoming less and less probable, even impossible. The economies of the great powers were so intertwined that it seemed that none of them could support a war against the other. The fact that the heads of England, Russia and Germany were all first cousins, directly or by marriage, also appeared to be a reassuring sign.

Despite these factors, there was a great sense of unease in Europe. Germany and Austria-Hungary were bound by alliance, as were France and Russia. Though England was not officially allied with France, it spoke up sharply in defense of French interests in Morocco and pointedly warned Germany to back off during the Agadir crisis. England was concerned over the kaiser's open ambitions to equal it as a naval power and

---

17. Arthur Herzberg, *The Jews in America*, New York, 1989, pp. 240-1.

colonial empire. Reluctantly but unavoidably, England became an ally of France, though no formal treaty of alliance was ever signed between the two countries.

Germany had begun a major shipbuilding program in the early 1900's in order to obtain a degree of parity with the British navy. This touched off a battleship-building race between the two powers. In 1906, under the direction of the fiery and single-minded First Sea Lord, John Arbuthnot (Jacky) Fisher, England constructed the world's largest battleship, the *H.M.S. Dreadnought*,[18] to serve as a deterrent to the rapidly expanding German High Fleet. While it rendered most of the German High Fleet useless, this monster ship also had the unwanted effect of making most of the other 40 battleships in the British navy obsolete as well.[19] By the time Winston Churchill became the head of the British Admiralty in 1911, the British navy had eighteen dreadnoughts in its fleet. Germany, in turn, began to build its own version of monster ships and Churchill attempted to negotiate a halt to the armament race. Two Jews, Albert Ballin[20] of Hamburg and Ernest Cassel[21] of London had the ears of their respective monarchs and they devised a plan to begin negotiations. Richard Burdon Haldane, a dour Scotsman, was dispatched to Germany as a result of their efforts. After three months of intensive negotiation in early 1912, the "Haldane Mission" was deemed a failure and the dreaded armament race continued. The failure of the "Haldane Mission" was a damaging blow to the cause of peace, because England now viewed the growing German threat of naval parity as a mortal threat to its imperial status.

Waxing stronger in nationalist feeling, Germany felt itself hemmed in by the Franco-Russian alliance. Its military and diplomatic policy now was based on the inevitability of conflict with Russia and France, a psychological as much as a geopolitical decision. Kaiser Wilhelm II, a man of moods, impetuosity and terrible inferiority frustration (due to his withered arm, it is thought) wished to be the emperor of the greatest of the great powers. But the armaments race in which Germany was engaged, particularly the

---

18. Dreadnought soon entered the English vocabulary as a synonym for any super-battleship.

19. The former First Sea Lord, Sir Frederick Richards, loudly complained that, "The whole British fleet was ... morally scrapped and labeled obsolete at the moment when it was at the zenith of its efficiency and equal not to two, but practically to all of the other navies of the world combined." Robert K. Massie, *Dreadnought*, New York, 1991, p. 487.

20. He was the owner of the Hamburg-American shipping company that transported millions of Jewish and other immigrants to the United States.

21. Born Jewish, he converted to Roman Catholicism when he married. He was a wealthy investment banker and well known for his penchant for risky ventures, most of which turned out to be highly profitable. He was a close friend of Jacob Schiff, the American Jewish financier and a confidant of King Edward VII of England.

building of super-warships, was draining her economy. During this period, open anti-Semitism gained much ground in Germany. No matter how hard Jews struggled to prove themselves loyal to the kaiser, they were continually subject to anti-Semitic abuse, though not to violence.

Niall Ferguson, in *The Pity of War*, writes:

> *In February 1914, the American ambassador Walter Page warned the State Department: "Some government [probably Germany] will see bankruptcy staring it in the face and the easiest way out will seem a great war. Bankruptcy before a war would be ignominious; after a war it could be charged to 'Glory.'" [At around this time]his eye was caught by an article in the Berlin Post ... urging an immediate war, on the grounds "that Germany is in a more favorable position today than she will be shortly."* [22]

At an unguarded moment in 1913, the kaiser told the Austrian chief of staff that Germany was prepared for a "great war."[23] But no one imagined what such a "great war" would entail. Germany's strategy was based on a quick and crushing victory over France before England could effectively intervene. England was not a signatory to any diplomatic document that would require it to come to the aid of France and Germany felt that England would not unnecessarily involve itself in a land war on the European continent, but Germany was prepared to fight Great Britain if need be. This was only one of the major miscalculations of the great powers of Europe that led to the First World War.[24] In its grand scheme, Germany assumed that once France and England were no longer a threat, it would be able to fight Russia on its Eastern front, removing that menace to its expansionist future.

Dangerous Trends Surface

IN RUSSIA, THE GOVERNMENT WAS PARALYZED BY THE STRENGTH OF THE right wing that thwarted all efforts of Petr Stolypin, the more liberal chief minister of the czar's government, to affect reforms. Stolypin attempted to alleviate the desperate situation of the Russian Jews as well as the justified complaints of the various ethnic nations, such as the Poles, being governed by Russia. Stolypin was undercut by the czar (and especially the czarina) however, and publicly repudiated and humiliated. In August, 1911, Stolypin was shot in Kiev by a Jewish anarchist (who was also sometimes a double agent for the czar's secret police) and he died of his wounds a

---

22. Niall Ferguson, *The Pity of War: Explaining World War I*, New York, 1999, p.140.

23. J.M. Roberts, *Twentieth Century*, New York, 1999, p.205.

24. For an in-depth study of these miscalculations, see Niall Ferguson's, *The Pity of War*, New York, 1999.

month later. The reactionaries took complete power. Nicholas II made his famous declaration asserting that most revolutionaries and socialists in Russia were Jews,[25] and pogroms swept Russia again.

In 1913, a poor Jew from Kiev, Mendel Beilis, was placed on trial for the "ritual murder" of a Ukranian youth. He was charged in the indictment with having killed the Christian child in order to extract his blood for the baking of matzoh. This preposterous charge brought Russia the scorn and protests of the other great powers of the world. Undaunted, the Russian authorities proceeded with the trial and with the anti-Semitic public furor it caused. As did the Dreyfus trial twenty years earlier, the Beilis trial deepened Jewish fears regarding their future in Europe and quickened Jewish emigration. Even though Beilis was eventually acquitted by the Russian court (despite intense governmental and Church pressure to find him guilty), it was clear that the oppression of the Jews by the czar and his government would continue unabated. This realization only further radicalized Russian Jewish youth, who now preached open rebellion and violence to solve their bitter problem. (As for Beilis himself: he left Russia for Palestine after his acquital and emigrated to the United States in 1920. Settling on the Lower East Side of New York City, he sank into anonymity.)

Ideas and ideologies seep through even the most strongly sealed ghetto doors. The two most powerful idealistic forces that gained impetus at the beginning of the twentieth century — nationalism and Marxism — swept mightily over the Jewish world. Zionism was the beneficiary of the nationalist sentiments that enflamed Europe at the time. The traditional Jewish world, with its attitude of patience, submission and pious behavior, was unable to compete effectively for the hearts and hands of much of the Jewish youth of Eastern Europe. Given the poverty and persecution of Jewry, the spiritual grandeur of Torah study and traditional observance was no match for the glamour and allure of revolutionary creeds and movements. The desertion of many young Jews from Orthodoxy to the cause of secular Zionism influenced all Jewish life for the rest of the century. A smaller, but more radical and intense segment of Jewish youth raised the red banner of socialism/communism/bolshevism as their ideal. Zionism/nationalism was an expression of particularization and was meant to solve the "Jewish problem" solely, no matter how that solution may affect others. The Marxist solution was universal for all human beings, and the "Jewish problem" would be solved only as

---

25. However, there were only twelve Jews (out of the 524 delegates) in the Duma representing the six million Jews then in Russia. For a description of the life of one of the Jewish Duma delegates while the Duma was in session see *Galut u'Mered,* Shmaryahu Levin, Tel Aviv, 1967, pp.284-292.

part of the general salvation of humankind by the implementation of Marxist ideology. Both movements sapped much of the strength and numbers of traditional Jewry. Only when the fire would eventually die under both Zionist nationalism and Marxism at the end of the century, would the Jewish world again realize the eternal strength of traditional Jewish life, and a slow reverse flow of Jewish youth back to Jewish tradition would begin to occur.

Russia was a land that had one hundred million peasant farmers. The vast majority of them were illiterate and there was a very high rate of chronic alcoholism among them. They were religious, superstitious and easily given to violence. Most of the Russian army was made up of peasants, and the discipline used to keep them in line was ferocious. Even when not in the army, the peasants seemingly responded only to iron force. They preferred cruel, but efficient, masters to kindly but ineffective ones.[26] Due to this prevalent mentality, the Russian governments tolerated no political opposition, fearing that the peasants would view tolerance as weakness: any government concessions or reforms would encourage peasant revolt. Sergei Witte, one of the leading politicians of Nicholas' Russia, wrote about the uncertain future:

> [Russia] in one respect represents an exception to all the countries in the world ... The exception consists in this: that the people have been systematically, over ... generations, brought up without a sense of property and legality ... What historical consequences will result from this, I hesitate now to say, but I feel they will be very serious ... [Legal relations among the peasants] are regulated not by precise, written laws, but by custom, which often "no one knows" ... Under these conditions, I see one gigantic question mark: What is an empire with one hundred million peasants who have been educated neither in the concept of landed property nor that of the firmness of law in general?[27]

The Jews of Eastern Europe lived among this dangerous peasantry, even when they moved to the cities, for the peasant population of Russia also began to leave the family village to search for a better life there. It was clear that the old system of traditional *shtetl* life was collapsing. Yet, traditional Jewish leadership provided no clear-cut program to chart a new social and national course. Even though the majority of Jews in Eastern Europe were still religiously observant in behavior and traditional in outlook, much of the pre-World War I generation of young Jews broke away from its Orthodox past. They were

26. Richard Pipes, *The Russian Revolution*, New York, 1990, p.119.
27. Ibid. p.120.

One of the many pre-war followers of the Haskalah movement

unwilling to accept the suffering of the Exile any longer, and they violently revolted against their Jewish past. They became atheists, anarchists, secularists, Zionists, socialists, communists, "enlightened" *maskilim*, internationalists and nationalists — and they carried their traditional Jewish fervor into their new "faiths." Jewish atheists are fanatically religious atheists. Though *mussar*, yeshivos, *Chasidus* and religious Zionism all valiantly attempted to stem the tide, the younger generation in the main fled from its past, confusing the terrible conditions of physical Jewish life in Eastern Europe with the values of Torah and Jewish tradition. This development strongly influenced all later Jewish life in the twentieth century and guaranteed bitter strife within the Jewish world.

Hope and Despair Meet in the Promised Land

JEWISH IMMIGRATION TO THE LAND OF ISRAEL CONTINUED IN THE YEARS just before World War I. After Herzl's death and Max Nordau's presidency, the Zionist movement was headed by David Wolffsohn, a Lithuanian-born former yeshivah student who gained German citizenship and was seen as a natural heir to Herzl. Nevertheless, the Zionist movement was torn by divisions and personalities. Menachem Ussishkin, Chaim Weizmann, Zev Jabotinsky, Nachum Sokolow, Shmaryahu Levin and others emerged as leaders of the World Zionist movement, many times pulling in different directions at the same time; while in Palestine, Yitzchak Ben-Zvi and David Ben-Gurion were the leading figures in the establishment of the new *yishuv* (the Jewish settlement in Palestine).

Back in 1907, the Order of Sons of Zion was formed as a fraternal Jewish organization and it became the foundation of the General Zionist organization in the United States. In 1912, a women's group called Hadassah was created to "promote Jewish institutions and enterprises in Palestine and to foster Zionist ideals in America." The guiding spirit and president of Hadassah for over 30 years was Henrietta Szold, the daughter of Rabbi Benjamin Szold of Baltimore. She eventually became known as the "mother of the *yishuv*." Hadassah's first task was to promote the health of the inhabitants of Palestine, irrespective of creed or race. In 1913, it sent two trained American nurses to Jerusalem to open a health center. By 1914, the Zionist movement in America had formed a number of important organizations and Young Judea, a Zionist youth organization, came into effective influence. It boasted more than 175 branches with 5,000 members. Zionism was gaining a strong foothold in American Jewish life.

Nevertheless, there were many prominent American Jews who considered the Zionist idea to be anathema. Jacob H. Schiff, a leading Wall Street financier, stated that, "Speaking as an American, I cannot for a moment conceive that one can be at the same time a true American and an honest adherent of the Zionist movement."[28] Adolph Ochs, the Jewish owner and publisher of *The New York Times,* prohibited the mention of Zionism in the newspaper. Yet such influential figures in the Reform movement as Steven Wise and Judah Magnes[29] became active supporters of the Zionist movement, much to the dismay of their colleagues and official Reform movement policy leaders.

By the beginning of the Great War, there were more than 85,000 Jews living in Palestine and Hebrew had been officially established as the language of the Jewish community. The new all-Jewish city of Tel Aviv sprang forth from the old mixed-population city of Jaffa and numbered close to 1,500 souls by 1914. The legendary Orthodox personality, Dr. Moshe Wallach from Germany, had founded and was heading Shaarei Zedek Hospital in Jerusalem, the first modern hospital in the country. It operated within the full framework of Jewish *halachah* and tradition. The first Jewish agricultural settlements had been established all over the country, especially in the Galilee and the Sharon plain. A watchman's guild — *Hashomer* — was organized to defend the settlements from the many Arab marauders.

The new *yishuv* was strongly secular and Marxist and in the eyes of the new settlers, the old *yishuv* was to be left to wither on the vine. There were some attempts to bridge the gap between the two communities,[30] but no real progress was made on either side. The vehement rejection of tradition and faith by the young pioneers was matched by a rigidly defensive posture and unyielding view of Jewish life by the old settlers of Jerusalem and Safed. The positions of the two communities would harden even more in the coming decades.

---

28. Howard M. Sachar, *A History of the Jews in America*, New York, 1992, p. 249.

29. Magnes was discharged from his faculty position at Hebrew Union College because of his pro-Zionist views. He later became President of the Hebrew University in Jerusalem, where his support for a bi-national (Jewish and Arab) state in Palestine made him unpopular with the Zionists.

30. The "*teshuvah* trip" led by Rabbi Kook and Rabbi Yosef Chaim Sonnenfeld in 1913 to the kibbutzim in the Galilee was the most noteworthy and ambitious of these attempts. Rabbi Kook termed the journey a success. Rabbi Sonnenfeld did not.

The Ottoman Empire, which ruled Palestine at the time, was in the throes of collapse. It had been torn apart by internal rebellion and external wars. In the byzantine world of the Balkans, Serbia had great ambitions of uniting all of the southern Slavs under its flag. Austria moved to prevent this, and in 1908 formally annexed Bosnia-Herzegovina, thus blocking any Serbian expansion towards the Adriatic Sea. This not only angered Serbia, but it also disturbed the newly united Italy that also was looking for its place in the sun. But Italy could not expect satisfaction from Austria and it therefore turned its attention towards the weaker Ottoman Empire. In September 1911, Italy declared war on the Ottoman Turks, captured the port of Tripoli in Libya and landed an army on the Dodecanese.

When the Italians then proceeded to bombard the Dardanelles Straits, Russia became alarmed. As a riposte, Russia encouraged an alliance between Serbia and Bulgaria, who were later joined by Montenegro and Greece. In September 1912, these four "small powers" declared war against the Ottoman Empire. This First Balkan War ripped away almost all of the European territories under previous Ottoman control and the Ottoman Empire was seen as a dying carcass surrounded by jackals and vultures. The Jews in Palestine sensed that Ottoman weakness might now allow them to establish recognized Jewish national rights in Palestine. However, no Moslem government, no matter how feeble or crumbling, would then willingly acquiesce to a strong Jewish presence in the Middle East, especially in Palestine. Thus, the Ottoman Turks, paradoxically driven by their insecurities and weaknesses, turned against the Jewish settlers and the Jewish presence in Palestine. Until 1917, when the British captured Palestine, the Jews there lived under terrible economic, political and social persecution and duress.

Alliances Seal Europe's Fate

THE GREAT POWERS INTERVENED TO SETTLE THE FIRST BALKAN WAR. A new independent country, Albania, was created and its presence again effectively blocked any possible Serbian expansion to the Adriatic. But the victors of the First Balkan War soon fell out among themselves over the spoils and within a year, the Second Balkan War broke out. Bulgaria attacked Serbia, Rumania attacked Bulgaria, Turkey attacked Greece and Macedonia, then retook Adrianople. Bulgaria lost almost everything it gained in the first war, Serbia smoldered with resentment against Austria and Albania, and the Ottoman Turks desperately searched for allies to help prop up its collapsing empire. Germany came to its rescue, militarily, economically and diplomatically, and was the only major power in Europe that had not attempted to take pieces of the Ottoman Empire for itself. The strength of German influence in Constantinople was crucial in bringing the Ottoman Turks into the Great War on the side of the Central Powers.

The Balkan Wars were marked by unusual ferocity, cruelty and atrocities. Since there were Jewish communities in all of the nations involved in these wars and ethnic hatreds and nationalist fervor were the dominant motives in these struggles, the Jews suffered greatly. For the Jews were the ultimate outsider, the "other" who was distrusted and feared by all. The Jewish communities of the Balkans contained both Ashkenazic and Sephardic segments. They were originally tepid in their response to the Zionist movement. Though the vast majority of them were still Orthodox in practice, Reform and "modernization" of Jewish life had already penetrated the Ashkenazic communities of the area by the end of the nineteenth century. Sensing the precariousness of their status in the midst of the Balkan turmoil, many of these Jews now turned to Zionism, both the secular and religious forms of the movement, hoping to find safety and purpose in Jewish nationalism. It would be the destruction of the old order in Europe that would prove to be the strongest catalyst for the increasing momentum of Zionism.

The instability of the Ottoman Empire that was reflected in the revolt of the "Young Turks" continued throughout the decade of the Great War. The Turkish Empire was slowly being dismantled by its neighbors. Greece, Bulgaria and Serbia and most of the Turkish possessions in Europe west of the Bosporus were lost. Despised by the Turkish government as being potential troublemakers, the Jews of Turkey suffered mightily. The presence of the Zionists in Turkish-administered Palestine and Zionist influence exerted among the Jews in the Ottoman Empire further exacerbated the situation. It is not surprising, therefore, that during this decade the migration of Jews from Turkey to the West, and especially to America, began in earnest. Historian Howard M. Sachar estimates that as many as 25,000 Turkish Jews left during this time. Sephardic Jewish communities, composed primarily of Jews from Turkey, now began to appear on both coasts of the United States.

Meanwhile, a series of official and unofficial alliances were developing from the Balkan Wars that would spell doom for Europe. Russia was Serbia's patron, and the kaiser backed Austria and the Ottoman Empire in order to counterbalance Russia. As mentioned earlier, France was already officially allied with Russia, while England unofficially gave France backing against German threats. The Great Powers struggled to end the Balkan Wars and imposed settlements upon the belligerents in order to safeguard the general peace of Europe. The cooperation of the strong countries fanned a false hope that they would not allow themselves to be drawn into any general European war. But the instability of the Balkans and the weakness and vulnerability of the Ottoman Empire were factors that at any time could provoke a large European conflict. Psychologically, people and governments in Europe were tired of the torturous dance of diplomacy between the competing powers in Europe. The problems of the Great Powers were so complicated and the solutions so painfully obscure that diplomacy alone would no longer suffice. Many silently agreed with the statement of the bellicose Austrian Chief of Staff General Franz Conrad, that what Europe needed to settle its problems was "a short, brisk war."

EUROPE BEFORE WORLD WAR I (1914)

© 2001, Shaar Press. Reproduction prohibited

There would indeed be a war, but it would be neither short nor brisk. On June 28, 1914, that Great War was ignited when Archduke Franz Ferdinand, the heir to the Hapsburg throne of Austria-Hungary, was assassinated, together with his wife, by a nineteen-year-old Serb student, Gavrilo Princip.[31] A shudder passed through Europe as all realized that this murder carried the potential for war between Austria and Serbia.

---

31. Princip's cell can be seen today at Thereisenstadt (Terezin) in the Czech Republic. There are flowers that are still placed every day at the door of the cell by unknown admirers of that fatal deed.

While Austria debated its course, Serbia declared that it had nothing to do with the murder. (In fact, no evidence since has ever implicated Serbia in the assassination.) However, the kaiser encouraged Austria to take punitive action against Serbia and to permanently end "Serbian arrogance."[32] Because of this German backing, Austria sent an eleven-point ultimatum to Serbia for acceptance. The terms of the ultimatum were insulting and degrading to Serbia, but in order to prevent war, Serbia accepted ten of the eleven points and offered to negotiate the final point. Austria and Germany were of the opinion that Russia would not come to the aid of Serbia — a fatal miscalculation — and that Austria would therefore have a free hand in crushing Serbia.

On July 28, 1914, Austria declared war on Serbia and began to bombard Belgrade. Russia immediately started to mobilize its army, despite Germany's warnings to cease the mobilization. France mobilized four million soldiers in accordance with her agreement with Russia. Four million Austrian soldiers, five million German soldiers and six million Russian troops were also on the march. Germany's long-established military plan was to defeat France quickly and then, together with Austria, to destroy the czar's army in the east. On August 2, Germany invaded France, but the most significant German advance in the west was into Belgium, a country whose neutrality and borders were guaranteed by Britain. On August 4, England declared war on Germany. Accompanied by frenzied cheers and blaring bands, French, British, German, Austrian and Russian troops marched to trains and ships that would take them to the front. The "short, brisk war" was on.

Serbia was already in flames and Austrian troops crossed the Danube to occupy much of the country. However, Serbian resistance stiffened and by the end of autumn, Serbia was able to hold on to its western territories, establishing the front line along the Drina River. Serbia would eventually lose one-quarter of its entire population in the ensuing four years of war. The devil had been loosed on European civilization.

This war was destined to be a world war, not just a European one. On August 23, Japan entered the war against Germany and by the end of November captured the German enclaves in China and the German colonies in the Pacific island groups of the Marianas, Carolines, Marshalls and Palau. German and British navies fought sea battles off the coasts of Argentina and the Falkland Islands. Each side lost warships and over 3,000

---

32. The German ambassador in Vienna, Count Tschirschky, told an Austrian official: "The earlier Austria attacks [Serbia], the better. It would have been better to attack yesterday than today; and better to attack today than tomorrow." The kaiser told Austria: "Should war between Austria-Hungary and Russia prove unavoidable," Germany would fight on the side of Austria-Hungary. See Gilbert, pp. 310-311.

sailors drowned. Within 40 days of its invasion, German armies were only 30 miles from Paris. There the British and French armies rallied and forced the Germans back across the Marne River. The Germans would never enter Paris in this war. The Russian invasion of Prussia ended in complete disaster at Tannenburg, with tremendous Russian losses in men and materiel. The Russians advanced against the Austrians in Polish Galicia, capturing Lemberg (Lvov). Yet, their offensive there soon bogged down and further progress on that front was not forthcoming. After enormous expenditures of soldiers, civilians and armaments on both sides, the "short, brisk war" was now stalemated. Almost a million men had been killed in the first six months of the war, a third of them Frenchmen, and all for naught. D.H. Lawrence, the English author summed it all up: "The deluge of iron rain will destroy the world here, utterly."[33]

Victims of War

THE GERMAN-RUSSIAN STRUGGLES AND THE AUSTRIAN-RUSSIAN battlegrounds caused the uprooting of millions of civilians, among them a large percentage of Eastern European Jewry. After the defeat of the Russian armies in Prussia, Germany invaded Russia and captured large sections of Lithuania and Poland, areas with large Jewish populations. The Russians, always looking for a scapegoat to excuse their defeats, blamed the Jews. They accused the Jews of being disloyal to Russia and spying on behalf of Germany. This claim was believed by most Russians, even though large numbers of Jews were serving in the Russian army and no charges of Jewish espionage were ever proven. As a result of these accusations, the czar ordered the removal of hundreds of thousands of Jews from their centuries-old homes that were near the battlefront, moving them eastward into deeper Russia. The sufferings of the Jews at the hands of the Russians is described by an eyewitness:

> The Russians took many men, women and little children into captivity. They were forbidden to take anything with them and they were sent to Siberia — five hundred souls in all. Their sorrow was extremely great … We are now terribly afraid, the non-Jews are sharpening their teeth. They declared that the Jews have sent gold to Prussia and have caused the war. There are few police present and only God in heaven can help us. All the wealthy have fled and only the poor people, the weak and sick remain … No food was brought in. All the Russians know is how to oppress … The woods were full of Russians [who had deserted the army] and the brave act of one of these

---

33. Ferguson, ibid., p.xxviii

Russians is to meet a Jew on the road and beat him senseless ... The Jews were persecuted by the Russians because the Catholics [the Lithuanians] always accused the Jews of siding with the Germans, of giving them money. The Jews were accused of being spies and that caused great enmity, and of course the Jews had no answer. The non-Jews also told the Russians that the Jews had placed a curse on them. That day torn sifrei Torah *[scrolls of the Law], covered with dung, were brought to our town from Tzitavian [sic]. The Russians had driven out the Jews there and robbed them of everything.*[34]

When the Russians mounted successful counter-offensives against the Austrians or the Germans, the Jews were then treated harshly by the Austrians and the Germans. They were conscripted for labor, placed on very short rations, robbed and physically harmed. Nevertheless, compared to the treatment that they were receiving from the Russians, this treatment was considered relatively benign and many Jewish leaders and ordinary Jews hoped for a Russian defeat and for the toppling of the hated czarist government.

By the end of 1914, Russia had put out of commission one-third of the Austro-Hungarian army. But its own losses were catastrophic. Over 1,200,000 Russian soldiers had been killed, wounded or captured in the first four months of conflict. The Russian army was exhausted, ill equipped and demoralized. In early 1915, a strong German offensive overran the Russian army. By the fall of 1915, the Russian army was no longer capable of victory. Only one-third of the original 2.5 million-man front-line army survived. But in spite of all of its reverses, Russia did not sue for peace. In order to keep Russia in the war, Britain and France secretly promised Russia that it would have Constantinople and the Dardanelles as its own after an Allied victory. As long as Russia stayed in the war, it became increasingly apparent that Germany could not win a two-front war of attrition. As early as 1915, the German General Von Moltke despaired of winning the war and asked the kaiser to arrange the best peace possible. But the other German generals and the kaiser himself still felt that victory was only one more glorious offensive stroke away and the killing therefore continued apace.

The dislocation of the Jewish population in Eastern Europe and the invasion of Lithuania by the German army destroyed the life and influence of the yeshivos there. Most of these institutions were forced to either

---

34. Taken from the unpublished manuscript, *Diary of Eleazar Yankelevitch, 1913-1922*. Yankelevitch spent the war years in the two towns of Tavrig (Taurogen) and Rasseyn (Raseiniai) in Lithuania. The diary was afforded to me for my use for this book by Anna and Asher Finchas of Edgware, England.

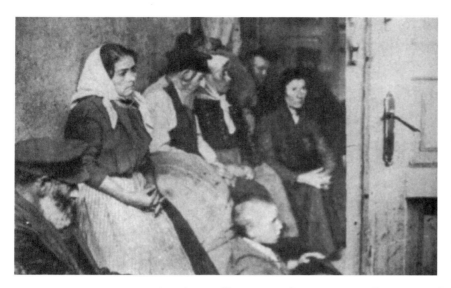

Jews of Kovno exiled during World War I by the Russian Army

close or go into a painful exile deep into Russia. The activities and influence of the great rabbis and Chasidic leaders were also drastically curtailed by the conditions of war. This further weakened the hold of tradition on Eastern European Jewry. Though there are no official figures available, it is estimated that over 250,000 Eastern European civilian Jews died during the First World War, most of them from malnutrition, disease and exposure. Pogroms by the local populace and anti-Jewish violence by all of the armies fighting in the area also took a large toll of Jewish life. Since war and armies by their very nature introduce a spirit of nihilism, rebellion, violence and a steely immunity to cruelty and horror, the occupation of the Jewish heartland of Eastern Europe by the German, Austrian and Russian armies hastened the movement of Jewish youth towards radical ideas and violent solutions to social problems. A dazed, angry, confused and ill-tempered Eastern European Jewry would emerge after the guns of World War I fell silent.

The British Take Palestine

THE JEWS IN PALESTINE ALSO FARED VERY POORLY DURING THE WAR. At the beginning of the hostilities, the 6,000 Russian Jewish residents of Jaffa were ordered to leave the city immediately. Many of them were forcibly deported to Alexandria, Egypt. Thousands of other Jews fled the country in the face of Turkish persecution. The Turks did not allow Palestinian Jews who were out of the country when the war started to return to their homes.[35] David Ben-Gurion and Yitzchak Ben-Zvi, among other leaders of the Jewish community, were expelled from the land. It is estimated that 8,000-10,000 Jews died in Palestine during the first two years of the war, most of them from hunger and disease. The Jewish community in Palestine shrank by more than a third during the war. The non-Jewish community also declined because of the brutality of

---

35. This was the fate of Rabbi Avraham Yitzchak Kook, then Rabbi of Jaffa, who had left for Poland to attend the world convention of Agudath Israel, which was cancelled by the outbreak of war. He would spend the next five years in Switzerland and London, England, until his return to Jaffa and Jerusalem after the war.

the Turkish authorities and the hunger occasioned by the effective British blockade of the ports on the eastern Mediterranean coast. The Jewish community was subjected to press-gang labor by the Turks and much of the newly-planted forestation and vegetation was torn up by the Turks for "military purposes."

Efforts of Henry Morgenthau, the Jewish ambassador from the United States to the Ottoman Turks, to bring American Jewish aid to the suffering Jews of Palestine were partially successful and helped prevent complete destruction of the Jewish community. The Jews in Palestine were embittered by their treatment at the hands of the Turks and most of them fervently hoped for an Allied victory. Nevertheless, the official statements of both the old and new *yishuv* insisted on continuing Jewish loyalty to the Ottoman Empire. Until 1917, Jewish sympathies worldwide were mixed because of the fact that anti-Semitic Russia was one of the Allied Powers. The Zionist movement therefore took a pointedly neutral stance in the war until the issuance of the Balfour Declaration in 1917.

In 1915, with the stalemate on the Western front confirmed beyond doubt in the enormous daily casualty lists posted in London, the British tried for an end run around the European armies of the Central Powers. England landed an army at Gallipoli, Turkey, in a bold attempt to cut through the "soft underbelly" of Europe and take the Austrian and German armies from the rear. The campaign failed after eight months and the British were forced to withdraw. One of the contingents that participated in the British effort was the Zion Mule Corps, a product of the insistence of Zev Jabotinsky and Joseph Trumpeldor that the Jews arm themselves and fight against the Turks. The 500-man Zion Mule Corps, insignificant as it was in the overall picture of forces aligned in the war, nevertheless was an important psychological step in the nationalist program of Zionism. A Jewish spy ring, NILI,[36] headed by members of the Aaronsohn family of Atlit, provided vital information to England about the military strength and disposition of the Turks in Palestine. Eventually, the members of the group were arrested, tortured and executed.[37] At this time, 1.5 million Armenians were being systematically exterminated by the Turks, and the Jews of Palestine feared that they would face the same tragedy. It was only the capture of Palestine by the British that forestalled such a fate.

After first crossing the Sinai Peninsula, the British army, under the command of General Edmund Allenby, invaded Palestine in October of

---

36. The Hebrew acronym for the verse in Samuel, "The Eternal One of Israel will not fail."

37. Their bodies were discovered and brought to honorable burial after the capture of the Gaza Strip by the Israelis in 1967.

British General Edmund Allenby reviewing an honor guard of British soldiers in Jerusalem's Old City

1917. Jabotinsky had once again organized a Jewish fighting group, this time called the Jewish Legion, to participate in the war against the Turks. Sixty-five hundred young Jews volunteered to serve in the Legion and the group joined in Allenby's final offensive. After early easy successes and later hard fighting, the British expelled the Turks from the land in 1918. The Jews were not the only non-British force fighting the Turks. Hussein, the Sharif of Mecca and the head of the Bedouin Hashemite tribe, mounted a rebellion with English encouragement and aid against the Turks and swept them out of the Arabian Peninsula and parts of Transjordan and Iraq. The British, the Jews and the Arabs would thus each have strong claims to parts of the disintegrating Ottoman Empire. That these claims would, of necessity, conflict with one another was perhaps unavoidable. These conflicts of interest would produce the palpable and unremitting tension that characterized the Middle East for the balance of the century.

The year 1917 marked the turning point of the war, though it may not have been apparent at the time. Desperate for victory after having spilled so much of its youths' blood, Germany threw the dice in a last mighty gamble. It announced that it would now pursue unrestricted submarine warfare in the Atlantic in order to bring Britain to its knees. The intended address for this announcement was the United States, for it had become the primary supplier of the Allied Powers.[38] When Germany sank a number of American merchant ships, America entered the war. Germany reckoned that it would be able to win the war before American power and armies could come to bear against it. This terrible miscalculation was based on the fact that Russia collapsed and freed the German army in the East for a great offensive in the West. Germany was certain that this effort would finally defeat the British and French forces.

The Bolshevik Revolution: Shortcut to Spiritual and Physical Devastation

RUSSIA COLLAPSED INTERNALLY: THE CITIZENS OF THE COUNTRY HAD had enough of the czar and his cruel and corrupt mismanagement of the nation, and the army no longer wanted to fight. Open citizen revolt and military mutiny forced the czar to abdicate in March (February, according to the old Russian calendar), 1917, and a parliamentary government was established, eventually headed by Alexander Kerensky, a moderate socialist. But the hardened revolutionaries of Russia led by the Bolsheviks and their leader, Vladimir Ilyich Lenin, were not satisfied with a sedate revolution or a middle-of-the-road government. Kerensky made the fatal error of committing Russia to continuing the war against Germany. The Russian people did not want to continue in a war that had already cost them five million casualties. In November (October, according to the old Russian calendar), 1917, 300 dedicated Bolshevik revolutionaries gained control over a country of almost one hundred fifty million people. Lenin and his Jewish assistant, Leon (Lev) Trotsky, ruthlessly eliminated all opposition to their elite ruling power. Lenin, in pursuit of building the Marxist paradise in Russia, needed to immediately end the Russian participation in the war. The 1917 treaty of Brest-Litovsk, negotiated by two Jewish communist leaders, Trotsky and Adolf Ioffe, contained shameful terms imposed by Germany on Russia. But the communist government officials signed the treaty because it allowed them to pursue their utopian goals within Russia. And now Germany had a free hand in the West.

---

38. By 1917, the Allied Powers owed the United States over two billion dollars. The Central Powers owed only twenty-seven million dollars. See Roberts, p.255.

Leon Trotsky as a young revolutionary.

The Bolshevik rise to power would severely impact on Jewish life in Russia. The communists paid lip service to the noble ideal of religious tolerance and freedom, but they immediately embarked on a ruthless campaign to make atheism the universal doctrine of its empire. By definition, all religious leaders were counterrevolutionaries. It would not be until the 1920's that the full force of communist oppression would be felt by the Jews: any remaining vestige of religious observance or tradition would be persecuted and stamped out. The irony that many of the leaders of the communist revolution and the subsequent Bolshevik government were Jews was especially painful. Prominent among them was Trotsky, but there were also other Jews in very high positions in the Bolshevik revolutionary government. These included Yakov Sverdlov, the first head of the Soviet state, Lev Kamenev and Grigory Zinoviev, powerful leaders of the Communist Party. The first Commissar for Jewish Affairs was Semeon Dimanshtain, a former Orthodox rabbi.[39] These Jewish revolutionaries were determined to build the new, glorious world that Marx had prophesied would come into being. To them, Marx was the new Isaiah and Lenin was Joshua. The stored genetic intellect of generations of Torah scholars and the inherited zeal and fervor of the Chasidic movement coalesced in the minds of these idealistic and ruthless Jews, then poured into the Marxist march to triumph. Millions of Jews were destroyed, physically and/or spiritually, by the results of that fateful Russian Revolution at the end of 1917.

By January 1918, Lenin had instituted a reign of terror that would characterize the communist government for the next 50 years. He established the secret police arm, Cheka,[40] under a sadistic and fanatical Polish communist, Felix Dzerzhinsky. This secret police arm was responsible to no one but Lenin himself — not to the party, not to the courts, not to the regular police forces. Lenin ordered it to ruthlessly kill all those who stood in the way of the revolution, including everyone who *may* conceivably stand in the way of the revolution due to their familial, class or professional background. On this basis, the merchant class, as well as those involved in religious education and practice and those of previous professional status under the czar's regime, were automatically classified as

---

39. Dimanshtain had been a student of Telshe Yeshiva and continued his rabbinic studies at Slobodka, Yeshiva Knesset Yisrael. He was ordained by the great Rabbi Chaim Ozer Grodzinski of Vilna. He joined the Bolsheviks in 1908, was imprisoned by the czar for five years and then escaped to the West. He returned to Russia in 1917 to help Lenin overthrow the Kerensky government and, because of his expertise in Jewish matters, was chosen to head the Jewish Affairs section of the government. The goal was the complete destruction of Jewish religious life.

40. Later initials for this dreaded terror organization would be NKVD and KGB, among others. Whatever the initials, the message was always terror, deportation to labor camps and murder.

counterrevolutionaries and "wreckers." As can well be understood, many Jews fell under this most undesirable classification. At that point, however, Jews were not yet singled out for special persecution solely for being Jews. By the end of 1920, when the Red Terror was only in its early stages, Cheka had killed more than 50,000 people.[41]

The Bolshevik Revolution threw Russia into a ferocious civil war that would last for almost four years. The Red Army, under Trotsky's leadership, eventually overcame the "Whites," as the anti-communist forces were called. In the Ukraine, the Ukrainian Nationalist Party took advantage of the Bolshevik's woes and declared Ukraine independent of Russia and Poland. In March 1919, soldiers of this Ukrainian national government, under the command of Semeon Petliura, a rabid anti-Semite, carried out the greatest slaughter of Jews since the massacres of 1648-9. In 1918-19 over 1,200 separate pogroms took place in the Ukraine alone. The Whites accused all of the Jews in Russia of siding with the Bolsheviks, though it was obvious that the overwhelming majority of Russian Jews had little love for the brutal communists and their heresies. Nevertheless, the Whites systematically destroyed hundreds of Jewish towns and thousands of Jewish dwellings and synagogues. Their frenzy of cruelty and inhumanity, rape, pillage and murder was a harbinger of the Holocaust twenty years later. The dean of the Russian Orthodox Church, Metropolitan Vostorgov, sided with the Whites and encouraged them to: "Bless yourselves, beat the Jews, overthrow the People's Commissars!"[42] The Red Army was only slightly less murderous than the Whites were towards the Jews. It also conducted pogroms, but Trotsky ruthlessly punished those involved in murders. There is no doubt that it was the greater cruelties of the Whites and the independent Ukrainians that turned many Jews towards the side of the Bolsheviks as the lesser of two evils.

T HE ZIONIST MOVEMENT UNDERWENT A REVOLUTION OF ITS OWN IN 1917, one that was far more pleasant and promising than that of the Bolsheviks. For a variety of reasons,[43] many of them not clearly understood by the British government of Lloyd George itself, the British Foreign Secretary and former Prime Minister, Arthur Balfour, wrote a letter to

Lord Balfour's Weighty Letter

41. Paul Johnson, *Modern Times*, New York, 1992, p.70.

42. John Shelton Curtiss, *The Russian Church and the Soviet State*, Boston, 1953, p.69.

43. Among the reasons advanced were: Chaim Weizmann had contributed to the British war effort by helping to develop a chemical that allowed artillery shell fuses to be more efficient; fear of an imminent German declaration that would support Zionism; the belief that Jewish pro-Allied opinion world-wide (and especially in America) would strengthen the cause of the Allies materially and

Lord Rothschild of London, declaring that "His Majesty's government view with favor the establishment of a national home for the Jewish people in Palestine, and will use their best endeavours to facilitate the achievement of this object .... " There was, however, a clause inserted immediately thereafter in the letter that seemed to cancel the commitment of His Majesty's government. That clause read " ... it being clearly understood that nothing shall be done which may prejudice the civil and religious rights of existing non-Jewish communities in Palestine ... " The origin of this last clause, which would later come back to haunt both the British and the Zionists, lay in the fierce opposition of Edwin Montagu, the Jewish member of the War Cabinet, to any declaration that would promote Zionist interests in Palestine. Montagu, who struggled all of his life to escape his Orthodox Jewish background and become an accepted member of English high society, raised the specter of English Jewry's dual loyalty if such a declaration were made. He declared Zionism to be "a mischievous political creed,"[44] and claimed that this type of an English governmental declaration would anger the Moslems of India and embarrass the non-Zionist Jews of England. Nevertheless, the Balfour Declaration, as the letter to Rothschild came to be called, was issued and was viewed by all concerned — England, Arabs and Jews[45] — as a triumph of Zionist diplomacy and a commitment by the world's greatest empire to help establish the Jews as an independent nation in their ancient homeland.

The original intent of the Balfour Declaration was clearly to create a Jewish state in Palestine under British sponsorship, as a member of the British Commonwealth. Lord Robert Cecil in 1918 stated: "Our wish is that Arabian countries shall be for the Arabs, Armenia for the Armenians

---

psychologically; a long-standing nineteenth century romantic idea about restoring Palestine to the Jews that was common in the upper-class circles of England; belief of certain Christian groups that the return of the Jews to the Land of Israel was a necessary prerequisite for the fulfillment of Christian prophecy; sympathy for the Jews due to their severe persecution by Christian Europe generally and the czarist government of Russia particularly; and that, after the war, the Zionists would gratefully and enthusiastically help Britain control the Middle East against French and other interests. Each of these reasons alone seems insufficient to justify such a bold declaration of support for Zionist aims, especially since many of the reasons advanced were in fact spurious. But the combination of these reasons and the desperation of the Allied military situation in the war apparently forced England's hand.

44. Howard M. Sachar, *A History of Israel*, New York, 1998, p.107.

45. Rabbi Yisrael Meir HaKohen Kagan – the Chafetz Chaim – treated the Balfour Declaration as a "heavenly awakening towards the redemption of Israel [from exile]." He added the warning, however, that the process could be aborted by Jewish misbehavior in the Land of Israel. See *Mikitvei Harav Chafetz Chaim,* by Aryeh Leib HaKohen Poupko Warsaw, 1937, Bnei Brak, 1986, p.178. Also see there at page 185 the statement of the Chafetz Chaim, "that due to the technological progress of the modern era, the redemption of Israel and the ingathering of the exiles could now take place by natural means."

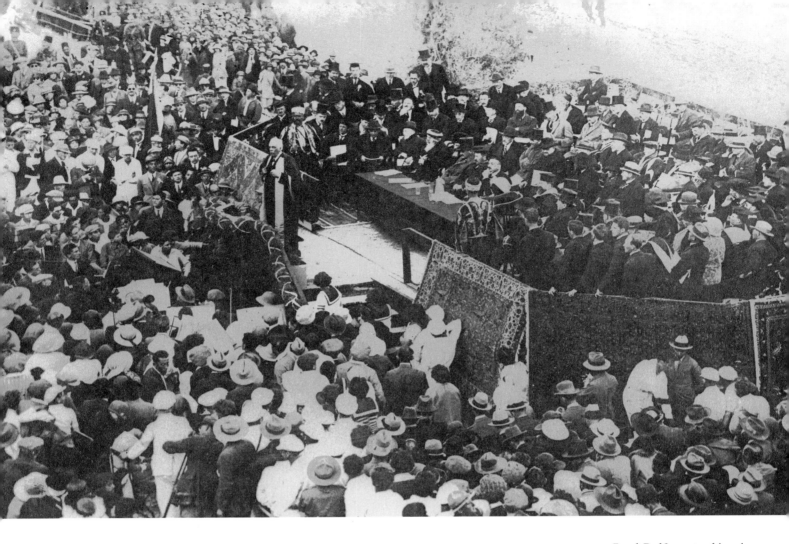

and Judea for the Jews."[46] Winston Churchill, as late as 1920, still envisioned "a Jewish state by the banks of the Jordan ... which might comprise three or four million Jews."[47] In fact, this was how the world generally understood the declaration. In response to the British move for Jewish support, Turkey immediately lifted restrictions on Jewish immigration to Palestine and issued a charter for a Jewish organization to help promote and speed Jewish immigration and colonization there. But the Jews of Palestine had suffered too long and too painfully under Turkish rule to be impressed by such a move so late in the game. Despite the Balfour Declaration, the Jews of Germany remained steadfastly loyal to Germany. The German Zionists attempted to influence the kaiser to issue a similar statement, but to no avail. To the Jews of America, the Balfour Declaration served to increase their fervor in support of America and its allies in the

Lord Balfour speaking in Jerusalem. This photo was taken at the opening of Hebrew University on Mount Scopus in 1925.

46. Sachar, *History of Israel*, p.110.
47. Ibid.

war.[48] The fact that the hated czar no longer ruled Russia allowed Jews the world over, except in Germany and Austria, to openly favor an Allied victory. The Balfour Declaration thus served to intensify international Jewish favoritism for the Allies. Jews now felt that at the end of the war they, too, would be the beneficiaries of a better world order.

The Bloody Aftermath of World War I

IN 1918, THE FINAL YEAR OF THE WAR, THE GERMANS REDEPLOYED their armies from the Eastern Front and mounted a supreme effort to break through the Allied defensive lines in the West. The Germans won the battle, pushing the Allied line back 40 miles in some places, but they lost the war because the effort completely exhausted their resources. They were once again stopped short of Paris. The newly arrived American Expeditionary Force was thrown into battle to plug the holes in the Allied lines. In June and July of that year, the Allies mounted strong counter-offensives, regaining all lost ground and tearing large gaps in the German army. The German home front was also collapsing, with the communists attempting to subvert the government and stage a revolution parallel to the one in Russia.

The Allied blockade of Germany had finally reduced much of the German population to hunger, though not yet starvation. There were mutinies in the German navy, in the shipyards and in some industrial plants. The German army still stood in the field, but its generals informed the kaiser that their army was no longer capable of effective offensive actions and thus winning the war would be impossible. A mood of depression and defeatism gripped Germany and in the fall of 1918, the German chancellor resigned and, with him, the ruling government. The new government, slightly left of center and moderate in its makeup, advised the kaiser to abdicate and leave for exile.[49] The army generals demanded an armistice to save their forces from an inevitable bloody mauling by the now numerically superior and infinitely stronger Allied forces. On

---

48. Not all American Jews were happy with the Balfour Declaration. The Reform movement's rabbinical body, The Central Conference of American Rabbis, passed a resolution at its 1917 convention stating its opposition to "a criterion of Jewish loyalty anything other than loyalty to Israel's God and Israel's religious mission." Nevertheless, in 1919, Kaufman Kohler, the President of the Reform Hebrew Union College stated: "Let Palestine, our ancient home, under the protection of the great nations or under the specific British suzerainty again become a center of Jewish culture and a safe refuge for the homeless. We shall welcome it and aid in the promotion of its work. Let the million or more [sic! BW] of Jewish citizens dwelling there … be empowered and encouraged to build up a commonwealth broad and liberal in spirit to serve as a school for international and interdenominational humanity. We shall all hail the undertaking and pray for its prosperity." Quoted in Michael A. Meyer's *Response to Modernity*, New York, 1988, p. 295.
49. The kaiser abdicated and left for lifelong exile in Holland in late November, 1918.

November 11, 1918, the armistice was signed on the Western Front, and not long after on the other battlefields as well. The guns fell silent and in that silence could now be heard the terrible groan of the human race, lamenting the carnage it had caused, for this war had no winners — only relative losers emerged from the blood-soaked years of 1914-18.

The big war may have ended in November 1918, but small, ferocious wars continued, especially in the Balkans and Eastern Europe. Lithuania, Poland, Russia, Rumania, Hungary, Ukraine and the various Balkan ethnic groups would continue to war among themselves even into the next decade. These brutal conflicts were fought in areas of dense Jewish population. From the end of the war in 1918 until 1920 in Ukraine and Poland, more than 2,000 pogroms occurred. Half a million Jews were left homeless, 30,000 Jews were killed directly in the pogroms and another 120,000 Jews died of starvation, disease and exposure.[50] This horrendous figure must be added to the quarter of a million Jews who died in Russia during World War I itself. Jews also continued to be victims in the wars that wracked the Balkans between the Serbs, Croats, Slovenes, Albanians, Kosovars, Bosnians and Montenegrins. Jews were singled out as victims in the wars for independence that Georgia and other Central Asian states waged unsuccessfully for separation from the Soviet Union. The Jews of Bessarabia, under Russian rule before the Great War, now found themselves part of an expanded and latently anti-Semitic Rumania after the war. It was not much of an improvement.

The peace conference at Versailles was beset by many difficulties. The nations involved could not be satisfied; eventually, great and bitter enmities were perpetuated by the peace treaty that was signed. The entire blame for the war was placed on Germany and strictures were placed upon it to make certain that it would never again be able to dominate Europe militarily. The Rhineland was demilitarized, Alsace and Lorraine were returned to French rule, the German colonies in Africa and Asia were divided between the victors, mainly Britain and France, and an onerous schedule of reparations payments was imposed on Germany. The German army was limited to 100,000 men and it was not allowed an air force or tanks. The Austro-Hungarian Empire was terminated and divided into the component states of Yugoslavia, Czechoslovakia, Hungary, and Austria. Parts of its former territories were annexed by Italy. The Ottoman Empire was also dismembered, with England taking the lion's share of the area in the Middle East under its domination or mandate.[51]

---

50. Zvi Gittelman, *Century of Ambivalence*, New York, 1988, p.106.

51. France ruled over Syria and Lebanon, both newly created entities. England then ruled, directly or indirectly, over Afghanistan, Iraq, Palestine (which included Transjordan), Egypt, Aden and Sudan. It also had strong influence on the rulers of Iran and Saudi Arabia as well as the Gulf States and Emirates.

Poland was made independent, as were Lithuania, Finland, Latvia and Estonia. Attempting to establish European order, Versailles guaranteed continuing chaos and instability in Europe. The whirlwind would not be long in coming.

Early in 1919, the Allies authorized Greek administration of the formerly Turkish Izmir, a city that had been home to Sephardic Jews for centuries. The Greek occupiers pillaged, looted and raped their way into control. The Turks were completely oppressed and the Jewish population of the area was treated as Turkish. Thus the fury of the occupation served to further destabilize the Sephardic Jewish community there. In 1922, the Turkish army defeated the Greeks in a brutal war of matching atrocities and reoccupied the area of Izmir. An exchange of populations then occurred, with Ottoman Greeks sent into Greece and Turkish Greeks forced to leave for Turkey. Many thousands of Jews shared this tragedy of dislocation and the Turkish Jewish communities were severely damaged — spiritually, physically and economically — by these measures.

As though the damage, death and destruction of the war were insufficient to make humankind completely miserable, a devastating plague of influenza swept the world in 1918-19. This viral disease, for which there was no known cure or preventative, carried away more than twelve million people to their deaths. More American soldiers — 62,000 of them — died of influenza in France than were killed by German bullets. We do not have exact figures from Eastern Europe as to the effects of the plague, but the deaths there were estimated to be in the hundreds of thousands. Entire towns were emptied of life in a week, in a manner reminiscent of the bubonic plague that stalked fourteenth-century Europe. The angel of death did not heed the bugle of the Armistice.

The year 1919 also saw a revolution of the Spartacists — a radical communist group — in parts of Germany. They attempted to take power in a Lenin-type coup in Bavaria, Berlin and other areas of Germany. Some of their leaders, notably Rosa Luxemburg (Red Rose), Ernst Toller, Eugen Levine and Kurt Eisner, were Jews. As in Russia, Jews became identified with the Bolshevik fever apparently sweeping other parts of Europe. The German government, with the aid of right-wing paramilitary groups formed from German army veterans, put down the ill-coordinated revolutions in carnage, blood and assassinations. Over 1,200 revolutionaries, including Luxemburg, were executed in Berlin alone. The revolutionary communist government that had succeeded in gaining power in Bavaria was destroyed by force. In Hungary, a communist revolution led by Bela Kun, also a Jew, took power through a coup and controlled the country for a number of months. Internal opposition forces, together with a Rumanian army that conquered and plundered Budapest, put an end to Kun's rule and his communist government in the fall of 1919. Kun eventually escaped to Russia and in 1936 was executed there by Stalin in the great purge of old-line communists. Even though all of these attempted communist uprisings throughout Europe after the war ended were forcibly put down, the Red flag of revolution haunted Europe during the post-war years. The association of Jews with that Red revolution was to prove grist for the mill of anti-Semitic propagandists who abounded in North America and in both Eastern and Western Europe in the years between the two World Wars.

One of the central agreements between the Allied powers at Versailles was to establish an international organization that would serve as a place of mediation between nations in conflict. This League of Nations would hopefully realize the optimistic prediction that World War I would be the "war to end all wars." President Woodrow Wilson was a strong backer of the League of Nations and knew that without American participation, the League would be ineffective. However, Wilson was greatly disturbed by many other details of the Versailles Treaty. He had hoped for a much less punitive and empire-protecting agreement. His very high-mindedness and pious manner infuriated Lloyd George and Georges Clemenceau, the British and French leaders at the peace conference. Subsequently, Wilson's effectiveness was dramatically curtailed by a stroke that he suffered in 1919. He was unable to sell the concept of the League of Nations to the American public or to the Congress. Americans had no more patience for European quarrels and wars. Too many American young men had died in France for reasons that now no longer seemed very clear. The Senate of the United States refused to ratify the Versailles Treaty or to allow the United States to join the League of Nations. The government and people of the United States entered an extended period of isolationism that would have sad effects on Europe, and eventually on America itself.

The Great War and the Bolshevik Revolution should be seen as the beginning of the end of Eastern European Jewry. Even though no one anticipated or could ever imagine the tragedy of the immense Holocaust that would occur only twenty years later, it was nevertheless obvious to many that the physical and spiritual pieces of the old Eastern European society could not be put together again. In the first flush of nationalist enthusiasm, most of the new countries of Eastern and Central Europe looked with hostility at their Jewish minorities.[52] Although the treaty crafted in Versailles explicitly guaranteed the rights of minorities to fair and equal treatment in the countries it had created, by 1920 it was already evident that Poland, Lithuania, Latvia, Rumania and Hungary harbored strong and powerful elements that were irrationally anti-Semitic and would not easily tolerate a Jewish population in their lands.

The situation of the Jews further deteriorated when the Russian army invaded Poland in late 1919. By August 1920, Trotsky and the Red Army stood at the gates of Warsaw. Under the command of Josef Pilsudski, the Polish army counterattacked and drove the Russians all the way back to Pinsk. Russia and Poland then reached an agreement as to where the border between them lay. The Poles accused the Jews of being Bolshevik sympathizers, even though thousands of Jews fought in the Polish army and the Jewish population generally had always supported Polish independence. The Bolshevik Revolution in Russia, so wrongly ascribed to the Jews, had so traumatized its neighbors that the Polish and Lithuanian Jews were seen by the masses (and even by the ruling elite) as being untrustworthy and potentially treacherous. This climate of suspi-

---

52. Czechoslovakia under Benes and Masaryk must be seen as an exception to this sad rule.

cion and assumptions of Jewish guilt would increase in the decades between the World Wars.

The Russian Jews were now under a tyranny as dark and destructive as that of the czars. Even though they were not officially persecuted, nor were they as yet singled out for special torment, all Jewish life was ruthlessly destroyed. The Bund, the Zionists, the yeshivos, the great rabbinic scholars and Chasidic masters, the *Haskalah* writers and poets, the intellectual dreamers, the *shtetl* and its traditional way of life, all were swept away by the communist regime. These Jewish groups, individual leaders and institutions were labeled as "wreckers," "saboteurs" and "counterrevolutionaries." There was an exodus of Russian Jews to Poland, Lithuania and America. Yeshivos and their faculties, many of which had been exiled into deep Russia during the war, attempted to return to Poland and Lithuania. By 1920, a number of them had successfully escaped, returned west and reestablished themselves anew. But the Russian exit door soon slammed shut, trapping millions of Jews in a Marxist exile for the next 70 years.

American Jewry mobilized in an attempt to aid their stricken European brethren. The Joint Distribution Committee[53] labored during the war years and thereafter to bring material relief to the impoverished Jews of Eastern Europe. A committee to raise and distribute large sums to rabbis and students of the yeshivos in Eastern Europe and Palestine was established in New York just prior to the outbreak of the First World War. Appropriately named Ezras Torah (Helper of Torah), it helped thousands of Jewish scholars to survive the terrible times of the war.[54]

Yet the Jews in Europe survived the war and its immediate aftermath primarily through the individual philanthropy of American Jews who helped their relatives. Jews who barely scraped together enough wages to support themselves and their families nevertheless set aside part of their money to send to their relatives in Europe. This sense of obligation became a hallmark of Jewish societal behavior and deeply imprinted itself on the American Jewish psyche and its view of Jewish life.[55]

---

53. So called because it was a combination of three Jewish organizations working to aid the Jews of Eastern Europe during the Great War. The three organizations were the American Jewish Committee, the Orthodox-sponsored Central Committee for the Relief of Jews Suffering Through the War and the secular labor group, People's Relief Committee. The "Joint" deserves a special place in the hearts of Jews for its work in the twentieth century.

54. Ezras Torah (The Torah Relief Society) was founded by Rabbi Yisrael Rosenberg, one of the great leaders of the American rabbinate at the beginning of the century. He was also one of the heads of the Union of Orthodox Rabbis of the United States and Canada. The executive head of Ezras Torah for most of the century was Rabbi Yosef Eliyahu Henkin, a noted scholar and a person of holy character and behavior.

55. I remember in the 1940's, in the midst of another war, my bitter childhood disappointment at my parents' refusal to buy an encyclopedia because they were sending money monthly to relatives in Palestine. I treasure the lesson that experience taught me about money, life and family.

The New Face of American Jewry

CHARITY, PHILANTHROPY, AND THE PRACTICE OF HELPING OTHERS became the prime, if not the only expression of Torah tradition for a large segment of American Jewry. Judaism became defined as brotherly conscience and charity, an attitude which was to characterize much of American Jewry in the twentieth century.

"Help the Suffering" Central Relief Committee ladies collecting for charity, 1919

Attempts at strengthening Jewish education in America also took place towards the end of the decade of the Great War. Almost all Jewish children attended American public schools, and the policy of those schools was to encourage total assimilation into American white, Protestant society. Yet organizations such as Young Israel and Zionist youth groups nevertheless influenced many Jewish youngsters. The key to the progress of these groups was their willingness to accept Americanization without materially compromising their basic halachic or idealistic principles. The ideal goals of a Young Israel synagogue were described in 1915:

> *A model synagogue is to be created where every atom of our time-honored traditions could be observed and at the same time prove an attraction particularly to the young men and women; a synagogue where with the exception of prayer, English would be spoken in delivering sermons and otherwise, complete congregational singing insti-*

tuted, shnoddering [the donating of money to the synagogue when one receives the honor of being called to the Torah, usually accompanied by long blessings to the family of the honoree] *eliminated, and decorum to the extent of almost 100% maintained.*[56]

Attempts to establish yeshivos outside of the New York area, with few exceptions, did not have long lasting success. One such exception was in Chicago, where the Hebrew Theological College (Beis Medrash LaTorah) was founded in 1919. In New York, Rabbi Isaac Elchanan Theological Seminary grew to be the main Modern Orthodox yeshivah in America. The appointment in 1915 of Rabbi Dr. Bernard Revel, a person of great scholarship, charisma and vision, as president of that yeshivah gave great impetus to the growth of the institution. One of the great pioneers of American Orthodoxy, Revel himself had been radicalized in the 1905 revolution against the czar and later imprisoned by the government, but soon after his release from jail returned to faith and traditional observance. At the end of the decade, Yeshiva Torah Vodaath was founded in the Williamsburg section of Brooklyn, New York. It would grow and, for many years, become the primary traditional Orthodox yeshivah in the country, assisting materially in the creation of other such institutions.

Both the American Conservative and Reform movements continued to grow, attracting many of the children and grandchildren of the Orthodox immigrant generation. Reform continued its radical streak, officially and vigorously opposing Zionism and denouncing all vestiges of Jewish ritual and tradition as anachronistic. Despite Reform's officially aggressive condemnation of Orthodoxy and its practices, one of the leading Reform laymen of the time, Jacob Schiff, defended his support of some Orthodox causes and of the Jewish Theological Seminary as follows: "There can be no healthy Reform that has not its origin in Orthodoxy; without the continuance of Orthodoxy, Reform would be in danger of disappearing."[57]

As noted in *Reform Judaism: A Historical Perspective*, edited by Joseph L. Blau: *Philosophically and theologically, the first period of American Jewish Reform was almost totally dominated by the German idealistic tradition stemming from Immanuel Kant and his followers ... Reform Judaism was still the liberalism of the Central European Jew transplanted to America ... The turning point from Reform Judaism's first American period to its second may have been America's entry into World War I as an enemy of the German-dominated Central Powers ... In the prevalent atmosphere it is not sur-*

56. Jeffrey S. Gurock, ed., *The History of Judaism in America*, New York, 1998, Vol. 5 (part I) p. 109.
57. Michael A. Meyer, *Response To Modernity*, New York, 1988, p.295.

prising that Reform Judaism, largely a movement of German ances-
try, made every effort to present itself as a bulwark of Americanism.
Among the papers presented before the CCAR [Central Conference of
American Rabbis, the Reform rabbinical movement] in 1920 there
are several that go to such extremes in identifying Judaism as
Americanism that they are almost embarrassing to read.[58]

Outwardly, Conservative Judaism strongly resembled Orthodoxy in its prayers and its stated demands on its constituents. It was eminently successful in selling itself as an Americanized Orthodoxy. There were those within the Conservative movement and on the faculty of the Jewish Theological Seminary who wished to liberalize the Conservative movement's theology and attitude more radically.[59] Yet, in the early part of the century they had scant popular backing. Conservative Judaism remained conservative.

Dr. Solomon Schechter opposed Reform, which asserted that the destruction of the Law is its fulfillment. He said, "It is not the highest praise for a rabbi that he is invited to preach in some church, or that he has succeeded in producing some high ecclesiastic or statesman to preach in the synagogue ... It does not help Judaism ... It rather reflects upon our sense of religious delicacy (weakness), upon our [lack] of confidence in our own cause, or even self-respect."[60] Nevertheless, Schechter himself proclaimed that, "The Torah is not in heaven. Its interpretation is left to the conscience of catholic [i.e. the general populaton of] Israel."[61] The United Synagogue, founded by Schechter at the helm of the Conservative movement in 1913, proclaimed a "tradition without Orthodoxy."[62] Because of the uncertainty of its theology, the Conservative movement was able to attract a large section of American Jewry. To be Conservative did not commit oneself on the major issues of contention between the Orthodox and the Reform — the divinity of Torah, the role of ritual observance in daily life, the requirement of a halachic framework for Jewish life and the uncertain definition of Judaism as either nation, faith or ethnic group, or as all of them at once. But this very ambiguity of the Conservative movement was its greatest weakness as well. As indicated by Abraham Karp in an essay quoted in Jeffrey S. Gurock's massive work *The History of Judaism in America*, "It is possible to see Conservative Judaism

---

58. Joseph L. Blau, ed., *Reform Judaism: A Historical Perspective*, New York, 1973 pp.10, 11, 12.

59. Mordecai M. Kaplan was chief among this group. At one time, he was the rabbi of the Orthodox Jewish Center in Manhattan. He later became the founder of the Reconstructionist movement.

60. Jeffrey S.Gurock, ed., *The History of Judaism in America*, Vol. 5, (part I), essay by Abraham Karp, p.209.

61. Gerald Sorin, *The Jewish People in America*, Baltimore, 1992, Vol. 3, p.187.

62. Ibid. p.190.

as a dilution of immigrant religious fervor, a middle-class stopover for Jews on the way from Orthodoxy to Reform or to secular assimilation."[63] A problem that would plague the movement throughout the century was the fact the its elitist leadership had created a very complicated and inexact definition of the movement's philosophy and goals, attempting to serve a disinterested and non-observant laity. In almost all religious and social issues that would confront the movement in the twentieth century, this leadership would have to bow to the wishes of its laity which was for the most part assimilated and Judaicly uneducated.

Due to the constant inflow of new Eastern European immigrants, Orthodox Jewish life in America appeared vital and plentiful,[64] as did Jewish cultural life. There were numerous Yiddish and *Haskalah* afternoon and Sunday schools as well as a thriving Yiddish theatre and literature. Schools and colleges such as the City College of New York helped

Hebrew Publishing Co. typesetters, 1909

63. Gurock, ibid.

64. Though the thrust of this immigration was to the United States, mention should be made of the fact that by 1914 over 100,000 Eastern European Jews immigrated to Canada. Settling primarily in Montreal, Toronto and Winnipeg, the Canadian Jewish community had an easier adjustment to the

Jewish young people climb the ladder into academia and the professions. Jewish society in America began to become upwardly mobile, socially and economically. Jews moved into better neighborhoods and out of the ghetto slums and tenements that housed their parents. The promise of America was becoming actualized.

American Jews earned their livelihoods in numerous ways. Above, a dinner reception of the Federation of Jewish Farmers of America in 1913. Note the Hebrew sign which means, "Those who weep when they plant, will sing for joy when they harvest."

Influential figures from outside America came to visit and and some stayed in the United States during the pre-war years. Of particular note among these visiting notables was Rabbi Meir Berlin, an extremely energetic and innovative person and the youngest son of the *Netziv* (Rabbi Nafatali Tzvi Yehuda Berlin) of Volozhin. He came to America early in the century and in 1912 helped found a successful and pioneering teacher's institute which was later absorbed into the Yeshiva University complex. He also was the driving force behind the organization of a large and powerful Mizrachi religious Zionist movement in America. Rabbi Berlin made important contributions in many areas of Jewish life in America in the war decade. His departure to the Land of Israel immediately after the war's end left a void in American Jewish society.

New World than did American Jewish immigrants. Canada had a smaller, more traditional general population than did the United States and the Jews there were successful early in building a strong traditional Jewish infrastructure that lessened the problems of Jewish assimilation and alienation.

There was also a substantial Jewish migration from Eastern Europe (mainly from Lithuania) to South Africa both before and after the Boer War. The Jewish community of South Africa would eventually grow to 125,000 people before shrinking dramatically at the end of the century.

Mention must also be made of the impact of new travel and communication technologies that began to be developed and distributed widely during the decade of the war. Radio, airplanes, automobiles and movies would all guarantee that the old world would quickly disappear. New and different ideas, strange foreign cultures, a quickening pace of life and increasing curiosity about the wider world would now seep into every corner of human habitation. Some of the items of technology — radios and movies, for instance — appeared as though they could be controlled and even banned, but their universal presence assured that eventually the messages and information they carried would touch everyone, no matter how isolated and secluded their society.

Like all new technological advances, there would be negative fallout from their use. Millions would die in automobile accidents as the century wore on. Thousands would be killed in airplane disasters. Movies and radio would be misused and manipulated, purveying anti-social behavior and attitudes. Nevertheless, the technology itself would prove beneficial to humans, increasing their comfort and knowledge. The true effect of this new technology would not be felt until a decade or two later, but indications of the power of these new inventions were already recognized in the early decades of the century. The self-contained society, which was the basis of the Jewish social world in Eastern Europe for many centuries, became extinct due in large part to these new technologies. Judaism, like many other forces and faiths in the world, would now have to compete for loyalty from its erstwhile adherents in an ever more open world of competitive ideas. This would be its greatest educational and social challenge during the latter 80 years of the twentieth century.

Chapter Three

Distortions and Illusions

1921-1930

HE DECADE THAT FOLLOWED THE GREAT WAR WAS ONE OF FALSE hopes and clouded vision. This was the case for humanity generally, but it is an even more apt description of the Jewish world of that time. The main areas of Jewish communal concern and settlement would continue to be in Eastern Europe, the Land of Israel and the United States of America. Due to improved conditions of communication and travel, these three major Jewish settlements would become more tightly bound and would influence each other in a way unprecedented in the earlier decades of the century.

But the Jewish world was held hostage by the events and power structures that surrounded it and it would take on a structure of its own only in the context of the unfolding themes of the general societies around it. In all major areas of Jewish population distribution, the Jews would encounter increasing bigotry and deprivation of their self-perceived rights as citizens.

The yeshivos that fled into Russian exile during the World War I fighting in Lithuania and Poland attempted to return to the newly independent countries of Poland and Lithuania, enduring many hardships on the way. The Russian communists were not anxious to let the yeshivah students leave Russia, since they saw in them material for potentially idealistic comrades. Those whom the communists could not convert, they would attempt to destroy. The *Yevsektzia* (Jewish Section of the Communist Party) was determined not only to eradicate Judaism from Russian Jews, but in the true fanaticism of the believing atheist, was also determined to suppress Judaism (and all religions) the world over. Thus, confiscating the minds and bodies of the yeshivah students and faculty

SOME YESHIVAH LOCATIONS
AND MAJOR JEWISH POPULATION
CENTERS IN EASTERN EUROPE

© 2001, Shaar Press. Reproduction prohibited

was a prime goal of these hardened Jewish communists. In some instances, they were successful, but in the main the young men and their teachers of the pre-war yeshivos of Lithuania and Poland were resourceful in maintaining their faith and in "smuggling" themselves over the border from Russia and returning to their original homes. This smuggling was a most serious business since Poland, Russia and Lithuania were all at war with each other in the early 1920's. The yeshivah students and faculty members were treated suspiciously by all sides and constantly accused of spying for the enemy, among other anti-Semitic fabrications. A number of yeshivah students were killed trying to cross the borders back into Lithuania and Poland. But most of them survived the harrowing experience and by the early part of the 1920's the yeshivah world of Torah study in Eastern Europe was reconstituted and rebuilt with a new enthusiasm and determination to survive and succeed.

The leading yeshivos in Lithuania and Poland in the 1920's were located on the towns of Mir, Slobodka, Telshe, Grodno, Radin, Baranovitch, Ponovezh, Lomzeh, Bialystok, Kaminetz, Kletzk, Slonim, Kelm and Kobrin. The Chasidic network of yeshivos included those of Lubavitch, Radomsk and the *shtieblach* of Warsaw (which were primarily composed of Chasidim of Gur as well as other Polish Chasidic dynasties.) There were also other Chasidic yeshivos beside Radomsk, in Galicia, in western Poland. At the end of the decade, in June 1930, the great yeshivah in Lublin was established amidst worldwide recognition and support. (See the Survey of European Yeshivos at the end of this chapter.)

There were also numerous yeshivos in Rumania, Hungary and Czechoslovakia and important institutions of Torah learning in Germany and Belgium. The growth and strength of the yeshivah movement in Europe, and especially in Eastern Europe, in the years between the World Wars was providential, if unexpected by many, for it was these yeshivos that trained and produced the men who rebuilt the Torah world after the Holocaust.

The 1920's would be a very turbulent time for Orthodox Jewry in Eastern Europe. The basic town/*shtetl* infrastructure upon which much of traditional Jewish society was based had been destroyed by the ravages of World War I. The new world of technology — telephone, electricity, radio, even movies — was slowly infiltrating even the most staunchly isolated groups of Jews. Zionism, communism and socialism all provided alternative faiths and ways of life for the young Jewish postwar generation. Because of this, secular Jewish parties and organizations gained strength and in the elections for representatives to the Jewish councils in Poland and Lithuania, the secular parties slowly gained dominance. Even in those communities where Orthodox Jews were the majority of the population, the Orthodox political parties rarely did well at the polls. Major contributing factors to this phenomenon were the continuing disaffection of many of the younger generation from the traditional Jewish life of the past, as well as the influence that these young people then had on their parents. In those fast-changing times, the influence of children on parents was far greater than the influence of parents on children.

All of the changes of the modern world that had not yet reached czarist Russia and the Jewish heartland in the nineteenth century were now released in full force in the aftermath of the Great War and the upheavals it engendered. The new always appears to be more attractive than the old, especially to the young. In retrospect, it was no surprise that Orthodoxy was placed on the defensive and thrust into a minority role in Jewish society, a position it had never before occupied in Jewish history.

As this pressure on the Orthodox community grew, there were new initiatives advanced to redress and improve the situation. In the field of education, there were attempts at modernization of the traditional *cheder* elementary school system. This system was long under attack by the czarist authorities and the Jewish secular *maskilim* in pre-World War I Russia and Poland. The major objections that were raised against the *cheder* system were the inadequacy, and sometimes cruelty, of the teachers, the use of corporal punishment to enforce discipline, the overcrowded physical conditions of the classroom and the lack of any general secular education in the curriculum. Each of these complaints may have had individual merit, but since the source of these suggestions for improvement was either a hated anti-Semitic government or hardened secularist Jews who were viewed as enemies of traditional Jewry, the Orthodox camp was loath to adopt any of their suggestions. In fact, in certain circles of Orthodoxy, any change whatever, no matter how minor or logical, in the traditional method of instruction was now viewed as heresy. Nevertheless, educational change was on the way for the Orthodox Jewish world in this decade.

A SIGNIFICANT SOCIAL REVOLUTION OF THE TWENTIETH CENTURY WAS the changed attitude towards women in most societies. The drive for the rights of women to vote, work outside of the house or the farm, and to achieve professional education and economic status on a par with men was universal in the twentieth century, however the results of that drive were uneven in different parts of the world. Women's suffrage was attained in the Western World, the Soviet Union and other parts of Eastern Europe by the end of the 1920's. However, in the election for public offices of the *yishuv* and the Chief Rabbinate in Palestine in the

The Critical Need of the Hour: Women's Jewish Education

1920's, Rabbi Kook and almost all of the other leading rabbis of the country opposed (unsuccessfully) giving women the right to vote. But the burning issue in the Orthodox world after the Great War was not the right to vote, but women's education.

In an unpublished report (in the author's possession) prepared by Mercaz Bais Yaakov in Israel in 1999, the postwar situation of Jewish girls is described:

> *[In Jewish Poland and Lithuania] the lure of the street prevailed over the influence of the home and a painful process began of an ideological separation of the young from their parents, the "older generation." The boys were harmed less, as most of them were instructed in Torah institutions that provided some protection from the dangers of the street environment. On the other hand, many of the girls who were supposedly sheltered in their parents' homes were detrimentally influenced by the atmosphere of the street. Their social and moral deterioration was sharp and quick. Many Orthodox girls completely abandoned observance of Torah ritual and Jewish modesty in dress, speech and behavior, as well as rebelling against the hitherto accepted social conventions of that time.[1]*

> *The situation posed a serious threat to the continued spiritual existence of the Jewish nation. Not only was the future of these Jewish girls in jeopardy, but the entire existence of the traditional Jewish home and family hung in the balance. Entire generations of yeshivah students throughout Lithuania and thousands of Chasidic youth in Poland were helpless, for no one would marry them. Most of the girls now had no desire to marry a young man with Torah views, and certainly not someone who saw his future within the Torah world.[2]*

Education of women in the pre-World War I Orthodox Jewish world was at best a haphazard event. Especially in Chasidic circles, there was no formal schooling for girls and many, if not most, of the Jewish women in the early 1900's in Eastern Europe were functionally illiterate. With the rise of idealistic movements in the twentieth century, this situation rapidly changed. Jewish girls flocked to the schools and *gymnasia* of the secular Zionist and socialist movements, as well as to the non-Jewish and Christian schools.

---

1. In 1921, the Rebbe of Gur was reported to have brokenheartedly told his followers: "The father and sons of the family come to my Shabbos *tisch* — and the daughters go to the theater!" (*Tisch* means literally table, the traditional Friday night Chasidic gathering at which the Rebbe delivers a Torah discourse.)

2. From the same report in the possession of the author, issued by Mercaz Bais Yaakov; prepared in Israel in 1999 on the history of the girls' schools movement.

One brave and farsighted woman, Sarah Schnierer, founded an Orthodox network of schools for young women that changed the face of Orthodox Jewry for the balance of the century, and undoubtedly beyond it as well. The first school of her Bais Yaakov movement opened in Krakow, Poland, in a small rented room. A seamstress by trade, Mrs. Schnierer wrote in her diary: "They are 25 girls in all, most of them girls for whom I sewed dresses. And now I am also sewing their spiritual garments."[3]

> Later, she would write in the same diary: When I sew dresses for Jewish girls, I ask their mothers if they would like to put their daughters in my care in order to revive their souls. Most mothers agree. I rented a humble house with an upright Jewish woman and gave my first lesson. Every day now, new girls come to register. However, our tranquility in that house did not last. The landlord became angry with us since he objects to there being a school on the premises and we had to move. We rented a second hall and now a third hall, which also serves as my residence. The school has grown (in three years) to 280 girls, 80 of whom are under my personal care. More and more students join from day to day. I am afraid that I will have to end up inevitably neglecting some of them. What should be done? To accept teachers from another school — that I do not want. Therefore, I choose my two most diligent students, stand them up in front of the class and they teach. They are not yet thirteen years old, yet they are aware of the heavy responsibility upon their shoulders.[4]

Despite initial formidable rabbinic and Chasidic opposition to the burgeoning school network,[5] within four years after the establishment of the school in Krakow, another two schools, one in Tarnow and another in Ostrowice, were opened. By the end of 1925, there were eighteen Bais Yaakov schools in Poland with a total enrollment of over 2,300 students. As the Bais Yaakov movement grew, opposition towards it moderated. In 1924, Agudath Israel, the non-Zionist Orthodox political party, adopted the Bais Yaakov schools and its network of educational facilities. The construction of a major building (six levels high) in Krakow to house the main Bais Yaakov teachers-training seminary was begun in 1929. By the 1930's, the Bais Yaakov network in Poland numbered approximately 250 schools and 40,000 students.

---

3. Ibid.

4. Ibid.

5. Sarah Schnierer said that the Bais Yaakov schools were "saved" by the unrelenting publicly expressed support of the Rebbe of Gur and the Chafetz Chaim (Rabbi Yisrael Meir Kagan).

After the death of Sarah Schnierer, Rabbi Yehuda Leib Orlean became the head of the school system in 1935.[6]

The example set by Poland in pioneering Jewish women's education was replicated in the 1920's in other Jewish communities in Europe as well. In Lithuania, there were sixteen schools for women with an enrollment of over 2,000 students. The leading teachers' seminaries were in Kovno and Telshe. In Austria, there were eleven schools with an enrollment of 950 students. In Czechoslovakia, eighteen schools were established, with an enrollment of 1,569 students. And in Rumania, there were eighteen schools with an enrollment of 1,292 students, including a teachers' seminary in Chernowitz. It is estimated that by the time of World War II, the enrollment in the Bais Yaakov system of girls' schools in Eastern and Central Europe reached 80,000.

In a related project, Agudath Israel created a girls' youth organization called Bnos Bais Yaakov Batya (Bnos Agudath Israel). This grassroots organization, founded by Eliezer Gershon Friedenson, organized Sabbath social and learning groups, conventions, seminars and other activities for young Jewish women. By 1930, it had 150,000 young people enrolled in its almost 300 branches scattered throughout Poland. In 1934, it claimed a membership of 200,000 girls. Together with the Bais Yaakov schools, Bnos helped restore Jewish pride and observance of tradition to many of the young generation of Jewish women.

Zionist and Yiddish Schools Carve Their Niches

OTHER NEW TYPES OF SCHOOLS ALSO EMERGED IN THE 1920's. A religious Zionist school system called Tachkamoni (a Biblical term referring to Torah knowledge) gained prominence in Poland. Its network of elementary and secondary schools (sometimes called Yavneh) included over 16,000 students in 238 schools by the end of the decade. It also maintained special schools (vocational, non-coed, etc.) that serviced 7,567 other students.[7] The pride of the Tachkamoni system was its rabbinical seminary in Warsaw. It was founded in 1920, with the goal of producing scholars and leaders who would be able to cope with the changing times and circumstances in the Polish Jewish world. Originally, Rabbi Chaim Heller was appointed as dean, but he soon resigned because of his dissatisfaction with the standards of

---

6. There was a strong debate over the propriety of appointing a man to head a women's institution. The opinion of Jacob Rosenheim, the German Jew who was the titular head of Agudath Israel, prevailed and Orlean, who was a most remarkable and talented person, became the head of the school network, especially of the Krakow teachers' seminary.

7. Mirsky, p.588.

admission to the school. Rabbi Yehuda Leib Graubardt (later of Toronto, Canada) succeeded Rabbi Heller. But after a year, Rabbi Moshe Soloveitchik, the son of Rabbi Chaim Soloveitchik and a most formidable Talmudic scholar in his own right, became the head of the Torah studies department of the seminary; and Professor Meir Balaban, the foremost Jewish historian of Poland, headed the secular studies department. The first classes in 1920-21 had only 48 students in all. But by 1930 the school had over 220 students from all over Poland and from many different religious and social backgrounds. Tachkamoni supplied a significant number of teachers and rabbis to the Jewish world in its 20 years of existence.

There was also a large secular Zionist school system called Tarbut (literally, the name means "culture"). As the name implied, the curriculum of the school was geared towards the ideas and goals of the earlier Hebrew *Haskalah* that were absorbed into the dynamic of the Zionist movement. Hebrew language, knowledge of the Bible (though not of Mishnah or Talmud), modern Hebrew literature and geography of the Land of Israel formed the core of this curriculum. In many instances, the individual Tarbut school also was socialist in its orientation and as such, Marxist texts were also taught.

All of these major school systems, Agudah/Bais Yaakov, Mizrachi/Tachkemoni and Tarbut were affiliated with and sponsored by Jewish political parties in Poland. This unhappy precedent would be slavishly followed in the Land of Israel and later enshrined in law in the State of Israel itself. It would be difficult, if not impossible, for Jewish children to receive an apolitical education in Eastern Europe or in the Land of Israel in the twentieth century.

There were also smaller Jewish school systems that functioned in Poland, and Lithuania during the period between the World Wars. There were Yiddish schools, based on the culture and language of Yiddish. These schools were avidly secular and anti-religious. They were usually affiliated with the Jewish labor union party, the Bund, and taught that solidarity with the working class of the world takes precedence over Jewish particulars. Much of their curriculum was based on the writings of the Yiddish *Haskalah* and their social science emphasized the "class struggle" aspect of human history. The Bund continued to be anti-Zionist. It felt that Zionism was a dangerous distraction in the ongoing struggle for the rights of the universal proletariat.

A very large number of Jewish children attended non-Jewish schools in Poland, and Roman Catholic schools in the large cities had meaningful numbers of Jewish registrants. This was especially true among the children of the more assimilated Jewish families of Poland

*Jewish public school
Gambin, Poland, 1929*

who aspired to be "Poles of the Mosaic persuasion." They opposed Zionism, viewing it as a diminution of the Jewish future in Poland. As Reform was not a viable option for Polish Jewry, these families either rapidly drifted out of any sort of Jewish life or remained superficially "traditional," though assimilationist in practice and belief. Large synagogues — called "choir synagogues" because of the cantor and choir that officiated there — catered to these assimilating Jews. These synagogues met minimal traditional halachic standards, but they were more modern in their services. Though they could not be judged as being nearly as radical as the Reform temples of Germany, they were shunned by the Orthodox Jews in Poland. The largest of these synagogues was in central Warsaw and had a seating capacity in the thousands.

Division Marks Jewish Communal Life

JEWISH POLAND AND LITHUANIA WERE BECOMING FRACTIONALIZED AND riven with dissension. Not only were the strong divisions between secular and religious, Zionist and anti-Zionist, socialist/communist and capitalist proving divisive, but each of these groups suffered further fragmentation. The General Zionists and the Labor Zionists quarreled bitterly. The Mizrachi religious Zionist movement was split by the formation of a more socialist oriented youth movement that became known as Hapoel HaMizrachi (The Workers of Mizrachi) which attempted to combine the ideas of Marxist collectivism with devotion to Torah and Zionism.[8] This movement established kibbutzim and other farming settlements in the Land of Israel. Its popular youth movement, Bnei Akiva, indoctrinated Orthodox youth with a combination of the ideals of farming, Zionism, immigration to the Land of Israel and Torah observance. Hapoel HaMizrachi also gave birth to a youth movement called Hashomer Hadati (The Religious Watchman) which was much more inclined to kibbutz/socialist ideology. Each of these youth movements had branches in Palestine, Eastern Europe and North America.

---

8. The motto of the movement was *Torah V'Avodah* – Torah and Labor.

World Jewish Congress of Orthodox Jews convened by Agudath Israel World Organization, Vienna, 1929

Session of first Orthodox Women's Conference, Vienna, 1929

Agudath Israel also faced a restive youth within its ranks. The 1920's saw the formation of the Zeirei Agudath Israel (Agudath Israel Youth) and of Poalei Agudath Israel (The Workers of Agudath Israel). These two groups exhibited a high degree of independence in their goals and actions, often bringing them into conflict with the parent organization. Poalei Agudath Israel battled for the rights of religious Jewish workers in Poland, often against the religious establishment and its lay leadership who were the employers of these workers. It also trained workers and farmers for emigration from Eastern Europe to settle in the Land of Israel, and it would eventually establish kibbutzim and settlements there under its banner.

Rabbi Meir Shapiro

One of the leading figures in Polish and world Jewish society in the 1920's was Rabbi Meir Shapiro. He was a genius of note, a gifted orator and an innovative and dynamic leader. One of the key leaders of Agudath Israel, he was one of its most important spokesmen in the Polish parliament. He was a man of ideas and action and constantly searched for ways to improve the lot of Polish Jewry, physically and spiritually. He was the founder of the *Daf HaYomi* program — a method by which a given page of the Talmud would be studied daily by Jews all over the world. He saw this activity as not only an aid to Jewish scholarship, but as importantly, a means of creating Jewish unity among different factions and communities throughout the Jewish world.

Rabbi Shapiro dreamt of establishing a great yeshivah in Poland that would become the creative base of leadership which would enable Polish Orthodoxy to meet the challenges it now faced from both without and within. Almost all of the great rabbinic and Chasidic leaders of Poland

Students of Yeshivas Chachmei Lublin in the 1930's

supported Rabbi Shapiro's great educational project. During his visit to the United States to raise funds for the project, he made a great impression on the American Jewish community, and it responded warmly to his appeal for help in building the yeshivah. The foundation of the building of Yeshivas Chachmei Lublin was laid in 1928, the school opened in 1930, and it attracted a very high caliber of student. The yeshivah building of Chachmei Lublin was one of the most impressive Jewish structures in Poland: Its library of tens of thousands of books became a magnet for some of the greatest scholars in Poland who served on the faculty. Rabbi Shapiro's dynamism and creativity had inspired Orthodoxy in Poland to a new self-confidence in the face of its problems and foes.

Political Loyalties Create Enduring Rifts

ALTHOUGH THE ORTHODOX POPULATION WAS DOMINANT IN MANY cities, including Warsaw, the Bund would eventually emerge as the most powerful Jewish party in elections, despite the fact that it rarely supported any particular Jewish interests. The Zionists were also strongly represented in the Jewish governing bodies, as were the assimilationist Jewish groups and the strongly secular parties. All of these groups also had representation in the Polish and Lithuanian parliaments. Typical of the division of power was the breakdown of representation on the Warsaw Jewish Council after the elections of 1926: Agudath Israel, 15; Zionist Bloc, 11; Mizrachi, 5; Bund, 5; Chasidic parties, 5; People's Party (Polish assimilationist oriented), 3; Labor Zionist, 2; Workers' Party, 1; Independents, 1.[9] The Orthodox parties maintained a bare majority on the council and because of continued infighting within the Orthodox group itself, the secular parties were able to impose their will on many communal issues.

A particularly divisive battle within Orthodoxy occurred as a result of the insistence of the Polish government that the Jewish community of Vilna elect a rabbi. Vilna had been without an official rabbi for over 150 years, since the bitter dispute in the 1700's between Rabbi Shmuel Avigdor and the lay leaders of the community. However, the great scholar and Jewish leader of Lithuania and beyond, Rabbi Chaim Ozer Grodzinski, was unofficially recognized as the rabbinic authority in Vilna in the early 1900's. Most of the Orthodox leaders in Vilna assumed that Rabbi Grodzinski would be elected without opposition as their official rabbi. Yet, when the election itself was forced on the community, the Mizrachi party nominated Rabbi Yitzchak Rubenstein for the post. Rabbi

---

9. Dr. Hillel Zaidman, *Ishim Shehikarti*, Jerusalem, 1970, p.82.

Rubenstein was a scholar, a talented orator and a well-known religious Zionist writer. In the ensuing election, the Mizrachi, with the aid of the secular Jewish parties in Vilna, prevailed and Rabbi Rubenstein was elected over Rabbi Grodzinski. This election and its result, which was seen within much of the Orthodox camp as an unwarranted insult to the great sage, engendered a great deal of animosity between Agudath Israel and Mizrachi. This animosity intensified in Poland and Lithuania in the decades before World War II and it also marked the less than cordial relations between the two parties during the entire century in the Land of Israel as well.

The behavior of the Jewish parties in the parliaments of Lithuania and Poland also caused a good deal of strife within Eastern European Jewish society. The Leftist Jewish parties slavishly voted with the overall Left on all issues, many times to the detriment of large sections of the local Jewish community. Agudath Israel often voted with the government parties (which were in the main blatantly anti-Semitic and xenophobic) in crucial parliamentary votes, in order to receive allowances from the government for Jewish religious schools and practices. The other Jewish groups denounced them for not seeing the forest for the trees. The Zionists were attacked by the non-Jewish parties and some of the Jewish parties as being a force of treachery against the resurgent Polish and Lithuanian national interests. These bitter party squabbles left the overall Jewish community in a state of disarray and ill-prepared to deal with the terrible challenges that would soon beset them.

Jewish Life is Crushed in the Communist Paradise

THE SITUATION OF JEWS IN THE SOVIET UNION WORSENED IN THE 1920's. The Jewish subgroup of the Communist Party, *Yevsektzia,* completely destroyed the entire infrastructure of religious Jewish life. Great rabbis were arrested and sent to die in Siberian exile.[10] Synagogues were closed and their buildings confiscated. All Jewish ritual was banned. The only school system allowed to Jews was a secular, Yiddish-language, cultural educational network based on Marxist ideology. Eventually, even this type of "Jewish" education would disappear. The shifting economic and social policies of the Soviet government, coupled with its relentless and ruthless terror apparatus, destroyed the last vestiges of Jewish communal and religious life. The New Economic Plan promulgated at the beginning of the decade, which allowed the Russian peasant some meas-

---

10. Rabbi Yitzchak Schneerson, the Rebbe of Lubavitch, and Rabbi Yechezkel Abramsky are two examples of great rabbis imprisoned by the communists. They both were later released and expelled from the Soviet Union. Other great rabbis did not fare as well and died in Siberian labor camps.

ure of land ownership, was followed by its revocation later in the decade and the forced collectivization of the farms in the Soviet Union. It is estimated that twenty million people died during the famine and terror that Stalin unleashed in destroying the peasantry of Russia during the 1920's while creating the "paradise" of collective farming.[11]

A Yevsektzia conference in 1918

The Jewish *shtetl* was completely destroyed by the New Economic Plan and its consequent revocation. In 1924, less than one quarter of the 90,000 Jewish inhabitants of 43 *shtetlach* in White Russia had any sort of gainful employment or employable skills.[12] The starvation policies of the Soviet government reduced the Jewish population to less than what it had been 30 years earlier.[13] In the early part of the decade, the efforts of Jewish American relief agencies, especially that of the Joint Distribution Committee, were intensified, operating more or less freely due to the Soviet government's desperate need for hard capital. However, by the end of the decade, it was removed from the Russian scene by Stalin. The flight from the *shtetl* intensified and with its disappearance, the reservoir of Jewish tradition and memory in Russia evaporated.

The communists, especially the Jewish communists, viewed the Jewish communities of Russia as unreliable partners in the pursuit of the dream of creating the proletariat's heaven on earth. The communists were certain that the future was theirs. They destroyed all forms of Zionism, even the Marxist Labor Zionists; suppressed Hebrew; eliminated the study and schools of Torah and the observance of Jewish tradition; disbanded the Bund and declared that there was no longer any need for the existence of a Jewish subculture in the Soviet Union.

But in spite of these "achievements," and the claim of the *Yevsektzia* that there no longer existed a Jewish bourgeoisie, the communist government always eyed the Jews under their domain suspiciously. In 1920,

---

11. The definitive work on the collectivization of the farms in Russia under Stalin is the book *The Great Famine*, written by Robert Conquest. The story is a harrowing one and not for those with a weak stomach.

12. Zvi Gitelman, *A Century of Ambivalence*, New York, 1988, p.124.

13. Ibid. p.108.

it was a radical left-wing revolutionary Jewess who attempted to assassinate communist leader Vladimir Ilyich Lenin, and he never really recovered from his wounds. His last years in office were marked by callous murder, policy indecision and the slipping of power from his hands into those of Josef Stalin. Stalin was perpetually paranoid about his Jewish cohorts. Leon Trotsky, a Jew, was Stalin's main rival for power after the death of Lenin in 1924. Exiled from Russia by Stalin, Trotsky kept up a campaign of invective against Stalin from foreign shores.[14] No matter how many Jewish communists declared their loyalty to the government and no matter how ruthlessly these Jews destroyed their Jewish brethren physically and spiritually, they never were trusted by Stalin. Eventually (with the exception of Lazar Kaganovitch), even the Jewish leaders in the hierarchy of the Communist Party, the "old Bolsheviks," were purged from the party and killed. This same fate befell the leaders and shock troops of the *Yevsektzia*, all of whom were also destroyed in the great purges and terror of the 1930's. Ironically, many Jewish "true believers" in communism left Western Europe, Poland, North America and the Land of Israel and came to Russia in the 1920's to help build the workers' paradise. Almost all of them were promptly shipped off to the labor camps of Siberia, there to be worked to death.

The Jewish world was slow to react to the true situation of their brothers and sisters in the Soviet Union. The Jewish Left pursued a policy of "see-no-evil, hear-no-evil, speak-no-evil" regarding the Soviet Union. Ideologically speaking, by Marxist definition, there could be no injustice or evil in a Marxist state. Any evidence of the murderous ruthlessness of Lenin, and later Stalin, was either dismissed as "capitalist propaganda" or justified as being necessary to destroy the counterrevolutionaries and the enemies of the state. The other groupings within the Jewish people — the Zionists, the religious, the Western assimilated, all looked on helplessly as the destruction of the old Russian Jewish community took place. In hindsight, one can make a case that there should have been greater public protests against Soviet policy towards the Jews. But Jews in the 1920's, the world over, found themselves in great difficulties, awash in anti-Semitism (which was not only tolerated, but socially encouraged), without much political influence over events or statesmen and generally very uncertain of their future. It would only be decades later that the Jewish communities of the world would successfully mount the great battle to free their brethren from the tyranny of Soviet Russian Communist rule.

14. A Stalinist agent eventually caught up to Trotsky in his hiding place in Mexico and deposited a pickaxe in his skull.

UNNOTICED AND ALMOST UNSEEN, THE IMMEDIATE FATE OF THE world was being decided in Germany. The German army retired from the field after World War I intact and, in the minds of many Germans, undefeated. The sense in the country was that the army had not been defeated and that the country had been betrayed by its leaders in asking for an armistice and submitting to Allied peace terms at Versailles. The truth was that it was the German general staff — the army itself — which had sought the armistice and felt defeated and exhausted. But that truth was never made public to the German masses. The harsh peace terms imposed by the Allies on Germany, the ruinous schedule of reparations demanded by the victors and the specter of Bolshevik revolution in Germany all combined to create a witches' brew of politics and government. The German government headquartered in Weimar struggled mightily to control the situation. The communist uprisings in Bavaria, Berlin and other German cities (led by communist Jews) were quelled. The reparations demands were satisfied by the printing of worthless German marks, so that all private German savings and pensions were obliterated by the raging inflation that ensued.

Scapegoats were needed to help explain how such an orderly society as Germany had been brought to the brink of chaos and decadence.[15] Strong anti-Semitism flourished among the right-wing nationalist parties and groups, especially among the members of the *Freikorps* (veterans of the German army of World War I) and the *Volkists* (the xenophobic German nationalist parties). In 1922, Walter Rathenau, the Jewish banker and government minister in the wartime German government, who actually signed the Versailles peace treaty representing Germany, was assassinated by three nationalist extremists who considered him to be a traitor to Germany. His Jewishness was deemed to be the major contributing factor to his treachery.

In spite of all of its problems, the democratic Weimar Republic governing Germany began to make progress on restoring the social and economic health of the country. By 1923, the raging inflation of the currency abated, unemployment decreased and German cultural and economic life began to flourish. The Bolshevik threat within Germany was crushed by brute force, though millions of Germans still claimed to be loyal to the Red banner of Marxism.[16]

Embers of German Anti-Semitism Burst into Flame

---

15. In the "Roaring Twenties," a decade whose hallmark was depravity and decadence, Berlin was the capital of this social phenomenon.

16. One of the more amazing things to contemplate regarding the rise of Hitler and Nazism is how millions of Marxists became loyal Fascists and Nazis overnight. Apparently, to those committed to totalitarianism, it ultimately makes little difference which totalitarianism one serves.

The Jewish population of Germany increased due to the immigration of large numbers of Polish Jews to Germany. These *ostjuden* (eastern Jews) were hardly welcome guests in Germany. Even the German Jewish communities were lukewarm to their eastern brothers and sisters. Language, custom, dress, social manners and intensity of religious observance differentiated these newcomers from the long-established Jewish communities and typical Jewish figure in Germany. Yet, the *ostjuden* had an important influence on German Jewish life. Their very exoticism proved attractive to many young German Jews. Small numbers of German Jews traveled to Lithuania to study in the great yeshivos there. The Rabbinical Seminary in Berlin founded by Rabbi Azriel Hildesheimer was headed in the 1920's by *ostjuden* scholars from Lithuania.[17] Jews in Chasidic garb began to appear on the streets of German cities. Their obvious presence only heightened the already strong current of anti-Semitism then running in Germany.

For all of the evidence of rising anti-Semitism in Germany, world Jewry, and even German Jews, remained blindly sanguine to the situation that would soon engulf them. No one in the Jewish world publicly warned of an impending Holocaust. In fact, if there was a country in the world where Jews felt relatively secure in the 1920's, that country was Germany. The feeling was best summed up in the remarks of David Philipson, a leader of American Reform Judaism, at the conference of the World Union for Progressive Judaism held in Berlin in 1928. The conference took place in the Herrenhaus, the former Prussian House of Lords chamber. He said: "How significant of the change that the years have wrought in the position of the Jews (that) this Jewish gathering is in the hall of Junkerthum whose walls resounded so frequently with anti-Semitic tirades in the Imperial days."[18] One reads these remarks, made in sincerity and apparent wisdom, with a shudder.

Adolph Hitler, a wounded veteran of World War I (who had been gassed and temporarily blinded weeks before the end of the war), became a figure in the rightist *volkische* parties very early in the decade. Hitler was a demagogic orator and able to hold the attention of large audiences for hours-long harangues. An Austrian by birth, Hitler was a rabid anti-Semite who demanded that Germany receive her "rightful place in the sun." To

---

17. Talmudic-intensive yeshivos also began to appear, according to Hungarian or Lithuanian style, in the Orthodox Jewish communities of Germany. The community of Rabbi S.R. Hirsch in Frankfort am Main, which had no such type of yeshivah existing during Hirsch's lifetime, now sponsored a major yeshivah under the leadership of its rabbi and Hirsch's son in law, Rabbi Solomon Breuer.

18. Quoted in *Reform Judaism — A Historical Perspective*, edited by Joseph L. Blau, New York, 1973, p.112.

him, and to many others in Europe, Bolshevism was a Jewish plot to rule the world. But he alone promised to do something about it. In 1923, his Nazi party, in cooperation with other *volkische* organizations and with the active leadership and presence of World War I hero General Eric Von Ludendorf, attempted a *putsch* (revolutionary coup) in Munich, aimed at establishing a new government in Bavaria and eventually in all Germany.

Heinrich Himmler (fourth from left) with some of Hitler's Storm Troops behind barricades in front of the War Ministry during the Munich Putsch, November 9, 1923

The *putsch* failed, several Nazis were killed and Hitler was arrested and jailed for nine months in a fairly comfortable fortress. During his time in jail,[19] Hitler wrote his political and diplomatic plan in the book, *Mein Kampf* (*My Struggle*). The book eventually sold millions of copies and had a profound, malicious influence on Germany, Europe and the rest of the world. Hitler's outlined program blatantly included: the annihilation of the Jews; the destruction of Bolshevism; the uniting of all "Germanic peoples" under Nazi rule; *lebensraum* (room for German expansion and colonization) in the east, at the expense of Poland and Russia; and the glorification of the master Aryan race.[20] The book idealized war and violence as justified and desirable means of attaining political goals and mocked democratic systems of government and life. In retrospect, what is most disturbing is that Hitler did not hide his agenda, yet his monstrous plans were not taken seriously by most Jews. He meant every word written in *Mein Kampf* and never deviated from this program when he eventually came to power.

By the end of the decade, the Nazi party and Adolph Hitler had gained great popular support throughout Germany. Hitler organized a private army of Brown Shirts which regularly brawled on the streets of Germany's cities. Hitler was very impressed by Benito Mussolini and his Fascist party that took power in Italy in 1922.[21] He imitated Mussolini's methods — demagoguery, violent political methods, forming of a militia and encouraging criminal thugs to lead it — and he attempted to emulate Mussolini's march on Rome to power and glory, by doing so himself, to Berlin. In the 1920's, Hitler failed in his power grab but in the 1930's, he would succeed. Nevertheless,

---

19. Hitler's jail term resembled house arrest more than hard time in prison. He had regular access to his party colleagues, to books and help in the writing of *Mein Kampf*.

20. The theory of racial superiority and inferiority, and especially of the dominance of the Aryan race, was advanced and popularized by the eccentric English aristocrat Houston Chamberlain in the late nineteenth century. Like many other crackpot social theories, millions would eventually suffer because of its madness.

21. Hitler's admiration of Mussolini would begin to pale when he actually met the Italian leader face to face.

much of Germany and most of the world powers viewed Hitler, with his ridiculous moustache and tousled hair, as a clown and a nuisance, but not really as a serious threat to German and world order.

The Nazi party gained considerable ground in Germany in 1929. Pitched battles between the Nazis and the communists, with scores of dead littering the streets, became commonplace in German cities. Hitler made a number of unholy alliances with leading German industrialists and businessmen, all the while exhorting the mob to rise against the "capitalist Jews." He promised the wealthy that he would restore law and order to Germany and thereby protect their capital investments. He promised the laborer and the poor revenge against the "American Jewish bankers" who had supposedly exploited them and enslaved them financially. In Thuringia province, the Nazis elected the first provincial government under their control. Even though the Nazi Party only had 12 of the 491 seats in the German parliament, by allying itself with other right-wing factions, it became influential and powerful.

Throughout 1929 and 1930, Nazi thugs regularly attacked Jews, synagogues and Jewish institutions. In January of 1930, eight Jews were killed by Nazi Brown Shirts in Berlin. The terror against German Jewry thus began, years before Hitler finally came to power. In the parliamentary elections of 1930, the Nazi party received over six million votes and elected 107 deputies to parliament. It was now the second largest party in Germany. The wave of attacks on Jews intensified. The other political parties, except for the communists, sought to appease Hitler and the Nazis rather than oppose them. Hitler felt that his dream of controlling Germany, and eventually all of Europe, was nearing realization.

Anti-Semitism was by no means limited to Hitler and the German Nazis. A general spirit of anti-Semitism pervaded Europe, from Poland and Russia to France and England. There were sporadic acts of violence against Jews and Jewish institutions throughout Europe in the 1920's. As will be discussed below in this chapter, the issue of Zionism and Jewish nationalism, as well as the association of some Jews with the Bolshevik cause, caused much of the civil service and numerous decision-makers even in the democratic governments of Europe to view Jews with suspicion and distrust.

Becoming Americans: A Turbulent Transition

As indicated in an earlier chapter, bigotry was rampant in the United States of the 1920's, laden with hatred of foreigners, immigrants, Jews, Catholics, Blacks and Hispanics. The Ku Klux Klan attained membership in the millions, and lynchings and cross-burnings were common throughout the southern and midwestern states. Henry Ford, a leading American industrialist, revealed himself as an open bigot and anti-

Semite. He sponsored and distributed millions of copies of the bogus screed, *The Protocols of The Elders of Zion*, and he constantly railed about a Jewish conspiracy to destroy true "Americanism." Eventually, Ford was forced to publicly apologize to the American Jewish community for his words and behavior, but most American Jews felt that the apology was coerced and insincere.

This increasing xenophobia and bigotry in America gave rise in 1921 to congressional legislation, the Quota Act, which severely limited immigration to the United States, especially from Central and Eastern Europe, the heartland of Jewish population in Europe. This legislation was followed by the Johnson-Reed Act of 1924, which limited immigration to a quota of 2% of any nationality residing in the United States in 1890. For European Jewry, this legislation and its strict enforcement would prove murderous in the coming decades. The ill-fated social experiment of the prohibition of liquor production and sales in America allowed for underworld crime gangs to wax fat, profiting in the bootleg liquor trade. Italian, Irish and Jewish immigrants[22] were represented in the leadership of these gangs, thus contribuing to the myth that all foreigners were undesirable in American society. In actuality, the opposite was true. America prospered in the 1920's as never before, due to the contributions of millions of immigrants who had voted with their feet against Old Europe and its closed societies.

During this period, Jews were the pioneers of the motion picture industry[23] who furthered the new "Americanism" of the "melting-pot" assimilationist culture through the movies. Jewish characters in the movies of the decade were essentially caricatures. Indicative of the attitude of the Jewish moviemakers was the first sound movie, "The Jazz Singer," which starred Al Jolson as an assimilated cantor's son who marries a non-Jew, but who is eventually regarded as a hero by the Jewish community, and even by his own family. The drive to become American at all costs and to willfully discard Jewish heritage was given strong impetus by the growing popularity of movies.

The foremost yeshivah in America in the 1920's was Rabbi Isaac Elchanan Theological Seminary in New York. Under the dynamic leadership of Rabbi Dr. Bernard Revel and with the continuing support of the Union of Orthodox Rabbis of the United States and Canada (headed by Rabbi Eliezer Silver of Cincinnati), RIETS produced most of the English-speaking Orthodox rabbis for American Jewry in the 1920's and 1930's.

---

22. Rich Cohen wrote about Jewish gangs and gangsters in his book, *Tough Jews*, New York, 1998.

23. Neal Gabler's book, *An Empire of Their Own: How the Jews Invented Hollywood*, New York, 1988, develops the role of Jews in the early era of movies most convincingly.

The yeshivah was bolstered by the addition of Rabbi Moshe Soloveitchik, the son of the famed Rabbi Chaim Soloveitchik, in 1926 as the head of its faculty. During the decade of the 1920's, many great European rabbis visited the United States and lectured at RIETS. Rabbi Shimon Shkop, the eldest and most respected of the deans of the Lithuanian yeshivos, delivered Talmud lectures on a regular basis in RIETS at the end of the decade.

Conference of Orthodox Rabbis of America at Hebrew Theological College, Chicago, Illinois, November, 1922

Rabbi Shraga Feivel Mendlowitz

In Chicago, the Hebrew Theological College, founded by Rabbi Chaim Zvi Rubenstein and headed by Rabbi Saul Silber, was organized and began to function in 1921. It also produced English-speaking rabbis to serve the Orthodox and general communities of American Jewry. Rabbi Nissan Yablonsky of Slobodka was its first *rosh yeshivah*. After his untimely death in the middle of the decade, Rabbi Chaim Korb, a noted Talmudic scholar, headed the school. In New York, Yeshiva U'Mesivta Torah Vodaath began to grow into a major educational institution and under the leadership of Rabbi Shraga Feivel Mendlowitz, one of the seminal leaders of American Orthodoxy of the twentieth century, it would become a national bastion of Torah education. Yeshivah Rabbi Jacob Joseph and Yeshiva U'Mesivta Rabbeinu Chaim Berlin, both in New York, also served the Jewish community in the 1920's, though their glory days were yet ahead of them.

These important efforts and institutions notwithstanding, Jewish education in America was in sad shape. The basic system of congrega-

24. These schools were described by an observer of the scene as "unenthusiastic teachers holding boring classes for unwilling students."

tional or communal afternoon or Sunday schools[24] did not reach the vast majority of American Jewish youth who grew up without any formal Jewish education whatsoever. Very few boys received any Jewish education after their bar mitzvah lessons ended and Jewish education for girls on any meaningful level simply did not exist. The home, however, still played a powerful role in the lives of Jewish children in the 1920's, helping many of them to retain some vestige of Jewish culture, faith and tradition. But the flight from Yiddish language, *shtetl* culture and mores, the influence of the American public school system's "melting pot" mentality, the peer pressure of the street, the glamour of the movies and of baseball teams, the determination to "get ahead" financially, educationally and professionally, and the omnipresent atmosphere of institutionalized class anti-Semitism, all combined to drive a deep wedge between American Jewish youth and the value systems and traditions of Jewish life. American Jews desperately wanted to "belong" and there was nothing that they would not discard in attempting to achieve this goal.

The secular American Jewish community — the socialists, communists and Bundists — also were unable to hold their youth. A network of secular Yiddish schools was established to indoctrinate the beauties of Marxism to the young. However, these schools were unsuccessful in their mission. Socialism, communism and any other form of Marxism were foreign to the American environment. And even though the Socialist Party attracted 6% of the popular vote in 1912 for its presidential candidate, Eugene V. Debs, it declined rapidly thereafter. The anti-Zionist and anti-religious agenda of Jewish socialism in America also contributed to its declining popularity among Jews. The children of the Jewish socialists and communists wanted to be successful Americans above all else, and that meant discarding all of the theoretical nonsense concocted by Marx. Nevertheless, the largest Jewish newspaper in the United States remained *The Daily Forward* with its combination of socialist rhetoric, old-world nostalgia and Yiddish literature. There were other Yiddish newspapers as well — *Der Tag* and the *Morgen Journal* in New York and the *Courier* in Chicago, among others — but by the end of the 1920's, they were all losing readership, influence and revenue.

Explosive growth characterized the Conservative movement in the 1920's. United Synagogues of America, the movement's synagogue organization, numbered 50 congregations in 1916. By 1922, that number had risen to 156 and by 1927 the number of United Synagogues congregations was 230.[25] The Conservative movement seemed to young, Americanized Jews an answer to the needs of their emerging society. It

---

25. Pamella S. Nadell, *Conservative Judaism in America*, New York, 1988, pp.330-1.

was in this decade that the tendency of the Conservative movement to be guided by the wishes of its laity and congregants rather than by the principles of its leaders and scholars became increasingly evident. This created continuing tension between the Jewish Theological Seminary faculty/administration and the lay leadership of the United Synagogues. Nevertheless, the Conservative movement proved itself dynamic and popular. It was yet extremely traditional in its orientation to observance of ritual and Jewish custom. It promoted intensive observance of the dietary laws and strict observance of the Sabbath.[26] The first extensive guide to kosher eating places in America was published by the United Synagogues of America in the early 1920's. The organization raised a large sum of money for the construction of the Central Yeshurun synagogue in Jerusalem, an Orthodox congregation.

In 1915, Cyrus Adler had succeeded Dr. Solomon Schechter as the chancellor of the Jewish Theological Seminary. He would serve in that position until 1940. He was non-Zionist, disdainful of Eastern European Jews, but in a general way was quite traditional in Jewish outlook and observance of ritual and custom.[27] Defining the Conservative movement, he commented:

> *Conservative is a general term which nearly everybody uses but which is, I believe, technically applied to those congregations which have departed somewhat in practice from the Orthodox, but not in any great extent in theory. Speaking for myself, I may say without qualification that the old prayer book and the old service without any innovation whatsoever are entirely satisfactory to me and that I do not feel at home anywhere else.*[28]

The Conservative constituency, however, slowly, but inexorably, demanded less and less tradition, and the movement was never able to stem this tide of disaffection from Jewish ritual and observance in its ranks. Despite these inconsistencies, the Conservative movement would see steady growth in numbers and influence on American Jewry for the next 40 years.

Reform was still seen as too non-traditional for most second-generation American Jews. Its strong denial of any Jewish ritual, its strident anti-Zionism, and its tacit sanctioning of intermarriage were as yet still too deviant for the children of Eastern European Jews to easily accept and join. In the 1920's under the presidency of Julian Morgenstern, Hebrew Union College added to its faculty a number of impressive Eastern European Jewish scholars, almost all of them former students of the great

---

26. Herbert Parzen, *Architects of Conservative Judaism*, New York, 1964, p.110.
27. Ibid, p.94.
28. Ibid, p.99.

Lithuanian yeshivos. These scholars, though not personally Reform, found Hebrew Union College a haven for pursuing their scholarly careers. In addition, Reform in America was undergoing change, no longer aping nineteenth century German customs and mores. Hebrew Union College had a relatively small student body during this decade, never numbering more than 120 students. Many requests from Reform temples for rabbis went unanswered during this period. Morgenstern himself expressed his vision for American Jewry when he wrote in 1919: "The period of dominant foreign ideas and principles in the Judaism of America is passing ... The new day of one, united, common American Judaism is dawning for us and our children."[29] That vision never came to pass. The Reform movement itself suffered a division when Stephen S. Wise opened a competing Reform seminary in New York in the 1920's called the Jewish Institute of Religion. Wise was a dynamic person and an ardent Zionist. He was a thorn in the side of the official Reform establishment based in Cincinnati. After several rancorous decades of competition and criticism, Hebrew Union College and the Jewish Institute of Religion merged after World War II.

As noted earlier, Rabbi Meir Berlin had helped establish religious Zionism in the previous decade in Orthodox circles, and in fact, most of the leading rabbinic figures and heads of yeshivos in American Orthodoxy were affiliated with Mizrachi and religious Zionism. This would remain true until the 1950's, when the situation changed dramatically.

Although it was fiercely opposed by the Reform movement, the Zionist movement in America began to take root in American Jewish society. Zionism was considered acceptable to the masses of Jews undergoing rapid Americanization due to the open support of Supreme Court Justice Louis D. Brandeis.[30] When he was appointed to the Supreme Court, Brandeis resigned from his many organizational affiliations except for his leadership role in Zionism. More than that, he seriously considered resigning his seat on the Supreme Court in 1920 to accept the presidency of the World Zionist Organization, a position that had been offered to him. Though he had many fundamental disagreements with Chaim Weizmann, and certainly with David Ben-Gurion, regarding the tactics and social philosophy of Zionism, he never wavered in support of the Zionist ideal of achieving a Jewish homeland in Palestine. Brandeis did much to dispel the myth of dual loyalty, which always colored the rela-

---

29. Samuel E. Karff, *Hebrew Union College – Jewish Institute of Religion – At 100 Years*, Cincinnati, 1976, p.85.

30. Professor Robert A. Burt, Professor of Law at Yale University, wrote an excellent review of Brandeis' life, career and beliefs in his book, *Two Jewish Justices: Outcasts in the Promised Land*, University of California, 1988.

tionship of American Jewry to Zionism. American Jews reasoned that if a member of the United States Supreme Court could be an open and leading Zionist, then they could feel safe in so doing as well.[31] As far as most American Jews were concerned, however, it was clear to them that America was the "Promised Land," and not Palestine.

Jewish Heritage in Turkey Devastated

WHILE THE AMERICAN JEWS WERE SLOWLY LOSING THEIR GRIP ON traditional Judaism, the Sephardic Jews of Greece and Turkey had it wrested from their hands. They had suffered mightily during the Greek war with Turkey in the early 1920's. The Turkish authorities, led by Kemal Ataturk, the victor at Gallipoli and now the dictator over Turkey, behaved brutally towards non-Turkish minorities. As stated earlier, the Turks conducted a genocidal campaign against the Armenian Christians living in their midst in the previous decade. In 1922, Ataturk defeated the Greek army occupying parts of western Turkey and he now forced over a million people of Greek descent to vacate their homes in Turkish territory and relocate to Greece. With the absence of the Armenians and Greeks, the Jews, numbering some 120,000, constituted the largest remaining non-Turkish minority in Turkey.

Ataturk's drive was to create a secular, "democratic," Turkish republic, though in fact he was a dictator of the highest order and would run the country almost single-handedly. He would not tolerate officially recognized "minorities" operating in the new Turkey that he was fashioning. He forced the Jews to give up their protected minority rights and their previous right to guaranteed representation in the Turkish parliament. A fanatic secularist, Ataturk abolished the caliphate, removed Islam as the official religion of the country and abolished the country's religious school systems. This campaign against religion and ethnicity carried over to the Jewish community of Turkey as well, wounding the community deeply.

Turkish now became the sole language of instruction permissible in Jewish schools. The Alliance schools were banned from teaching in French and the religious schools were not allowed to teach Hebrew or any subject in the Hebrew language. Whereas in 1927, 80% of Jews in Turkey listed Ladino as their language of speech, by 1935, this percentage had declined to only 54.[32] The secularization of Turkish Jewry was now in full force and this ancient home of rabbinic scholarship and Sephardic Torah

---

31. Despite his success, Brandeis experienced the scourge of anti-Semitism before and during his tenure on the Supreme Court. Justice McReynolds, a bigot and anti-Semite, never spoke one word to Brandeis during the entire time that they both served as "brethren" on the Supreme Court.

32. Howard M. Sachar, *Farewell Espana*, New York, 1994, p.104.

life rapidly collapsed in the face of the coerced modernity foisted upon their community by the government. It was a replay of what was happening to traditional Judaism in the neighboring Soviet Union, though the Turkish government's methods of policy enforcement were more subtle and less brutal than in Stalin's paradise. Nonetheless, the effects on Jewish life were just as catastrophic. Turkish Jews were not allowed to be members of Zionist organizations and their participation in general world Jewish bodies was also forbidden.[33] The Sephardic community in Turkey began to erode through emigration, assimilation, apathy and ignorance.

THE COLLAPSE OF THE OTTOMAN EMPIRE IN THE FIRST WORLD WAR was followed by chaos, as England, France, Russia, Italy, Greece, Turkey, Persia, Afghanistan, the Armenians, Kurds, Maronite and Eastern Christians, the Jews (Zionist and non-Zionist) and the Arabs struggled against each other to carve out the new Middle East.[34] When all of the pieces finally fell into place in 1922, Turkey, Iran (Persia) and Afghanistan became the buffer states between Russia and the Middle East. Turkey

Jewish Settlement in Palestine Continues Despite Hostility

British High Commisioner Herbert Samuel (left) with Home Secretary Winston Churchill (right) in Jerusalem

---

33. Ibid.

34. David Fromkin's book, *A Peace to End All Peace*, New York, 1989, will be an invaluable aid in understanding the process that led to the creation of the modern Middle East and its seemingly intractable problems and tensions.

The Grand Mufti of Jerusalem (left) calling on Adolph Hitler

retained control over Istanbul (Constantinople) and the Dardanelles. France controlled Lebanon and Syria, two new artificial countries created out of former Ottoman territory. England held the mandate over Palestine, an area that originally included Transjordan. British influence, though not official control, was dominant in Saudi Arabia, the Gulf States, Iraq and Egypt. Winston Churchill, the British Colonial Secretary, separated Palestine into two parts at the Jordan River, and the British installed the Hashemite sheik Abdullah as the ruler over Transjordan. Churchill always claimed that it was his intent that the part of Palestine west of the Jordan River should be dedicated to fulfilling England's commitment to the Jews in the Balfour Declaration. Towards that end, Lord Herbert Samuel, a prominent Jewish leader and politician, was appointed as the High Commissioner for Palestine. The Jews hoped he would be a second Nechemiah, the Jewish leader of ancient times who led the nation back from Babylonia. It didn't quite turn out that way.

Opposition to Jewish settlement in Palestine was formidable. British military officers and civil servants posted in Palestine, middle-level officers of the Colonial Office in London, diplomats at the London Foreign Office, as well as the administration of British India, were all pro-Arab, anti-Zionist and, in most cases, anti-Semitic. They simply refused to enforce or advance the promises contained in the Balfour Declaration on behalf of the establishment of a Jewish national homeland in Palestine. Colonel Ernest Richmond, who made "all cooperation with the Jews impossible,"[35] championed the appointment of Amin el Husseini, a radical Arab xenophobe and Jew hater, as Grand Mufti of Jerusalem. Even though the results of Husseini's election victory were highly tainted, Lord Samuel confirmed him in the post. He became the leading Arab opponent of the Jews, constantly calling for violence. During World War II he found refuge in Berlin, where he encouraged Hitler to apply his "final solution" to the Jewish problem in Palestine. Husseini was the wrong man in the wrong place at the wrong time, not only for the Jews

35. Howard Sachar, *A History of Israel*, New York, 1998, p.168. Also see Fromkin, p.518.

but for the Arabs as well. His personal hatreds, violence towards other Arab leaders and unrealistic political positions doomed him to be an ineffective leader.

The Jewish population in Palestine at the end of World War I had fallen from 85,000 to 55,000. By 1923, it had almost doubled, however, due primarily to the influx of 37,000 Jews from Poland and Russia. These Jews were young, idealistic, leftist and Marxist in belief, opposed to the "old" Jew and his Judaism. The leftist character of their leadership set the tone throughout most of the balance of the century. During this time, the kibbutz movement and Jewish defense organizations emerged to help prevent Arab attacks on Jewish farming settlements.[36] As early as August, 1920, under Arab pressure, the British restricted Jewish immigration to Palestine to 16,500 people per year. Nevertheless, clandestine Jewish immigration swelled those numbers. Goaded on by the Grand Mufti, the Arabs responded with a wave of riots throughout Palestine in 1921. The British were hard-pressed to restore order and Lord Samuel responded to the violence by banning all Jewish immigration temporarily. The lesson of that appeasement response was not lost on the Arabs.

At the beginning of the decade, Tel Aviv had a population of 3,600 and close to 50,000 by 1930. Jewish urban centers in Jerusalem and Haifa developed in the 1920's as well. The Histadrut labor union was formed in 1920 and for many decades influenced, if not controlled, the economic and political development of the *yishuv*. It created a health plan for Jewish workers — *kupat cholim* — which became the model for all subsequent general population health care programs in Israel. Based on the nineteenth-century attitude of Jewish freethinkers about the holiness of manual labor and its "socialist aim of establishing a Jewish workers' society in Palestine,"[37] it followed a policy of "Jewish labor only" to work in agriculture, industry and construction. This exclusionary policy increased the tensions between the Arab and Jewish communities. Tens of thousands of Arabs had streamed into Palestine in the 1920's, seeking to benefit from the economic opportunities created by the Jews. When they could not find work, most of them nevertheless remained in the country, disgruntled, disappointed and hostile.

The Zionist movement suffered a split in its ranks in 1925, when Vladimir Zev Jabotinsky, the organizer of the Jewish legion in World War I, established the Revisionist Zionist movement. He claimed both parts of Palestine, east as well as west of the Jordan River, for the forthcoming

---

36. Joseph Trumpeldor, one of the founders of the *Hechalutz* movement was killed at Tel Chai in one of those attacks.

37. Sachar, p.157.

Jewish state. He presumed that Arab hostility would continue, and was scornful of Labor Zionist attempts to accommodate them. Jabotinsky was a powerful orator and an impassioned campaigner for his policies; and his movement grew in size and influence. Its youth organization, Betar, grew quickly. Openly militant in speech and action, Betar tended to be more radical than Jabotinsky. Together with his movement, Jabotinsky was criticized, reviled[38] and eventually ostracized by the Labor Zionists who controlled the governing institutions of the *yishuv*. It was not just his program that the Labor Zionists opposed. They hated him for telling them things about themselves, the Arabs and the British that made them uncomfortable: The Jewish state, he maintained, could only come about by force and the Arabs would not easily come to terms with its existence. Furthermore, he surmised that the British would renege on the Balfour Declaration. It is always easier to kill the messenger than to do something about the message. The bitterness of the feud between the Revisionists and the Labor Zionists left scars on the Jewish body politic that persisted until the end of the century.

At the end of the decade, there were 162,000 Jews in Palestine, constituting 17% of the total population. The enlarged Jewish Agency for Palestine, comprised of both Zionist and non-Zionist representation, was founded in 1929. Jewish school systems were established, hospitals and welfare agencies created and an internal Jewish government of sorts formed, which operated autonomously from the British mandatory power. The power structure of the Jewish community lay in the hands of the Labor Zionist/Histadrut faction. The leadership of this faction was concentrated in the political party Mapai, led by David Ben-Gurion, Yitzchak Ben-Zvi, Berel Katzenelson and Moshe Sprinzak (later Sharett). Other than Ben-Zvi, these leaders were in the main secular and leftist-oriented. Yet they were pragmatic people who concentrated on building the Jewish infrastructure in the Land of Israel, and did not press for the extreme Marxist doctrines of the far left faction in the Labor Zionist movement.

Orthodox Leadership in the New Yishuv

IN ADDITION TO THIS IMMIGRATION OF SECULAR JEWS, THERE WAS ALSO a group of young, equally idealistic religious Jews who came to the country. There were enough of them to make a difference in the makeup of the *yishuv*, but there were too few of them to make *the* difference in the newly building society. Great sages from Eastern Europe, such as

---

38. "Fascists" was the usual term used by the Labor Zionists to refer to the Revisionists. Ben-Gurion called Jabotinsky "Vladimir Hitler!"

Rabbi Isser Zalman   *Rabbi Nosson Zvi*   *Rabbi Moshe Mordechai*
Meltzer   *Finkel*   *Epstein*

Rabbi Isser Zalman Meltzer, immigrated to Palestine in this decade. Foremost among the religious newcomers to the country was the Slobodka Yeshivah. In 1923, Rabbi Nosson Zvi Finkel, the head of the school and the leading sage of the *Mussar* movement, and Rabbi Moshe Mordechai Epstein, the *rosh yeshivah*, along with more than 100 students, left Lithuania and settled in Jerusalem. The yeshivah moved soon thereafter to Hebron[39] and became internationally famous. It was the beginning of the Lithuanian yeshivah movement in the Land of Israel. In the Arab riots of 1929, the yeshivah in Hebron was destroyed and many of its students were murdered or maimed. The remnants of the yeshivah limped back to Jerusalem, reorganized themselves and developed into the famous Yeshivas Chevron, albeit in a different location.

Young people from Hapoel HaMizrachi and from Poalei Agudath Israel left Eastern and Central Europe and established religious settlements and kibbutzim in the land. Even though the gap in ideology between the religious and secular communities in the *yishuv* was already quite large, the social gap was still manageable. The Eastern European Jews, religious and secular, who comprised the largest component of the *yishuv*, were still all basically *shtetl*-oriented family, with common memories, traditions and friendships. It would be their grandchildren and great-grandchildren who would no longer have affinity one for the other.

Rabbi Avraham Yitzchak HaKohen Kook, the Rabbi of Jaffa, had not been allowed by the Turks to return to Palestine after his journey to Poland to attend the Agudath Israel conference which was to be held there (and was later aborted). He spent part of the war years in St. Galen,

---

39. One of the reasons that Rabbi Finkel moved the yeshivah to Hebron was that the dress, manners and outlook of the Lithuanian students was too "modern" for the tastes of the old *yishuv* in Jerusalem.

Switzerland, and later became Chief Rabbi for the Federation of Jewish Synagogues in London. At the beginning of the decade, he returned from his Swiss and British exile. In an election that was controversial, but with nearly unanimous results, he was appointed Rabbi of Jerusalem. A charismatic, spiritual scholar of extraordinary talents, he believed that the Zionist movement, and the subsequent flow of Jews to the Land of Israel, represented the beginning of the Jewish redemption from exile foretold by the prophets of old. He injected a note of messianism into the Zionist enterprise, something which the previous religious leaders of the Zionist movement (and certainly the non-Zionist religious leaders) were clearly loath to do. He saw the physical redemption of the Jewish people in the Land of Israel — the wresting of fertile land from desert, the creation of a physically strong youth, Jewish self-defense organizations, and the emergence of an autonomous Jewish self-government — as positive and necessary steps in the process of the redemption of Israel. He believed that the spiritual redemption of Israel — the return of all Jews to Judaism and its values and observances — would eventually follow the accomplishment of the physical redemption. Thus, he was able to ignore the atheism, socialism, secularism and bitter anti-religious fervor of the Labor Zionist camp and see the distant Promised Land rather than the immediate desert of thorns and spite. Rabbi Kook's declarations of seeming support for organized Jewish sport activities and for the establishment of the Hebrew University in Jerusalem were misinterpreted and distorted by his opponents, and made him even more controversial. He was accused of ignoring the negative effect of organized sports on youth and the desecration of the Sabbath that the leagues engendered. He was also wrongly accused of accommodating Biblical Criticism studies at Hebrew University. It is therefore not surprising that he was almost alone in the rabbinic world of Jerusalem in his visionary approach to the realities of secular Zionism.

In 1923, in cooperation with the British mandatory authorities, Rabbi Kook created the institution of the Chief Rabbinate to govern the religious affairs of the *yishuv*. The structure of the Chief Rabbinate in Palestine was patterned after that institution in the British Empire, specifically in England. The Zionist leadership pressured many rabbis to support the institution of the Chief Rabbinate, hoping that this new rabbinic structure would help "modernize" Judaism. Rabbi Kook's influence was quite strong in this regard as well, and almost all of the rabbis and scholars in Palestine at the time joined this official rabbinate.

Rabbi Kook had high hopes for this institution, not only as an administrative and legal structure to facilitate and standardize rabbinic and religious court procedures, but just as importantly, as a means to influence all of Jewish society in a moral, spiritual and traditional manner.

He wanted the Chief Rabbinate to serve as the conscience, the apolitical voice of morality for the *yishuv* and for Jews the world over. During his lifetime, the institution did achieve these lofty goals, at least partially. In the coming decades, however, it would be devoured by the monsters of politics and bureaucracy, becoming more administration than inspiration.

A minority group dissented from Rabbi Kook's election as Rabbi of Jerusalem and from the establishment of the Chief Rabbinate. Though most of the members of the *yishuv hayashan* supported Rabbi Kook's candidacy, a significant group broke away from the established Jerusalem community after his election and formed their own community called Eidah HaChareidis. This group elected Rabbi Yosef Chaim Sonnenfeld as its Chief Rabbi and it boycotted the Chief Rabbinate, its activities and *kashrus* supervision. The Eidah was fiercely, but not violently, anti-Zionist and shared none of Rabbi Kook's views. It refused to become part of the Zionist governing structure of the *yishuv* and mounted an unrelenting stream of criticism on Mizrachi for its participation in the Zionist governing bodies of the *yishuv*. Most of the adherents of Agudath Israel in Jerusalem joined the Eidah HaChareidis. However, the Zeirei Agudath Israel and Poalei Agudath Israel remained independent of both the Chief Rabbinate and the Eidah HaChareidis. In 1923, an extreme faction broke away from the Eidah HaChareidis itself, charging that it was too moderate in its anti-Zionist stance and behavior. This group, Neturei Karta (Guardians of the City), never numbering more than a few hundred adherents in Jerusalem, became notorious for its anti-Zionist fervor and behavior.[40]

Though Rabbi Kook was personally honored and respected by the rabbis of the Jewish world, many of his actions and his vision of redemption were widely contested. The Rabbi of Gur visited Rabbi Kook in Jerusalem in 1925 and held long discussions with him. Though praising Rabbi Kook as a scholar and noble leader, he disassociated himself from his views, especially his assessment of Zionism, the Labor Zionists and kibbutzim.

Rabbi Kook was determined to create a new generation of rabbinic leadership that would share his vision of the rebuilding of the Jewish people in the Land of Israel. To that end, he founded the yeshivah Mercaz HaRav Kook in Jerusalem. The yeshivah attracted stellar students from yeshivos in Lithuania, Jerusalem and Hebron and became a major Torah force in the country. Rabbi Kook hoped that the yeshivah, together with the Chief Rabbinate, would provide the resources for a broad-based revival of Judaic practice in the *yishuv*.

---

40. One of the leaders of Neturei Karta was a member of the Palestinian Authority's Legislative Council in the late 1990's.

The "Even-handed" British

HERBERT SAMUEL WAS SUCCEEDED AS HIGH COMMISSIONER FOR Palestine by Viscount Plumer, a tough, no-nonsense administrator. As he was not Jewish, he was not handicapped by the need to be "even-handed" in his dealings with the Arabs and Jews. The Arab riots of 1925 were put down quickly and firmly by the British forces and relative calm ensued for the next four years. However in September of 1928, the Mufti of Jerusalem objected to the *mechitzah* (curtain or screen used to separate the men's and women's sections for prayer) erected at the Western Wall by the Jews preparatory to the High Holiday services. He charged that the Jews were thereby somehow endangering the mosques at the top of the Temple Mount; and the Arabs imediately mounted a campaign of intimidation and interference with Jewish prayer services at the Western Wall. Jewish demonstrations and Arab counter-demonstrations developed.

On August 24, 1929, after a particularly provocative and inflammatory speech by the Mufti against the Jews, Arab mobs attacked Jewish quarters[41] in Jerusalem, Hebron and throughout the country. As noted earlier, 60 Jews, including yeshivah students, were murdered in Hebron and scores were injured. The Jewish community there was forced to abandon its homes and institutions. The British were unable to restore order until four days later, when 87 Arabs were killed by the British forces and 91 others were wounded. In all, 133 Jews were killed in the riots and 399 were wounded. Sir John Chancellor, then High Commissioner, issued a statement condemning the Arab atrocities. The Mufti protested this declaration and threatened more violence. Chancellor hastily withdrew his words and promised an inquiry into the behavior of both sides. The Jews protested now, but to no avail. Britain was inexorably moving towards formal repudiation of its obligations to the Jews under the Balfour Declaration.

In England, the Labor Party took over control of the British government in 1929. It was decidedly anti-Zionist in sentiment and practice. As it had not been party to the Balfour Declaration twelve years earlier, it did not feel itself bound to enforce its promises. The wife of the new Colonial Secretary, Lord Passfield (Sidney Webb), told Chaim Weizmann: "I can't understand why the Jews make such a fuss over a few dozen of their people killed in Palestine. As many [people] are killed every week in London in traffic accidents, and no one pays any attention."[42]

In 1930 a new commission, headed by Sir Walter Shaw, reported that the Arabs were responsible for the 1929 riots, but that the only way to prevent further trouble was by preventing any more large-scale Jewish

---

41. Most of the attacks of the Arabs centered on quarters populated by Orthodox Jews of the *yishuv hayashan*.
42. Sachar, p.174.

immigration. The British authorities promptly revoked immigration permits for 3,300 Jews who were due to arrive in Palestine shortly. Another British commission, headed by Sir John Hope Simpson, stated that there was room in Palestine for only another 100,000 people and that not more than half of them should be Jews.[43] The population then in Palestine was less than a million people. In October of 1930, Lord Passfield issued a White Paper (an official pronouncement of British policy issued, as the name implies, on white paper) that negated the Balfour Declaration and declared that Palestine did not contain sufficient land or resources to successfully absorb new immigration. The decade, which had begun with so much promise for the cause of the Jews' settlement in their ancient homeland, ended in seeming defeat and disappointment.

The Great Depression Fuels Worldwide Anti-Semitism

COMMODITY PRICES THROUGHOUT THE WORLD HAD BEEN FALLING since 1927. In October 1929, the New York stock market, which was the victim of rampant speculation and the purchasing of stocks with borrowed funds, collapsed under the weight of overvaluation and margin calls. Supply of commodities far exceeded demand and consumption. The index of the 30 leading industrial companies in America stood at 380 on September 3. By November 19, it had fallen to 198. Savings were lost, banks failed, homes and farms were foreclosed and foreign trade could not be sustained. In many industries the domestic consumer market disappeared, and soon the manufacturers and importers had goods stocked in their warehouses that could not be sold. Plants closed and unemployment skyrocketed. In the United States, more than 22,000 businesses failed in 1929 and an additional 26,000 in 1930. 1929 saw 434 bank failures. In 1930, another 1,326 banks failed. Over five million American workers were unemployed in 1930, out of a total population of 122 million.[44]

The virus of this "Great Depression" then swept the world. Europe was particularly hard hit. German unemployment and economic stagnation undoubtedly played a major role in the Nazi success at the polls in 1930, as Hitler was able to convince millions of people, inside and outside of Germany, that the Depression was caused and sponsored by Jewish money interests. In the United States, Jews were blamed by many for the stock market crash, and overt anti-Semitism increased. The decade of the greatest American prosperity — the Roaring Twenties — ended with the greatest financial catastrophe in economic

---

43. Ibid, p.176.
44. Martin Gilbert, *A History of the Twentieth Century*, New York, 1997, Vol. 1, p.788.

history. 1920 had been year of hope and optimism. 1930 was a year of depression and foreboding.

A Survey of European Yeshivos in the 1920's

Mir   RABBI ELIEZER YEHUDA FINKEL WAS THE HEAD OF THE YESHIVAH AND Rabbi Yechezkel Levenshtein was the *mashgiach ruchani* (the official title for the person charged with the teachings and behavior of *mussar*, i.e. ethical thought, punctilious observance of ritual, and sensitive and compassionate human behavior).[45] Rabbi Avraham Zvi Kamai, the Rabbi of Mir, also delivered weekly lectures in the yeshivah. Rabbi Kamai was a pharmacist before assuming his position as rabbi in Mir, and in his pre-World War I days as a druggist he prepared remedies for the chief Russian minister, Petr Stolypin. When Rabbi Levenshtein left Mir in 1924, Rabbi Yerucham Levovitz arrived as the new *mashgiach ruchani*. A man of unusual talents, deep piety, great personal charisma and iron will, he stamped his imprint on Mir and on the other Lithuanian yeshivos as well. His influence and reputation were enormous, and largely due to him Mir was a magnet for students from other yeshivos in Lithuania and Poland as well as a small number from Germany, Belgium, England, Switzerland, Sweden, Latvia, Finland, Rumania, Hungary and the United States. Due to the almost constant influx of former students of Rabbi Yitzchak Zev Soloveitchik, the son and successor of Rabbi Chaim Soloveitchik as the Rabbi of Brisk, and of Rabbi Baruch Ber Leibowitz, Rabbi Chaim's main disciple, Mir was a bastion of Talmudic study in "Rabbi Chaim's way." The number of students in the yeshivah during the decade of the 1920's fluctuated between 250 and 400. Almost all of the great Torah scholars and leaders of the post-World War II yeshivah world studied at Mir for some period of time.

Slobodka   IN 1914, THE YESHIVAH KNESSES YISRAEL WAS EXILED TO KREMENCHUG in Russia. In 1916, the yeshivah was reopened in Slobodka, then under German occupation, by Rabbis Nissan Yablonsky and Baruch

---

45. The students and faculty returned to Mir in the summer of 1921.

Horowitz. Rabbi Yerucham Levovitz (see above) served as *mashgiach ruchani*. After the war, Rabbi Yablonsky left Slobodka to serve as the head of the Beis Medrash LeTorah in Chicago and Rabbi Levovitz moved to the yeshivah in Ponovezh. In the fall of 1921, Rabbi Nosson Zvi Finkel and Rabbi Moshe Mordechai Epstein, together with the remaining original faculty and many of the students, returned to Slobodka. The yeshivah soon regained its preeminent position as the leading yeshivah in Lithuania. Rabbi Finkel also reestablished the famous *kollel* of Kovno/Slobodka. This institution for select married students trained many of the leading heads of the yeshivos of the next generation worldwide. It was headed by the Rabbi of Kovno, Rabbi Avraham Dovber Kahana-Shapiro and Rabbi Yitzchak Sher, Rabbi Finkel's son-in-law. Rabbi Avrohom Grodzinski was the *mashgiach ruchani* in Slobodka in the 1920's, with a student body numbering approximately 350. The continuing policy of Rabbi Nosson Zvi Finkel was that select students from Slobodka were "loaned" to other yeshivos in Lithuania to help the yeshivos rebuild themselves.

Telshe

UNLIKE MOST OF THE OTHER LITHUANIAN YESHIVOS, THE YESHIVAH in Telshe, under the leadership of Rabbi Yosef Leib Bloch, did not taste exile during the Great War. However, most of its students were dispersed and it maintained itself with very few students during the war years. By 1920, many students, new and old, found their way to Telshe. The growth of the yeshivah was accompanied by the establishment of a number of institutions affiliated with the main school in the decade following the Great War. These included a preparatory school — *mechinah* — for preparation of younger students before entry into the main yeshivah; a *kollel* for graduate married students; a teachers' seminary to train male teachers for the religious schools of Lithuanian Jewry (this was a daring innovation at the time); a religious "gymnasium" school for women (an even more daring and controversial innovation for the time); a teachers' seminary to train female teachers; and an educational network of religious elementary schools in the area of Telshe. The Telshe yeshivah was also prominent in the social and political life of Lithuanian Jewry, and it was active in sponsoring religious newspapers and magazines in Yiddish and Hebrew. Assisting Rabbi Yosef Leib Bloch in leading the yeshivah and all of its institutions were his son and successor Rabbi Avrohom Yitzchok Bloch, Rabbi Azriel Rabinowitz, Rabbi Eliyahu Meir Bloch and Rabbi Zalman Bloch. The yeshivah numbered approximately 300 students with an additional 300 students enrolled in its affiliated institutions.

Grodno

IN THE MIDST OF THE GERMAN OCCUPATION OF GRODNO IN 1915, A number of students of various Lithuanian yeshivos were trapped in Grodno, unable to leave. With the encouragement of the Jewish community of Grodno and with the help of a German army chaplain, Rabbi Dr. Winter, these refugee students remained in Grodno and formed an ad hoc yeshivah. When the new Poland established final control over the fortress city in 1920, the famed Rabbi Shimon Shkop arrived in Grodno and headed the fledgling institution. His prowess as a teacher of Torah and his saintly personality soon attracted many young men to his yeshivah. Rabbi Shkop's analytical method of Talmudic study and his guidance in the deep understanding of the nuances of Talmudic thought created an alternative, if somewhat parallel, method of study to "Rabbi Chaim's way" in the Lithuanian yeshivos. Rabbi B.Z. Olshvang and Rabbi Moshe Shkop were leading members of the early faculty. When Rabbi Olshvang left for Chicago in 1922, Rabbi Shlomo Harkavy came to the yeshivah as *mashgiach ruchani*. A native of Grodno, Rabbi Harkavy was a person of great, though gently unobtrusive, influence on the students of the yeshivah. The combination of Rabbi Shimon Shkop and Rabbi Shlomo Harkavy helped create an aristocratic, analytical, loyal student body that made Grodno one of the outstanding houses of learning in Lithuania. In 1924, Rabbi Shraga Feivel Hindes became the executive head of the yeshivah, but the yeshivah always struggled mightily for its physical survival. The number of students in Grodno varied between 200 and 300 during the 1920's.[46]

Radin

THE ORIGINAL FAME OF THE YESHIVAH IN RADIN WAS BASED ON THE presence of the sainted Chafetz Chaim, Rabbi Yisrael Meir Kagan, in the hamlet. He had no official position in the community or in the yeshivah, but he was nevertheless the inspirational force there, if not in all Lithuanian Jewry. In 1915, the yeshivah and Rabbi Kagan were exiled by the Russians from Radin. In one of his letters, written in 1921, Rabbi Kagan wrote of the experience: "Behold, I have suffered wanderings and exile in Russia for the last six years. With the yeshivah, I wandered to three separate locations in Russia — Shmelovitz, Sumitatz and Snovsk. [In Snovsk] the Bolsheviks forced all of the people of the town to work for them seven days a week. Even the students in the yeshivah were forced to labor on the Sabbath and I was not able to save them from this. Therefore, I decided to escape with the yeshivah from that place where the Name of God was being publicly desecrated and come to a location [Poland] where the Torah could yet be observed." The students and fac-

---

46. One of those students in Grodno was my father, Rabbi Zev W. Wein.

ulty were successfully "smuggled" across the border and reestablished the yeshivah in Radin in 1921. However, the leader of the yeshivah and the son-in-law of Rabbi Kagan, Rabbi Hirsch Levinson, passed away in 1921 and this blow endangered the continued existence of the school. Because the yeshivah building had been used by the German occupiers as a horse stable, arms depot and grain storage area during World War I, the entire interior had been destroyed. The yeshivah began its studies in the local synagogue. The leading heads of the yeshivah in the 1920's were Rabbi Naftali Trop, Rabbi Moshe Landinsky and Rabbi Eliezer Zev Kaplan. The yeshivah reflected the personality traits of the Chafetz Chaim: simplicity, innocence, deep faith and an unflinching commitment to Torah study and life. The student body grew to a number close to 300.[47]

Baranovitch

THE YESHIVAH IN BARANOVITCH WAS FOUNDED IN 1907 BY Rabbi Yosef Yoizel Horowitz, the founder of the *mussar* educational network of Navaradok. Until the end of World War I, the yeshivah was small and served primarily a local population. However, in 1921, Rabbi Elchanan Wasserman, the great student of Rabbi Eliezer Gordon, Rabbi Chaim Soloveitchik, and of the Chafetz Chaim, came to head the yeshivah in Baranovitch. Under his direction, it became an international yeshivah. His method of teaching combined clarity of thought and expression, brevity (never more than a 45 minute lecture) and exactitude of interpretation of the text. Rabbi Wasserman's influence was not limited by the walls of his yeshivah: He became one of the key leaders of Orthodox Jewry in Eastern Europe and throughout the Jewish world. Other leading members of the faculty were Rabbi Shlomo Heyman, Rabbi Dovid Rapaport and Rabbi Yisrael Yakov Lubtchansky, the *mashgiach ruchani*. The executive head of the yeshivah was Rabbi Zvi Hirsch Goodman. The student body in the 1920's numbered between 200 to 250.

Ponovezh

THE YESHIVAH IN PONOVEZH WAS FOUNDED IN 1917 BY THE DYNAMIC visionary, Rabbi Yosef Shlomo Kahaneman, known in the Jewish world as the *Ponovezher Rav*. As Vilna had been annexed by the Poles, Ponovezh was the second largest city in Lithuania after Kaunas. It had a substantial Jewish population and was blessed with great rabbinic personalities as its leaders. Due to the ongoing battles near the city in 1917, the yeshivah closed. However, when the position of rabbi of the community became available in 1919, Rabbi Kahaneman became the

---

47. One of the students of Radin was my father-in-law, Rabbi Eliezer Levin.

rabbi as well as the head of the newly reopened yeshivah. His enormous personal charisma and prodigious scholarship attracted many students from all over Lithuania. His worldwide trips on behalf of the yeshivah also spread the fame of the institution. In the 1920's, the number of students in Ponovezh averaged 250. Its greatest success and fame would come after World War II, when the yeshivah was rebuilt in Bnei Brak, Israel.

Lomzeh

RABBI ELIEZER SHULEVITZ, A DISCIPLE OF RABBI YISRAEL LIPKIN OF Salant, founded the yeshivah in the 1880's. During the First World War, this yeshivah also wandered into Russian exile. In 1922, after returning to Lomzeh, Rabbi Shulevitz left Europe to settle in the Land of Israel. He brought with him 40 students and founded a second "Lomzeh Yeshivah" in Petach Tikva. The yeshivah in Lomzeh itself was now headed by Rabbi Shulevitz' eldest son-in-law, Rabbi Yechiel Mordechai Gordon. Known in the Jewish world as the *Lomzehr Rav*, Rabbi Gordon was an outstanding Talmudic scholar and a warm and caring person. His personal involvement and concern regarding each of his students was legendary, as were his patience and gentle manner. The yeshivah also benefited greatly from the presence of Rabbi Yehoshua Zelig Roch, a great scholar who taught Talmud there on a regular basis. Rabbi Moshe Rosenstein was the *mashgiach ruchani* of the yeshivah. He was a saintly and mystical person who devoted himself completely to the students of Lomzeh. The yeshivah numbered 150-200 students in the 1920's.

Bialystok

THE EDUCATIONAL SYSTEM OF NAVARADOK, FOUNDED BY RABBI YOSEF Yoizel Horowitz in the late nineteenth century, had almost one 100 branches by the end of World War I. Most of these were in Russia and were unfortunately destroyed by the Bolsheviks after the 1917 revolution. Rabbi Horowitz died in Kiev in the winter of 1920. After his death, the surviving students and faculty of the system smuggled themselves across the Polish border. The main successor yeshivah to Navoradok was established in 1922 in Bialystok, under the leadership of Rabbi Avrohom Yoffen. A branch of Bialystok was also established then in Mezritch, with other branches in Warsaw and Pinsk. These were large yeshivos that served young men in their late teens and twenties. In addition, Bialystok established a network of 80 schools throughout Poland for younger students. Thirty of these schools were under the direct control of Bialystok, while the other 50 schools were operated by the three other main branches of Bialystok. Rabbis Nisson Ruzanker and Nisson Putashinsky were on the faculty of Bialystok. The yeshivah in Bialystok numbered 150-200 students in the 1920's, while the entire educational network of Bialystok had thousands of students.

Kaminetz

THE YESHIVAH IN POST-WAR KAMINETZ HAD ITS ORIGINS IN 1904 Slobodka. The great Rabbi Baruch Ber Levovitz, the chief disciple of Rabbi Chaim Soloveitchik, was its head. His method of study was a further refinement of "Rabbi Chaim's way" and his deep analysis of the Talmudic subject matter was unique. In 1914, the yeshivah was exiled from Slobodka and it settled, together with Rabbi Levovitz, in Kremenchug in 1917 in the Ukraine. Following the Bolshevik Revolution, the war between the Ukrainian nationalists and the Russians, and then the civil war between the Reds and the Whites, the city and its Jews were overcome by a wave of bloodshed. Persecuted and hounded by the communists, the yeshivah attempted to escape Russia. From 1921 until 1926, the yeshivah and Rabbi Levovitz were in Vilna. But the transfer of the city from Lithuania to Poland brought hard times, and the constant bustle of city life was not to Rabbi Levovitz' liking. In the autumn of 1926, the yeshivah reestablished itself, this time in Kaminetz, a much smaller and quieter town than Vilna. There Rabbi Levovitz was aided in the operation of the yeshivah by his two sons-in-law, Rabbi Reuven Grozovsky and Rabbi Moshe Bernstein. The yeshivah numbered 350-400 students by 1930. This number included 50 students in the preparatory school (*mechinah*) and seven members of the *kollel*.

Kletzk

THE YESHIVAH HAD ITS ORIGINS IN SLUTZK, WHERE ITS HEAD, RABBI Isser Zalman Meltzer, was rabbi from 1903 to 1923. He was forced to flee from Slutzk by the communists and smuggled himself across the border to the Polish town of Kletzk. His son-in-law, Rabbi Aharon Kotler, had escaped there in 1921 and reopened the yeshivah in Kletzk. Until 1925, Rabbi Issar Zalman Meltzer once again headed the school. When he then left for the Land of Israel, Rabbi Kotler became the head of the yeshivah. Under his inspired leadership, the yeshivah grew and prospered. It was the second largest yeshivah in Poland and was considered one of the most important schools there, second only to Mir. Rabbi Kotler was one of the leaders of Polish Jewry and was involved in many projects outside of the yeshivah on behalf of strengthening Torah life in Polish and world Jewry. The *mashgiach ruchani* in Kletzk was Rabbi Pesach Pruskin. Rabbis Nosson Wachtfogel and Yosef Leib Nendik served on the faculty. In the 1920's, the enrollment in the yeshivah was approximately 200 students.

Slonim

THE HOME OF A FAMOUS CHASIDIC DYNASTY, SLONIM WAS A TOWN ON the border of Lithuania, White Russia and Poland. After the Great War, it was part of Poland. Rabbi Shabsai Yagel headed the yeshivah, aided by his son, Rabbi Peretz Yagel (later in America) and the *mashgiach ruchani* was Rabbi Avraham Zvi Litovsky. The yeshivah was a typical non-Chasidic "Lithuanian type" institution, but it nevertheless had the constant support of the Chasidic masters of Slonim, the Weinberg family. The yeshivah was very influential in its area of Poland and maintained an excellent reputation for scholarship and character building. In the 1920's, its student enrollment varied between 125 and 175 students.

Kelm

A BASTION OF THE *MUSSAR* MOVEMENT, THE KELM YESHIVAH WAS founded by Rabbi Simcha Zissel Ziv, a disciple of Rabbi Yisrael Salanter. The yeshivah was in exile during World War I. When it returned to Kelm, Lithuania, after the war it reestablished itself under the leadership of Rabbis Eliyahu and Reuven Dessler and Daniel Moshovitz. The yeshivah was famous for the order, discipline, aristocracy of character and nobility of soul of its faculty and students. Its reputation for *mussar* overshadowed (unfairly and inaccurately) its accomplishments in Torah scholarship. Kelm was pristine, pure and the quintessential Lithuanian *mussar* institution. In the 1920's, the number of students in Kelm ranged from 250 to 300.

Kobrin

THE TOWN OF KOBRIN WAS A NEIGHBOR OF THE FAMOUS CITY OF BRISK. In 1923, the Rabbi of Kobrin, Rabbi Pesach Pruskin, founded the yeshivah there. The yeshivah served primarily as a preparatory school for younger students (thirteen to seventeen years old) before their entering one of the major Lithuanian yeshivos, though certain select students did remain in Kobrin until their mid-twenties. The number of students in the yeshivah never exceeded much more than 100 in the decade of the 1920's. For most of its existence this atmosphere of smallness and intimacy was the hallmark of the institution, allowing the students to develop strong bonds with their teachers, especially with Rabbi Pruskin. For many years, the *mashgiach ruchani* was Rabbi Yosef Leib Nendik. Rabbi Shlomo Mattes was also a member of the faculty. The students of Kobrin, even after leaving for study in other yeshivos, were famous for their fierce loyalty to the yeshivah of Kobrin.

Lubavitch

THE NETWORK OF YESHIVOS OF CHABAD/LUBAVITCH WAS CALLED Tomchei Temimim. Before the Great War, this network was concentrated in Mohilev, Vohlin, Kremenchug, Zhelubin and Shedretzin,

Russia. There were also Lubavitch schools in Ukraine, Crimea, Uzbekistan and Georgia. Its home base was naturally the town of Lubavitch in Russia, where the Rebbe resided. These yeshivos combined the analytical method of Talmud study of the Lithuanian yeshivos, which by then had become traditional, with the study of *Tanya* and Chasidic thought. In 1916, when the town of Lubavitch was overrun by the Germans, the Rebbe and the yeshivah escaped to Kremenchug. There, the Russian revolution overtook them and they were subjected to the unrelenting persecutions of the Bolsheviks, especially of the *Yevsektzia* — the Jewish communists. In 1920, the Rebbe Shalom Ber died and was succeeded by his son, the Rebbe Yosef Yitzchak (the *"frierdige Rebbe"*). The three main Lubavitch yeshivos remaining in Russia at the time were in Rostov on the Don, Poltava and Kharkov. These institutions were unable to operate publicly and by 1922, the entire Lubavitch movement and educational system went underground. (Somehow Lubavitch, alone among all Jewish religious organizations, was able to maintain an underground Jewish religious life in the Soviet Union for the entire 75 year period until the collapse of the communist system.) The Lubavitch educational system was very active in Lithuania, Latvia and Poland in the 1920's. Many of its students and activists escaped from the Soviet Union and reestablished Tomchei Temimim schools in all of these countries. A Lubavitch yeshivah was established in Warsaw in 1921 with twelve students. It rapidly grew into a school of hundreds of students. Lubavitch schools were also prominent in Lodz, Vilna, Kovno, Rakshik, Chamelnik, Riga and Chelm. The head of the school system was Rabbi Shmaryahu Gur Aryeh, the elder son-in-law of the Rebbe.

Radomsk

BEFORE WORLD WAR I, LITHUANIAN-STYLE YESHIVOS DID NOT EXIST IN Poland or Galicia. After the war ended, it became apparent that the old style of private learning had broken down and that the Chasidic world would be severely damaged if new educational approaches to teaching Torah were not formulated and implemented. In 1926, the famous Rebbe of Radomsk, Rabbi Shlomo HaKohen Rabinowitz, inaugurated a school system for his and other Chasidim. The first yeshivah in this new educational system was established in Krakow. The Radomsk system of yeshivos was named Kesser Torah and soon grew into a network of 35 yeshivos servicing 4,000 students in towns and cities all over Poland and Galicia. The Rebbe of Radomsk was personally wealthy and he was the chief financial supporter of this educational system.

The method of study in these yeshivos differed from that in vogue in the Lithuanian yeshivos: less time was spent on detailed analysis

("Rabbi Chaim's way" did not find its way into Poland and Galicia.) and the emphasis was more on broad knowledge of the source material itself. Radomsk, unlike the Lithuanian-type yeshivos, did not concentrate only on the portions of the Talmud dealing with torts, commerce and domestic relations, but also included in its curriculum the Talmudic study of the Temple service and the laws of purity. Radomsk was not intended to serve only the elite student (as were the Lithuanian yeshivos) but had a broader and more representative student body. Rabbi Moshe Rabinowitz, the son-in-law of the Rebbe of Radomsk, was the educational head of the school system, but it was the Rebbe himself who was the living fire behind the growth and accomplishments of the educational network and the individual schools.

Warsaw

WARSAW WAS THE LARGEST JEWISH CITY IN EUROPE. BECAUSE OF ITS size and the fiery, independent temperament of the Warsaw Jews, there was no organized educational system of yeshivos in Warsaw. The learning was done in *shtieblach* — small houses of prayer and study. There were many hundreds of such places in Warsaw. There was no set curriculum of study nor were there different classes. Rather, groups of three or four younger students studied with an older student who was their guide, mentor and teacher. It was a laissez-faire educational system with no attendance taken, no administrative discipline enforced and no major educational budgets required. Despite, or perhaps because of, the apparent laxness of discipline and freedom of the system, thousands of great Talmudic scholars were educated this way in Warsaw and throughout Poland in the post-World War I years. The leading scholars of Poland during that time —Rabbis Menachem Ziemba, Nosson Spiegelglass, Avraham Vanberg, Shlomo Dovid Kahana and Yaakov Meir Biderman — were all products of the *shtieblach*. Almost all of the students in the *shtieblach* were Chasidim and the *shtieblach* themselves were differentiated and segregated by the loyalty of the students to a particular Chasidic dynasty. Naturally, the works of the great Polish Chasidic masters were part of the study program in all of the Warsaw *shtieblach*. One of the advantages was that by their very nature and flexible structure, *shtieblach* allowed for ongoing part-time study of Torah, while the Lithuanian-type yeshivos demanded full-time application and devotion to the Torah studies. The number of students who attended study sessions — full or part time — in the Warsaw *shtieblach* in the 1920's is estimated to have been in the many thousands.[48]

---

48. See the article on the Warsaw *shtieblach* by Rabbi Avraham Ziemba in *Mosdos Torah B'Eiropa*, edited by Samuel K. Mirsky, New York, 1956, p.355.

Mention must be made of the Warsaw Mesivta. This institution was a structured school and had the support of the great rabbinic and Chasidic leaders of Poland, including that of the Rebbe of Gur. The school was established in 1919 under the leadership of Rabbis Meir Dan Plotzki, Menachem Ziemba, Menachem Mendel Kasher and Meir Warshaviak. The established curriculum demanded the study of 1,735 folios of the Talmud in five years as well as the standard commentaries and books of laws and *halachah*. The method of study was a synthesis of the analytical method of the Lithuanian yeshivos and the broad knowledge and peppery discussions of the Polish study method. The Warsaw Mesivta also included two hours of secular studies in its daily learning schedule. This raised the ire of certain rabbis in Hungary who attacked the institution as being a "rabbinic seminary." The Rebbe of Gur forcefully defended the Mesivta, and it was highly regarded in all Polish circles.

In the late 1920's, especially after the death of Rabbi Meir Dan Plotzki in 1928, the school declined in numbers and influence. New yeshivos arose, especially Yeshivas Chachmei Lublin, and these new lights dimmed the luster of the Mesivta. The institution serviced many hundreds of students in the 1920's and tens of them later became rabbis or educators throughout Jewish Poland. It was officially identified with the Agudath Israel movement in Poland.

Kishinev

RABBI YEHUDA LEIB TZIRILSON WAS THE RABBI OF KISHINEV FROM 1910 till his death at the hands of the Germans in 1941. A man of great dynamism and strength, he created a strong yeshivah in Kishinev which attracted hundreds of students from Bessarabia as well as other parts of Europe. Under the auspices of Agudath Israel, Rabbi Tzirilson established a religious "gymnasium" high school in Kishinev in 1923. He was a gifted writer and orator and the dominant figure in Jewish life in that area of Europe.

Chernowitz

IN 1923, THE YESHIVAH BE'ER MAYIM CHAYIM WAS ESTABLISHED IN Chernowitz, with Rabbi Kutai at its head. This yeshivah was classical in its nature and curriculum, though it also included some secular studies in its schedule. There were between 60 and 120 students in the 1920's. The yeshivah closed in 1934.

Vizhnitz

THE LARGEST CHASIDIC YESHIVAH IN BUKOVINIA (RUMANIA) WAS THAT of the dynasty of Vizhnitz. The yeshivah opened in 1923 with 30 students and by 1925, numbered 50. By 1930, the number of students reached 100. The yeshivah had a set curriculum, a system of promotions from one class level to the next and vocational training. The Rebbe of Vizhnitz personally supervised the faculty and students. There were other even larger Vizhnitz yeshivos in Seret-Bukovinia and Ober-Vishiva-Transylvania, that were under the guidance of the brothers of the Rebbe. By the end of the decade, there were yeshivos operating in Satmar, Sighet-Marmorush, Munkacz, Toshnad, Halmin, Kroli, Sikilihad, Spinka, Dej, Klausenberg and Grossverdein. Almost all of these yeshivos included vocational training in their curriculum. The most popular vocational training courses were in textile weaving and printing. These yeshivos were conducted in the spirit of Chasidic fervor and thought: The method of study was far from that of the Lithuanian yeshivos, and "Rabbi Chaim's way" of Talmudic analysis was practically unknown in Rumania and Hungary. Broad knowledge, study of certain *sugyos* (concentration on certain topics that entailed study in a number of different volumes of the Talmud simultaneously), and practical decisions in *halachah* formed the basic method of Torah study. Most of the yeshivos averaged an enrollment of between 100 — 150 students.

Pressburg

THE LARGEST AND OLDEST YESHIVAH IN CENTRAL EUROPE WAS IN Bratislava (Pressburg), headed by Rabbi Akiva Sofer-Schreiber. Even in the midst of the Great War in 1915, the yeshivah in Pressburg numbered over 500 students. The Pressburg yeshivah supplied the Austro-Hungarian army with its Jewish chaplains during World War I. After the war, the yeshivah found that it was now located in Czechoslovakia. Because of the continuing tension between Czechoslovakia, Austria and Hungary, many of the Austrian and Hungarian students were unable to obtain visas to study in Bratislava. However, a new source of students came from the Carpathian mountains; Jews who suddenly were no longer officially Russian, but either Rumanian or Czechoslovakian. The yeshivah maintained its enrollment of 400-500 students during the 1920's. The method of study was heavily oriented towards understanding the different *shittos* (opinions of differing halachic viewpoints) in the Talmud and to arrive at practical halachic decisions through the study of the Talmud. This study method was different from the one employed in the Lithuanian yeshivos. Most of the leading non-Chasidic rabbis of Central Europe were graduates of Pressburg. It was a place of great scholarship and aristocracy of character and behavior.

Frankfort am Main

RABBI SOLOMON BREUER, THE SON-IN-LAW AND SUCCESSOR OF RABBI Samson Raphael Hirsch, founded the yeshivah of Frankfort, Germany. Though there were German students in the yeshivah, a large number of the students were from Hungary, Moravia and Austria. The yeshivah included a full program of secular studies as well as courses in Jewish history and Prophets. In 1921, the yeshivah was divided into five levels of study with approximately 30 students at each level. The method of study was close to the Hungarian model of *sugyos* — following the subject matter of a topic throughout the pages of the Talmud. There was also an emphasis on the study of the laws of the Sabbath, *kashrus,* prayers and blessings. Needless to say, this was not the curriculum or method of study of the Lithuanian yeshivos. In the early 1920's, two more yeshivos were founded in Frankfort. They served the Eastern European Jews who migrated to Frankfort before, during and after World War I. One of these was founded by Rabbi Moshe Schneider and was a Lithuanian-style school. Its student enrollment reached 40. The second yeshivah was headed by Rabbi Yaakov Hoffman. It served approximately 100 students and its curriculum was a mix of German and Lithuanian educational concepts. There were also other small yeshivos formed in the 1920's in Nuremberg, Hamburg, Leipzig and, for a short time, in Breslau.

T HE OTHER IMPORTANT GERMAN YESHIVAH WAS THE RABBINICAL Seminary in Berlin founded by Rabbi Azriel Hildesheimer. After Rabbi Hildesheimer's death, the institution was headed by Rabbi Dovid Zvi Hoffman. The impact of the war caused great changes in the yeshivah. The institution was later headed by Rabbi Avraham Eliyahu Kaplan. After his untimely death, Rabbi Yechiel Yakov Weinberg headed the Seminary from the 1920's until its closing in 1938. It produced rabbis for Germany and other parts of the Western world, as well as for Israel.

Berlin

T WO JEWISH BUSINESSMEN FROM ARGENTINA FOUNDED A YESHIVAH IN Antwerp, Belgium, in 1927, then moved it to the resort city of Heide, fifteen miles north of Antwerp, in 1929. Headed by Rabbi Shraga Feivel Shapiro, a student of the Kelm yeshivah, the Heide yeshivah was a Lithuanian-style institution. It opened with only 20 students, but it grew dramatically. Most of its students were from Holland, England, France and Germany and the enrollment reached 120 students. Rabbi Yosef Beigun, one of the outstanding graduates of Mir, became the *mashgiach ruchani* of the yeshivah. Heide was one of the few bastions of intensive Torah study in Western Europe in the period between the World Wars.

Heide

Chapter Four

The Ominous Sky

1931-1940

ONE OF THE WORST DECADES OF HUMAN EXISTENCE AND JEWISH history began with the dreary report of bad news on all social fronts — economic, diplomatic and human. At the end of World War I, both Germany and Austria wished to unite as one country. Fearing the power and size of such a union, the Allies participating in the Versailles Treaty explicitly forbade such a combination. Yet the Weimar Republic's Chancellor Bruning, attempting to dull Hitler's growing popularity by strengthening the German economy, proposed a customs union to neighboring Austria. He claimed that this effort was a purely economic move and had no political or nationalistic overtones to it. The French saw Bruning's proposal as the beginning of a process of annexation of Austria by Germany. To show its displeasure, France withdrew its considerable deposits from the Kreditanstalt Bank, the largest bank in Austria.[1] This move immediately precipitated a run on the bank, and the bank soon failed. The Austrian bank crisis spilled over into Germany and soon economic panic gripped both countries.

---

1. The bank was owned by members of the Rothschild family, and its failure, leaving thousands of depositors bereft of their savings, spurred greater anti-Semitism in an already anti-Semitic society.

At that time, the countries of the world and their currencies were based on the gold standard. To conserve their gold reserves and prevent the flight of capital, the industrial powers raised their tariff rates and limited withdrawals of gold. This action only further intensified the instability of the world economy. International trade almost came to a standstill as each nation attempted to save itself at the expense of its neighbor. To stem the tide, American President Herbert Hoover, in June 1931, proposed a moratorium on "all payments on intergovernmental debts, reparations and relief debts, both principal and interest."[2] The proposal, eventually approved by Congress, was too little and too late. In September 1931, England, drained of its capital and gold reserves, declared that it would no longer remain on the gold standard. Germany and other countries soon followed suit, restricting imports and trade as well.[3]

The flight of gold and capital now crippled the American banking system. Nearly 2,300 American banks collapsed and closed in 1931, 522 in one month alone, following England's abandonment of the gold standard.[4] Deflation destroyed the American economy: commodities sold for less than their cost; factories closed; farm loans were defaulted, and the land was repossessed by banks. Drought, coupled with poor land use, further crippled American agriculture. Mass migration of people from the impoverished rural areas to the only slightly less impoverished urban centers and to the West occurred. More than ten million people were unemployed. The American economy was devastated, and the economy of Europe was no better.

The Soviet Union, now under Stalin's full terror and control, rejoiced at the capitalist debacle. The Soviets trumpeted the Great Depression as the precursor of the collapse of the West and its capitalist system, and of the inevitable triumph of communism in world society. In 1931 "show trials" of the old Bolsheviks, now accused of aiding counterrevolution, began and would continue throughout the decade.[5] Many of those put on trial and convicted on shabby evidence and coerced confessions were Jews. The *Yevsektzia* was eliminated during the 1930's, with most of its operatives sent to Siberia or executed immediately. The former members of the Bund, who had seemingly turned themselves into super-loyal Bolsheviks, were weeded out of Soviet society and eventually elimi-

---

2. Herbert Hoover, *The Memoirs of Herbert Hoover: The Great Depression, 1929-1941*, New York, 1952, p.70

3. David M. Kennedy, *Freedom From Fear,* New York, 1999, p.77. He notes that world trade was $36 billion in 1929 and had shrunk to $12 billion by 1932.

4. Ibid.

5. Robert Conquest's book, *The Great Terror*, is the best recording of the chilling events of the 1930's in Stalin's Russia.

nated in the slave labor camps of Siberia. The old Bolshevik and former yeshivah student, Semeon Dimanshtain, who had served Stalin loyally and ruthlessly as commissioner of nationalities, was accused in 1931 of "being profoundly revisionist and hateful to Leninism"[6] and was executed by the Soviet secret police in 1938. Moishe Litvakov, also a former yeshivah student and Talmudic scholar, became the editor of the Yiddish newspaper, *Der Emes* (*The Truth*), and slavishly followed Stalin's line as it twisted back and forth in the 1930's. It availed him naught, for he was also arrested and died in prison in 1937. These are only a few examples of the thousands of loyal Bolsheviks, many of them Jews, who disappeared from the scene in Stalin's purge campaign in the 1930's.

The true face of Stalin and his callous attitude towards life can be seen from the following incident, told by Anton Antonov-Ovseyenko (in *The Time of Stalin: Portrait of a Tyranny*): "Lady Astor, on a visit to Moscow in December 1931, had the rare honor of being received by the New Leader [Stalin]. During their conversation, she asked a question no one else would have dared: 'How long will you keep killing people?' Stalin's interpreter froze. But the Boss insisted on hearing the question and, without a pause, as though he had been expecting a question like that, replied to the naïve lady that 'the process would continue as long as necessary' to establish communist society."

Lazar Kaganovich, Stalin's erstwhile brother-in-law and a leading Jewish communist and Politboro member, explained the justice of Lenin's and Stalin's mass murders to an American nephew thusly: "...You must think of humanity as one great body, but one that requires constant surgery. Need I remind you that surgery cannot be performed without cutting membranes, without destroying tissues, without the spilling of blood? Thus we must destroy whatever is superfluous. These are unpleasant acts, granted, but we do not find any of this immoral. You see, all acts that further history and socialism are moral acts." (Quoted by Stuart Kahan in *The Wolf in the Kremlin*, London, 1987.)

During Stalin's terror, the Jewish population became completely isolated from the world Jewish community, for even a postcard from a relative in the West was sufficient to have the recipient arrested as a "foreign agent."[7] The head of the secret police and one of the chief purgers, Genrikh Yagoda, was himself a Jew, as were many of the employees of the secret service. But many more Jews — suspected Zionists, religious teachers, rabbis and innocent people who were merely visibly Jewish — were caught in the net of terror and became its victims. Yagoda himself

6. Zvi Gitelman, *A Century of Ambivalence*, New York, 1988, p.163.
7. Ibid. pp.170-1.

was purged and killed in 1936. His successor, Nikolai Yezhov, was in turn purged in 1938. Tens of thousands of Russians were shot during the times of the purges and show trials. Untold numbers were shipped off to slow death in the labor camps of Siberia.

Paradoxically, some Jews continued to hold high public office in the Soviet Union during the 1930's. Isser Meir Wallach, renamed Maxim Litvinov, served as Stalin's foreign minister until 1939. Instead of a purge, he was rather shunted aside, sent to serve as ambassador to Washington, D.C. during World War II. There were also numerous Jewish officers in the Soviet Army, some of them achieving the rank of general. This was a matter of particular pride to many Jews, even outside of Russia, since there were no Jewish generals in abundance anywhere else in the world at that time. In fact, the Jewish communists in the United States and in the Land of Israel pointed to these generals as proof of the earthly paradise that existed for Jews under Soviet rule. However, during Stalin's purge of the Red Army in 1937, many of these Jews were removed from their positions and killed. Although Stalin's purge of the army was not particularly aimed at Jews per se, the destruction of the Jewish generals nevertheless further terrorized the already frightened Jews of Russia.

The Soviet Union was the active ally of Germany in circumventing the restrictions that the Versailles Treaty placed upon German rearmament following the First World War. The Weimar German government was not a pacifist entity and it looked forward to the day when Germany would again be the strongest military power in Europe. The Soviet government aided and abetted these ambitions. German officers, commanders and pilots underwent training with the Red Army. Russian factories produced and storaged weapons, including airplanes and tanks, then clandestinely delivered them to the German army. Stalin saw England and France — especially England — as Russia's greatest and most permanent enemies. A strong Germany would turn against those capitalistic, imperialistic countries. Amazingly, and to his later shame and immense cost, Stalin did not reckon that a strong Germany would turn against Russia as well.

I F THE SITUATION OF JEWS IN RUSSIA IN THE 1930's WAS LESS THAN idyllic, it turned truly catastrophic in the rest of Europe. All of the economic and social ills of Poland between the wars — and there were many — were blamed on the Jews. The repeated accusation was that the Jews were Bolsheviks and therefore traitorous to the Polish regime, nation and the Roman Catholic Church. Official anti-Semitism was enshrined in the platforms of the leading Polish political parties and public acts of anti-Semitism were condoned. Though clearly not Bolsheviks,

Harbingers of Tragedy Go Unheeded

it was the visibly observant Jews who were usually singled out for abuse and injury. Jews were beaten on the streets of Warsaw and other large cities, and the police somehow never found the attackers. They were thrown off of moving trains and forced to suffer indignities on a regular basis. Jewish political parties in the Polish Parliament fought with each other bitterly, each seeking to gain its narrow vested interest, many times at the expense of not seeing the larger picture of what was happening to Polish Jewry as a whole. Despite the daily persecution, Jewish leadership, both religious and secular, naively thought that Jews still had a future in Poland. It was hard to give up on a home that had sustained a large and respected Jewish community for seven centuries.

One of the factors that weakened the resolve of Eastern European Jewry in the decade of the 1930's was the changing of the guard in the religious Jewish world. The great Chafetz Chaim, Rabbi Yisrael Meir Kagan, died in 1933, as did Rabbi Meir Shapiro of Lublin. Almost all of the Lithuanian *yeshivos* were now headed by younger men who, though great in scholarship and piety, had not yet acquired the authority and stature of their predecessors. Rabbis Shimon Shkop and Chaim Ozer Grodzinski were aged and both died in 1940, just after World War II had begun.

In the world of the Lithuanian yeshivos and in Chasidic Poland, emigration to Palestine[8] or America was not encouraged and many times it was discouraged. The main exception to this rule was the Rebbe of Gur, who did promote emigration. Of course, even if wholesale emigration from Eastern Europe had been promoted by the Jewish leaders, it would not have succeeded: In the 1930's the doors of refuge were pretty well locked against the emigration of tens of thousands, let alone millions of Jews from Eastern Europe.

Dire warnings about the future of Eastern European Jewry were sounded in this decade by the leader of the Revisionist Zionists, Vladimir Zev Jabotinsky. He urged the emigration of hundreds of thousands of Jews from Eastern Europe to Palestine, fully aware that a war against the British Mandate and against the Arabs would be necessary to realize that goal. He petitioned the anti-Semitic Smigly-Ridz government of Poland to press England to allow the emigration of Poland's "surplus Jews" to Palestine.[9] The Revisionists organized their own illegal immigration process and by 1939 had smuggled 15,000 Jewish illegals into Palestine.[10] The Revisionist's

---

8. Rabbi Avrohom Yeshaya Karelitz, the Chazon Ish, emigrated from Vilna to Palestine in the early 1930's on the basis of a special immigration permit obtained from the British for him and his family by Rabbi Kook.

9. Howard M. Sachar, *A History of Israel From the Rise of Zionism*, New York, 1998, p.187.

10. Ibid.

active military arm, Irgun Z'vai Leumi (The National Military Organization)[11] staged reprisals against Arab marauders and attempted to avenge Arab attacks on Jews. Jabotinsky was tarred by the Jewish Left and the mainstream Zionist organizations as a Fascist.[12] But he was nothing of the kind. He simply despaired of any meaningful Jewish future in the ancient heartland of Eastern Europe and believed that Jews would have to fight for their national

Zev Jabotinsky (bottom right) meeting with Betar leaders in Warsaw, Poland — Menachem Begin is at bottom left.

homeland. To him, war with the Arabs was unavoidable and he therefore encouraged the Jews to prepare for it by arming and training themselves for battle. Much of Jabotinsky's gloomy prophecy was to be soon fulfilled in a manner that even he could not dare to envision.

The events in Germany were truly ominous, not only for Jews, but for the world at large. Curiously, no one in the early 1930's seemed to take Hitler and his Nazi thugs too seriously. The Left and the Right, the industrialists and the army, the intellectuals and the politicians, all seriously underestimated his abilities, determination and utter ruthlessness. His anti-Semitism was shared by many in Germany, but his promise to rid Germany and Europe of its Jews was seen by many German and European leaders as hyperbole and rhetoric excess.

This hatred was demonstrated on Rosh Hashanah night in 1931, when Jews returning from synagogue services were beaten in the streets of Berlin and other German cities. The police did not interfere. The deliberate choice of a Jewish holiday for outrages against Jews would become a familiar trademark of Nazi brutality.[13] The year before, in the general elections of 1930, the Nazis had obtained 18% of the total vote. In the regional elections held in Oldenburg and Hesse in 1931, the Nazi vote exceeded 37%. The momentum in Germany was swinging Hitler's way.

In Austria, there was an attempted Nazi revolt in 1931. It failed, but none of the participants were ever arrested or punished. The forces of

11. Popularly known by its acronym, Etzel.

12. Mussolini himself called Jabotinsky "your [Jewish] Fascist." Sachar, p.187. The Left in Israel traditionally has been loose in calling its political opponents "fascists." They continued to do so until the end of the century.

13. Martin Gilbert, *A History of the Twentieth Century*, Vol. 1, New York, 1997, p.797.

democracy, though officially in power in Austria and Germany, were paralyzed in the face of the growing popularity and brute force of Nazism. As unemployment and unrest grew in Germany in response to the worldwide Depression, Hitler's promises of a united and strong Germany, free of the Versailles Treaty and all "foreign" influences, became increasingly persuasive. Nazi attacks on the streets increased. Not only Jews were targeted, but all political opponents of Nazism were fair game for the violence of Hitler's Brown Shirts. Hundreds of Germans, many of them Jews, were killed by the Nazis in unprovoked street violence. As the situation became more chaotic, Chancellor Bruning resigned and President von Hindenburg appointed Franz Von Papen as chancellor. Von Papen was an oily character, a schemer and an opportunist. Like many others, he thought that he could win Hitler over to his side and control him. Von Papen suspended Parliament and attempted to rule by decree, unwittingly creating the precedent that Hitler would use later to become the dictator over Germany.

In the elections for Parliament in July 1931, the Nazi party became the largest in the Reichstag. More than thirteen and a half million Germans — 37.1% of the total vote — cast their ballots for the Nazis. Hitler demanded to be appointed chancellor. Hindenburg refused to do so, reportedly remarking: "That man for chancellor? I'll make him a postmaster, and he can lick stamps with my head on them."[14]

Nazi violence continued, now within the legislative halls of Parliament itself. Prominent socialists, communists and leaders of the democratic parties were assassinated by the Brown Shirts. A campaign against Jewish-owned shops and businesses began in earnest; their windows smashed, their premises looted and their owners impoverished. Using unabashed violence and parliamentary maneuvers, the Nazis forced the dissolution of Parliament and issued a call for new elections. In those elections, held in November 1932, the vote for the Nazi party declined by over 4% and their representation in Parliament fell from 230 seats to 197. But they were still the largest party in the Reichstag.

Hitler again demanded the post of chancellor for himself and Hindenburg now had to consider the matter seriously. In addition, Hitler demanded the right to govern by presidential fiat, free of any parliamentary restraints. Hindenburg still bore a grudge against Hitler, due to Hitler's run for the presidency against him in April of 1932. Though Hindenburg had won convincingly on that occasion, he bore enmity towards the "little corporal," as he snidely referred to him. Refusing Hitler's audacious request, Hindenburg instead appointed General von Schleicher as chancellor.

---

14. Gilbert, p.816.

Fieldmarshal Hindenburg, President of Germany (right), greeting Hitler after his appointment as chancellor.

In 1932, Austrian Nazi thugs, as vicious and violent as their German cohorts, were let loose on the streets of Austrian cities. Again, Jews — usually Orthodox, bearded, visibly Jewish — were routinely beaten. Chancellor Dolfuss of Austria attempted to placate the Nazis by including them in his governing cabinet. But, as in Germany, this morsel of power only whetted their appetite for more and they continued to intensify their violent tactics throughout the country. The influence and pressure of German Nazis on their Austrian comrades, and vice versa, radicalized the respective Nazi parties even further.

After only 54 days in office, Schleicher pronounced Germany ungovernable and resigned. Without any other choices, and constitutionally bound to offer the chancellorship to the leader of the largest party in Parliament, Hindenburg appointed Hitler as chancellor on January 30, 1933. Armageddon was fast approaching.

Hitler's Maniacal Mechanisms Set in Motion

UPON ASSUMING OFFICE, HITLER IMMEDIATELY ACTED ON HIS MAD plans. The Nazis rammed through an Enabling Law in Parliament that gave him dictatorial powers. Communist, socialist and democratic leaders were arrested. March 9, 1933 marked the opening of the concentration camp at Dachau. It is estimated that 40,000 people were killed by the Nazis in their first months in power.

The terror against the Jews continued and strengthened. Jews were beaten by roving gangs of Nazi thugs throughout Germany. Jewish pro-

AN DIE DEUTSCHEN
MÜTTER!

72.000
jüdische Soldaten
sind für das Vaterland
auf dem Felde der Ehre
gefallen.

Christliche und jüdische Helden haben gemeinsam
gekämpft und ruhen gemeinsam in fremder Erde.

12.000 Juden fielen im Kampf!
Blindwütiger Parteihaß macht vor den Gräbern
der Toten nicht Halt.

Deutsche Frauen,
duldet nicht, daß die jüdische Mutter in ihrem
Schmerz verhöhnt wird.

Reichsbund jüdischer Frontsoldaten E. V.

A leaflet issued by the Federal Association of Jewish Frontline Soldiers in the early 1930's in response to anti-Semitic propaganda. It points out to German mothers that 12,000 Jewish soldiers died defending Germany in World War I.

fessors and students were expelled from the universities. Jewish civil servants were removed from their positions. The Nazis proclaimed a boycott of all Jewish stores and commercial ventures. At a mass rally in Madison Square Garden in New York, the Jews of the United States threatened a counter-boycott of German goods. Cowed for an instant, the Nazis restricted their boycott of Jewish commerce to a one-day affair.[15] The Jewish community in America was split over the wisdom of such a counter-boycott against German goods. Strong opposition to the proposed boycott was expressed by the Orthodox Jewish community of Germany itself. It feared that the Nazis would use the excuse of the counter-boycott to further intensify their anti-Jewish campaign.[16]

Hitler introduced his "scientific" racial theories into everyday practice. The "Aryan" race, of which the German nation was the leading representative species, was enshrined at the top of the list of human beings. Jews, Slavs, Gypsies and other *untermenschen* (sub-humans) were the lowest of animals designated for slavery and extinction. Hitler began his deadly program by "mercy killings" of the insane and the terminally ill in Germany. Over 50,000 people were exterminated in this program. (Eventually, more than half a million Gypsies would be exterminated by the Germans, according to Godfrey Hodgson in *People's Century*.) In addition to Dachau, there were other concentration camps established in 1933 at Erstwegen and Sachsenhausen. Although the majority of inmates in these camps were non-Jews, the Jews were singled out for particularly brutal treatment. Not many survived the ordeal for long.

---

15. Gilbert, p.838.

16. See the letter from Jacob Rosenheim, then president of the World Agudath Israel Organization, strongly opposing the idea of a boycott of German goods, in Marc B. Shapiro, *Between the Yeshiva World and Modern Orthodoxy*, London, 1999, pp.234-5. Also on page 117 of that book, footnote 29, there appears a detailed list of Orthodox Jewish leaders and rabbis who objected to any Jewish boycott of German goods.

I believe that all judgments regarding Jewish behavior in the 1930's in response to the Nazis' rise to power should be reserved since the Holocaust itself was as yet an unthinkable event, even after Hitler's cruelty towards the Jews was evident. For an example of Jewish innocence on the true intent of the Nazis, see the poignant and amazing letter written to Hitler in October 1933 by the leaders of the Orthodox Jewish communities of Germany quoted by Shapiro, pp.225-33. I was particularly struck by the following sentences in that letter: "…we have learned to love the German people. They have occasionally caused us sorrow, especially during the Middle Ages. But we also shared in their [the German people's] resurrection. We have close bonds with their culture. It is part of our spiritual life and has set a special stamp upon us German Jews."

The Jewish community in Germany was left bewildered and shocked by the turn of events. Jews had lived in Germany for a thousand years![17] Numerous provinces in Germany had been the first major areas in Europe to give Jews civil rights in the eighteenth and nineteenth centuries. In the main, German Jews had assimilated completely into German life by the twentieth century. More recently, more than 12,000 Jews had died fighting in World War I in the service of Germany, a proportion of dead far higher than their numerical proportion in the German population itself. Even the Orthodox population, though remaining strictly observant, was German to the core. Most German Jews felt that the situation would eventually stabilize and were therefore determined to ride out the storm.

As the situation continually worsened in the 1930's, however, many Jews began to leave Germany.[18] Where to go and how to get there were major obstacles in their path. Many escaped to France, Belgium, Czechoslovakia, Austria and Eastern Europe; places of refuge that would prove temporary and eventually valueless. The fortunate ones reached the Land of Israel, America and England, where true refuge existed. Almost all German Jews arrived at their new locations destitute, robbed by the Nazis before their departure.

In 1933, the famed Rabbinical Seminary of Berlin, founded by Rabbi Azriel Hildesheimer, and now headed by Rabbi Yakov Yechiel Weinberg, attempted to leave Berlin and move to Jerusalem. Rabbi Hildesheimer's son, Meir Hildesheimer, who was one of the directors of the Seminary, traveled to Palestine to make arrangements for the move. There he found strong objection to the idea among the rabbis of Jerusalem, both from the Eidah HaChareidis and from the Chief Rabbinate: both felt that German-style "modernity," even under Orthodox auspices, had no place in the Holy Land. But the strongest opposition to the move came from the Eastern European rabbis, led by Rabbi Chaim Ozer Grodzinski of Vilna. They believed that what was perhaps acceptable in Germany, dominated as it was by Reform, should not be exported to Jerusalem. Their objections were so strong, that the Seminary eventually dropped the idea.[19]

---

17. Leo Baeck, the leading Reform spokesman in Germany at the time, commented bitterly on Hitler's rise to power: "The thousand-year history of German Jewry has come to an end."

18. A *Kindertransport* – the transport of over 1,000 Jewish children to England — took place in the late 1930's. Almost all of these children never saw their parents again. Many of them were raised in non-Jewish homes in England, and some eventually underwent conversion to Christianity. Others remained fiercely observant Jews.

19. Another factor preventing the move of the Seminary to Jerusalem at that time was the unwillingness of many of its directors and members of the faculty to "desert" German Jewry in its hour of travail. The Seminary itself was closed by the German government in 1938 and its students and faculty members imprisoned. Some, including Rabbi Weinberg, survived the war. Most did not.

The German government attacked the institution of *shechitah* — the method of Jewish ritual slaughter of meat and poultry — almost immediately upon assuming power. *Shechitah* was deemed insufficiently humane for the compassionate Nazis to countenance. The law in Germany now demanded that the animal be stunned electrically before slaughter. Such a process of stunning prior to *shechitah* raised enormous halachic problems.[20] It soon became apparent that the real issue in Germany was not kosher meat but whether the Nazis would allow any Jewish life to survive on German soil. And it was becoming increasingly apparent that the answer to that question was negative.

Germany sponsored Nazi groups in all of its neighboring territories, especially in Czechoslovakia, and in the areas of the Saar, Memel and Danzig, which had large German populations. Austria's Nazi party was growing and becoming more openly violent. In 1934, Chancellor Dolfuss of Austria was assassinated by the Austrian Nazis.

A Nazi mass meeting in 1934 (location unknown)

20. See Volume One of *Seridei Aish*, a collection of rabbinic responsa by Rabbi Yakov Yechiel Weinberg, for a thorough discussion of the problem of stunning before *shechitah*. Rabbi Weinberg addressed the problem to the leading rabbinic scholars of the time and their responses are organized in that volume.

Vicious Nazi anti-Semitism spread to other areas of Europe as well. Attacks against Jewish university students became commonplace in the colleges of Hungary. The Iron Guard, a Fascist anti-Semitic militia, took to the streets of Rumania, fighting pitched battles with the police. Civilized Europe was fast disappearing, to be replaced by a reign of terror and blood unequaled in its sad history. In 1934, on the "Night of the Long Knives," Hitler purged people he felt were not blindly loyal to him among his Brown Shirts, the Nazi Party and other German organizations. Like Stalin of Russia, his unlimited use of terror intimidated any possible opposition into submissiveness.

Hitler's racial theories of superiority and inferiority were set into law in 1935. The Nuremberg Laws enshrined the superiority of the Aryan race and spelled the doom of anyone who had Jewish ancestors, even four generations back. Marriages between Jews and non-Jews were invalidated and Jews were forbidden to fly the German flag. Jews no longer had any official standing or civil rights in Germany. Hitler ended the illusion that the Reform movement had trumpeted a century earlier — that Jews were simply "Germans of the Mosaic persuasion." The Nuremberg Laws threatened even those Jews who had converted to Christianity, and their descendants. Barred from jobs in universities, hospitals, government offices, banks and major companies, more than 100,000 Jews were deprived of their ability to make a living. A brief respite occurred when official persecution of Jews abated somewhat in 1936 because of the Olympic Games in Berlin,[21] but it intensified again after the spectacle was over.

Anti-Semitic propaganda and increasing violence culminated in a mass pogrom on November 9, 1938, — when *Kristallnacht,* the "Night of Broken Glass" — overwhelmed German Jewry. Synagogues were torched; Jews were killed in the hundreds and arrested in the thousands. Many ordinary Germans agreed with these anti-Jewish atrocities.[22] Hitler's propaganda machine had been broadcasting vastly inflated figures as to the number of Jewish doctors, lawyers, bankers and teachers in Germany, thus fanning German resentment. Anti-Semitism and the belief that Jews somehow "had gone too far" in integrating themselves into German society were deeply ingrained in the minds and hearts of the German citizenry.

All hope for any Jewish survival in Germany was dashed that awful November *Kristallnacht* night. By then, Hitler had made Germany so powerful in the eyes of the world, that he seemed to be unstoppable.

---

21. Jewish athletes from a number of countries, including the United States, were prevented from participating in the games by their own countries, out of deference to German "sensitivities." Ironically, the star of the games was a Black American, Jesse Owens, who won four gold medals. Hitler refused to personally present them to him.

22. Martin Gilbert, *A History of the Twentieth Century*, Vol. 2, New York, 1998, p. 208.

Kristallnacht. Burning of the synagogue in Rostock

The interior of the Fasanenstrasse Synagogue in Berlin after Kristallnacht

A Brazen Scheme for World Domination

A MAJOR CIVIL WAR BETWEEN THE RIGHT AND LEFT ERUPTED IN SPAIN in 1936. The Soviet Union supported the Left with weapons, military advisors, an intensive propaganda campaign and communist volunteers from all over the world.[23] Hitler and Mussolini backed the Right, which was headed by General Francisco Franco. The German and Italian air forces participated in the war and Franco eventually conquered the whole country, setting in place his dictatorship, which lasted well over 30 years. That same year, Germany officially renounced the Versailles Treaty and reoccupied the previously demilitarized and French-administered Rhineland. Hitler ignored French protestations, correctly surmising that "the French will not move an inch." He had only scorn for the Western democracies and was convinced that no action would ever be taken by them against his aggression.

---

23. The Lincoln Brigade was composed of Leftist volunteers from America, many of them Jewish. Jewish volunteers from Palestine, Poland and other countries also fought for the Left in the Spanish Civil War.

Germany had rearmed itself rapidly and massively in the 1930's. In 1937 and 1938, Hitler bullied the German army's General Staff into accepting his will and vision of European conquest. Generals who refused to agree to his schemes of immediate armed action against Austria and Czechoslovakia were discharged, though not murdered.[24] The newly appointed Chancellor Kurt von Schuschnigg of Austria was brutally treated by Hitler at a meeting in February 1938. In spite of Schuschnigg's concessions to Hitler, the German army invaded Austria in March and *Anschluss* — the annexation of Austria by Germany — was proclaimed. The name of Austria was erased from German maps of Europe and it was now known as the German province of Ostmark.

With the *Anschluss* in place, Jews in Vienna were beaten and killed at will. Rabbis, professors, the aged and the visibly Jewish were made to scrub the streets with their bare hands, sometimes from pails of water mixed with acid, in front of jeering, spitting, kicking mobs. Many Jews, despairing of any hope, committed suicide, as did many Catholic activists, socialists and others who were opposed to Nazism. Hitler immediately purged the Austrian Nazi Party of "undesirable" elements and most of the governing positions in Ostmark went to German Nazis. He did, however, place many Austrians in the SS, where they would play pivotal roles in the impending destruction of European Jewry. "SS" was the designation for the black-shirted *Schutzstaffel*, or "Protective Echelon," which was Hitler's private elite corps, known to be the most fanatical and cruel of the Nazi forces.

Hitler's next target was Czechoslovakia. Both France and England had guaranteed its borders and France made strong statements about defending Czechoslovakia's integrity. Yet as Hitler warned Czechoslovakia against continuing alleged persecution of Germans living in Czech Sudetenland and demanded its territorial unification with Germany, England wavered. Germany mobilized for war against Czechoslovakia. British Prime Minister Neville Chamberlain flew to Germany and in the infamous Munich Conference agreed to appease Hitler and dismember Czechoslovakia. In 1938, Sudetenland was annexed to Germany and in early 1939, the entire country of Czechoslovakia was overrun by the Germans. Poland and Hungary joined in tearing away bits of Czechoslovakian territory. Jews were subjected to the usual Nazi treatment in Prague and other Czech cities.

All of these triumphs came with ease, as the democratic world stood absolutely powerless in will and action.[25] Hitler sensed that the Jews of the

---

24. Hitler was not yet Stalin's equal in this matter.

25. In the immortal words of Winston Churchill, commenting on "appeasement:" "If mortal catastrophe should overtake the British Nation and the British Empire, historians a thousand years hence

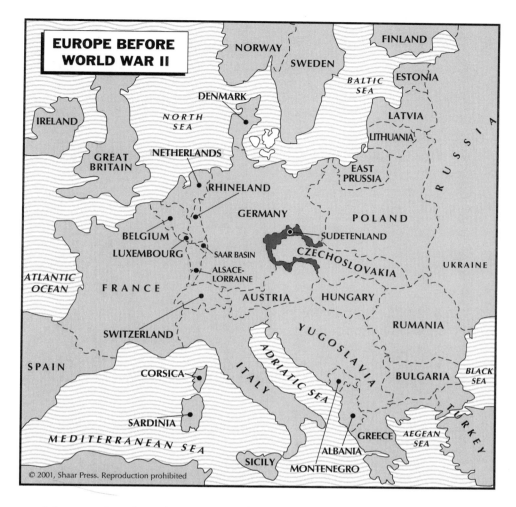

EUROPE BEFORE WORLD WAR II

world were abandoned to their fate and that no one would ever fight on their behalf. He was also convinced that the democracies of France and England did not possess the will and spirit necessary to oppose him. He intuitively understood that the British government still felt him to be a lesser evil than Stalin and communist Russia. Aware that the enthusiasm of the German people for war — created after the first flush of his triumphant Austrian and Czech adventures — was rapidly declining, he determined that unleashing his war for European domination should be done as soon as possible.[26] Brushing aside the advice of his generals that Germany could not be ready for total war until 1943, he placed his plans for the conquest of Poland on the military table for immediate action. He

---

will still be baffled by the mystery of our affairs. They will never understand how it was that a victorious nation, with everything in hand, suffered itself to be brought low, and to cast away all that they had gained by measureless sacrifice and absolute victory – gone with the wind! Now the victors are the vanquished, and those who threw down their arms in the field and sued for an armistice are striding on to world mastery."

26. Paul Johnson, *Modern Times*, New York, 1991, p.356.

was also hungry for the destruction of the three and a half million Jews living in Poland whom he had already earmarked in his poisonous mind for annihilation. Only one thing stood in his way as far as the conquest of Poland was concerned: the enormous presence of the Soviet Union.

Russian Premier Stalin talks with his Foreign Minister Molotov

Stalin signaled to Hitler that he was amenable to a deal with Germany by removing Maxim Litvinov from the position of foreign minister and appointing a non-Jew, V.M. Molotov, in his stead. Stalin was fearful of any confrontation with Germany and he silently watched as Germany took away the city of Memel from Lithuania in the spring of 1939. Hitler made immediate demands on Poland for the return of Danzig and the Polish Corridor to German rule.[27] But Stalin also had eyes on Poland and was sufficiently intimidating to Hitler that the German dictator decided to conciliate Russia. At the end of August 1939, Hitler sent Joachim von Ribbentrop, the German foreign minister, to Moscow. There, on August 23, the Russo-German Treaty of Friendship and Non-Aggression was signed. In a secret protocol to the treaty, Hitler and Stalin agreed to divide Poland between themselves and wipe it off the face of the world map. England and France nevertheless reiterated their commitment to Poland and declared that they would go to war if Germany invaded. Hitler was not impressed with their threats, quipping: "Our opponents are little worms. I saw them in Munich."[28]

On September 1, 1939, he invaded Poland. England and France immediately declared war on Germany. World War II had begun.

The communist faithful throughout the world now had to reverse course from fanatical anti-Nazism to support of Hitler and Germany. For true believers, such a sudden reversal of policy and direction posed no problem. Thus, many communists became enthusiastic supporters of

27. A finger of land which divided German East Prussia from Germany proper and gave Poland access to the Baltic Sea and the port of Danzig. The Polish Corridor was a creation of the Versailles Treaty.
28. Johnson, p.360.

Hitler and the head of the French Communist Party urged French soldiers not to fire against the Germans in case of attack. Yet many communists were sickened by Stalin's duplicity. Most Jewish communists never wavered in their faith in Stalin, but there were some notable defections. The virus of Marxism was so deeply ingrained in the Jewish Left that it continued to infect the Jewish people throughout the century. Jews were such "believers" that some found it within themselves to justify Stalin's aims and policies, even after the Hitler-Stalin pact! But Hitler and Stalin would both do their best to eventually cure them of their delusions.

Within six weeks of the German invasion of Poland, the Polish army was smashed and Poland was occupied by the Germans. On September 17, the Russian army invaded Poland from the east and occupied the territory allotted to it by the secret protocol of the German-Russian Non-Aggression Treaty. The German *Luftwaffe* (air force) particularly targeted the Jewish neighborhoods of Warsaw and other major Polish cities for severe bombing. This bombardment coincided with the Jewish holidays of Rosh Hashanah and Yom Kippur that fell in September of that year. As the German army moved into the Jewish areas of Poland, violence against the Jews began. Special squads of SS killers, *Einsatzgruppen*, shot to death more than 90,000 Jews in the first nine months of 1940.

Jews were hounded and persecuted by the local Polish population as well. The anti-Semitism of many Poles now found violent expression in their cruelty to the hapless Jews and in their systematic looting of Jewish property. The bitter irony of the situation was that the Poles themselves were also treated as subhumans by the German occupiers.[29] As often happens among those persecuted, the victims war with each other instead of with the tyranny that rules them.

In 1939 and 1940, Stalin attempted to conquer Finland. The Russian army was subjected to a number of humiliating defeats at the hands of the plucky Finnish forces. Eventually the Russian preponderance in numbers and arms took hold and an armistice was signed. Under its terms, Finland ceded part of its territory to Russia and made other concessions to its giant neighbor. However, the lackluster performance of the Russian army against Finland was not lost on Hitler. He was now convinced that one strong German *blitzkrieg* campaign would destroy the Russian army and with it Bolshevism and Russian sovereignty. His falsely optimistic assessment of the true nature of Russia and its armed forces was the beginning of his undoing.[30]

---

29. Over six million non-Jewish Poles would be killed in World War II.
30. Contemptuous underestimation of his adversaries was one of Hitler's great weaknesses.

In 1940, Russia invaded and annexed the three Baltic republics, Lithuania, Latvia and Estonia. Puppet communist governments were installed and the Bolshevik "purification" of these areas began in earnest.[31] The yeshivos, their faculties, students, and many major rabbinic figures gathered in Vilna and Kaunas, attempting to escape their fate and continue the chain of Torah study. In these two cities, as well as in Stockholm, they were aided by a number of consular officials from Holland, Japan and other small countries that granted transit and entry visas to thousands of petitioning Jews. Only a relatively small number of Jews were able to successfully use these patently illegal visas to traverse Russia and arrive in Kobe, Japan, later moving on to Shanghai. The fear of Russian deportation to Siberian labor camps, if caught at the railroad station to board trains going east,[32] coupled with the natural inertia that grips people at times of fateful decisions, caused many Jews not to apply for visas or not to use them once they obtained them. This hesitance surfaced even regarding the small number of immigration certificates to Palestine that the Jewish Agency was able to wangle out of the British authorities, many of which tragically went unused.

In May 1940, Hitler unleashed the full fury of his armored corps, air force and infantry against France, Belgium, Netherlands and Denmark. Norway also was invaded and conquered. The vaunted Maginot Line that was to protect France from German invasion was outflanked and rendered useless by the German armored assault through the Ardennes Forest. In six weeks, the German army achieved what it had not accomplished in the four years of World War I. The British Expeditionary Force sent to France to aid the French was itself cut off and trapped with its back to the English Channel. (In a miraculously successful effort, 337,000 British and French soldiers were saved from the beaches of Dunkirk and brought back to England to be regrouped and rearmed to fight another day. Winston Churchill realistically assessed the situation, however. "Wars," he stated grumpily, "are not won by successful evacuations."[33])

The French were forced to sign a humiliating peace treaty with Germany, ceding half of France to German control and setting up a collaborationist government over the remaining half in Vichy that would do

---

31. Soviet commissars shot my uncle, Rabbi Aaron Yehuda Wein (who was the rabbi of a small, but prestigious, community in Lithuania), as well as my aunt and cousins in 1940, because they were "incurable counterrevolutionaries."

32. Thousands of Lithuanian and Polish Jews, mainly observant ones, were shipped to the Gulag from Lithuania and Poland in 1940. Most were never heard from again. There were Jews who wandered all the way to Asiatic Russia and survived the war there, though under conditions of extreme privation and hardship.

33. Winston Churchill, *The Second World War*, reprinted by Houghton/Mifflin Co., January, 1986.

Hitler's bidding. Hitler now ruled mainland Europe. He was confident that England also would come to terms with him and that would leave him free to pursue his war with Russia and Bolshevism. His dream of world domination was within reach.

Hitler's wait for British capitulation would be in vain. Churchill became the prime minister of England and his bulldog determination to defeat Hitler rallied the British people to the dreadful task at hand. In 1940, Hitler waited for British peace overtures, which never came. Convinced that he could destroy the English will to resist by aerial bombing, Hitler planned the *Luftwaffe*'s Battle of Britain. In the interim, Stalin continued to supply Germany with enormous amounts of commodities and supplies. This kept the German home front quiet and its economy robust. Much of the German populace had seen enough of war by now, however, and longed for a settlement that would consolidate Germany's victorious gains and end the fighting.[34] But Hitler had hijacked Germany and no opposition to his maniacal dreams of conquest and destruction of "inferior peoples" would be tolerated.

Jewish Leadership in America Stymied

As MENTIONED ABOVE, OPEN ANTI-SEMITISM WAS PART OF AMERICAN political and economic life in the period after World War I. Immigration restrictions, job and university quotas and rabid anti-Jewish demagoguery combined to create a climate of Jewish reserve and reticence. However, when the Great Depression ushered in the 1930's (and it lasted for the entire 1930's in America), the situation of the Jews in America changed somewhat. Franklin Delano Roosevelt defeated Herbert Hoover in the 1932 election, promising a "New Deal" for America. Roosevelt himself had the mildly anti-Semitic attitudes of his patrician class. Nevertheless, he included in his "brain trust" many Jews, most notably Samuel Rosenman, Henry Morgenthau Jr., Benjamin V. Cohen, Felix Frankfurter and

Franklin D. Roosevelt (left) and Henry Morgenthau Jr.

---

34. See Johnson, p.356, for a description of the German public's gloomy mood despite their military successes.

Jerome Frank. There were hundreds of Jews in the civil service and administration of the "New Deal" and its numerous bureaucracies. Roosevelt's enemies dubbed his program the "Jew Deal." Never before had there been such an influx of Jews into positions of influence and power in American life.

Though the policies of the New Deal created new programs and furious active spending, they began to disappoint many as they did little to cure the Depression in the short run; and the Depression begged for scapegoats. An enormously strong current of American anti-Semitism nationwide was fed by the bigotry of such demagogues as Gerald L.K. Smith, Huey Long and Theodore Bilbo. The drive for the exclusion of Jews from important financial or professional positions gained momentum in tandem with the opposing great influx of Jews into government and policy-making roles.

Forceful and bloody struggles for the recognition of labor unions racked the manufacturing industries of America. Jews were prominent in organizing labor unions and in supporting their aims for worker improvement. This naturally brought about an anti-Jewish backlash from the opponents of labor. A Roman Catholic priest in Michigan, Father Coughlin, broadcast his simplistic, anti-Semitic and demagogic message to millions of listeners every Sunday. The German-American Bund, and similar organizations that supported Hitler and his policies, was prominent and powerful in American life. Charles Lindbergh, one of America's heroes after his solo plane flight from New York to Paris, visited Hitler and was vociferous in his pro-German statements. By 1936, the United States Olympic team decided not to allow Jewish athletes to compete in the Games in Berlin, out of deference to Hitler's biases.

Because of these pressures and anti-Semitic trends, the official representatives of the Jewish community in America took a low profile on any "Jewish" issues. This attitude would continue, with few exceptions, throughout the period of World War II. Even the condemnation of Hitler and his brutality towards the Jews of Germany was muted. Very little was done to attempt to influence the United States government to accept Jewish refugees searching for safe haven. In the midst of a Depression that left many millions of Americans without jobs, it was most difficult to persuade the government to allow tens of thousands more people, especially Jews, to come into the depressed American job market. (While not successful in changing government policies, communal attempts to save as many Jews as possible were initiated. These will be discussed in the next chapter.)

Jewish leadership in America was unsure of itself. At this point, the vast majority of American Jews became followers of the Democratic Party and believers in FDR,[35] trusting that Roosevelt and the Democratic Party would be their economic and social saviors. This faith in Roosevelt would be sorely tested later by the revelation of his negative attitude and behavior towards the Jews of Europe and of Palestine during World War II.

Yet Roosevelt was the sole hope of England, and indirectly of the Jews worldwide, in the terrible war against Hitler. If the United States entered the war against Hitler, Germany could eventually be defeated. If America left England in the lurch to face Germany alone, who knows if it would able to withstand Hitler's onslaught? Thus, Roosevelt would become both a hero and a villain in the eyes of many Jews throughout the balance of the century.

An international conference on the problem of the Jewish refugees from Germany and Austria was convened in Evian, France, in 1938. The conference exposed British and American refusals to expand their immigration quotas to allow the Jews refuge in their countries. Only Holland, Denmark and the Dominican Republic agreed to allow unrestricted Jewish immigration. No hope for a large-scale solution, even a partial one, emerged. On hearing of this, Hitler boasted that "no one wants Jews!" and he was not far wrong. The only solution for Jewish refugees seemed to be Palestine, but Palestine was also to become closed to major Jewish immigration for the next decade. The noose of death tightened around European Jewry.

Strife Erupts in the Yishuv

THE *YISHUV* IN PALESTINE WAS IN TURMOIL THROUGHOUT THE 1930's. It was obvious to all that England had reneged completely on its obligations under the Balfour Declaration and on its stated aims under the League of Nations mandate for Palestine. England realized, perhaps more clearly than did the Jewish leaders then in Palestine, that Arab intransigence and violent behavior would not allow for the peaceful establishment of a Jewish national homeland in Palestine. That homeland could only come into being by force, and the British were unwilling, and perhaps unable, to expend the necessary force to create it. In the 1930's, the Jews in Palestine were also unwilling and unable to exert such force on their own. The great project of Zionist national redemption appeared to be aborted.

The decade was a violent time for the *yishuv*. The Arabs objected not only to the concept of a Jewish national home in Palestine, they opposed a

---

35. A situation that would continue for the balance of the century, though in a more diminished fashion.

Inside the Jewish Quarter of the Old City of Jerusalem, 1934

sizable Jewish population existing there at all. Jewish immigration in the '30's, both legal and illegal,[36] continued at what seemed an alarming rate and the Arab population feared becoming a minority in Palestine. In 1918, the Jews constituted barely 7% of the population of Palestine. By 1936, only eighteen years later, the Jews constituted almost 30% of the population.[37] Under the constraints of continued Arab rioting in 1931 and 1933, the British attempted to control and reduce Jewish immigration.

Yet Hitler's butchery was forcing Jews to leave Germany, Austria and Central Europe in significant numbers, and many of these Jews somehow reached Palestine. This new group of Jewish immigrants, mainly secular, assimilated, Westernized, bourgeoisie city folk, was not only unwelcome to the Arabs, they were viewed askance by the socialist Zionists who governed the *yishuv* as well. Since Jewish life in Palestine was controlled by political parties, and the political parties of the Left were the strongest, non-Leftist Jewish immigration was hardly encouraged. Chaim Weizmann himself was afraid of bringing "undesirable elements" (read: non-Leftist Jews) into the country. Yet, the non-Leftist immigrants of the 1930's laid the basis for a strong economic foundation in Jewish Palestine, developing mercantile skills and industrial projects that would greatly expand the development of the *yishuv*.

The strife between the Labor Left and Jabotinsky's Revisionist followers caused a deep rift within the *yishuv* and world Jewry. In 1933, Chaim Arlosoroff, one of the leaders of the Left and a high official in the Jewish Agency, was shot down by unknown persons while taking a stroll with his wife on a Tel Aviv beach. Jabotinsky's followers were immediately accused of arranging the assassination.[38] A Revisionist Zionist, Avraham

---

36. For example, many of the Jewish athletes who participated in the first Maccabiah Games in 1936 stayed in Palestine after their temporary visas expired.

37. Sachar, p.198.

38. Unfortunately, political assassination was not unknown in the *yishuv*. Jacob De Haan, a mysterious Dutch Jew who became the "foreign minister" of Agudath Israel in Palestine, was shot dead by unknown killers in the 1920's. The religious community perceived De Haan's killing as political assassination.

Stavsky, was arrested, tried by the British court and convicted of the murder. Rabbi Kook vigorously defended Stavsky, stating that he knew the man was incapable of such a crime. (In fact, the conviction was reversed on appeal and later evidence seems to exonerate him completely.) The rabbi's outspoken defense brought him the withering criticism of the Left that insisted on Stavsky's guilt and punishment. Cries against "rabbinic interference" in political matters were heard throughout the secular community. The bitter enmity, both personal and ideological, between the Left and the Right in Zionist politics was cemented by the Arlosoroff tragedy. This bitterness and potential violence would lie just below the surface of Israeli politics and governmental action for the rest of the century.

Rabbi Kook died in 1935 and was succeeded by Rabbi Isaac Halevy Herzog, formerly of Dublin, Ireland. A great scholar and Talmudist, Rabbi Herzog was also a Ph.D. graduate of Cambridge University. The appointment of a "Doctor" as the Chief Rabbi was vehemently opposed by some of the rabbis of the country. Ultimately, Rabbi Herzog proved to be a far less controversial figure than was Rabbi Kook. The Religious Zionist movement — Mizrachi — and its fractious, socialist-oriented child, Hapoel HaMizrachi, (though it yet maintained its independence from Mizrachi) gained in strength both in Palestine and in the Diaspora. It created its own school system in Palestine, dominated the Chief Rabbinate and occupied major positions of importance and influence in the Jewish Agency and the World Zionist Organization. It was far larger and more powerful than Agudath Israel was in Palestine, though Agudath Israel obtained recognition from the ruling British authorities as a separate community, outside the leadership of the Zionist *yishuv*. Both Mizrachi and Agudath Israel were pilloried by anti-Zionist elements of the Orthodox community in Palestine and in the Diaspora. These groups were ideologically opposed to any cooperation whatsoever with the Zionist enterprise in Palestine and even Agudath Israel was found wanting by their standards.

Proposed Solutions to the "Palestine Problem" Guarantee Continued Violence

PROTESTING JEWISH IMMIGRATION TO THE COUNTRY, ARAB LEADERS IN Palestine called for a general strike on April 15, 1936. On that day, three Jews were killed on the roads by Arab gangs. The Irgun Z'vai Leumi retaliated by slaying three Arab workers near Jaffa. The situation spiraled out of control. Within the next month, 80 Jews were killed by Arab violence, thousands of *dunam* of Jewish farms were vandalized and their crops burned. The British, attempting to restore order, killed over 140 Arab rioters while themselves suffering 33 dead. The official leadership of the *yishuv* condemned the Irgun for its attack on the Arabs and pleaded with the British authorities to impose order. It also began to seriously train and equip its own official Jewish defense unit, Haganah,[39] and to counterattack against Arab marauders.

In May 1937, Britain established yet another commission to study the problem of Palestine, appointing Lord Peel as its chairman. He and other members of the commission visited Palestine a number of times, finally recommending the partition of the area into Jewish and Arab sections. The Jewish section, which was to be small and truncated, could never become a viable national entity. The entire idea of partition was a bitter pill for the Zionist movement to swallow.[40] Zionist leaders argued that the land already had been partitioned in the 1920's, when Trans-Jordan was formed on the eastern side of the Jordan River. The Peel Commission also restricted Jewish immigration to the country, though it did not completely eliminate it.[41]

While the Jews were displeased by the report of the Peel Commission, the Arabs were outraged even more. By the end of 1937, Arab violence again spread throughout the country. In the preceding few years, the Jews had established "tower and stockade" settlements in key strategic spots in Palestine. These settlements were established literally overnight and were the Zionist response to Arab opposition. All of the settlements were established on land that the Jewish National Fund had previously purchased from Arab landowners. Most of these Arab landowners were absentee landlords and the Arabs who tilled the land were little more than serfs. However, the establishment of these Jewish settlements provoked these

---

39. Yitzchak Sadeh (Landsberg), a former officer in the Red Army, became the driving force behind the newly aggressive tactics of the Haganah, and a British army officer, Orde Wingate, helped train the Haganah fighters in commando tactics and night fighting. Wingate, who was killed in an air crash in Burma during World War II, was a devoted believer in the Zionist cause and risked his life and career to help the Jews protect themselves against Arab violence.

40. Aside from the practical grounds of opposition to the Peel Commission's partition of the Land of Israel there were strong emotional ones as well. Berel Katzenelson, one of the leading Labor Zionists of the time, in a speech that he made just before the opening of the Twentieth Zionist Congress in 1937, said: "Let us ask ourselves, is our love for our 'homeland' dependent on actual life experience? Is it based on land that we physically walked on when we were young, on the scent of real flowers that we once held in our hands, to nature's scenery in which we were raised, to an actual sunset that we saw? Certainly not! The plains where we were raised were always secondary in our hearts to the hills of Judah and the flowers that we held were only symbols of the rose of Sharon. The fresh air of the forests where we hiked were harbingers of our imaginary but yet so real 'homeland.' Is not our love of 'homeland' therefore unique from all others? We are loyal to a 'homeland' of the 'Book,' to a 'homeland' of far distant memory, to a 'homeland' that transcends reality. It is not for naught that we have preserved in our memory names of places that we never saw, some names being magical and inspirational and some strange and mysterious. These names have waited for us till we gave them actuality again. How can we now give them up and agree to the partition plan of the Peel Commission?"
Kitvei Berel Katzenelson, Tel Aviv, 1956, pp.350-1.

41. Jewish immigration was to be limited to 1,000 immigrants per month for the next five years.

Arab workers who realized, and correctly so, that their days of sharecropper farming were now ending. Because of this continuing Arab enmity, these settlements had to fight off marauders regularly and were seen by both Arabs and Jews as the testing point of Jewish determination in Palestine.

Due to British policy and openly anti-Semitic British bureaucrats, the Jewish population of Palestine grew by less than 5,000 in 1938-39, while the Arab population increased then by more than 65,000. Still not placated, Arab violence against the Jews intensified during this time. The actions of the Irgun escalated in response to the continuing and horrific random Arab violence against Jews. Though the Irgun was consistently ostracized and condemned by the leaders of the *yishuv*, it ignored this strong disapproval of its tactics. Claiming that only force could contain Arab violence, Irgun leaders were unwilling to sit idly by while Arabs slaughtered Jews.

The situation reached a boiling point when the British Colonial Office issued a White Paper in 1939 closing

An Arab gaffier (super-numerary policeman) in Jerusalem, 1938

off almost all Jewish immigration to Palestine. This, at the time of greatest need for Jewish escape from Germany and Europe! The White Paper met with revulsion in the Jewish world and it also sparked strong dissent in England itself.[42] But the deepest blow to Jewish hopes was struck by the announcement of the Russian-German Non-Aggression Treaty. The doom of Poland and its Jews was now clear, though the extent of that destruction was still unimaginable. The Russian-German deal was announced at the Twenty-First Zionist Congress, then convening in Geneva. "The news exploded like a bomb," says historian Martin

---

42. The members of the Peel Commission wrote a strongly worded criticism of the White Paper and published it in the *Times* of London. Churchill, Duff Cooper and others attacked Neville Chamberlain in the House of Commons debate over the White Paper policy.

The Damascus Gate
locked during a curfew in
the Old City of Jerusalem
in 1938. In response to
Arab rioting, curfews
were imposed by the
British to prevent the
movement of armed
gangs. The curfew later
was used to restrain Lechi
and Irgun as well.

Gilbert.[43] With even greater fervor than before, illegal Jewish immigration into Palestine continued, and more than 25,000 illegal immigrants were brought in at the start of World War II.

Hitler's war reached Palestine with deadly swiftness. On September 9, 1939, Italian bombers struck Tel Aviv and 107 Jews were killed in that air raid.[44] Despite Britain's entry into the war, the British Foreign Office continued to pressure neutral nations, such as Turkey, to prevent any Jewish immigration to Palestine. The attitude of the *yishuv* to these depressing events was summed up by David Ben-Gurion in his famous statement: "We will fight with the British against Hitler as if there were no White Paper; we will fight the White Paper as if there were no war!" The British policy makers were counting on the fact that the Jews had no choice but to support England in its war against Germany.

By publishing the White Paper at this juncture, the British hoped to rally Arab support to their side as well. In this hope, they were consider-

---

43. Martin Gilbert, *Israel: A History*, New York, 1998, p.99.
44. Ibid. p.100.

ably disappointed. The Palestinian Arabs publicly proclaimed their confidence that Hitler would triumph. Arab sentiment generally throughout the Middle East was at best neutral, and in many cases openly pro-German. The Grand Mufti of Jerusalem became an enthusiastic collaborator with the Germans and was forced by the British to leave Palestine. In addition to the Jews and the British, the Mufti was fighting an internal war against his Arab political opponents, particularly the al-Nashashibi family clan. From 1938 to 1941 more than 3,000 Arabs died in this mini-civil war. Another 18,000 Arabs fled Palestine to Egypt and Lebanon (the first Arab "refugees" from Palestine) to escape the terror and violence unleashed by the Mufti.[45]

American Jewish Life Crystallizes

THE ZIONIST MOVEMENT IN THE UNITED STATES GAINED STRENGTH IN the 1930's. The apparent helplessness of European Jewry in the face of Hitler's actions strengthened the realization among many American Jews that an independent Jewish state was a necessity. Emmanuel Newman, Abba Hillel Silver and Stephen Wise (the latter two Reform rabbis who ignored their movement's opposition to Zionism), spearheaded the effort to supply moral, political and financial support to the *yishuv*. The Mizrachi religious Zionist movement represented the majority of Orthodox Jews in America and its various unofficial affiliates (Hapoel HaMizrachi, Bnei Akiva, Hashomer Hadati) were active and strong. The youth groups affiliated with the Labor Zionist parties (such as Habonim, Hashomer Hatzair, etc.) also gained wide acceptance among American Jewish youth. The Zionist youth movements of the 1930's provided an alternative social group and outlet for these young American Jews who still faced anti-Semitism and were often excluded from the social groups of general American society in this decade.

Because of this still-widespread rejection of Jews in American society, intermarriage and mass assimilation were still not rampant. The Conservative movement continued to grow during this period of time. An alternative Orthodox rabbinical group was founded in the 1930's, weakening the hegemony of the Union of Orthodox Rabbis of the United States and Canada (Agudas HaRabanim), This new group, the Rabbinical Council of America (Histadrut HaRabanim), was primarily composed of graduates of Rabbi Isaac Elchanan Theological Seminary in New York and Hebrew Theological College in Chicago. The new group was composed of English-speaking, American-born and trained,

Abba Hillel Silver

Stephen Wise

45. Sachar, p.213.

English classes were given in various American cities between the World Wars.

younger rabbis who felt excluded from the older rabbinical group, who were predominantly older, European-born and trained, Yiddish-speaking rabbis. The emergence of the new rabbinical group placed a painful strain on the formerly warm and cordial relationship between the Union of Orthodox Rabbis and Rabbi Isaac Elchanan Theological Seminary. The creation of Yeshiva College, later Yeshiva University, by Rabbi Dr. Bernard Revel under the auspices of the Seminary also created heated rabbinic controversy. The whole question of higher secular studies as part of a Torah curriculum, and as part of a Torah institution, now became a focal point of disagreement in the Orthodox world. It would continue to be a divisive issue within American Orthodoxy throughout the balance of the century.

In 1932, Rabbi Joseph Dov Soloveitchik, the son of Rabbi Moshe Soloveitchik and the grandson of Rabbi Chaim Soloveitchik, arrived in America from Europe. He became the rabbi of the United Orthodox Synagogues of Boston. His father was then the *rosh yeshivah* of Rabbi Isaac Elchanan Theological Seminary. For nearly the next half-century, Rabbi Joseph Dov Soloveitchik would play an influential role in the development of Orthodox Jewry in America and in the education of many of its leaders. His Talmudic erudition, general knowledge, great oratorical skills and pedagogic mastery stamped him as a unique figure in American Orthodoxy.

Other outstanding religious leaders came to America in this era and would wield enormous influence. Rabbi Moshe Feinstein became the head of Yeshiva Tiferes Yerushalayim,[46] while Rabbi Yitzchak Hutner became the leader of Yeshiva U'Mesivta Rabbeinu Chaim Berlin.[47] Frantic efforts were made by the Union of Orthodox Rabbis to provide entrance visas for great rabbis trapped in Europe. Rabbi Yaakov Kamenetsky came to San Francisco, then Seattle, before finally settling in Toronto. Later in life he headed Yeshiva U'Mesivta Torah Vodaath in New York. In 1940, the dynamic Rabbi Aharon Kotler arrived in America and immediately became a driving force in American

Rabbi Isaac Elchanan Theological Seminary Semichah Class with Rabbi Moshe Soloveitchik (third from left), Dr. Bernard Revel (center) and Rabbi Benjamin Aranowitz (third from right)

46. He would later become the recognized *posek* (decisor of Jewish law) for much of the Jewish world.

47. He was a Polish Chasid, who traveled to Lithuania and became a student of the Yeshivah Knesses Yisrael in Slobodka. He later journeyed to Jerusalem and studied under Rabbi Kook before coming to America. A person of genius and immense physical presence and charisma, he incorporated within himself the traits of *Chasidus, mussar* and Jewish philosophy. His influence in American Orthodox life over the next decades would be strong and profound.

Rabbi Moshe Feinstein

Rabbi Yaakov Kamenetsky

Rabbi Aharon Kotler

Rabbi Yitzchak Hutner

Orthodoxy. He would soon found, in an old mansion in Lakewood, New Jersey, what was to become the internationally famous yeshivah, Bais Medrash Govoha.

Rabbi Eliezer Levin arrived in Erie, Pennsylvania in 1937 and soon moved to Detroit where he would lead the Jewish community for over 50 years. Rabbi Pinchas Teitz succeeded his father-in-law, Rabbi Elazar Preill, as rabbi in Elizabeth, New Jersey. Under his leadership, the community became a model Jewish *kehillah* (organized community), a rarity in America. Rabbi Dr. Joseph Breuer, the grandson of Rabbi Samson Raphael Hirsch, arrived in New York towards the end of the decade and the renowned German Jewish community of Frankfurt am Main was reestablished in Washington Heights under his steadfast leadership. All of these personalities infused into American Orthodoxy a new strength and determination to survive and prosper. Their presence also marked a new confidence in Orthodoxy and an aversion to compromise with "America" and its Orthodox norms in the United States and Canada.

Non-Orthodox groups also incorporated personalities of scholarship and influence into their seminaries. Professor Shaul Lieberman,[48] an outstanding Talmudist and classical languages scholar, became the head of the Talmud department at the Conservative Jewish Theological Seminary. Dr. Abraham Joshua Heschel[49] came to the faculty of the

---

48. He was the son-in-law of Rabbi Meir Berlin (Bar-Ilan) and one of the outstanding students of Yeshivah Knesses Yisrael in Slobodka. He headed the Harry Fischel Torah Institute in Jerusalem before coming to America.

49. He was a scion of a distinguished family of Chasidic masters. Heschel was an elegant author, an accomplished scholar in all fields of Jewish thought and a person of charisma and leadership. He

Reform Hebrew Union College at the very end of the decade, and would soon go from there to the Jewish Theological Seminary. Samuel Atlas, a former student of Slobodka like Professor Lieberman, was then professor of Talmud at Hebrew Union College, having arrived in America earlier in the decade.

By the 1930's, the Reform movement in America began to shed some of the more radical positions that Isaac Mayer Wise had formulated for it in the late nineteenth century. Though its opposition to Zionism was still strong, it was no longer universal in the movement since, as mentioned above, Abba Hillel Silver and Stephen Wise were Zionist leaders. In general, the 1937 formulation of Reform beliefs was much more moderate than the declaration of the 1880's. However, as the formulation itself stated, Reform still maintained that in terms of belief in a personal God, or belief in God Himself, observance of ritual and Jewish tradition, the obligation of prayer and the commemoration of the Sabbath, "each age has the obligation to adapt the teachings of the Torah to its basic needs." Thus, Reform continued to espouse its message of non-binding Judaism, though the presence of a more traditional faculty at Hebrew Union College was now a source of friction between that faculty and the lay leadership of Reform. The events of the 1930's in Germany also caused Reform to throttle back on its definition of Jewry as being exclusively a "religious community." In any event, Hitler was changing many Jewish minds about long-cherished beliefs of the nineteenth century "enlightenment" and of the progressive world that it was meant to create.

---

did not stay long at Hebrew Union College and his career and fame flourished upon his transfer to the Jewish Theological Seminary at the beginning of the next decade.

Chapter Five

World War II and the Holocaust

1941-1945

A s Hitler surveyed Europe and the world at the beginning of 1941, he felt confident of victory. It was true that England had not sued for peace after the fall of France as he had expected, and that the murderous British Air Force now regularly bombed German cities, but these were merely pinpricks in the overall strategic superiority of dominant German might. Hitler was annoyed by the inept campaign that the Italian army was conducting against British forces in Libya. But that also was a mere diversion from the reality of German power, which as of yet had never tasted military defeat. Hitler's goal of obtaining *lebensraum* for Germany in the East, coupled with his desire to annihilate the Jews of Europe, blinded his rational thinking.

He now proposed Operation Barbarossa — an enormous military assault on the Soviet Union. Hitler believed that German armored *blitzkrieg* warfare would destroy the Soviet Red Army in a matter of months. The Bolshevik government of Stalin would be deposed easily, communism would be destroyed forever, and the eastern borders of Germany would extend to the Ural Mountains. And millions more Jews would be destroyed.

Hitler wanted the invasion of Russia to begin in the early spring of 1941. Stalin received repeated warnings about German preparations for war against the Soviet Union, but he ignored them all. Dismissing the mounting evidence of Hitler's treacherous duplicity, Stalin kept supplying Germany with grain, oil and war materiel right up until the day of the German invasion of Russia. He had hoped that by scrupulously living up to his part of the Russian-German Treaty, he would induce Hitler to live up to his part of that agreement as well. The ruthless realist in the Kremlin was naive beyond belief in this vital matter that threatened Russian and communist survival.

Hitler was buoyed in his hopes for a relatively easy victory over Russia by the poor performance of the Russian Army against Finland in 1940. He was convinced that England was powerless to aid Russia: submarine warfare — the Battle of the Atlantic — was going Germany's way in 1941. Hundreds of thousands of shipping tonnage and thousands of British and American seamen were sent to the bottom of the Atlantic by German submarines operating in "wolf packs." If the submarine attacks would continue without pause, England would be starved into submission, for she was wholly dependent on American aid. Franklin D. Roosevelt, elected to an unprecedented third term in November 1940, had ingeniously circumvented the Neutrality Act as well as the isolationist spirit of Congress and the American public with his "Lend-Lease" program to help Britain. Despite its reluctance to be drawn into the war, the American public was slowly coming to the realization that Hitler had to be defeated. Lurking in the background was the growing crisis in the Pacific caused by the aggressiveness of Japanese imperialism and militarism. The United States, which was then more of a Pacific than European power, was seen as the main obstacle to the Japanese dream of dominating Asia. 1941 was to prove to be the fateful watershed year of the future of the century.

In February 1941, Hitler created the *Afrika Korps* to salvage Libya from the debacle of Italian defeat at the hands of the British. General Erwin Rommel[1] arrived with a sizable contingent of German troops and armor in Libya, and soon the British forces were in full retreat towards Egypt and the Suez Canal. German propaganda beamed to the Arab world promised a "just solution" to Arab grievances against the Jews in Palestine. The Jews of Palestine had organized a military unit to fight alongside the British. Jewish units fought in Libya against the Italians and the Germans and in Lebanon and Syria against the Vichy French forces allied with Germany.[2]

---

1. He would gain fame as the "Desert Fox."
2. Moshe Dayan lost his eye in one of these battles against the French.

But the *yishuv* felt itself threatened by Rommel's advance and it looked on with great trepidation as British officials began to make arrangements to withdraw to Iraq in case of a German breakthrough in Egypt. For almost six months in 1941, it seemed that the very survival of the Jews in the Land of Israel hung in the balance.

With clear hindsight, it is obvious today that had Hitler committed even half of the forces that he had arrayed against Russia in 1941 to conquer the Middle East, he would have been successful and reached India. In fact, many of his naval advisers begged him to do so. But Hitler's personal obsession with Russia, Bolshevism and Eastern European Jewry would not allow him to be deflected from the Russian campaign. Thus the *yishuv* was spared the fate of its fellow Jews of Europe.

There were desultory efforts to raise an Arab Legion to fight along with the German Army, but in spite of the Mufti's appeals, his efforts in this regard were not successful. However, he was able to recruit about 6,000 Bosnian Moslems into a fighting unit that eventually fought on the German side in Russia. The Mufti was confident that an Arab uprising throughout the Middle East against Britain was imminent. The British were very concerned about the likelihood of just such an uprising and therefore downplayed any official use of Jewish manpower and resources in the fight against Germany. Even though the Jewish Brigade had shown outstanding courage and skill in Libya and Syria, the British were very cool to the idea of expanding it and properly arming it.[3] The fear of Arab violence governed all British policy regarding the Middle East and the *yishuv*.

Despite their frustrations with British policies, approximately 11,000 Jews from Palestine were part of the British army in the Middle East in early 1942. Eventually England agreed to the organization of military units that were composed exclusively of Jews from the Land of Israel. By the end of the summer of 1942, approximately 18,000 Jews were members of these wholly Jewish military units within the British army. These soldiers, and especially their officers, eventually became the core of the Haganah and ultimately of the Israel Defense Forces. The Haganah then also established a commando group, Palmach, to help protect Jewish settlements from Arab attack in the event of a British evacuation of Palestine.

The *yishuv* also prepared for the worst. It devised a strategy — the Carmel Plan — to resist an actual German occupation of Palestine. The plan entailed the establishment of an enclave in the Carmel mountain range near Haifa where all Jews would gather. Organized there under a Jewish government, they would fight to the end against the German invader. The

---

3. It should be noted that Leslie Hore-Belisha, the British War Secretary, led the opposition to any form of Jewish Brigade whatsoever. Hore-Belisha was Jewish.

British were aware of this plan and gave it their active approval. In retrospect, the formula appears foolhardy and wildly optimistic regarding Haganah capabilities against the Germans. Nevertheless, it was an expression of the determination of the *yishuv* to fight on and survive.

The Carmel Plan never came into operation because of the defeat of the *Afrika Korps* in 1942 at El Alamein by General Bernard Montgomery and the British Eighth Army. The Germans retreated westward across North Africa; and an American amphibious landing in Morocco eventually forced the Germans to leave North Africa and the Middle East completely. After these Allied successes, with the immediate Axis threat ended, the British administration in Palestine reverted to its traditional anti-Zionist and anti-Jewish stance. The Haganah then became an underground, illegal organization and the relationship between the Zionist heads of the *yishuv* and the British administration of Palestine became strained and bitter. It would remain so until the end of the British Mandate over Palestine in 1948.

The Jews Fight Great Britain...And Each Other

THE DESPERATE PLIGHT OF EUROPEAN JEWS ATTEMPTING TO REACH Palestine in late 1940 was accentuated by the tragedy of aging, unseaworthy ships arriving at Haifa harbor crammed with illegal immigrants. England transshipped many of these refugees to Mauritius Island in the Indian Ocean and even attempted to send some of them back to their cruel fate in Bulgaria and other European countries. One of the ships, *Patria*, intentionally was sunk in Haifa harbor by the Haganah in order to prevent the deportation of its 1,900 passengers to Mauritius. The ship sank too quickly for the planned rescue to be successful, and 240 Jews drowned together with twelve British military policemen.[4] Hundreds of other Jews drowned in other failed attempts to find sanctuary in Palestine.

In December 1941, a decrepit vessel, *Struma*, arrived in Istanbul with 769 Jewish refugees aboard. For two months, it lay in the harbor, with Turkish authorities refusing to grant permission for the Jews to land. The British

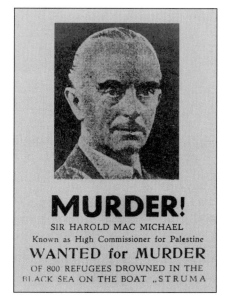

MURDER!
SIR HAROLD MAC MICHAEL
Known as High Commissioner for Palestine
WANTED for MURDER
OF 800 REFUGEES DROWNED IN THE
BLACK SEA ON THE BOAT „STRUMA

The Jewish underground in Palestine accused Sir Harold MacMichael, the British High Commissioner, of murdering the passengers of the "Struma" by refusing to grant them entry visas to Palestine.

---

4. Howard M. Sachar, *A History of Israel From the Rise of Zionism*, New York, 1998, p.237.

in Palestine refused to allow the ship to enter Palestine, even for transshipment of the refugees to Mauritius. The Turks eventually forced the ship to leave Istanbul and it soon sank in the Mediterranean with the loss of almost all the passengers aboard.[5] The Jews of Palestine were horrified by the incident and their bitterness towards the British deepened.

British policy regarding the Jews of Palestine was shaped by a deep rift within the British government itself on that issue. Winston Churchill was sympathetic to Zionist aspirations and he envisioned some sort of Jewish independent entity that would arise in Palestine after the war, yet as the old imperialist that he always was and always remained, he never agreed to England relinquishing overall sovereignty over Palestine. As he envisioned the arrangement, the Jewish and Arab entities that would arise after the war would be either under benevolent British control or, at the very least, be part of the British Commonwealth of Nations.

This policy of Churchill's was strongly opposed and undermined by the British Foreign Secretary, Anthony Eden, who was no friend of Jewish hopes in Palestine. The pro-Arab staff of the Foreign Office counseled against agreeing to any Jewish demands for increased Jewish immigration to Palestine and certainly opposed the establishment of any autonomous Jewish entity in Palestine. The result of this clash of ideas and attitudes within the wartime British government was to freeze British policy and administration in Palestine in its pro-Arab, anti-Zionist mode. The insensitivity of British policy and behavior toward the Jews, who were just then beginning to learn of the horrorible destruction of their families in the Holocaust, created a new and strong militancy against the British rule in Palestine.

In 1941, a Polish Jew who had immigrated to Palestine, Avraham Stern, formed an underground military organization, Lochamei Cherut Yisrael (Lechi) — Fighters for the Freedom of Israel. The British referred to the group contemptuously as the "Stern Gang." Viewing England as the chief obstruction to Jewish ambitions in Palestine, Stern unleashed a string of attacks against British police, soldiers and government offices. His group never consisted of more than a few hundred youths, but their unwavering devotion to the cause compensated for their lack of numbers. Stern himself was killed by British policemen in 1942 and the leadership of the group passed to Nathan Friedman-Yellin and Israel Eldad-Scheib. Yitzchak Shamir, a future prime minister of Israel, was also a member of Lechi. Many of their attacks wildly misfired, often killing as many Jews as British.

---

5. 428 men, 269 women, 70 children. Sachar, ibid.

Lechi was widely condemned by leaders of the *yishuv,* and the British found willing helpers among the Zionist leadership in Palestine in their drive to uproot and destroy Lechi and its members. The members of Lechi never forgave Ben-Gurion and the Zionist leadership of the *yishuv* for their active cooperation with the British authorities in the war against Lechi. This was especially true after the British hanged a number of captured Lechi fighters.

Along with Lechi there emerged another military group who despaired of ousting the British from Palestine except by armed struggle. Etzel was composed of followers of Jabotinsky and it was initially led by David Raziel. Despite his hatred of the British, in 1941 he served as a commando on a special secret mission for them in Iraq. He was killed during that mission, some say by the British themselves.[6] The leadership of Etzel passed to Menachem Begin. A Polish Jew, Begin was a disciple of Jabotinsky who was arrested and imprisoned as a Zionist agitator by the communist authorities on their takeover of Poland. He later was allowed, with other imprisoned Polish Jews, to join the Polish Army in Exile. He reached Palestine, deserted the Polish Army, and by 1943 he was the head of Etzel. A gifted orator, a devoted ideologue to Jabotinsky's dream of a Jewish state created by force of arms, Begin built Etzel into an effective guerilla fighting group.

Etzel was also sharply condemned by Ben-Gurion and the Zionist leadership, and here again the Zionist leadership actively cooperated with the British police in hunting down the members of Etzel. The guerilla group retaliated by executing Jewish "informers." The personal enmity between Begin and Ben-Gurion was fierce and unending. In hindsight, one must acknowledge how remarkable it was that all-out civil war did not erupt between the different Jewish groups.

An Invincible War Machine Delivers Mass Murder

WHILE THE *YISHUV* WAS SPARED THE HORROR OF GERMAN OCCUPATION, the Jews of Europe were being methodically destroyed. The Holocaust has been one of the most studied and analyzed events in human history, yet it remains a mystery. It is unfathomable that so many civilized leaders and ordinary citizens could have cold-bloodedly perpetrated a crime of such immense magnitude. We must surmise that Hitler had unleashed the monster that lay beneath the pretensions of civilized Europe. He found willing helpers in his genocidal acts in every country

---

6. So bitter was the relationship of Etzel, Haganah and the British towards one another that Etzel accused the other two parties of "setting up" Raziel to be killed in the battle.

of Europe that he dominated, with perhaps the only exceptions being Denmark and Greece.[7]

A statement made in 1941 to the Iron Guard militia by General Ion Antonescu, the dictator of Rumania and a Hitler ally, set the tone for the depravity that characterized Europe during World War II:

> *I beg you to have no mercy. At the risk of being misunderstood by some traditionalists, I am supporting the idea of the compulsory eviction of Jews from Bessarabia and Bukovinia. They shall be pushed outside the borders ... I do not know when, in how many centuries, the Rumanian nation will benefit from the same liberty of action for its ethnic purification. Nowadays we are owners of our territory. Let us make use of it. It does not matter if we are treated as barbarians ... We never had a more proper moment ... If necessary, fire with machine guns ... I give you the full liberty ...Go on with this ... Let American Jews call me to account.[8]*

In the spring of 1941 Hitler was prepared for his invasion of Russia, but his plans for the Russian war were delayed by the necessity of saving Italy from Mussolini's foiled invasion of Greece. German forces eventually overcame Greek and British resistance, conquering both Greece and Crete. Later that spring, when an anti-German government came to power in Yugoslavia, Hitler invaded and subdued Yugoslavia in six weeks. As a result, tens of thousands of Jews who previously had thought themselves to be relatively safe now fell into German hands. Most of them were destroyed by the Germans and their Croatian and other ethnic Balkan allies.[9] The Jews of Greece, including the large and centuries-old Jewish community of Salonika, were obliterated in Auschwitz.

Mussolini (left) and Hitler

---

7. On the night of September 29, 1943, almost all of Denmark's 7,400 Jews were stealthily ferried across the sea to Sweden by intrepid Danish fishermen. However, there was a special Danish Legion in the SS, composed of volunteers from Denmark, that participated in the slaughter of Eastern European Jews. The courageous Danish king and government branded these SS volunteers as traitors and revoked their Danish citizenship. The people of Athens, led by the example of the royal family, hid over 3,000 Greek Jews among them, sparing them deportation to Auschwitz.

8. Martin Gilbert, *A History of the Twentieth Century*, Volume 2, p.385. The Rumanian Army, while fighting alongside the Germans in Russia, had a policy of executing 200 Jews for every Rumanian soldier killed and 100 Jews for every Rumanian soldier wounded by partisan action within the territory that they occupied.

9. Two rival guerilla/partisan groups arose in Yugoslavia to fight the German occupation. The Chetniks were supported by England and America while Joseph Broz Tito's partisans enjoyed Russian support. Even though Jews fought in their ranks, both groups were notorious for their anti-Semitism and their cruelty towards Jews.

Germany invaded the Soviet Union on June 22, 1941, predicting, "We have only to kick in the door and the whole rotten structure will come crashing down." Finland, Hungary and later Rumania all joined in the war against Russia. In the first month of the war, Russia suffered enormously, sustaining almost a million casualties in dead, wounded and captured soldiers.[10] The Baltic States, Poland, White Russia and much of the Ukraine fell to the advancing German forces. Leningrad was surrounded and the German push towards Moscow seemed unstoppable.

Stalin reeled from the blow struck by his trusted partner. He initially fell into a deep depression and it was not until July 3 till he could broadcast a message of toughness and resistance to his people. Regaining his cunning, Stalin transformed Hitler's war against Bolshevism into a war of Russian patriotism and survival.[11] This brilliant propaganda stroke was little noticed in the original flood of German victories. Eventually it would become the self-righteous basis for the Russian triumph over Germany, as well as for the survival of the tyrannical Soviet system for decades after the end of World War II.

As was the case in Poland, the German killing of Jews began immediately with the advance of the German army. Hundreds of thousands of Jews were killed by the SS, the German army and the *Einsatzgruppen* forces (a separate group nominally under the SS). Lithuanian, Latvian, Ukrainian and other local populations were also brutally active in the killing of Jews and the looting of their property. In fact, the guards and killers in many of the German death camps were of these various Baltic and Slavic ethnic groups. The SS organized special Lithuanian and Latvian battalions composed of volunteers to their cause.[12] Over 80% of the *Einsatzgruppen* killers in Lithuania were Lithuanians. In Kaunas (Kovno), Lithuania, more than 2,000 Jews were massacred by local Lithuanians even before the Germans reached the city. Among them was the spiritual giant, Rabbi Elchanan Wasserman, the head of the yeshivah of Baranovitch. In July and August of 1941, in Kaunas alone, more than 42,000 Jews were murdered by the *Einsatzgruppen*.

Rabbi Elchanan Wasserman

---

10. The vast majority of Soviet prisoners of war who fell into German hands in World War II were starved, beaten and/or worked to death. Stalin would treat German prisoners of war with the same barbarism.

11. The populations of Ukraine, Lithuania, Latvia and White Russia were ripe to throw off the yoke of Stalin and Bolshevism and cooperate with the Germans. But the Germans treated these native populations so brutally that they turned against their new oppressors and became part of the Russian people's effort to defeat Germany. What would have been the result of a more benevolent attitude towards the Slavic populations by Germany is one of the unanswered questions of World War II. Hitler's racial convictions about the "subhuman" Slavs drove his murderous policies regarding the conquered populations of Eastern Europe.

12. Lenin also had Latvian battalions as the shock troops for his Bolshevist revolution.

There was no place in Eastern Europe that provided any refuge for Jews. Only the Jews who could retreat far enough east into Russia to avoid eventual German occupation had a good chance of surviving the war. And even they were the constant victims of privation, hunger, disease and endemic anti-Semitism.

The Fuhrer's Two Fatal Miscalculations

HITLER HAD DETERMINED THAT THE WAR IN THE EAST WOULD BE a war of annihilation. The Russians responded with a scorched earth policy that frustrated the results of many German victories. Russia also organized a large and ferocious partisan warfare that flickered behind German lines. The partisan war was brutal beyond description and the worst atrocities were committed in its conduct. Many of the partisan bands sheltered Jews and included Jews in their ranks. There were partisan bands composed exclusively of Jews. Yet many of the Russian partisans were openly anti-Semitic and many a Jew met his end from a partisan bullet or bayonet.

Stalin also moved major Russian war production factories east of the Ural Mountains. In a prodigious effort of will and labor that cost the lives of thousands of Russian workers, whole factories and plants were dismantled and shipped east, then reassembled and put back into production. Initially Russia was dependant on British and American materiel aid, but as the war continued, Russia became more than self-sufficient in war production. Its immense territory and manpower reserves would eventually thwart Hitler's plans for its destruction. Hitler's invasion of Russia was the first of his colossal blunders in 1941. By 1943, Russia was easily outproducing Germany in all of the vital weapons of war.

The second terrible miscalculation of Hitler was his unnecessary declaration of war against the United States after the Japanese attack on the U.S. naval base at Pearl Harbor, Hawaii, on December 7, 1941. Japan risked all on its plan to first destroy the American Pacific fleet, quickly conquer all of the island territories up to Australia, and then force the United States and England to accept its gains, allowing it to become the major Pacific power. The American Congress, which until the Japanese attack had been decidedly isolationist, declared war against Japan and Japan only. With his contempt for America and the perceived weakness of all democracies, Hitler jumped the gun and declared war against the United States.[13] When America responded in kind, it became impossible

---

13. German Information Minister Joseph Goebbels turned the American declaration of war into a rousing propaganda episode proclaiming that the Jews had forced America into declaring war against Germany: Now the liquidation of the Jewish people was justified because of their "incessant warmongering."

for Germany to win the war. As Churchill phrased it: "It is not yet the beginning of the end, but it may well be the end of the beginning."

By November of 1941 the spires of Moscow were spied through German field glasses, but the Germans would never capture the city. The fearsome Russian winter descended with a vengeance on the ill-clothed and unprepared German army. Their supply lines were stretched to the limit, the frontline troops had absorbed enormous casualties and they were badly battle weary. A strong Russian counterattack drove the Germans back from Moscow, signaling the end of the *blitzkrieg* and the beginning of a battle of attrition. In 1942 and 1943 Germany would mount additional mass offensives on the southern and central Russian fronts, capture Crimea, reach the Volga at Stalingrad and threaten the conquest of the oil fields of the Caucasus. In this enormous effort, millions of casualties would be sustained on both sides. But Russia was too big for anyone to swallow easily and it prevailed, pushing back the German tide. By the end of 1943, Germany was in retreat in both Africa and Russia. The German generals realized the war was lost, but Hitler would not allow any room for compromise or armistice.

"Final Solution" Too Atrocious to Believe

IF HITLER'S WAR AGAINST RUSSIA DID NOT PROCEED SMOOTHLY according to plan, his war against the Jews was far more efficient. The Germans realized that the system of murder by starvation, random violence and *Einsatzgruppen* killing was unequal to the task of liquidating all of Europe's Jews. In January 1942, the Wannsee Conference was held at which the leaders of the SS and of the German railway system, together with assorted government bureaucrats, reviewed the destruction of Europe's Jews up to that time and planned the most effective "Final Solution" to the "Jewish problem." Experiments with euthanasia by gas had been successful in killing more than 100,000 German children who were judged too mentally ill, retarded or physically handicapped to be of value to the new German state. The medical doctors who had conducted that mass murder were sent to Poland to implement the German plan. Dr. Irmfried Eberl became the commander at Treblinka;[14] while Dr. Horst Schumann, together with Dr. Josef Mengele, conducted gruesome medical experiments on helpless inmates at Auschwitz.[15]

The "Final Solution" strategy entailed the herding of Europe's Jews into ghettoes and isolated camps, where many would die of starvation and disease.[16] These ghettoes and camps were administered primarily by Jews — the *Judenrat* — who were responsible to their German masters. The ghettoes had a Jewish police force, which usually aided the Germans in the roundup of Jews for deportations to the killing camps. Many members of the *Judenrat* committed suicide when they finally realized the true purpose of the ghettoes and the deportations. Others continued in their posts till they themselves were shot or deported when their ghetto was emptied.

Deported Jews were shipped by rail in cattle cars to the death camps. Many died in the cattle cars of asphyxiation, hunger or thirst, as well as suicide. When the trains arrived, the Jews were stripped of their meager belongings and clothing and herded into the gas chambers. Most Jews

---

14. More than 800,000 Jews, mostly from the Warsaw ghetto, would be gassed to death at Treblinka. The camp was destroyed and all evidence of its existence eliminated by the Germans in 1943. However, approximately 70 Jews survived Treblinka and reconstructed the scene after the German defeat.

15. Over 30% of all of the commandants and higher German officers who operated the death and concentration camps in World War II possessed either an M.D. or Ph.D. degree. So much for the moral saving grace of higher education.

16. In the early months of 1942, while awaiting the completion of the death camp at Treblinka, 4,500 Jews a month were dying in the Warsaw ghetto of "natural causes."

arriving in Treblinka were dead within three hours of their arrival. Their bodies were then buried in mass graves or burned in crematoria.[17]

Originally the systematic killing entailed poison gas, introduced by exhaust fumes from vehicles specially constructed to kill about 100 Jews at a time. This proved to be unequal to the numbers of Jews being sent to the camps, and the more sophisticated "shower room" system was adopted. A special pesticide poison gas, Zyklon B, was used to induce death in those "shower rooms." The enormous purchases by the SS of this chemical, manufactured by a subsidiary of I.G.Farben, doubled that company's dividends to its stockholders from 1942 to 1944.[18]

The deportees were always told that they were being sent to "resettlement in the East" or to labor camps where they would engage in "productive work." Most Jews went to their deaths deceived completely, not even immediately realizing in the "shower room" that it was gas and not water that was descending upon them.

> *Then they would feel the gas and crowd together away from the menacing columns and finally stampede towards the huge metal door with its little window, where they piled up in one blue clammy blood-spattered pyramid, clawing and mauling at each other even in death. Twenty-five minutes later the "exhauster" electric pumps removed the gas-laden air, the great metal door slid open, and the men of the Jewish* Sonderkommando *entered. Wearing gas masks and gumboots and carrying hoses, their first task was to remove the blood and defecations before dragging the clawing dead apart with nooses and hooks, the prelude to the ghastly search for gold and the removal of the teeth and hair which were regarded by the Germans as strategic materials. Then the journey by lift or rail-waggon to the furnaces, the mill that ground the clinker to fine ash, and the lorry that scattered the ashes in the stream of the Sola.* (Quoted by Paul Johnson in *Modern Times*.)[19]

By the middle of 1943, however, many Jews were aware of the true destination and nature of the deportations. The first large killing camps were Treblinka, Belzec, Sobibor, Chmelno, Majdanek and Maly Trostenets. This latter camp was just outside of Minsk in White Russia. It was the only large killing camp not on Polish soil. It boasted a record of no known survivors.[20] But these camps, murderous as they were (over two

---

17. Before burial or cremation, any gold teeth in the mouths of the corpses were first extracted. The gold was melted down into ingots and shipped to the Reichsbank in Berlin or to Swiss banks that cooperated with the Germans during the war.

18. Paul Johnson, *Modern Times*, New York, 1991, p.415.

19. Ibid.

20. Gilbert, Vol. 2, p.421

million people, mostly Jews, died in them), were minor league in comparison to the enormous killing camp built at Auschwitz-Birkenau in southern Poland. From 1941 until its closing in 1944 when the Red Army stood at its gates, more than 2,500,000 people were killed at the camp. It was also a work camp where the thousands who were not killed immediately were nevertheless worked to death slowly and painfully. Fritz Saukel, the head of the German slave-labor apparatus, described his goals succinctly: "All the inmates must be fed, sheltered and treated in such a way as to exploit them to the fullest possible extent, at the lowest conceivable degree of expenditure."[21] It is no wonder that in 1943, in Auschwitz alone, 25,000 workers died of "natural causes." Ironically, the slave-labor factories remained uniformly unsuccessful economically. The Germans set up concentration camps in France, Holland, Czechoslovakia, Germany and the Baltic States. Although some of these camps were not officially killing camps,[22] innocent people died in vast numbers in all of them.

Reports of the Germans' genocide of the Jews in Europe began to reach the outside world in 1941, and generally were met with skepticism. However, by 1942, the reports were confirmed from various sources and there was no doubt that Hitler's hideous promises were now actually being fulfilled. At the World Jewish Congress meeting in Lausanne, Switzerland, in August 1942, the scope of the continuing killings was reported to the disbelieving delegates. Jewish response to news of the Holocaust was muted and weak, as leaders were fearful of an anti-Semitic backlash in their own countries if they made public demands on their governments to intervene to stop the killings. In the United States, the official leaders of American Jewry parroted the official government line that priority had to be given to the winning of the war and that therefore not much could really be done to stop the mass murders. Many of these prominent Jews downplayed the killings and were openly skeptical of the numbers of victims involved.[23]

---

21. Johnson, p.417, quoting the records of the Nuremberg War Trials.

22. Theresenstadt (Terezin), in the Czech Republic, is an example of such a holding and transport camp where nevertheless death was a daily and constant visitor.

23. This story of Supreme Court Justice Felix Frankfurter's reaction to the Holocaust is illustrative of this attitude. The story appears in Robert A. Burt's excellent little book, *Two Jewish Justices* (Brandeis and Frankfurter) — *Outcasts in the Promised Land. ... in 1942, a member of the Polish underground, Jan Karski, secretly came to Washington and the ambassador of the Polish government in exile arranged a meeting with Frankfurter. Karski, according to his subsequent account, described Nazi genocide in the concentration camps. Frankfurter responded, "A man like me talking to a man like you must be totally honest. So I am. I do not believe you." The Polish ambassador rejoined, "Felix, how can you say such a thing? You know he is saying the truth. He was checked and rechecked in London and here. Felix, what are you saying?" Frankfurter answered, "I did not say that he's lying. I said that I didn't believe him. There is a difference. My mind, my heart, they are made in such a way that I cannot conceive it."... Frankfurter's protestations of disbelief were not merely rhetorical; he did not use his access to President Roosevelt to convey Karski's allegations about genocide or to express concern generally about the concentration camps.*

In November 1943, Churchill, Stalin and Roosevelt issued an official statement warning against the continuance of the genocide and promised to hold all of those responsible for it to just retribution. Roosevelt reiterated the warning in March of 1944. But the killing continued briskly and undeterred. In spite of pleas from Chaim Weizmann and promises from Churchill, the Allied air forces did not bomb Auschwitz or the railroad lines that led to it when they had the opportunity to do so in 1944.[24]

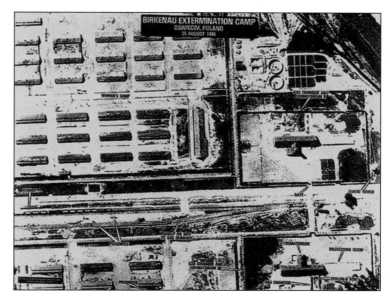

This aerial photo of the Auschwitz-Birkenau extermination camp was taken from an American plane in August, 1944, giving the lie to the American government's insistence that its bombers could not reach the extermination camps, or that they did not know their purpose. After the photo was developed, American intelligence identified a transport train, groups of prisoners, gas chambers and crematoria.

The Allies also did precious little to try and extricate those Jews still living from Hitler's control. The U.S. State Department and Immigration Service were both notoriously anti-Semitic and refused to grant asylum to Jews. For most of world Jewry, the gates of America were sealed shut. In 1944, Roosevelt finally agreed to the establishment of the War Refugee Board, through whose efforts about 100,000 European Jews were saved from the Holocaust. Eventually, thousands of Jews did find some shelter in the United States in places such as Oswego, New York.

One of the saddest incidents in the Holocaust story occurred in the last year of the war. The German Army invaded and took control of Hungary in the spring of 1944, after a failed attempt by the Hungarian government to extricate itself from the war and its alliance with Germany. Adolf Eichmann, the SS officer in charge of the "Final Solution," immediately moved to Hungary to plan the extermination of more than 400,000 Hungarian Jews newly under German rule. The death trains from Hungary to Auschwitz rolled on throughout the spring and summer of 1944, despite the obvious fact that Germany had lost the war. The average number of Hungarian Jews killed during these few months was 12,000 per day. Yet, even Eichmann hesitated for a moment. He negotiated a deal with the Hungarian Jewish leadership, represented by Dr. Rudolf Kastner, the head of the Hungarian Zionist organization, by which the remaining Hungarian Jews would be spared if the Jews would see to it that the Western Allies would provide Germany with 10,000 trucks and other items for use against Russia.

The Nazis believed their own propaganda that the Jews controlled the Allies and thus would be able to deliver on such a preposterous

24. Johnson, p.421.

arrangement. A Hungarian Jew, Joel Brand, was dispatched to deliver the terms of this deal to the Zionists in Palestine and to the British. As a goodwill gesture, Eichmann allowed a train bearing over 1,500 hand-picked Jews (chosen by Kastner and his associates) to leave the Bergen-Belsen concentration camp and arrive safely in Switzerland.[25] Brand was arrested by the British, the offer of Eichmann was scorned by all and the death trains renewed their tragic journeys. In response to British apathy towards saving Jewish emigres, the British Minister of State for the Middle East, Lord Moyne, was assassinated by Lechi gunmen on November 6, 1944. The assassins were tried and hanged by the British. They, too, were victims of the failed mission of Joel Brand.

A number of Orthodox Jewish organizations, spearheaded by the Union of Orthodox Rabbis, Young Israel and Ezras Torah, created the Vaad Hatzala (Committee for Rescue) to help the Jews of Europe. The Joint Distribution Committee also labored mightily to save Jews from the pit of destruction by whatever means possible. The Vaad Hatzala, together with a small but active Revisionist Zionist group headed by Hillel Kook,[26] who went under the pseudonym of Peter Bergson, lobbied Congress and the American administration to help the Jews. A mass rally of more than 200 Orthodox rabbis visited Congress before Yom Kippur, 1943.

The delegation of rabbis visits Washington, D.C. in 1943. Rabbi Eliezer Silver is in the front row, center, holding papers.

_____

25. Among others who were so saved was Rabbi Yoel Teitelbaum, the Rabbi of Satmar.

26. He was a member of the extended family of Rabbi A.Y. Kook, the first Chief Rabbi of Palestine.

Mass demonstration protesting Nazi murder, Madison Square, New York, July 31, 1944

The only member of the Roosevelt administration who reacted positively to the appeals of the Jewish groups was Secretary of the Treasury Henry Morgenthau Jr., himself a Jew.[27] Generally, it must be admitted that American Jewry was quite intimidated by the specter of American anti-Semitism and did not respond forcefully or speedily to the disaster engulfing their European brethren.

The Germans had willing allies in the implementation of the "Final Solution" of the Jewish problem in the countries that they occupied. The French police and Vichy government sent 72,000 French Jews to their

This window of a kosher butcher store was subject to anti-Semitism in New York, 1943-44.

27. The personal and emotional appeal made to Morgenthau by Rabbi Kalmanowitz, a Brooklyn rabbi, himself an escapee from Hitler's Europe, made a profound impression on the patrician, assimilated Jewish secretary of the Treasury.

deaths in Auschwitz, with the French National Railway System sending the transportation bill to Berlin for payment. There were active collaborators in the Holocaust in almost every European country, the main exception being Denmark, where 97% of its Jewish population was saved.

Neutral countries also were implicated in the Holocaust. Switzerland guarded its borders zealously, and relatively few Jewish refugees found safe haven there during the war. Turkey, under German pressure and because of its own distrust of "minorities," imposed a punitive tax on its Jewish citizens in 1942. This *Varlik Vergisi*, as it was called, impoverished the Jewish community in Turkey. By the time the tax was lifted in the spring of 1944, the Jewish community there had been brought to its knees, financially and socially. The old canard about "Jewish money controlling the country's economy" and the Jewish "exploiters" had been used to justify this persecution of the Jewish population. After the war, the Turkish Jewish community was only a shell of its former great self and emigration from the country to the West and to the Land of Israel picked up pace.

Jewish women of Salonika in peacetime. Sixty thousand Jews of that city were deported to Auschwitz.

Though most of Sephardic Jewry escaped the ravages of the Holocaust, there were ancient and strong Sephardic communities in the Balkans that were decimated and destroyed. The thriving Jewish community in the Greek port city of Salonika was shipped en masse to Auschwitz. About 90,000 Greek Jews were killed by the German murder machine. The Jews in Yugoslavia were killed not only by the Germans, but by the warring partisan groups as well. The Croatians and Slovenians were particularly cruel to their Jewish neighbors, while the Serbs on the whole behaved more fairly and sympathetically to them. As Arabs were openly pro-German, Jews kept a very low profile in the Arab countries of North Africa and the Middle East. It was nothing short of miraculous that there were no major killings of Jews in the Arab lands during the war. Sporadic violence against Jews did exist, however, and was accepted in the Arab societies throughout the war years.

As it became certain that the Allies would win the war, Jewish organizational focus began to shift towards the goal of establishing a Jewish state in Palestine after the war. This was done, both in the United States and in Palestine, subconsciously and perhaps even unknowingly, at the expense of greater rescue efforts for European Jewry.

At the Zionist Conference convened on May 9, 1942 in New York's Biltmore Hotel, which was attended by Ben-Gurion and Weizmann, a resolution was passed demanding "the establishment of Palestine as a Jewish Commonwealth integrated in the structure of the new democratic world." Ben-Gurion and his Jewish Agency allies were no longer willing to accommodate Weizmann's more cautious idea of Jewish autonomy under British sovereignty. Territorial compromise in Palestine was possible and, in fact, expected. But Weizmann's gradualist position on Jewish statehood and incomplete independence was rejected. It was to be complete Jewish self-rule or nothing. Ben-Gurion now believed, as did Jabotinsky before him, that the new Jewish state would have to be born in blood. He wrote to the members of the Jewish Agency in 1942 regarding the achievement of statehood by means other than British fiat: "[We must] be ready, also, for another way, the way of armed struggle … Our youth must be prepared to do everything possible when the right moment comes."[28]

U.S. troops land at Normandy Beach June 6, 1944

28. Sachar, p.244.

The eyes of the Zionist leadership were no longer fixed on the present but on the future. They envisioned unlimited Jewish immigration into the Land of Israel. By 1946, there were 560,000 Jews living in Palestine.[29] The war had helped strengthen the Jewish economy and many new settlements and enterprises had been created. The idea of a Jewish state gained wide acceptance throughout the *yishuv* and among Jews the world over.

General Charles DeGaulle (center, in uniform) leads a victory parade in Paris, August 25, 1944

The Western Allies invaded France in June 1944, and successfully established a beachhead on its shores. By August, Paris had fallen and the British and Americans were approaching the Rhine. On the Eastern front, the Germans never recovered from their defeat at Stalingrad. The German army was being mauled by the overwhelming numbers and firepower of the Soviet Union. Yet all the while, the German killing apparatus which was obliterating the Jews of Europe never abated in its will or

29. Ibid., p.246.

work. As late as April of 1945, as the Russian army was battering the gates of Berlin, the surviving Jewish inmates of concentration camps, including Bergen-Belsen and Buchenwald, were forced to undertake inhuman marches by their captors, lest they be liberated by the advancing Allied troops. Thousands died on these marches, even to the last day of the war.

Hitler committed suicide in his underground bunker under wrecked and burning Berlin and the German forces surrendered unconditionally on May 7, 1945. The "Thousand Year Reich" came to its end after twelve years. It is estimated that over twenty million people died in the process of Germany's rise and fall. Almost a third of that number were Jews.

Allied troops view concentration camp inmates slaughtered just before the liberation.

German citzens, under the
direction of U.S. medical
officers, walk past a group
of 30 Jewish women starved
to death by SS Troops in
a 300 mile march
through Czechoslovakia.

German officers sign unconditional surrender in Reims, France

The War Ends in a Mushroom Cloud

THE WAR IN THE PACIFIC WAS NO LESS HORRIFIC THAN THE COMBAT IN Europe. The Japanese were brutal and murderous in their treatment of local populations in the vast areas of the Pacific that they conquered at the beginning of the war. Their treatment of American and British war prisoners was so atrocious that eventually Allied soldiers refused to surrender, preferring death at their own hands to the tortures which otherwise awaited them. The Allies also took very few Japanese prisoners and many of those who attempted to surrender were summarily shot.

General MacArthur's strategy of "island hopping" brought Japan within range of the American Air Force by 1944. Firestorms created by the enormous tonnage of incendiary bombs dropped during the incessant American air raids literally razed major Japanese cities. But the Japanese code of honor — *bushido* — forced Japan to fight on although it was apparent that it could no longer hope to win the war. Japanese resistance remained fierce and unyielding, especially in the battle for Okinawa, where Japan employed kamikaze suicide pilots in a desperate effort to destroy the American naval fleet. General MacArthur estimated that the United States would suffer a million casualties in the invasion of Japan itself.

The Yalta Conference of February 1945, marked the begining of the Cold War.

In the midst of this, in April 1945, Franklin D. Roosevelt died and was succeeded by Harry Truman, a little known senator from Missouri whom Roosevelt had chosen as his vice-president. American Jewry, as a whole, was crushed by the death of Roosevelt. Because of the wartime alliance with Stalin, the leftist sentiments among the Jewish intelligentsia in America were reinforced. Roosevelt's statement that he could "do business with Uncle Joe [Stalin]" further endeared him to the Jewish Left, who were highly critical of Churchill's obvious anti-communist stance.[30] American Jewry was as yet unaware of his apathy towards the Jews of Europe during the Holocaust and his assurances to Ibn Saud of Arabia that the United States would oppose a postwar Jewish state in Palestine. Roosevelt was a great president, but he certainly was not a friend of the Jewish people in its hour of need. As is now abundantly clear with vivid hindsight, that Roosevelt's death and Truman's succession to power were pivotal events in the course of Jewish life and history after World War II.

Although the Japanese were brutal to their enemies, they rather benignly treated the Jewish war refugees from Europe who came first to Kobe, and later to Shanghai (which was under Japanese rule at the time). Jews who had reached their shores were never persecuted and German requests for the handover of the Jews under Japanese control were finessed and ignored.[31] The Mir Yeshivah was allowed to function in Shanghai, though physical conditions were difficult and the city was subject to numerous American bombing attacks. Nevertheless, thousands of Jewish refugees were able to survive the war there, and many of these someday would play a leading role in the postwar revival of Jewish life in America and in the Land of Israel. In Shanghai, a Jewish printing press was established and copies of the Bible and the Talmud, as well as prayer books and other Hebrew books, were produced there. A Yiddish theater, literary cultural activities and a clandestine Zionist organization also operated in Shanghai during the war.

The possibilities of atomic energy being harnessed as a military weapon or as a source of energy power were being explored in the 1920's and 1930's. There were those who scoffed at the idea that atomic research could produce tangible practical results. In September of 1933, *The Times* of London quoted Lord Rutherford, a leading British scientist, who stated that "[Nuclear fission] was a very poor and inefficient way of producing

---

30. I remember how everyone on my block in the Lawndale area of Chicago — a fully Jewish neighborhood — wept openly at the news of Roosevelt's death.

31. The Japanese officer handling the affairs of the Jewish refugees called in two leading rabbis from the refugee community and asked them point blank, "Why do the Germans hate you so?" One of the rabbis, Rabbi Shimon Kalish, the *Amshinover Rebbe,* answered: "Because we are Orientals!" The matter was never discussed again.

Atomic bomb, August 8, 1945

energy, and anyone who looked for a source of power in the transformation of atoms was talking moonshine." Despite Hitler's fascination and drive for inventing new weapons of mass destruction, he was wary of supporting atomic research, as he considered nuclear physics to be a "Jewish science."

Nevertheless, German Nobel-prize physicists were engaged in atomic research throughout the war and there was a distinct possibility that Germany would produce an atomic bomb. Based on this possibility, Albert Einstein was prompted to personally write to President Roosevelt to advocate an American atomic energy program. Under Roosevelt, the United States undertook the building of an atomic weapon. The "Manhattan Project," as it was called, employed thousands of scientists and technicians in a frenzied effort to create this ultimate weapon of mass destruction. Most of the leading physicists who worked on the project were Jews, many of them refugees from Hitler's Europe. Because of the German laws against the Jews, the best German and Hungarian physicists had fled Europe and placed their talents at the disposal of the Americans.

In late July of 1945, Truman was informed of the successful test explosion of an atomic bomb in the western American desert: The power of the sun had been released in an awesome explosion. To spare the loss of millions of American and Japanese lives that a conventional invasion of Japan would entail, Truman decided to use an atomic bomb on Japan in order to force its unconditional surrender. The first bomb was dropped on Hiroshima in the first week of August 1945.[32] When surrender did not immediately follow, a second bomb fell on Nagasaki a few days later.[33] The awesome destruction wrought by these two bombs — between them killing more than 100,000

Cheering crowds welcomed General Dwight D. Eisenhower (standing in car), Commander of the Allied Forces in Europe, on his return home after WWII. At least four million New Yorkers participated in this historic reception. June 19, 1945

---

32. Hiroshima was one of the few relatively undamaged cities remaining on the Japanese mainland islands.

33. There were no more atomic bombs ready in the American arsenal after the one dropped on Nagasaki and it would have taken considerable time to prepare another one. The Japanese were unaware of this. Whether knowledge of this fact would have changed Emperor Hirohito's decision to surrender is a moot point.

people immediately and many tens of thousands more over time — forced the Emperor of Japan to overrule his warlords and surrender.

World War II was at an end, but much of the world was in ruins. The Jewish world was particularly devastated, disheartened and distressed.

A NUMBER OF SIGNIFICANT CHANGES WERE OCCURRING WITHIN American Jewry during the war years. The growth of the Conservative movement was slowed because of the focus on the war effort, but it would experience phenomenal growth in the immediate postwar decades. Jewish neighborhoods in the major cities — New York, Boston, Chicago, Detroit and Los Angeles, to name a few — were stable during the war years because of the lack of new or alternative domestic housing. But the subsequent migration of millions of Southern Blacks to work in the war factories of major Northern cities and industrial centers put pressure on the Jewish neighborhoods. After the war, when housing, especially suburban housing, became available, the Jews fled from their old neighborhoods to these new, more comfortable surroundings.

Orthodoxy would suffer greatly from this migration. The old societal bond to the Orthodox synagogue of one's parents and grandparents was broken permanently. Synagogues that were within easy walking dis-

Scattered Seeds Take Root in the United States

tance of densely populated apartment buildings would no longer be so easily accessible on foot in suburban single-family-home tracts. The Conservative movement, whose constituents could drive to the synagogue on the Sabbath without guilt, would be the main beneficiary of this social upheaval. In general, ritual and observance of tradition played a much smaller role in the non-Orthodox world. As such, Conservative and Reform were deemed more "American" than Orthodoxy.[34]

At the same time, a number of new significant personalities emerged in American Orthodox life. In 1941, after the death of Rabbi Dr. Bernard Revel, Rabbi Dr. Samuel Belkin became the head of Rabbi Isaac Elchanan Theological Seminary and Yeshiva College. A product of the famous Lithuanian yeshivos, Belkin had arrived in America in 1929 and obtained a doctorate from Brown University in Providence, Rhode Island. His reputation for scholarship became widely recognized. Under his leadership, Yeshiva College would become Yeshiva University. It would eventually house graduate schools, a medical school and a law school, all under Orthodox Jewish auspices. Rabbi Dr. Belkin was a man of vision, a skilled fundraiser and a shrewd judge of educational and administrative talent. In that same year of 1941, Rabbi Dr. Joseph B. Soloveitchik was appointed as the new *rosh yeshivah*, in fact, if not in title, of Rabbi Isaac Elchanan Theological Seminary, after the death of his father, Rabbi Moshe Soloveitchik. He retained his rabbinic position in Boston, but he spent most of his week at RIETS, teaching Talmud in his extraordinary fashion. Over the decades, he dazzled thousands of students with his knowledge and personality. He soon became the clearly recognized leader of "Modern Orthodoxy" in America and his influence spread far past the confines of his classroom. Other prominent European Torah scholars. including the *Suvalker Rav* Rabbi Dovid Lifschitz and Rabbi Mendel Zaks, son-in-law of the Chafetz Chaim, among others, also found themselves at RIETS under Dr. Belkin's protective wing.

A number of illustrious Eastern European *roshei yeshivah* were able to escape and find asylum in America just before America's entry into the war. These scholars had a profound influence on the development of Orthodox Jewish life in America. They were determined to reconstruct Torah life in America as it had existed in Eastern Europe, rather than support Modern Orthodoxy as a substitute for the intensive Jewish life they had known. They were devoted to the cause of rebuilding their lives and institutions, albeit on what they had previously considered the hostile soil of America.

---

34. Herman Wouk, in his novel *Marjorie Morningstar*, presents an accurate, if sometimes withering, portrayal of American Jewry and its social mores immediately after World War II.

Rabbi Aharon Kotler

Rabbi Aharon Kotler was the strongest force among them. Previously a *rosh yeshivah* in Kletzk, Poland, he and Rabbi Avraham Kalmanowitz spearheaded the work of the Vaad Hatzala. His yeshivah in Lakewood, New Jersey, initially was small in numbers, but it represented a dramatic change in American Orthodoxy. It allowed for no secular studies and demanded the same curriculum and devotion of time and effort from its students that had previously existed in Europe. It eventually became the largest yeshivah in the United States, with thousands of students. Rabbi Kotler's influence on all sections of Orthodox Jewry was enormous. He was the driving force behind the expansion of the Chinuch Atzmai school system in *Eretz Yisrael*. He was the ultimate decision-maker for Torah U'mesorah in America and tirelessly campaigned for the day school movement.

Rabbis Eliyahu Meir Bloch and Chaim Mordechai Katz founded the Telshe Yeshiva in Cleveland, Ohio in 1941. In spite of initial community apathy and the overt opposition of some Jewish leaders in the community, the Telshe Yeshiva took root and thrived. In Baltimore, the Talmudic Academy Chofetz Chaim, under the leadership of Rabbi Chaim E. Samson, also succeeded in establishing itself in what had previously been thought to be a hostile environment. Talmudic Academy was soon joined in Baltimore by Ner Israel Rabbinical College, under the direction of Rabbi Yaakov Yitzchok Ruderman. This yeshivah, which was a successor

Student of Yeshivah Chofetz Chaim in Baltimore with Rabbi Samson, rosh yeshivah, c.1941

institution to previously unsuccessful yeshivos in New Haven, Connecticut and Cleveland, Ohio, would grow into an important bulwark of Torah learning in America.

In Brooklyn, Rabbi Kalmanowitz reestablished the Mirrer Yeshiva, with Rabbi Mordechai Ginsberg as the *rosh yeshivah,* and they built it into a much larger institution (in numbers) than it had been in Europe. (The Mirrer Yeshiva in Jerusalem was established by Rabbi Eliezer Yehuda Finkel upon his arrival there from Vilna during the war.) Rabbi Shraga Feivel Mendlowitz founded Beis Medrash Elyon in Monsey, New York as a post-graduate and *kollel* branch of Mesivta Torah Vodaath. This school was a parallel institution to Rabbi Kotler's yeshivah in Lakewood. It was headed by Rabbi Reuven Grozovsky, formerly of Kaminetz Yeshivah in Poland, the son-in-law of the famed Rabbi Baruch Ber Leibowitz, *rosh yeshivah* of Kaminetz. Rabbi Yosef Yitzchok Schneerson, the sixth Lubavitcher Rebbe, established the world headquarters of Chabad in Brooklyn upon his arrival in America at the beginning of the decade.

Rabbi Reuven Grozovsky

An important yeshivah was also established in the small, out-of-the-way English town of Gateshead. Rabbi Eliyahu Eliezer Dessler and the two great "lions," the brothers-in-law Rabbis Aryeh Leib Gurewitz and Aryeh Leib Lopian, nurtured their yeshivah into the leading yeshivah in Western Europe. Strictly Lithuanian in style and outlook, it nonetheless has a strong influence on Anglo Jewry and produced many of its rabbis and rabbinical judges.

When a raging forest fire consumes the standing trees, seeds from those destroyed trees are left on the ground and from those scattered seeds the forest regenerates itself. So too did the fire destroying Eastern European Jewish life spare a few eminent people who would devote themselves to rebuilding the lost world of the Eastern European yeshivos and Chasidic courts on American and Western European ground.

Rabbi Eliyahu Eliezer Dessler

Chapter Six

The Jewish State

1946-1950

T THE END OF WORLD WAR II, THE JEWISH PEOPLE WERE AT THEIR lowest ebb since the destruction of the Second Temple in Jerusalem. The European heartland of Ashkenazic Jewry, where it had resided for a millenium, was now one vast Jewish graveyard. Though precise numbers regarding the victims of the Holocaust are impossible to ascertain, the murder of approximately six million Jews has been widely accepted, and it is known that another half million were left homeless, stateless and traumatized by their experiences.

The Allies initiated a public war crimes trial against 22 leading German Nazis[1] in Nuremberg which conclusively demonstrated the guilt of the German regime. Even though the German general staff was not itself found guilty of war crimes, it was shown "that the leadership was more than a gaggle of tactical geniuses, and that many of its most admired

---

1. Hitler, Goebbels, Himmler and other Nazis escaped trial and execution for their war crimes by committing suicide at the end of the war. Hermann Goering, who was tried at Nuremberg and sentenced to die, foiled his captors by killing himself in his prison cell with a smuggled cyanide pill before his scheduled execution. Many Nazis, including Dr. Josef Mengele and Adolf Eichmann, escaped to South America where they found easy refuge, and others found refuge in Syria. Eichmann was later captured, stood trial in Israel and was executed.

Nazi defendants at the Nuremberg Trials. Seen in the defendants' box are (second row, right to left): Julius Streicher (standing), Wilhelm Frick, Hans Frank (third row): Albert Speer, Franz von Papen, Alfred Jodl

commanders had been waist-deep in war crimes."[2] Similar war crimes trials were held throughout Europe; and the worst criminals were hanged while lesser lights were sentenced to prison terms.[3] Hundreds of camp guards and other brutes were killed summarily by their former wards when the German army retreated from the camps and occupied territories.

But all of this was of little comfort to the surviving Jews who had nowhere to go. Revenge can only bring temporary satisfaction. Only a home, a purpose, a future, can bring comfort that is more permanent.

Help for refugees organized by American yeshivah students

The surviving Jews wandered over the face of Europe seeking refuge and a chance to rebuild their shattered lives. They were offered little encouragement by the Europeans, for Europe generally was in shambles and the devastation in many places was complete. Jews attempting to return to their former homes in Poland were met with open and vicious anti-Semitism. "They didn't finish you off yet?" and "You're still alive?" were the greetings they received from their former neighbors in Poland.

---

2. Martin Gilbert, *A History of the Twentieth Century*, New York, 1998, Vol. 2, p.721.

3. Most of the prison sentences were later commuted or substantially shortened. Rudolf Hess, the erstwhile number two man in the Nazi hierarchy, had the distinction of serving out his full life sentence, due to a Russian refusal to pardon him.

Vaad Hatzala poster

In Kielce in early 1946, a heinous pogrom killed 46 Jews, four of them teenagers and two others mere children. The news of the Kielce pogrom spread quickly throughout Poland. A very short time thereafter, almost all of the Jews fled Poland.

Anti-Semitism also was quite prevalent in the Baltic states, which were dominated by and virtually annexed to the Soviet Union, but the communist authorities refused to allow pogroms to take place on their watch, allowing some Jews to return to Vilna, Kaunas, Riga and other smaller Baltic states cities. Eventually, Poland came under the control of the Soviet Union through the Communist Party of Poland and thanks to a large Russian army that was stationed on Polish soil. The Communists "won" a sham election in Poland and for the next 35 years, Poland was under complete Russian domination. Though there were very few Jews living in Poland immediately after World War II,[4] there was a dispro-portionate number of Jews in the Communist Party leadership and governmental apparatus in postwar Poland. This fact only increased the inbred hatred of Jews carried by most of the Polish populace, which resented Russian rule and communist ideology.

For a brief period after the war, Jews were allowed to leave the Soviet Union and head west into Europe. This was especially true for Polish, Lithuanian and Russian Jews who were exiled into central and Asiatic Russia during the war. The Displaced Persons Camps set up by the Western Allies after the war to house the stateless and homeless survivors of Hitler's ravages soon were filled to overflowing. The living conditions within the camps deteriorated rapidly: Sickness and depression haunted the inhabitants. In both the British and American sectors of occupied Germany and Austria where DP camps were located, the initial sympathy for the Jews soon waned and bureaucratic anti-Semitism took its place. Claiming that the inmates were disease-ridden, American General George S. Patton ordered the camps sealed and guarded, and they began to resemble the German concentration camps of the Holocaust. General Eisenhower eventually countermanded Patton's orders, but the psychological damage

4. In 1946, there were approximately 25,000 Jews on Polish soil, the remnants of a prewar Polish Jewish population of over 3,500,000.

In a Displaced Persons camp in Austria

Teaching Torah in Paris, 1947

inflicted on the depressed inmates was already quite significant. It was obvious that the vast majority of Jewish inmates of the DP camps wanted to leave European soil as soon as possible and embark for Palestine. World Jewry mobilized for this struggle.

The Battle for Immigration to Palestine

WHEN ERNEST BEVIN BECAME FOREIGN MINISTER OF BRITAIN IN mid-1945, he immediately repudiated the prewar, pre-White Paper British policy that allowed for the immigration of 18,000 Jews per year into Palestine. Britain now clamped a tight lid on Palestine, forbidding anything but token Jewish immigration.[5] President Truman had

---

5. In the summer of 1946, England granted immigration certificates to 400 Jewish teenagers, survivors of the concentration camps.

requested that Britain allow 100,000 refugee Jews into Palestine. In refusing this "impertinent" request, Bevin snorted: "That is because he does not want too many of them in New York!"[6]

The *yishuv* organized a far-flung operation named *Brichah* ("Escape") which attempted to smuggle tens of thousands of "illegals" into the country. In the early months of Operation *Brichah* in the summer of 1946, more than 4,000 illegal immigrants succeeded in reaching Palestine. Success was short-lived, for the British soon committed overwhelming force to the prevention of any further mass-scale illegal immigration. There were now over 80,000 British troops in Palestine and the bulk of the Mediterranean Fleet of the Royal Navy was committed to the blockade of Palestine. The *Brichah* operation had the clandestine support of the French and Italian governments, out of a combination of sympathy for the Jews and bitter antipathy towards Britain. England created vast detention camps in Cyprus for the "illegals" who were caught in their blockade's dragnet, and by the middle of 1947 more than 50,000 Jews were confined in them. The living conditions in the camps were appalling.

In 1946, under pressure from President Truman, an Anglo-American Committee of Inquiry was established to deal with the problem of the Jewish refugees in the DP camps. The committee's report confirmed that the only logical solution to the problem was to allow them to go to Palestine. Great Britian adamantly refused to cooperate with such a plan.

Another facet of the Anglo-American report was that Palestine should remain under British trusteeship, but with separate Jewish and Arab sections in the country. This plan would necessitate a transfer of populations, since Jew and Arab lived in close proximity to each other in Palestine. The Jewish section would comprise only 17% of the country's area. England then agreed that 100,000 Jews would be allowed to come into the country, but only over a five-year period. All later Jewish immigration would remain under the control of the British.

The plan was staunchly rejected by the Zionist leadership and even more vehemently by the Arabs. The Arab stance was unyielding: There could be no Jewish autonomy, let alone a Jewish state, anywhere on the soil of Palestine. Throughout late 1946 and early 1947, England attempted to find some type of settlement that would preserve British interests in the area and mollify both the Jews and the Arabs. This proved impossible and in February 1947, Bevin finally gave up, declaring that England was

---

6. The outrage against Bevin at this remark was not confined to Jews. The stevedores at the Port of New York refused to load Bevin's baggage on board the ship that he was then taking to return to London. Howard M. Sachar, *A History of Israel*, New York, 1996, p.264.

transferring the problem of Palestine to the United Nations for a solution. British foreign policy makers hoped that the United Nations would decide that Palestine should remain under British control and that whatever compromise the UN formulated would be under the trusteeship of Britain.

Chief Rabbis Yitzchak Herzog and Meir Uziel visit Jerusalem during the tense years of the British Mandate

All of this diplomatic maneuvering was taking place in the midst of a bloody guerrilla war that Lechi, Etzel and sometimes Haganah were conducting against the British forces in Palestine. Bombings, ambushes, killings and retaliatory murders were now daily events. Arab terrorism was also on the rise. The *Palestine Post* (now *Jerusalem Post*) building in the center of Jerusalem's commercial district was blown up by the Arabs, as well as a wing of the Jewish Agency's main headquarters in the heart of western Jerusalem. A section of the King David Hotel housing the British governmental authority's offices was blown up by Etzel, killing more than 90 people, some of them Jews. Etzel had warned the British to evacuate the building, but the warning was ignored. The British blockaded a large section of central Jerusalem's streets to prevent further attacks.[7] They also arrested almost all of the Jewish leaders of the *yishuv* (with the exception of David Ben-Gurion, who was out of the country) on Saturday, June 29, 1946 — later known as "Black Sabbath." Many of the Jewish fighters and leaders arrested were deported to Central Africa. The bitter Jewish assessment of British policies was reflected in Chaim Weizmann's terse statement: "The Mufti — the murderer — in an Egyptian palace; the Jews behind barbed wire in Palestine."[8]

---

7. The Jews promptly named the blockaded area Bevingrad.
8. Quoted by Carl Herman Voss, *Servant of the People*, Philadelphia, 1969, p.274.

David Ben-Gurion and the official leaders of the *yishuv* condemned and disassociated themselves from what they considered to be the excessive and almost random violence of Lechi and Etzel. Menachem Begin,[9] the leader of Etzel, was not easily cowed, not by the British nor by Ben-Gurion. The military blows struck against the British forces in Palestine undoubtedly contributed to Bevin's decision to extricate Britain from this mire by referring Palestine and its problems to the United Nations. England made some conciliatory gestures to the Zionists, such as releasing the leaders of the movement who were arrested on Black Sabbath. But the Zionist leadership had had enough of British promises and rule. Ben-Gurion was now determined to press for the establishment of a Jewish state in Palestine. There were many Jews who were opposed to such a radical step,[10] but Ben-Gurion's determination would eventually carry the day.

FOLLOWING WORLD WAR II, THE WESTERN ALLIES WERE CONFRONTED with an expansionist, aggressive Soviet foreign policy. An enormous Russian army, flushed with its total victory over Germany, backed this policy. By 1948, the Soviet Union had annexed the Baltic states of Lithuania, Latvia and Estonia and made them "republics" within the Soviet Union. It also moved the prewar border between Poland and Russia hundreds of kilometers west. It compensated Poland for the loss of its eastern territories by similarly moving the prewar Polish-German border hundreds of kilometers west. Prussia, the seat of German militarism and strength for 150 years, disappeared from the map of Europe. Poland, Hungary, Rumania, Czechoslovakia, Yugoslavia, Bulgaria and Albania became communist countries and obedient satellites of the Soviet Union in domestic and foreign affairs. Russia also controlled a third of Germany, which it kept under its occupation, installing a ruthless communist government. In the immortal words of Winston Churchill's speech in Fulton, Missouri in 1946, an "iron curtain" had descended, dividing Europe in two.

Rare Circumstances Bolster the Zionist Cause

---

9. Begin was able to escape the British search for him by disguising himself as a *kollel* student, "Rabbi Sossover," and living a religious lifestyle in a religious neighborhood in which he hid. It was his tradional upbringing in Poland that allowed him to assume this cover identity and carry it flawlessly.

10. Practical opposition came from Ben-Gurion's own colleagues in the Jewish Agency who were justifiably fearful that a fledgling Jewish state would be overwhelmed by Arabs who would undoubtly attempt to crush it at birth. The philosophical opposition to a Jewish state came from the Hebrew University intellectuals, Dr. Judah Magnes, Martin Buber, Yeshayahu Leibowitz, Gershom Scholem and others. They felt that a Jewish state would be an unjustified and unnecessary excursion of the Jewish people into nationalism, whereas Jewish talent should instead be directed into more intellectual pursuits and universalistic goals.

Stalin's paranoia of the West locked the people dwelling in the Soviet sphere in an enormous prison. Any contact with the West, no matter how innocent or understandable, could be fatal. The Jews of Eastern Europe who had survived the war in the Soviet Union rapidly were becoming isolated from their brethren outside the Soviet Union.

The Cold War between the United States and the Soviet Union had begun. Stalin underestimated Truman's pluck and determination. Like Hitler, Stalin scornfully thought the democracies innately soft. Yet, to his vast discomfort, the "Truman Doctrine" saved Iran, Greece and Turkey from Soviet domination in 1947. The Marshall Plan of American foreign aid funds, food and material goods saved Western Europe from starvation, bankruptcy and communism. America developed a foreign policy based on the "containment" of the Soviet Union and communism. As the United States was the only nuclear power in the world at the onset of the Cold War, it had a decided military edge over the Soviet Union. But Stalin played his hand boldly and constantly probed to increase Soviet influence anywhere he could. One of the aims of Soviet foreign policy was to oust Britain from the Middle East, thus creating a vacuum that Russia would fill. The fact that England was now withdrawing from India and from most of its other colonial possessions, and that these emerging countries would be independent of their previous Western masters, persuaded Stalin that there would be no one capable of contesting Soviet ambitions in the Middle East once England withdrew. Stalin also believed that the Jewish communists in Palestine

Emir (King) Abdullah (center) and British High Commissioner Cunningham end their meeting at "Government House" in Jerusalem, May 6, 1947

would be able to dominate any Jewish or bi-national state that would be formed there.[11] Thus, in 1947, the Soviet Union supported the idea of the termination of the British Mandate and the creation of a Jewish state in Palestine. This window of Soviet support for a Jewish state would be open only for a short time.

Under intense Zionist lobbying pressure in America, President Truman was coming to the conclusion that the creation of a Jewish state

11. Meir Wilner-Kovner, the head of the Communist Party in the *yishuv*, signed the Israeli Declaration of Independence.

After Israel was established as a state, President Truman (right) was presented with a Torah by Israeli Ambassador Eliyahu Elath, in the name of Chaim Weizmann.

was a necessary solution to the problem of Jewish refugees in Europe. The State Department, under the direction of Secretary of State George Marshall, objected strongly to the creation of a Jewish state. At one point, Marshall threatened to resign and publicly campaign against Truman in the coming 1948 elections over this issue. James Forrestal, Truman's Secretary of Defense, also was a bitter foe of Zionist aspirations. Balancing Marshall and Forrestal were members of the President's inner circle, led by Clark Clifford, who wholeheartedly backed the idea of a Jewish state. As Truman wavered between the varying assessments of his advisors, he grew testy and annoyed with the pressure placed on him by American Zionists. He refused the aged, ailing and almost blind Chaim Weizmann's request for an appointment to talk with him about the matter. The Zionists, desperate and despairing of Truman's support if Weizmann did not visit with him, arranged to have Truman's former partner in a failed haberdashery store venture, Eddie Jacobson, intercede with Truman on Weizmann's behalf. Truman, loyal to a friend to a fault, berated Jacobson for raising the issue but nevertheless granted Weizmann the desired interview. By the end of their talk, Weizmann had obtained Truman's commitment to support the creation of a Jewish state in Palestine, and Truman never went back on his word to him.

After months of hearings, the special United Nations committee dealing with the Palestine issue recommended that the country be partitioned between the Jews and the Arabs, each of whom would establish separate independent states on their territories. England was to leave the country permanently. The partition map drawn by the UN was hardly favorable to the Jews, giving them a disjointed, sometimes unconnected, gerrymandered country. It also separated Jerusalem territorially from the rest of the Jewish state and placed it under UN international trusteeship. Yet, in spite of these drawbacks and disappointments, the Zionists quickly agreed to the UN plan. The Arabs, on the other hand, totally rejected the committee's recommendations and announced that partition meant war and that they would "push the Jews into the sea." The partition plan had to be ratified by a two-thirds vote of approval of the UN General Assembly. Due to constantly shifting policies in the State Department, the American delegation wavered in its support of the partition plan. Truman overruled them and personally lobbied a number of undecided countries to vote for the partition resolution.

In a rare measure of Soviet-American cooperation, the resolution for the partition of Palestine and the establishment of a Jewish state therein was passed on November 29, 1947 by a vote of 33 to 13. The world powers declared a Jewish State in Palestine to be legitimate. Herzl's 50-year-old statement that "at Basel (the meeting place of the first Zionist Congress in 1897) I founded the Jewish State. It will take 50 years for it to become a reality" proved eerily accurate.

A State Born in Blood

WHILE MOST OF THE JEWISH WORLD REJOICED AT THE RESULT OF the United Nations vote,[12] the Arabs immediately began their war against the *yishuv*. The British were particularly stung by the UN's insistence that they leave the country. They now hoped that the Arabs would have initial success in their attempt to drive the Jews into the sea: The Zionists would have no choice but to beg the British to return and save the Jews from annihilation. The condition for such British help would then be a final pledge by the Zionists to relinquish their claim to a Jewish State in Palestine. In line with this policy, the British openly sided with the Arabs in their fight against the Jews. British arms were supplied to the Arabs, while Jewish arms caches were confiscated. Many deserters from the British Army joined the Arab forces. Britain first stated that it would leave Palestine at the end of August 1948. As the fighting began to take an unexpected turn against the Arab irregulars, England moved up the date of its departure to one minute to midnight, April 14, 1948, confident that the neighboring Arab armies would invade and overwhelm the Jews before they could consolidate their gains.

---

12. I vividly remember the joy and the tears that were part of the morning prayer service in the yeshivah I attended that next morning, November 30, 1947.

The Western Wall in Jerusalem's Old City prior to Jewish defeat and evacuation of the city

The five months between the passage of the UN resolution and the declaration of the Jewish State were tense, painful and bloody. England's embargo against Jewish immigration and Jewish arms continued unabated, while a large number of Arab infiltrators from Jordan, Syria, Egypt and Lebanon entered the country without any British attempt to stop them. British forts, army installations and military camps were turned over to the Arab fighters. The Jewish city of Jerusalem was cut off from the rest of the *yishuv* by the Arab blockade of the Jerusalem-Tel Aviv road, and Jewish settlements in the Galilee were under attack and siege. The Jewish Quarter of the Old City of Jerusalem was besieged, bombarded, and after a fierce struggle, would eventually fall to the Arabs.[13] Meanwhile, the British stood by and never interfered with the Arab attacks.

Arab violence against Jews was not limited to Palestine. In Aleppo, Syria, hundreds of Jewish homes, eleven synagogues and many Jewish stores were looted and burned.[14] Half of its Jewish population immediately fled from this city that had been home to a Jewish community for a millennium.[15] The rest would leave within a decade. In Yemen and Aden, Jews were slaughtered in Arab rioting. It was now obvious that the creation of a Jewish state in Palestine would trigger a mass exodus of vast numbers of Jews living in the Moslem countries of the Middle East and the Mediterranean basin.

Arab disunity in Palestine was a boon to the Jewish population. Arab forces were badly led and subject to the bitter political and traditional personal rivalries of the powerful families in the country. The Mufti's family, the Husseinis, warred with the Nashashibi clan. To counteract the Mufti's control of the Arab fighters, an "Arab Liberation Army" was created by the Arab League, meeting in Lebanon in the fall of 1947. As a result, thousands of volunteers, seeking easy victory and spoils, were infiltrated into Palestine via Syria. Fawzi el-Kawukji, who led the Arab rioting in 1936 against the Jews, was appointed field commander of this force. Kawukji established his headquarters in Tiberias and soon had 7,000 men under his command. His goal was to drive the Jews out of the Galilee and all of northern Palestine. His allies in this struggle were to be the Lebanese and Syrian armies which were then poised to invade Palestine the instant the British left. Kawukji boasted that he needed no outside help and that his forces would make short work of the Jews.

---

13. This would not happen until the end of May 1948. For an outstanding pictorial record of the fall of the Jewish Quarter and the subsequent Arab looting and destruction of the Quarter and its 40 synagogues, see *A Will to Survive* by photojournalist John Phillips, Dial Press, New York, 1976.
14. The famed *Aleppo Codex*, the oldest existing masoretic text of the Bible, a text from which Maimonides himself had copied his own text of the Torah, was severely damaged and parts of it lost forever in the Arab riots.
15. Sachar, p.298.

The Mufti's nephew, Abdel Kadar el-Husseini, commanded the Arab forces that sealed off Jerusalem from the Jewish coastline. Very few Jewish convoys made it through to Jerusalem in that dark spring of 1948. The city was without electricity and running water. Canned water and food, medicine and other necessary supplies were all rationed and in very short supply. Fighting took place on the borders between Arab and Jewish neighborhoods in all parts of Jerusalem.

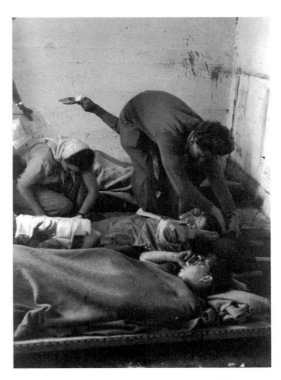

The Moslem Brotherhood, mostly fanatical Islamic volunteers from Egypt, fought in the Hebron hills and in the Negev. The Arab forces, with the cooperation of the British, dominated the roads of the country, isolating most Jewish settlements in the Galilee, Beit Shan Valley, Hebron hills and the Negev. Somehow, they grimly held on and turned back the repeated Arab attacks. Only the Etzion Bloc of settlements in the Hebron hills and the Revisionist kibbutz, Mishmar HaYarden on the Syrian border, fell to the Arab attackers.

The disparate Arab armies refused to cooperate with each other, sharing neither plans nor weapons with one another. Kawukji openly scorned Husseini and all Palestinian forces, saying that "for military operations they simply get in the way."[16] The Arab forces suffered a damaging blow to their morale in April 1948 when Husseini was killed in the battle for Kastel, a height commanding the Jerusalem road. The Arabs tem-

Nurses treating Haganah members wounded during the fighting in Jerusalem

porarily abandoned the position to attend Husseini's funeral in Jerusalem; and for a number of days, large Jewish convoys of food, water, medicine and arms reached Jerusalem. However, the Arabs were able to recapture Kastel shortly thereafter and the siege of Jerusalem was reimposed.

The Arabs sustained a further defeat in April when Jewish forces overran the port city of Haifa. Almost all of its Arab population — about half the

A Jewish convoy leaving Mt. Scopus

16. Ibid. p.306.

Wooden huts in a ma'abarah near Tel Aviv, put up for families displaced during the fighting in Tel Aviv-Jaffa

city population of 150,000 people — fled to Lebanon and other Arab countries. In early May, Jewish forces under the command of Yigal Allon attempted to capture Safed, the key position in the Upper Galilee. Although the Arabs numbered 10,000 fighters and Allon had only 1,400 soldiers under his command, the Arabs became demoralized and fled.[17] Most of the Arabs living in the Upper Galilee left for Lebanon and Syria.

A combined Etzel and Haganah offensive captured the Arab city of Jaffa adjacent to Tel Aviv. Southern Tel Aviv had been shelled repeatedly from gun emplacements placed in the minarets of mosques in Jaffa. The capture of Jaffa by the Jews drove another 70,000 Arabs into flight towards the Gaza Strip and Egypt. The borders of the new Jewish state were now emerging, not from UN resolutions, but from the bloody battles between Jew and Arab.

A great deal has been made of the flight of the Palestinian Arabs from their homes during the war of 1948. It gave the Arabs their greatest propaganda victory and allowed the world to forget that it was the Arabs who fomented the war that created these refugees. Their fate has remained a contentious issue for more than 50 years after the fact. No exact numbers

---

17. It was in the battle for Safed that the famous legend of the "Davidka" was born. The "Davidka" was a homemade mortar that made much more noise and flash than any real military damage that it could inflict. During the battle for Safed, a rare thundershower occurred and the "Davidka" was fired at regular intervals by the Jewish fighters. The Arabs panicked, some even fearing an atomic bomb attack, and the panic turned into a rout. The "Davidka" was also employed by the Jews in the battle for Jerusalem. There too, it served as a great psychological warfare weapon. There are monuments to the "Davidka" in prominent city squares in both Safed and Jerusalem.

Galilee Arabs leaving their villages

can be given to the number of Arab refugees from Palestine, though there were undoubtedly hundreds of thousands who fled Jewish-controlled territory. It has long been claimed by Israel that the Arabs were encouraged, and even ordered, to leave the areas of Jewish Palestine by their own leaders in order to provide the Arab armies freedom of action against the Jews.[18] The Arabs were promised loot and plunder, homes and possessions, when they would return in a few months after the expected military victory over the Jews. The Arabs claim that the Jews drove them from their homes and would not allow them to remain in their residences. As recorded in the memoirs of David Ben-Gurion in April of 1948, the Jewish leadership literally begged Arab residents to remain in Haifa and in many other areas of Palestine, but that the Arab League (and the Grand Mufti) at that time forbade Arabs to remain in territory where they would have to submit to Jewish rule. As the Arab flight turned from a trickle into a flood, however, the Arab High Command reversed itself and demanded that the Arabs now remain wherever they lived. But it was too late to stop the

18. There never has been any hard evidence advanced for or against this statement. There has been much anecdotal evidence to support the claim that the Arabs wanted their kinsmen to leave for military operational reasons, but there are no records of Arab orders or correspondence to that effect. For many years, this idea was taken for granted in Israeli society as true, though lately it has come into question.

panic. The leadership infrastructure and wealthy upper class of Palestinian Arab society had left the country. There was no person or institution left to guide the bewildered Arab community, and they ran away. Since the Arabs loudly proclaimed that they were bent on a "war of extermination" against the Jews, the Arab populace assumed that this would be the type of war waged by the Jews against them. Tales of Jewish reprisals against Arab villages, many of them exaggerated if not completely fanciful,[19] spread panic among the Arabs. All of these factors combined to create what soon would be called the "Palestinian refugee problem."

Israel Fights for Survival

ON MAY 14, 1948, THE FIFTH DAY OF IYAR 5708, A FEW HOURS before the Sabbath, David Ben-Gurion read the Declaration of Independence creating the State of Israel. It was Ben-Gurion above anyone else who had forced the issue. The executive committee of the Jewish Agency ratified Ben-Gurion's decision to announce the formation of the new state, but by a bare majority of six to four. It was Ben-Gurion's iron will that overcame the hesitations of his colleagues and the determined opposition of the intellectual elite in Israel who felt that declaring the independent State of Israel was a military, political and moral wrong.[20] An electric feeling passed through the entire Jewish people on that Friday afternoon. Jews wept openly on the streets of New York, London, Chicago, Sydney, Johannesburg and in the DP camps of Europe and Cyprus. A historic moment had occurred.[21]

That night, Egyptian bombers attacked Tel Aviv. Army units of Jordan, Egypt, Iraq, Syria, Lebanon and Saudi Arabia invaded the Land of Israel. The war for the survival of the State of Israel began in full force. The Jews were outnumbered and outgunned, but the Arab attacks were uncoordinated and the rivalries between the Arab leaders and armies weakened the ability of the Arabs to mount a truly effective attack. Nevertheless, the fighting was fierce and costly. More than 6,000 Jews — one percent of the entire population of the *yishuv* — were killed

---

19. The prime example of Jewish action against Arab civilians was the attack of Etzel and Lechi on the Arab village of Deir Yassin near Jerusalem. Over 200 Arab men, women and children were killed in the action. The attackers claimed that they were fired upon from civilian houses and that they thought the women and children had been evacuated. However, the Haganah and the Zionist leadership of the *yishuv* condemned the attack and arrested the commanders of the forces responsible for it. In the psyches of the Palestinian Arabs, the name Deir Yassin invoked panic, then bitterness and finally a need for revenge.

20. For a thorough review of this viewpoint, see Yoram Hazoni, *The Jewish State*, New York, 2000.

21. The headline in *Hamodia*, the newspaper of Agudath Israel on Sunday, May 16 was: "*Baruch Shecheyanu V'kiyamanu V'higianu lazman hazeh*" – Blessed be He Who has allowed us to live and preserved us to reach this time!

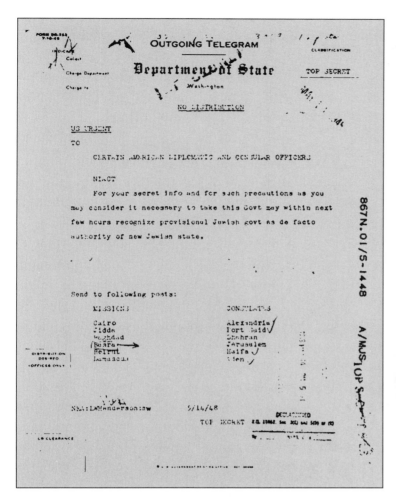

Top secret State Department memo of May 14 advising personnel in Middle Eastern offices that the United States would shortly recognize the Jewish government of Israel

David Ben-Gurion sitting below the portrait of Theodor Herzl just before reading the Declaration of Independence. Behind him at left is Rabbi Y. L. Fishman (Maimon)

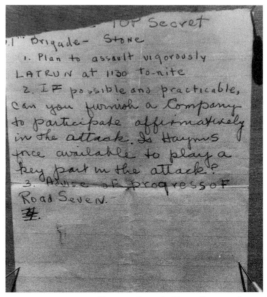

Operational directives written by American military volunteer Colonel Mickey Marcus.

in the war. Many newly arrived Jewish refugees were rushed into the fighting and died in the raging battles, after being in the country for only a few short days.

The Egyptian army reached Kibbutz Ramat Rachel on the southern outskirts of Jerusalem. Its patrols also came within sixteen miles of Tel Aviv on the coastal road. The Arab Legion of Jordan captured the entire Old City of Jerusalem as well as the Mount of Olives and all of eastern Jerusalem and the surrounding villages. The Jews were unable to break the Arab grip on the Tel Aviv-Jerusalem highway despite repeated attempts to dislodge the Arab Legion from the British police fort at Latrun, the point of the highway bottleneck.

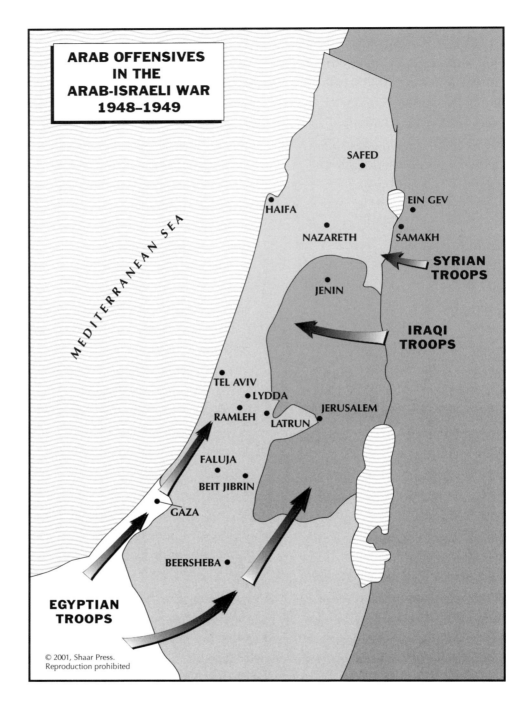

ARAB OFFENSIVES
IN THE
ARAB-ISRAELI WAR
1948–1949

SAFED

EIN GEV

HAIFA

NAZARETH

SAMAKH

SYRIAN TROOPS

JENIN

IRAQI TROOPS

MEDITERRANEAN SEA

TEL AVIV

LYDDA

RAMLEH

LATRUN

JERUSALEM

FALUJA

BEIT JIBRIN

GAZA

BEERSHEBA

EGYPTIAN
TROOPS

Despite these early Arab successes, the battle was slowly turning against them. There were few easy victories after May, and there were many casualties among their forces. The professional officers in the Arab armies were particularly bitter about their lack of success and placed the blame on the government corruption and mismanagement of the Arab countries engaged in the war against Israel. This attitude would lead to immediate consequences in the Arab world after the war ended.

The Jewish leadership was able to circumvent the arms embargo placed by Great Britain and the United States by purchasing weapons from Czechoslovakia. In April of 1948, ships and planes bringing in weapons, mainly purchased with the donations of American Jews, secretly arrived in Palestine, escaping the notice of the British blockade. After the State of Israel was declared, heavy weapons from Czechoslovakia, France and from independent arms dealers throughout Europe were bought and delivered to the ports of Haifa and Jaffa and to secret makeshift airports in the country.

Etzel attempted to bring in a shipload of French arms and Jewish refugees on a refitted LST vessel named *Altalena* — the pen name of Zev Jabotinsky. In June 1948, the ship attempted to dock at Tel Aviv harbor. Though Ben-Gurion had originally consented to the arms delivery, he became incensed when Etzel demanded that part of the arms shipment on board be reserved for their own militias. Desperately trying to fashion a united Jewish army, Ben-Gurion refused permission for the ship to dock under those conditions. In the ensuing melee between the Etzel officers on board the *Altalena* and the Haganah troops at the port, firing broke out. The ship caught fire, 82 people on the ship died and much of the arms cargo was lost.[22] The incident also brought about the disbanding of Etzel as an independent fighting force, because Menachem Begin refused to be drawn into a civil war. The struggle between Begin and Ben-Gurion now became a political one, but it was no less fierce and personal than it would have been under military conditions. Ben-Gurion also terminated the

The shelling and burning of Etzel's ship, "Altalena"

22. In an incident of numerous ironies, Avraham Stavsky, the Revisionist Zionist accused and later acquitted in the previous decade of the murder of Labor Zionist leader Chaim Arlosoroff, died on the *Altalena*. The young Haganah officer who led in the firing on the *Altalena* was Yitzchak Rabin.

Haganah and created the Israel Defense Forces which would operate under the direct control of the Minister of Defense — Ben-Gurion himself.

Weapons from the United States, including B-17 bombers, were also smuggled to Israel.[23] The fledgling Israeli Air Force consisted of a range of planes from Piper Cubs, German Messerchmidts and British Spitfire fighters, to American Dakota cargo planes and the aforementioned B-17 bombers. The Air Force would play a greater role in the struggle as it continued. The inflow of men, arms and planes bolstered Israel's beleaguered forces, and the Arabs, despairing of a quick victory, agreed to a temporary cease-fire in June 1948. Both sides would use the respite to prepare themselves for the next round of the struggle.

The United Nations attempted to use the cease-fire period to impose a settlement on the warring parties. It appointed a Swedish diplomat (a member of the royal family), Count Folke Bernadotte, to serve as mediator in the Arab-Israeli war. Bernadotte was active in World War II on behalf of European Jewry and other refugees and he was a well-respected person in Jewish and Western circles. He proposed a radical solution to the problem, in effect ignoring the previous UN partition plan and the facts on the ground that the war had already created. He proposed that Jordan rule over Arab Palestine, including Jerusalem; territories in the Negev and the Galilee would be exchanged between Israel and Jordan; unlimited Jewish immigration would be allowed for two years; the airport at Lydda and the seaports of Jaffa and Haifa would be internationalized; all Arab refugees would return to their original homes; and that the Jewish population in Arab sections of the country would be granted full autonomy. Bernadotte would later modify his suggestions in light of the successes of Israeli arms, but Ben-Gurion still had no interest in the plan. The Arabs, for their part, refused to even discuss the matter with him. Egypt and Syria were not interested in a settlement that enlarged Jordan and left them with nothing to show for their severe war losses.

In September 1948, Bernadotte was visiting Jerusalem to advocate his plan when he was assassinated by men dressed in the khaki uniforms of the Jewish fighters. His murderers were never found. Ben-Gurion accused Lechi of the crime and used the tragedy as justification for a vicious crackdown against Lechi, which effectively ended the group's military existence. Bernadotte's assassination earned for Israel its first taste of universal international disapproval.

---

23. Hank Greenspan, later editor and publisher of the *Las Vegas Sun* newspaper, was one of a number of American Jews who were imprisoned by the US government for participating in the smuggling of arms to Israel during its War of Independence.

After the expiration of the cease-fire, another two weeks of fighting ensued and a second cease-fire was called on July 18, 1948. Again, both sides used the cease-fire as an opportunity to prepare for further battle and not to initiate peace talks. When the fighting resumed in early August, the Israelis captured Lydda and its airport,[24] the town of Ramle, the entire upper and western Galilee, and succeeded in opening a road to Jerusalem to relieve the siege. This road, nicknamed the Burma Road, was based on an ancient Roman road known by Jewish shepherds. It was built under the noses of the Arab forces that controlled the main road at the Latrun junction. The Burma Road bypassed Latrun and rejoined the main road past Shaar Hagai in territory that had been wrested from the Arabs.

The Israeli forces attempted to enter the Old City of Jerusalem and drive the Arabs out of the Jewish Quarter, the Western Wall and Temple Mount areas, hoping to recapture the entire Old City and East Jerusalem. Although they successfully broke through the Zion Gate, the Israeli forces were unable to dislodge the Jordanian Arab Legion from its strong defensive positions and the Old City remained in Arab hands.

In August, the Israelis breached the Egyptian lines in the Negev and the 35,000 Egyptian soldiers fighting there were in danger of annihilation or entrapment. The "Faluja Pocket," as the Egyptian defense line was called, was the scene of very heavy fighting and grievous casualties on both sides. Realizing that the Egyptian forces were near total defeat, England pressed for another cease-fire and it was imposed by the United Nations in October. During this truce, the Israelis negotiated directly with the Egyptian ground commanders for the surrender of the Egyptian forces in the Faluja pocket. As a point of honor, the Arabs refused to surrender. One of the Egyptian officers taking part in the negotiations was Major Gamal Abdel Nasser. He was struck by the difference between the modern, technically advanced Israeli settlements that he visited during the negotiations and the feudal, poverty-ridden villages of rural Egypt. He became determined to someday free Egypt from the control of its corrupt and indolent ruler, King Farouk, and his equally corrupt, inefficient government, and then modernize his country.

As the Haganah was searching house to house for the enemy, this homeowner in Safed marked the door to his house as "Jewish property"

---

24. Ben-Gurion exulted: "When could we have been able to build such a fine airport as the one the British built for us?"

The Arab countries were in disarray: old loyalties and rivalries emerged. The annexation of much of Arab Palestine, including the Old City of Jerusalem, by Abdullah of Jordan was bitterly denounced by Egypt, the Arab League and the other Arab countries. The Egyptians convened an "All-Palestine Government" in Gaza and elected the Grand Mufti as its head. Lebanon, Syria and Iraq supported Egypt and the Mufti. But Abdullah had created the facts on the ground and it was his army, led by British officers,[25] that occupied the West Bank. Egypt refused to recognize the Hashemite annexations and Jordan refused to recognize the Mufti and his puppet government in Gaza. Eventually, Egypt got rid of the Mufti and took over the Gaza Strip itself.

The final portion of the War for Independence was fought in a dramatic series of battles that carried the fighting into Egyptian territory in the Sinai Desert. The Israeli forces reached El-Arish on the Mediterranean coast of Sinai and Abu Agheila in the interior of the desert peninsula. The Egyptian army was near collapse, and with it the Egyptian government. Rioting against the government and against Jews and Jewish businesses raged out of control in major Egyptian cities. It was at this moment that England intervened, demanding Jewish withdrawal from the Sinai and ominously threatening armed cooperation with Egypt in expelling Israel from there. Not wanting a confrontation with Britain, Ben-Gurion complied with the British request and withdrew from the Sinai. But the Israelis still retained the high ground that prevented the withdrawal of the Egyptian army from the trap of the Faluja Pocket, and Britain fumed about that as well. The United Nations had ordered another cease-fire, one that Israel chose to ignore in order to press its advantage against the trapped Egyptians. On January 7, 1949, four British Spitfire planes of the Royal Air Force, flying in support of the Egyptian forces, were shot down by Israeli Messerschmidts. Thereupon, England threatened to bring its forces guarding the Suez Canal to the borders of Palestine to save the trapped Egyptian forces. Against the entreaties of his generals, Ben-Gurion chose to raise the siege of the Egyptian forces and withdraw from the heights. The battered and demoralized Egyptian army in the Faluja Pocket left the soil of the Negev, returning in defeat to Egypt. By January 1949, the War for Independence was over and Israel was the surprise victor.[26]

Though very costly to Israel in terms of life and property, the war nevertheless accomplished a great deal. It gave Israel contiguous, if hardly eas-

---

25. The chief commander of the Arab Legion of Jordan was the British major, John Glubb. His book, *A Soldier Amongst the Arabs*, provides a fascinating portrait of the 1948 war as seen from the Arab side.

26. *Parade Magazine*, a Sunday supplement to many American newspapers, in its review of 1948, characterized the Israeli victory over the Arabs as "The Upset of the Year."

Chaim Weizmann takes the oath of office as President of Israel in the Jewish Agency building in Jerusalem

ily defensible borders; much more of the Land of Israel came under Jewish control than envisaged under the UN partition plan; and the flight of Arab populations opened up housing and territory for the settlement of the Jewish refugees. By March 1949, under the auspices of Dr. Ralph Bunche, the UN Middle East peace mediator, armistice agreements were signed by Israel with Lebanon, Egypt, Jordan and Syria. Iraq, which had no common border with Israel, refused to negotiate an armistice agreement.

Israel was admitted as a member of the United Nations in that same month. All of the armistice agreements stated specifically that they were preliminary agreements to the final peace agreements to be negotiated in the immediate future.

Under Arab pressure and United Nations administration, refugee camps to house the hundreds of thousands of Arabs who had fled Palestine during the war were established. These camps were located in Lebanon, the West Bank, Jordan and the Gaza Strip. The Arab nations, as a matter of policy and as a weapon against Israel, refused to assimilate their fellow Palestinian Arabs into their societies. The Arab countries, now with Russian support, pushed through a General Assembly resolution at the UN giving these refugees a "right of return" to their former homes. Israel rejected the resolution and considered it non-binding, since it never was passed by the UN Security Council.

The refugee camps received UN aid for the entire second half of the century, but because its residents for all practical purposes were unable to leave them to resume any normal life, the camps became havens for terrorists operating against Israel. The plight of the Arab refugees was constantly emphasized both by the UN and the Arabs, and it was mainly used as a political and diplomatic weapon with which to bludgeon Israel. The human tragedy of the refugees themselves was largely ignored by the UN, the Arabs and the nations of the world. Since the Arabs refused to recognize or deal with the Jewish state, Israel felt powerless to address this issue. The camps eventually became home to well over a million Arabs who were embittered by the squalor and purposelessness of life that the camps embodied.

The promised "final agreements" never happened, for the Arabs refused to accept the existence of Israel and instead used their territories for continuing unrelenting terror and war against Israel. Though perhaps not clear to the Israelis themselves, their struggle with the Arabs was not really a territorial one as much as it was an existential one. The terms of the armistice agreements were never adhered to by the Arabs. Jews were denied access to the Western Wall and the Mount of Olives by the Jordanians, in open defiance of the armistice agreement with Israel. Egypt used the Gaza Strip as a staging area for terrorist forays into Israel. Syria shelled the farmers of the eastern Galilee regularly and maliciously.

Internecine Religious Battles Set Future Agendas

ISRAEL SET ITS FACE TOWARDS BUILDING A NEW COUNTRY AMID THE realities in which it found itself. Hundreds of thousands of Jewish refugees from Europe and the Moslem countries came to Israel in its first few years of existence. On January 25, 1949, before the armistice agreements with the Arab countries were signed, the elections for the first Israeli legislature — the 120 seat Knesset — took place.[27] The election formula was based upon proportional representation in the Knesset in accordance with the percentage of the popular vote obtained in the election, with the public voting for parties and not directly for individuals. The Labor Zionists took 57 seats, the General Zionists together with Begin's Revisionists won 31 seats and the Religious Bloc captured 16 seats.[28] Ben-Gurion formed a wall-to-wall cabinet excluding only the communists and Begin's Revisionists (but not the General Zionists) from the government coalition. The Labor Zionists, especially Ben-Gurion and his Mapai party, controlled the government and the country's economy.

---

27. The name and number of members of the Israeli legislature were taken from the ancient governing body of Israel under Ezra at the beginning of the Second Temple Commonwealth. It was called the *Anshei Knesses Hagedolah,* The Men of the Great Assembly.

28. In the first election for the Knesset, all of the religious parties united in one election bloc. This act of unity was never repeated in subsequent elections.

29. The extreme Leftist Mapam party deserted Ben-Gurion because of its slavish adherence to Stalin and the Soviet Union in the Cold War confrontation with the West. Ben-Gurion opted for a pro-Western foreign policy.

Sensing that this broad coalition would not last long,[29] Ben-Gurion forged a strategic alliance with the religious parties, especially Mizrachi, to buttress his parliamentary majority and rule. Ben-Gurion was also convinced that the numbers and power of the religious parties would wane in time, as the magic of secularism and socialism would attract their young in ever-increasing numbers. He was very wrong in this assessment.[30] Perhaps because of his conviction that religion in the Jewish state would eventually give way to Labor Zionist socialist humanitarianism, Ben-Gurion was most accommodating to the religious parties. The *status quo* agreement regarding religious matters was established. In all major cities in Israel, the Sabbath was to be observed as far as businesses and public transportation were involved.[31] The Chief Rabbinate and Rabbinical Courts became part of the government structure and all matters of personal status — marriage, divorce, conversion, etc. — were governed by them. The religious school systems were to be supported by the Ministry of Education.[32] All public and governmental institutions, including the El Al national airline and the army, would serve kosher food exclusively. Exemptions and deferments from army service were granted to full-time yeshivah students.[33] Ben-Gurion later explained these concessions to the religious parties:

> *Any government leader must prescribe for himself priorities, must decide on first things first ... Where there was agreement on what was urgent to me, I was prepared to make concessions on what was urgent to others ... When I wanted to introduce national service conscription, the religious parties said they would of course support it, but they insisted that all army kitchens be kosher. Kosher kitchens to them were of paramount importance; to me they were of subsidiary interest. It was a price I was prepared to pay for their full-fledged support on a vital defense measure ... In the same way I agreed not to change the*

---

30. In the last elections for the Knesset at the end of the century, the religious parties won 27 seats and six other religious Jews were members of Knesset as well.

31. Haifa, which was half Arab before the war and a stronghold of the Jewish Left, continued to allow public transportation on the Sabbath, as it had before the war.

32. The Mizrachi school system was named Mamlachti Dati (governmental religious schools) and was an integral yet separate part of the general public school system. The Agudath Israel school system was established outside of the general public school system. It was called Chinuch Atzmai (independent school system) and originally received only a percentage of its budget from the government, the balance of the funds to be raised from private donors. Since then, the government's percentage has increased, but Chinuch Atzmai still must raise a substantial part of its budget.

33. Yeshivah deferments issued in 1949 and 1950 were negligible in number, estimated to range from only 27 to less than 300. It should be noted that during the War of Independence, many yeshivah students and Orthodox Jews fought in the war and died. They were wounded in numbers proportionate to their representation in the population.

status quo on religious authority for matters of personal status. I know that it was hard on some individuals. But I felt, again in the national interest, that it was wise to … pay the comparatively small price of religious status quo.[34]

The question of the place of religion in the State of Israel remains a vexing one till today. Ben-Gurion's *status quo* endured, though increasingly frayed, throughout the balance of the century. In truth, the *status quo* satisfied no one. For the religious population, it was never enough; and for the secular public, it was always too much. The very existence of religious political parties is a question unto itself. A strong case was and is still being made that religion in Israel would be much more influential and acceptable in the non-Orthodox society if it were not associated with the inevitable wheeling-dealing and scandals of political party life. Others maintain that if it were not for the existence of the religious parties, the national image of the country would become so secularized that Israel would not be a Jewish state whatsoever. As of this writing, the religious political parties in Israel are well entrenched and the debate regarding them still swirls on.

Among those who came to Israel immediately following the World War, were the remnants of the yeshivos and the great Chasidic courts of prewar Eastern Europe. They began the laborious task of rebuilding the world of Torah that was destroyed in the Holocaust. The yeshivos of Mir, Slabodka, Brisk and Ponovezh, among others, were reestablished in Israel. Though all of their beginnings in the 1940's were small and painful, they took root in Israeli soil and grew into prestigious institutions of Torah study, their student numbers by the end of the century far surpassing their enrollments in prewar Europe. The Chasidic dynasties that survived the war, led by Gur, Vizhnitz and Belz, were also reestablished in Israel. These groups joined with the old-time Jerusalem and Bnei Brak-based Orthodox leaders and became the backbone of Agudath Israel. In time, they would exert great influence on the Mizrachi sector of the Orthodox population as well.

Despite the efforts of the religious parties, most of the newly arrived immigrants to Israel were undergoing rapid secularization. The Labor Zionists and the Left[35] controlled the process of immigrant absorption and their mantra was that religion may have been necessary in the Diaspora, but that it had no place in the new Jewish state that was now being built. Thus

---

34. Sachar, pp.378-9.

35. In all fairness, it must be pointed out that the Right in Israel was generally no less secular than their Left counterparts. Since they were not in power at the time, it is impossible to know how they would have handled the absorption of the immigrants.

hundreds of thousands of Jewish adults and children were taught to discard their traditions and to separate themselves from their parents and their ethnic and spiritual roots. This was especially true in regard to the Sephardic Jews who immigrated to Israel from the Moslem countries of the Middle East.[36] Though the efforts of the Left to secularize these Jews were initially successful, eventually — decades later — Sephardic resentment of this treatment, and of their loss of self and tradition, would emerge and have a lasting effect on Israeli politics and society.

A split within the Orthodox camp regarding the State of Israel began to develop in the late 1940's. Mizrachi, which was then the largest grouping within Orthodoxy, supported the state wholeheartedly. The party held important cabinet positions in the government, urged its young to serve in the army and was a full partner in the Zionism that the state then espoused. It was under the aura of Mizrachi values that Rabbi Meir Bar-Ilan (Berlin) initiated a number of bold educational projects. One was the *Encyclopedia Talmudit* — a compendium of all Talmudic knowledge and its later commentators in encyclopedic format.[37] The second was the creation of the first university in Israel under Orthodox auspices. When the university opened, it was named Bar-Ilan in memory of its founder. In the late 1940's, Mizrachi itself sponsored few, if any, yeshivos. The largest independent one under its ideological influence was Yishuv Hachadash,[38] established by Rabbi Moshe Avigdor Amiel, the Chief Rabbi of Tel Aviv. Rabbi Kook's yeshivah, Merkaz HaRav, was never officially affiliated with Mizrachi, though it also fully subscribed to the idea of Orthodox participation in the process of Jewish statehood and saw such participation as a religious obligation. Mizrachi would soon develop its own networks of intensive Torah study: *hesder* yeshivos[39] and Bnei Akiva yeshivos.[40] These

36. Particularly scandalous was the policy towards the children of the Yemenite immigration. Not only were the distinctive *peyos* (sidelocks) of the Yemenite boys cut off, but Yemenite children were also forcibly taken from their parents and sent to Leftist kibbutzim to be raised by foster parents in the "proper" atmosphere of socialist values. The religious parties demanded that all of these children be enrolled in religious schools. For the first two years of the state, this demand was officially honored, though even then more in the breach than in fact. Beginning in 1951, however, the children were officially allowed "freedom of choice" and most of them were then registered in the secular school system.

37. The twenty-fifth volume of this proposed fifty-volume work was published in 1999.

38. This school was more in the nature of a high school than a yeshivah for older students. It included a broad range of general studies in its curriculum.

39. Rabbi Chaim Goldvicht, a student of Rabbi Yitzchak Zev Soloveitchik, the *Brisker Rav*, founded the first such school, Yeshivas Kerem B'Yavne. This yeshivah combined years of Torah study with full army service. It was to serve as the prototype for dozens of other such institutions over the coming decades.

40. These yeshivos were affiliated with the Mizrachi youth movement. The original school at *Kfar HaRoeh* was headed by Rabbi Moshe Zvi Neriyah, a disciple of Rabbi A.Y. Kook. This network of yeshivos also experienced enormous growth in the forthcoming decades of the century.

institutions would have a profound effect on Mizrachi policies and on the State of Israel generally. A strong leader of Mizrachi in this era was Moshe Chaim Shapiro, a student of Rabbi Shimon Shkop of Grodno and the leader of the Hapoel HaMizrachi faction of the movement.

Agudath Israel decided that even after the establishment of the State of Israel it would retain its previous anti-Zionist stance, but that it would nevertheless participate in the activities and government of the state, albeit on a limited basis. Rabbi Yitzchak Meir Levin, the head of Agudath Israel, served in Ben-Gurion's first cabinet as Minister of Welfare. Agudath Israel could not make peace with the overwhelmingly secular nature of the state, therefore choosing to deal with it and its government with the same policies that it had employed in dealing with any other country prior to World War II. This ambivalent attitude of being doctrinally anti-Zionist and yet somehow part of the State of Israel would cause many strains within Agudath Israel over the decades. Poalei Agudath Israel, on the other hand, became increasingly involved in Zionist and state activities and for a short period of time was quite influential in Israeli governmental and societal issues. This faction of Agudath Israel would disappear from the political scene by the 1960's.

There was another group within the Orthodox camp that opposed the existence of the State of Israel. Its ideology was that only the Messiah could establish a Jewish State in the Land of Israel. Otherwise, such a state should not be created and no permanent good for the Jewish people could come from it. This opinion was held valid even if all of the leaders of the State of Israel were to be religious Jews. The fact that the leaders were avowed secularists only reinforced their opposition to the state. Thus Neturei Karta, the most extreme anti-Zionist religious group before the creation of the state, became the strongest anti-state group.

The champion of this idea was Rabbi Yoel Teitelbaum, the *Satmar Rav*. Having survived the Holocaust, Rabbi Teitelbaum arrived in Israel in the mid-1940's and lived for a short time in Jerusalem before emigrating from there to America. His stay in Jerusalem and exposure to the non- and even anti-religious leadership of the Jewish Agency only hardened his already formidable anti-Zionism of prewar years. In his writings and speeches, he placed a significant degree of responsibility for the Holocaust on Zionism. He was an implacable foe of the idea of a Jewish State. Neturei Karta was small and of little influence in the late 1940's; however, it gained support that would make not only anti-Zionism but also anti-Israel policies acceptable for tens of thousands of Orthodox Jews by the end of the century. Neturei Karta itself remains a fringe, extremist group, but it has suceeded in influencing many Orthodox groups.

Jewish refugees arriving in New York, 1946

AMERICAN JEWRY BEGAN TO UNDERGO CHANGE AFTER THE END OF World War II, polarizing and moving in two very different directions. The influx of refugees and survivors of the Holocaust had a profound effect on American Jewry. The Orthodox scholars who had resided in Shanghai during the war revitalized the yeshivah movement in America, and sent it in a new direction. Though both Yeshiva University in New York and the Hebrew Theological College in Chicago added to their faculties from the great European scholars who now came to America, they retained their Modern Orthodox status and policies. The new yeshivos founded by many of the surviving Eastern European *roshei yeshivah* created a counterforce to the Modern Orthodox philosophy. New yeshivos such as Lakewood's Beth Medrash Govoha and the Brooklyn branch of Mir opened and joined the previously operating yeshivos of Telshe, Torah Vodaath and Chaim Berlin. Other yeshivos that gained strength in the early postwar years were the Rabbinical Seminary of America (Yeshivas

Jewish Polarization in the United States

Campers at Camp Agudah in Highmount, New York

Rabbi Yisrael Meir HaKohen — Chafetz Chaim), Bais Medrash Elyon and Ner Israel in Baltimore. These yeshivos would become catalysts in the restructuring and postwar reconstruction of American Orthodox Jewry.

At this point, the Jewish day school movement began to emerge. Visionary leaders of American Orthodoxy, notably Rabbi Shraga Feivel Mendlowitz (who preferred to be known simply as Mr. Mendlowitz) and Rabbi Dr. Samson R. Weiss (who was soon followed by Dr. Joseph Kamenetsky[41]), formed Torah U'Mesorah, the National Council for Jewish Day Schools.[42] These day schools provided an intensive Jewish

---

41. The prime mover behind the establishment of a national Jewish day school movement was Rabbi (Mr.) Shraga Feivel Mendlowitz, the head of Yeshiva Torah Vodaath in Brooklyn. His students were the pioneers of the movement, establishing and staffing the fledgling schools in different communities throughout America. The first director of Torah U'Mesorah, Dr. Joseph Kamenetsky, served as the catalyst for the spread of the day school movement throughout North America.

42. There were such schools established in New York, Baltimore, Boston and Chicago, even before World War II, but there was no national body to administer, encourage and foster a national network until the creation of Torah U'Mesorah.

education along with the fulfillment of the general studies requirements of the American public school system. The day schools had long hours, mostly inadequate physical facilities and were uniformly underfunded. They were opposed bitterly by the Reform and Conservative movements, as well as by the Jewish Federations and most major national Jewish organizations. The commitment then of the majority of American Jewry was to the American public school system: The accusation was leveled that the Orthodox day schools were unpatriotic, if not downright subversive. Despite vigorous opposition, and against the predictions of the educational and sociological experts (and the moans of naysayers), the day school movement survived, expanded and marked the beginning of a resurgent Orthodox Jewish life in America. American Orthodoxy could no longer depend on Europe for reinforcements, teachers and leaders. The day schools and the revitalized yeshivos made it possible to raise a homegrown cadre of American Jews who would build Orthodox Jewish life for the balance of the century.

Day school and yeshivah education for boys and girls became goals of Orthodox society in the postwar years.

As previously noted, one of the dominant personalities in American Orthodoxy immediately after the war was Rabbi Aharon Kotler (who was discussed briefly in the previous chapter). Lakewood, New Jersey, was a "winter resort" for New York Jews[43] and an aged house there was donated as the first building of his new yeshivah. Beth Medrash Govoha not only replicated the style and curriculum of the prewar Lithuanian yeshivos, it also introduced the idea of continuing yeshivah study for a number of years after the students married. This goal, the *kollel* system, was an innovation in American Jewish life. The institution of the *kollel* would have great, if perhaps unforeseen, influences on Orthodox Jewish family life, education, the role of women in the workplace and the strengthening of the intensity of ritual observance in American Orthodoxy. But all of this would not be apparent for another two decades.

43. The average winter temperature in Lakewood is five degrees higher than in Manhattan. This qualified it as a winter resort. Florida winters were still out of the question, socially and financially, for the overwhelming majority of New York Jews.

The end of the war also brought about a heretofore unknown prosperity in American life that impacted profoundly on American Jewish society. New housing developments were built in the suburbs of the major cities in America. The assumption of the "right" of every American family to own a home and an automobile fueled a new mobility in America. The changes in population composition of the inner cities brought about the abandonment of numerous Jewish neighborhoods. Orthodox synagogues were sold as churches or warehouses, and many of those synagogues were never rebuilt elsewhere. Other Orthodox synagogues were moved to the suburbs and rebuilt, but now declared themselves "Traditional"[44] or joined the Conservative movement outright.[45] In 1949, there were 365 congregations affiliated with the United Synagogues of America. By 1956, the number of affiliated congregations rose to 597.

The head of the Jewish Theological Seminary and of the Conservative movement was Professor Louis Finkelstein. A scholar of note, an indefatigable fund-raiser and innovator, he served as president and later as chancellor of the Seminary for 32 years, beginning in 1940. During his tenure, the Conservative movement grew and gained influence. It established the Jewish Museum in New York in 1947 and the University of Judaism, its West Coast branch, in Los Angeles in that same year. But the movement generally, and the Seminary particularly, was subject to wrenching internal strains due to its amorphous philosophy and its inability to define itself in the context of Jewish history and tradition. Milton Steinberg, one of the leading Conservative rabbis of the decade, said of the movement: "In practice it is kind of middle-of-the-roadism ... between Orthodox and Reform. This in a nutshell is the program. As to the theory, it is regrettably difficult to put it precisely. Truth to tell, Conservatism has still not formulated the philosophy on which it stands."[46] In 1946, the United Synagogue established a "Committee on the Philosophy of Conservative Judaism." At the end of the decade, it still

---

44. These synagogues retained the Orthodox prayer service and their rabbi was usually a graduate of an Orthodox yeshivah, but there was mixed seating during the services and many times there was no central *bimah* (reading stand) in the synagogue. The "Traditional" synagogue was especially popular in the American Midwest and West.

45. For example, out of the 42 Orthodox synagogues in the Lawndale area in Chicago in 1945, only about a half-dozen still existed as Orthodox synagogues in the Chicago area a decade later. Many times this conversion of a previously Orthodox synagogue to a Conservative synagogue was accompanied by great social and legal struggles. Court cases regarding this matter were brought concerning synagogues in New Orleans, Louisiana, and Mount Clemens, Michigan. See Baruch Litvin's book, *The Sanctity of the Synagogue,* for a full review of this struggle within American Jewry in the 1940's and 1950's. A cynic, commenting on the change in Jewish congregational affiliation that occurred during this time, remarked: "The Orthodox three-day-a-year Jew now became a Conservative three-day-a-year Jew."

46. Milton Steinberg, *A Partisan Guide to the Jewish Problem*, Indianapolis, 1945, p.165.

had not made a definitive report back to its constituents. Certain that the creation of Israel was a boon to the Jewish people, the movement was overwhelmingly pro-Zionist and organized substantial support for the fledgling State of Israel.[47]

The most radical member of the Seminary's faculty was Mordecai M. Kaplan. He would eventually leave the Seminary and the Conservative movement and found his own movement — Reconstructionist Judaism. In 1945 though, while still a member of the Seminary's faculty, Kaplan issued a new prayer book, removing God entirely. The prayer book reflected Kaplan's theology.[48] In a dramatic act of censure, the prayer book was burned at a meeting of the Agudas HaRabanim in New York. In what was perhaps a more sensitive act of criticism to Kaplan, Professors Saul Lieberman, Louis Ginzberg and Alexander Marx, all distinguished and well-respected members of the Seminary's faculty, denounced Kaplan and his prayer book in a paid ad in *Hadoar*, the Hebrew journal of American Jewry. The inner tensions of the Conservative movement would become stronger as the century advanced.

Perhaps the greatest departure from *halachah* and Jewish tradition that the movement took in the late 1940's was regarding the Sabbath. In 1948, the Committee on Jewish Law and Standards promulgated the following rulings:

"Having learned to adjust our strategy to the realities of our time and place … [we recommend] permitting travel in an automobile on *Shabbat*, solely for the purpose of riding to the synagogue to join in communal worship. At the same time, the Committee also permits the use of electricity [on *Shabbat*] … in order to enhance the observance of the Sabbath in the home. These permissions are tied to the Sabbath Revitalization Campaign, designed to encourage [our] members to recapture for themselves and their families the spirit of *Shabbat*."[49]

---

47. In a strange footnote to history, Seminary students battled [President] Finkelstein in the late 1940's when he refused to allow the playing of *Hatikvah*, the Zionist hymn and the new Israeli national anthem, at their graduation, because it was the national anthem of a "foreign country." Pamela S. Nadell, *Conservative Judaism in America*, New York, 1988, p.284.

48. "Kaplan proposed a total revolution in Jewish theology by accepting naturalism, teaching that Judaism must be 'reconstructed' from supernaturalism to naturalism. He rejected the notion of a supernatural God, redefining God as the Power in the universe that makes for salvation, the sum of the forces that help men and women make the most of their lives. For Judaism to survive the challenge of modernity there could be no miracles, no supernatural revelation … He replaced the mitzvot of Jewish law with the concept of folkways … Kaplan's rejection of the concept of the Jews as the chosen people also grew out of his rejection of supernaturalism. Furthermore, he felt that that the entire notion of chosenness was out of step with the ideals and democratic ethos of the dominant American society. It was especially these controversial theological reconstructions of fundamental Jewish beliefs … that created for Kaplan grave tensions and left deep scars within the Conservative movement." Nadell, p.153.

49. Ibid. pp.10-11.

Needless to say, this Orwellian document did little to revitalize Sabbath observance within the ranks of the Conservative laity and only served to compromise the legal authenticity of the movement in its future years.

The use of radio to promote Jewish identity was also a feature of American Jewry in the postwar years. Beginning in 1944, the Conservative movement sponsored a weekly dramatic program called "The Eternal Light." It was broadcast on a national radio network and had a wide following. Its main content dealt with the Holocaust and the emerging State of Israel, but it also promoted holiday and ritual observances. As the programs were of high professional quality, and they appeared non-denominational, they commanded a wide Orthodox listenership as well.

The coming of television, however, would soon put radio into virtual eclipse (albeit not permanently). Television would change the lives, politics and world-view of Americans, and eventually of the rest of the world, over the coming decades. Tragically, in its commercial greed it descended to pandering to the lowest common denominator of the "viewing public," and many Orthodox Jews, among other religious Americans, came to view it as an enemy rather than as a potential educational tool. Its influence was pervasive and in its own way, television abetted the rapid and devastating assimilation of American Jewry into its non-Jewish surroundings.

The Reform movement in America was undergoing serious self-evaluation in the wake of the Holocaust and the birth of Israel. William G. Braude, one of the leading Reform leaders, wrote:

> ... We 19th and 20th century Liberal Jews have annulled for ourselves and for others most of the commandments; we have paraphrased revelation as the religious genius of Israel; we are left essentially with the strident and clamorous plea that all men are brothers ... Obviously since the patriarchs did not exist and the daily religion of the prophets was lost beyond recovery, the God of the patriarchs and the prophets is a meaningless apostrophe ... We thus unwittingly reduced the dream of improving the world through the kingdom of God to a hollow non-sectarianism bristling with disavowals of strong faith. [We have come] forth with a panacea — Jewish nationalism ... The Hatikvah is now in the Union Hymnal, the highest officials of the [Reform Rabbinic] Conference are Zionists ... [But] the strength of Eretz Yisrael was in its sanctity and not in being a nursery for national culture ...[50]

---

50. Joseph Blau, ed., *Reform Judaism: A Historical Perspective*, New York, 1973, pp.107-110.

Much of Reform Judaism was reduced to the quest for social justice in American society. As important as that goal was and is, it did not mobilize most Reform Jews to any strong commitment to their faith. There were attempts as early as the 1940's to restore Hebrew prayers to Reform services. Braude himself proposed no riding in automobiles on the Sabbath for secular purposes, the banning of pork, fasting on Yom Kippur and Tisha B'Av, and no slanderous speech. His program for "A Fence of Holiness" within Reform was not adopted. There were strong disputes regarding Israel and the issue of dual loyalty, with many Reform rabbis and temples refusing to participate in fund raising drives on behalf of Israel. The direction of Reform was not clear, though it was obvious that the tenets of extreme Reform as promulgated 70 years earlier by Isaac Mayer Wise in his Pittsburgh Platform — discarding all Hebrew, abandoning all ritual, and identifying Jews as a religion, not as a nation — were no longer operative. Many of the fundamental beliefs that had propelled the program of American Reform in its earliest form went up the chimneys of Auschwitz. Nevertheless, Reform, numerically and financially, remained the largest group within American Jewry throughout the first half of the century.

THE BURGEONING COLD WAR BETWEEN THE WEST AND THE SOVIET Union placed the Jewish Left into a dilemma. The heroic and enormously costly struggle of the Soviet Union against Hitler's Germany helped erase the memory of Stalin's purges of the 1930's. The temporary postwar Soviet support for the creation and recognition of the State of Israel also strengthened the Jewish Left in Israel and worldwide in their faith in Stalin's benevolence and in the goal of bringing the "workers' paradise" to all mankind. The disproportionate number of Jewish intellectuals, professors, artists, actors, teachers and political leaders who identified themselves as allies of the Soviet Union in the early years of the Cold War was troublesome: It would revive the American "red-baiting" scare of the 1920's and make the Jewish community most uncomfortable.[51] There were many Jews who were active in the presidential campaign of former Vice President Henry Wallace and the Progressive Party in 1948. It was later shown that Wallace and his party were willing dupes of the Soviet

The Red Threat

---

51. The fact that secrets of the atomic bomb were transferred to Russia by two Jewish spies — Julius and Ethel Rosenberg — who were tried, convicted and executed for their espionage activities was most unsettling to the American Jewish community. Many of the witnesses in the trial and other suspects were also Jewish — as were the judge, the prosecutor and the defense attorney, so that no one could charge the government with being anti-Semitic.

Union in an attempt to subvert American will to oppose the expansionist policies of the Soviet Union.[52] Sympathy for the Soviet Union ran deep within large sectors of Jewish Leftist society.[53] In Israel, this pro-Soviet devotion occasioned a permanent split in the Labor Zionist movement and produced Israeli political and military leaders who actually supported the cause of the Soviet Union over that of the State of Israel.[54]

Stalin himself would be the one to cure this Jewish myopia and fantasy. After the "National Patriotic War" was won, many Soviet citizens hoped for a better life and the end of the institutionalized terror of the 1930's. But as Stalin's paranoia of the West increased, his anti-Semitism became more blatant and his tactics were ever more brutal in crushing real or imagined "counterrevolutionaries." His new head of the secret police, Lavrenty Beria, was a sadistic murderer and a supreme Stalin sycophant.[55] The policy of Stalin was to repress all signs of particularistic Jewish activity, even those that had the sponsorship of the Communist Party itself. Thus, Yiddish literature and the Yiddish theater were now described as degenerate because of their "*shtetl* attitudes." Solomon Mikhoels, a winner of the Stalin Prize and a leading actor in the Soviet Yiddish theater, was murdered by the secret police. The Yiddish theater in the Soviet Union was officially disbanded in 1949. The police closed the last Jewish publication house in Russia at the end of 1948. The leading Jewish poets and writers, all of whom had extolled communism and Stalin to the heavens for decades through all the shifting policies of the state, were arrested and sent into hard-labor exile or executed immediately. They were accused of "bourgeois nationalism," slandering the Soviet Union by implying that anti-Semitism still existed in their country, or of espionage on behalf of the West.[56]

---

52. Truman said of Wallace: "Wallace is a pacifist one hundred percent. He wants us to disband our armed forces, give Russia our atomic secrets and trust a bunch of adventurers in the Kremlin Politburo … The Reds, phonies and parlor Pinks seem to be banded together and are becoming a national danger. I am afraid they are a sabotage front for Uncle Joe Stalin." Quoted by Johnson, p.438.

53. Nearly 50,000 Jews gathered at the Polo Grounds in New York in the mid-1940's to hear Sholom Asch, the noted Yiddish author, praise the Soviet Union for eliminating anti-Semitism. Ben Zion Goldberg, a Yiddish journalist and son-in-law of Sholom Aleichem, heaped praise on "the great leader Marshal Stalin." Paul Robeson concluded the evening by singing Russian and Yiddish folksongs. Millions of dollars were raised for Russia that evening. See Zvi Gitelman, *A Century of Ambivalence*, New York, 1988, p.230.

54. The Israeli Communist Party — Maki — was blindly pro-Stalin in all of its pronouncements and policies. However, Mapam, the more extremist Left faction of the Labor Zionist movement, was also totally pro-Soviet in the immediate postwar years. One of its leaders was jailed for spying on Israel on behalf of Soviet intelligence. A number of Leftist kibbutzim split asunder and physically separated into two different communes on the issue of the rectitude of Stalin and Soviet policy. Stalin, communism and the Soviet Union are all now long gone, but the separation in the kibbutz movement still remains as of this writing.

55. Like all of Stalin's secret service heads, he would also be murdered (but not until Stalin was dead) by the very killing apparatus that he headed.

56. Gitelman, p.235.

What really caught Stalin's attention and raised his considerable ire was the reception given by the Jews of Moscow to Golda Meir, the first Israeli ambassador to the Soviet Union. Tens of thousands of jubilant Jews thronged the streets outside the embassy building when she arrived to assume her post, and hundreds of well-wishers mobbed the ambassador herself on the day she attended Rosh Hashanah services at Moscow's main synagogue. Stalin may have agreed to the creation of the Jewish state, but he was not prepared to tolerate pro-Zionist sentiments among Russia's Jews. He soon turned against Israel itself. The official communist newspaper, *Pravda,*[57] published an article in September 1948 that stated: "The State of Israel is not headed by representatives of the working people. [In the Soviet Union,] Jewish toilers, like all others, are strongly attached to the land where they were born and where they grew up. [They] can never envy [those who live under] the yoke of capitalist exploitation. [Soviet Jews] are working to build up their socialist homeland ... and are not looking to the Near East."[58]

Stalin and his government now sank into the abyss of openly expressed anti-Semitism. Leading Jews in the government, army, arts and the Communist Party suddenly disappeared from the scene. All Jewish religious practices were banned on pain of Siberian exile. Jews who had "Russified" their names now saw their original Jewish names published in the newspapers. Accused of being part of a "Zionist conspiracy," V. M. Molotov's Jewish wife, Polina, was exiled to Kazakhstan. Stalin hated Jews and was immensely displeased that so many of his relatives had married Jews. He refused to meet five of his eight grandchildren because they were tainted by Jewish blood.[59] As Stalin's megalomania deepened and his paranoia increased, he focused more and more on Jews as his personal enemies. The cartoons in the Russian newspapers portrayed the "capitalist enemies" of Russia with hooked noses and other recognizable Jewish features, although none of these "enemy leaders" were in fact Jewish. As with Hitler, Stalin was fading into a stupor of fantasy, rage and murder as his own end neared. It seemed that the Jews in Russia were doomed to extinction one way or another.

In June 1950, Russia sponsored the invasion of South Korea by its puppet government in North Korea. The United States, under the cover of the United Nations, entered the war and was driven further and further south, until it finally was able to create a small defense perimeter on

---

57. *Pravda* was the official government communist newspaper that always reflected the current Stalinist line on all matters. In typical Orwellian irony, the Russian word *pravda* means truth.

58. Gitelman, p.241.

59. Paul Johnson, *Modern Times*, Revised Edition, New York, 1992, p.455.

the southwest corner of the Korean peninsula. The American forces then made a brilliantly successful amphibious landing in the north of the country, trapping most of the North Korean army. This maneuver turned the tide. The American forces charged northward, eventually invading North Korea. As the Americans reached the border of China and North Korea, the Chinese Communist Army entered North Korea and drove the Americans back again. By the end of the year, the war was a bloody stalemate. It coincided with the investigations and accusations of Senator Joseph McCarthy against spies, "Reds, pinks, subversives and fellow travelers" in the government, arts, judiciary and military of the United States. Because many of the accused were Jews, and McCarthy himself had Jewish assistants who served as his chief surrogate prosecutors, American Jews felt disturbed and frightened. The Jewish community felt compelled to assume a lower profile than it had in the previous few years during the struggle for the creation of the State of Israel. It would soon recover its voice, for Israel once again would be in need of vigorous support.

Chapter Seven

A Changed World

1951-1960

A S THE SECOND HALF OF THE CENTURY BEGAN, THE JEWISH WORLD had been radically changed by the events of the previous decade. European Jewry was virtually gone from the scene. Six million Jews had been slaughtered in the Holocaust, and the surviving European Jews were either locked away in Stalin's prisons in the Soviet Union or in its satellite communist-controlled countries, or were bent on leaving Europe for Israel or North America.

The United States now housed the largest Jewish community in the world, almost six million people. The Jewish population of Israel rose to nearly one million at the beginning of the decade due to the influx of European and Middle Eastern Jewish refugees immediately after the declaration of the State of Israel and its victory in the War of Independence.

As the full horror of the Holocaust settled on the Jewish people, two different reactions occurred. One was a feeling of bone-weary sadness and depression; a passionate, if passively expressed, attempt to give up the Jewish ghost, once and for all. Many of the Holocaust survivors simply retreated within themselves and did not speak of their past or experiences. Shucking off reminders of their Jewishness, they threw themselves into constructing new lives, new families and new wealth on a basis of secular assimilation into their new societies.

Even many who did not themselves experience the Holocaust were shaken to the roots of their faith by revelations of the disaster. Such books as *Night,* by Elie Weisel, brought home the tragedy of European Jewry to Jews who had spent the war years safely in the United States and unoccupied Allied countries. The test of faith in the God of Israel and belief in Jewish tradition engendered by the Holocaust was a factor in the decline of Orthodox Jewish life in America in the immediate postwar years. Whether the Holocaust was only a rationalization for succumbing to the lure of assimilation is a point that is yet debated.[1]

On the other hand, there emerged from among the Holocaust survivors a cadre of driven people who were determined to rebuild the Jewish people and the lost Jewish world at all costs and with devoted personal sacrifice. In the Orthodox world, they were represented by the Chasidic leaders, the heads of the Lithuanian European yeshivos, and the European-trained rabbis who somehow escaped the German genocide and reached Israel and/or America. Their utter tenacity and strength of will laid the foundation for the unexpected resurgence of Orthodoxy in the Jewish world in the second half of the century.[2] In the main, these new immigrants to both America and Israel refused to accommodate their views and practices of Jewish life to the pressures of the vastly different modern society in which they now found themselves. They doggedly hung on to their Orthodox mores and attempted to form American and Israeli Orthodox Jewry in their mold. Their faith and beliefs had annealed in the fire of Hitler's hell, and they were not fazed by the difficulties and naysayers confronting them. As time passed, they prevailed to an extent that no one originally thought possible.

The State of Israel and the memorialization of the Holocaust became a substitute Judaism for large numbers of Jews, both survivors of the Holocaust and others who otherwise were estranged from Jewish custom and practice. The support for both projects, the living state and the memory of the dead, would occupy most of the agenda of Jewish public life for the next 50 years. Huge fundraising organizations, led by the United Jewish Appeal and Israel Bonds,[3] supplied desperately needed cash

---

1. Many Orthodox acquaintances of mine in the early 1950's deserted the fold and almost all claimed that the Holocaust was a prime cause in their change of attitude and behavior.

2. The *American Jewish Yearbook,* in one of its editions in the early 1950's, confidently predicted the demise of Orthodoxy in America within a few decades.

3. In 1951, the American government gave Israel permission to float bonds in the American marketplace. The Israel Bonds Organization became an important source of cash flow to the fledgling state then hovering near bankruptcy. Over the years, the Israel Bonds effort has become an important source of investment in capital projects in Israel. Israel Bonds is, by far, the most successful foreign government bond sale in the history of the United States and Canada.

to the Israeli economy in the first decade of the state's existence. Strong American Jewish support for Israel also helped the country obtain a loan of $100 million from the American government in 1950. It continued to receive further American government loans, grants and other forms of assistance every year thereafter until the end of the century. Holocaust memorial projects began in the 1950's, though they would not achieve prominence and wide publicity until much later. Thus, a large section of the Jewish world was transfixed by the twin gigantic events of the age, the Holocaust and Israel. To many, the degree of support and commitment to these causes was the barometer of one's Jewish affiliation.

At the very same time, the creeping scourge of mass assimilation gained momentum among world Jewry, especially in the United States. The end of the war had released tremendous pent-up energy, resulting in wealth and societal mobility. The relaxation of anti-Semitism and Jewish quotas in universities and professional schools, coupled with the ability of World War II veterans to attend colleges under the GI Bill of Rights[4] without great financial hardship, created a flood of Jewish young people pursuing admittance into the professions. The dominance of American Jewish society by the entrepreneur, the merchant and the small manufacturer waned, to be replaced by the great numbers and success of Jewish doctors, lawyers, accountants and real estate developers.[5] The downside of this phenomenon was that mass entry into the professional non-Jewish world increased the pressures of assimilation. Yet there was still enough residual anti-Semitism present in the 1950's to keep the intermarriage rate in the Jewish community negligible.[6]

---

4. The GI Bill of Rights was a law passed by the United States Congress allowing armed forces veterans to attend colleges and vocational schools with tuition subsidized by the government. It was one of the most visionary and effective pieces of legislation passed in postwar America and had great positive impact on American society and its economic growth.

5. In order to combat the quotas that prevented many Jewish students from attending medical schools, Jewish groups established their own medical schools in these early postwar years. Prominent among these schools was Chicago Medical College, founded in the late 1940's, and Albert Einstein College of Medicine, founded in the early 1950's. The latter school, located in Bronx, New York, was established under the auspices of Yeshiva University. It pioneered study and internship programs that allowed its Jewish students to participate without violation of the Sabbath and other Jewish ritual obligations. It became one of the premier medical schools in the country; and the Orthodox Jewish doctor became a fixture in American medicine through its leadership.

6. Estimated to be between 5-6% of Jews marrying in that decade. Intermarriage is a two-way street in that the non-Jew has to find it socially acceptable to marry a Jew. Wide non-Jewish social acceptance would not be found until the latter part of the century, but when it arrived, the Jewish rate of intermarriage skyrocketed to 50-70%.

Diaspora Jews Return Home

ISRAEL WAS FLOODED WITH JEWISH REFUGEES IN THE EARLY 1950's. Operation "Magic Carpet" brought 50,000 Jews from Yemen to Israel. These Jews, with their distinctive Jewish appearance of flowing robes and long curled *peyos* (sidelocks) were subject to intense efforts at secularization by the dominant Ashkenazic socialist government and absorption agencies. In 1950 and 1951, in "Operation Ezra/Nechemia," 114,000 Jews arrived in Israel from Iraq. As in the case of Yemen and Aden, the Jews of Iraq were "encouraged" to leave their home of thousands of years by the local Arabs and government. In Iraq, Jewish property was confiscated and riots against Jews occurred in Baghdad and other major cities. The Egyptian Jewish community, which numbered 80,000 at the end of World War II,[7] was also severely restricted by the Arab rulers of the country, particularly after the defeat of the Egyptian army in the 1948 war. In the 1950's, 30,000 of these Jews reached Israel,[8] with the rest settling in France, the United States and Central and South America.

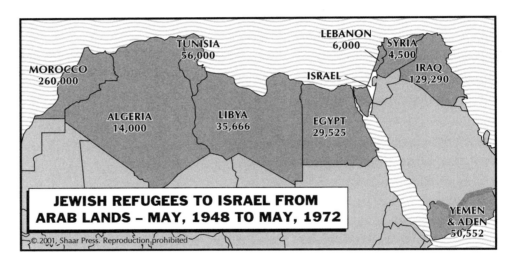

JEWISH REFUGEES TO ISRAEL FROM ARAB LANDS – MAY, 1948 TO MAY, 1972

©.2001, Shaar Press. Reproduction prohibited

Thus, approximately a half million Jews were expelled from the Arab countries of the Middle East and resettled in Israel. The largest Sephardic immigration came from North Africa. In several waves of immigration, 180,000 Jews arrived from Morocco, Algeria and Tunisia. Approximately 35,000 Jews remained in North Africa and close to 250,000 immigrated to France. More than 30,000 Jews arrived in Israel from Libya during this decade. From Syria and Lebanon, approximately

---

7. Interestingly enough, 10% of the Egyptian Jewish community was Ashkenazic.

8. One of the immigrants from Egypt to Israel at this time was the famed Torah scholar, Rabbi Ovadiah Yosef. Born in Baghdad, he was brought to Jerusalem when he was four years old. He later served as Deputy Chief Rabbi of Egypt from 1947-50. He then returned to Israel where he later became the Sephardic Chief Rabbi of Israel. Towards the end of the century he would become the spiritual mentor of the *Shas* political party.

6,000 Jews settled in Israel, with another 10,000 Jews immigrating to North and South America.

Israel claimed, in effect, that an exchange of populations occurred between the Jewish state and the neighboring Arab countries. Israel claimed that 520,000 Arabs left Israel during the 1948 war. England put the figure at 650,000; the United Nations said 700,000; and the Arabs claimed the number to be 800,000.

The largest number of immigrants to Israel in the 1950's still came from Europe. Seventy percent of the Jews of Bulgaria, approximately 40,000 in number, immigrated to Israel. Although Bulgaria, like Rumania, Hungary and Poland, was a satellite of the Soviet Union, Stalin's iron curtain policy that blocked Jewish immigration from Russia to Israel apparently was not enforced in those countries. More than 130,000 Jews came from Rumania and another 100,000 came from Poland and Central Europe. After the failed Hungarian revolution of 1956, 42,000 Jews came to Israel from Hungary. The remnants of the European refugee/DP camps continued to straggle into the country and 60,000 more finally settled in Israel during this decade.

Thus, the Jewish population of Israel, which numbered 650,000 at the beginning of the 1950's, was 2,436,000 by 1960. The country's population had quadrupled in only ten years. The astounding feat of absorbing this enormous population — many, if not most of whom arrived in Israel destitute and bewildered — was accomplished. But the absorption process and experience was not uniform and certainly not without pain; and the upheaval it caused would leave lasting scars not only on the immigrants themselves, but on the entire Israeli body politic and national psyche.

The process of absorption first brought most of the new immigrants to an immigrant camp or transit camp — a *ma'abarah*.[9] The conditions in those camps ranged from bad to appalling. The government had very little monetary resources to invest in these transit camps. By May 1952, there were 111 such camps housing more than 250,000 people in makeshift tents and corrugated huts. Most immigrants spent twelve to eighteen months in the *ma'abarah* before being resettled in abandoned Arab homes in major cities, in fledgling settlements scattered throughout the country, or in *orei pituach* — development towns. The development

---

9. The various political parties in Israel also conducted immigration absorption programs for those who were officially affiliated and organized under their respective party banners while yet in the Diaspora. Although relatively few in number, these immigrants had vastly better absorption experiences than their less political brethren. These immigrant groups usually stayed together upon arrival in Israel and formed the nucleus of new settlements and kibbutzim. They tended to be skilled and enthusiastic people who escaped the feelings of ennui and depression that overwhelmed many of the immigrants enduring the *ma'abarah* experience.

towns were usually placed right on the armistice line borders of the country and were intended to serve as a first line of defense against Arab encroachment or attack. Almost invariably, these development towns developed neighborhoods with great pockets of endemic poverty and rising crime. During their stay in a *ma'abarah,* the immigrants were to learn Hebrew and vocational skills. These educational programs met with mixed success and a considerable hard core of unemployed and functionally unemployable people emerged from the system.

Most of the immigrants also had no choice as to where they were to be given permanent residence after leaving the *ma'abarah.* Sephardic immigrants were particularly hard-hit by these policies and complained bitterly about the discrimination, real or perceived, against them from the secular Ashkenazic establishment. The heavy-handed and blatant attempt by many of the people in charge of immigrant absorption to secularize the religious and traditional Sephardic communities, though initially successful, eventually became a source of bitter resentment and political backlash. Religion, respect for elders, teachers, rabbis and tradition were the cement that bound Sephardic families together, and its forced disappearance caused grave domestic and social problems to thousands of families.[10]

Ideological Clashes Confront the Young State

In the Israeli elections of November 1950, the left wing parties, Mapai (Ben-Gurion's) and Mapam (pro-Soviet and militantly anti-religious) garnered 60 seats, a decline of five seats from their showing eighteen months earlier. The religious parties, running independent of each of other and not as a united bloc as they did in the elections to the first Knesset, won fifteen seats, a loss of one from their previous numbers. Menachem Begin's Herut party declined even more strongly, retaining only eight of its previous fourteen seats. The big winner was the

---

10. This same process was experienced by the Ethiopian aliyah 40 years later. In an essay written in 2000 by a young Ethiopian, Tigbo (Amrah) Bitou, he wrote: "Respect for the father and the *kessim* (rabbis) was a virtue unto itself, but the most important virtue that we dreamed of daily was Jerusalem. The dream to go up to Jerusalem was an integral part of our lives. And behold! The dream was realized. We arrived in Israel. And we reached the holy city – Jerusalem. And here, all the important values of our community that we were so accustomed to were suddenly blown away. Thus began the changes that gnawed away at the position of the father, the mother and adults in general. The Israeli culture broke the Ethiopian mentality. As a result, a break has been created between adults and children. The respect given to the father is slowly disappearing, and particularly where the parents do not work and support their families. Therefore, the child seeks adult figures to admire, to imitate, to honor. From this point, it is only a short road to disputes with parents, arguments and shouting. The children are certain that their parents do not understand them, they are primitive and they are not "with it." It is no wonder then that the children drift toward bad influences. The generation gap is enormous! We, the younger generation, have to do some soul searching to change the atmosphere that was created in our homes."

General Zionist Party, which raised its representation to 20 seats from its previous number of seven. This party was capitalist-oriented and moderate in its social policies, though it also was firmly anti-religious. Ben-Gurion cobbled together a coalition government based on Mapai, the religious parties and the General Zionists. Mapam was excluded from the government due to its pro-Russian tilt in foreign policy.

Mapam suffered defections because of its inability to decide whether it should follow a pro-Soviet line completely or be primarily a Zionist party. In 1952, two of its fifteen parliamentary members defected to Ben-Gurion's Mapai party, and in 1954 another two of its parliamentarians left to join the Israeli Communist Party. The Left was further fragmented by the formation of a third Leftist party in August 1954, Achdut HaAvodah. Four other members of Mapam became the nucleus of this militantly leftist but strongly Zionistic party.

In the elections for the third Knesset in July 1955, Mapai garnered 40 seats; Mapam nine seats; Achdut HaAvodah ten seats; and the religious parties increased to seventeen seats. The General Zionists declined to thirteen seats while Herut took fifteen. Ben-Gurion's hostility to Menachem Begin remained as great as ever and he never once recognized or called Begin by name during his entire public governmental career.

This profusion of new parties, a changing and fickle electorate and the bitter infighting between and within the various political groupings made for difficult governing of the state. The basic government coalition in the 1950's consisted of Mapai and the National Religious Party with Agudath Israel also serving in three of the first four government coalitions. By the middle of the 1950's, Mapam and Achdut HaAvodah left the Russian camp and also became active partners in the government coalition. Because of the nature of these government coalitions, which included the religious and anti-religious parties under one umbrella, the basic social and religious divisions of the country were never addressed. Instead, they were papered over with the observance of an ill-defined *status quo* arrangement that continually caused bitter debate and a chain of government coalition crises.

In 1950, a committee under the leadership of Dr. Leo Kohn, the legal advisor for the Jewish Agency, prepared a draft constitution. It was never adopted by the Knesset because the religious parties objected to any constitution for a Jewish state that could override Torah law and Jewish tradition. The specter of a *kulturkampf* had haunted Israel since its inception and Ben-Gurion opted to avoid such a struggle at that time. The problems of stabilizing the new state were so overwhelming that he felt that this internal struggle had to be avoided at almost all costs.

David Zvi Pinkas of the Mizrachi Party was appointed Minister of Communications

Prime Minister David Ben-Gurion, accompanied by Abba Eban, Israeli Ambassador to the U.S., (center) visits President Harry Truman

In line with this policy, Ben-Gurion recognized the National Religious School System (Mamlachti Dati) as an official school system, equal to the general public school system. He also agreed to the government's financing of 80% of the basic budget of the Independent School System (Chinuch Atzmai) affiliated with Agudath Israel. In 1952, the Knesset considered a law to draft all Israeli women, including Orthodox women, into military or national service units. The religious parties objected very strongly to the terms of this legislation. The estrangement from home and religious environment; the fraternization with male soldiers; the general weakening of traditional moral values fostered by the army as part of its drive to assimilate everyone into a secular society, were all factors in the Orthodox opposition to the law. Because of this bitter opposition, the original law was modified.[11] Thereafter, many religious

---

11. It was regarding this issue that the famed meeting between Ben-Gurion and Rabbi Avraham Yeshayahu Karelitz (*Chazon Ish*) took place at the latter's home in Bnei Brak. Citing the Talmudic dictum that "a loaded animal has the right of way on a narrow path over an animal that does not bear a burden," Rabbi Karelitz stated that the traditional community should be allowed right of way on such social issues as women being forced to serve in the army because it bears millenia of Jewish history, observance and identity. The venerable rabbi insisted that Ben-Gurion give way on this issue and the prime minister eventually did so. The conversation between the two at that meeting has become the stuff of legend for a half century.

young women did serve in national non-army service as a substitute for army service, but Orthodox women who personally objected to even such service were exempted from its requirements. Chief Rabbi Herzog vehemently opposed compulsory military service for women and because of his influence, most women of the Mizrachi camp participated in national services programs. Agudist and Chasidic women chose not to participate in any of these programs.

Ben-Gurion also confirmed the acceptance and continuation of the *status quo* on matters of religion in public life regarding the Sabbath, marriage, divorce and *kashrus* in the country. As he himself ruefully commented: "The struggle has only been postponed, not ended." "Time is on our side;" — he is quoted to have said — "in a generation or two the ultra-Orthodox will disappear."

The place of public religious observance in an essentially secular state was not the only source of social conflict and tension in Israel in the early 1950's. Due to the Cold War between the Soviet Union and the West, two separate Germanys arose from the ashes of destruction of World War II. West Germany — the German Federal Republic — was created out of the territories of the American, British and French zones of occupation. Its capital was Bonn, a sleepy German university town. The chancellor of this Germany was Konrad Adenauer, an anti-Nazi Christian Democrat, who had miraculously survived the war as a political prisoner in Hitler's Germany. It was under his guidance and through massive American financial aid and military protection that West Germany became a true democracy and began rebuilding its industrial and economic strength. East Germany, the territory under Soviet military occupation, became a Soviet satellite, ironically named the German Democratic Republic. The East German government disclaimed any responsibility for the Holocaust, claiming that it was the work of "capitalist cannibals" for whom the "freedom-loving socialists" bore no blame. However, in a dramatic speech to the West German parliament in September 1951, Chancellor Adenauer expressed his conviction that the German nation must do penance for its crimes and advanced the idea of material reparations and restitution to the Jewish people and the State of Israel. Israeli and world Jewish society divided sharply on this issue of German reparations. Emotionally and ideologically, it was opposed by many groups and Jewish leaders. They felt that it was impossible to forgive Germany for its crimes against the Jews and that acceptance of reparations would be seen as a form of forgiveness. On a practical level, it was encouraged by Ben-Gurion and many other Jewish leaders.

Menachem Begin was adamantly against negotiating with the Germans. The debate in the Knesset over the issue took place in January

1952, with Ben-Gurion's pragmatic view carrying the vote. Begin took his case to the streets: Heated demonstrations, near-riots, erupted. Begin himself was suspended for a time from participating in Knesset sessions because of his emotional behavior and speeches. In spite of all objections, the treaty for German reparations was signed between Israel, a number of major Jewish organizations and the West German government.[12] Over the next four decades, billions of dollars worth of goods, money and raw materials were sent to Israel by the West German government.[13] The Israeli industrial infrastructure, waterworks, electricity grid, highway improvement programs, steel production, railway system and other projects were all helped, if not actually created, by German goods and help. Individual Jews the world over also qualified to receive reparation money. The issue of acceptance of German reparations was symptomatic of the deep and lasting trauma of the Holocaust in postwar Jewish life. That trauma and its effects would continue to be present in the Jewish world for the balance of the century.

The Pawns of Superpowers Ready for War

MUCH OF ISRAELI POLICY AND DIRECTION WAS SHAPED BY THE intensifying Cold War between the Soviet Union and the United States and its Western allies. Stalin's original ardor for the Jewish state rapidly cooled, and by the early 1950's Russia was the generous patron of the Arabs' continuing struggle against the existence of Israel.

Stalin's anti-Israel foreign policy was more than matched by his anti-Jewish domestic policy. He had always hated Jews, an instinct reinforced in his early years by his seminary training to be a priest. Numerous Jewish scientists were helping Russia become a nuclear power, but Stalin trusted none of them. Failed laboratory physics experiments oftentimes sent the scientist who performed them to the Gulag or worse. In his paranoid fantasy, Stalin went so far as to think that Beria, his murderous secret police

---

12. The leading negotiator for the Jewish side in the discussions with the Germans was Dr. Nachum Goldmann, the president of the World Jewish Congress. A long-time Zionist leader and an extremely creative and able administrator, he was frozen out of Israeli politics and government by Ben-Gurion, whose personal grudges were notorious and lasted forever. It was Goldmann's diplomatic skills, personal charm and hardheaded practicality that made the reparations agreement with Germany a beneficial deal for Israel as an entity. The industrial and transportation infrastructures of Israel were built through German reparation payments. Ironically, because of this agreement, Germany became Israel's best friend — economically, politically and diplomatically — among the European nations. Nevertheless, there never could be any real restitution for the horrors suffered by the Holocaust survivors personally.

13. Germany would not establish diplomatic relations with Israel in the 1950's. This was the price the Arab countries demanded and received for their refusal in return to recognize East Germany.

head, was Jewish.[14] He planned to kill Beria, as he had every other secret police chief who had served him. In the Party Congress of October 1952, Stalin made it clear that he planned to launch a new purge and wave of terror to "cleanse the party" of those who he felt were disloyal to him. During the infamous "Doctors' Trial" in November 1952, the physicians who served Stalin and the other high Kremlin officials were arrested and confessed, under beatings and torture, to all sorts of bizarre crimes. The overwhelming majority of these doctors were Jews and a massive anti-Jewish reign of terror was planned. Stalin seemed to have lost all touch with reality. Before he could begin his new reign of terror, his own mortality intervened: on March 2, 1953, he suffered a stroke, and he died on March 5, 1953.[15] Good communists the world over, including some Jews in Israel and other countries, wept when they heard that the "great progressive father" was gone. They would soon regret their misplaced tears.

General Dwight D. Eisenhower became the President of the United States in January 1953. He arranged for an armistice in the Korean War and attempted to create a better climate for Soviet-Western relations after the death of Stalin. At the same time, however, he strengthened the Western alliance against Soviet expansion in Europe and pursued an aggressive foreign policy of developing strategic alliances to counter communism throughout the world. In the Middle East, he was caught between the necessity of courting Arab favor and the developing American support for Israel's survival. This would be the tightrope upon which all American administrations would be forced to walk throughout the remainder of the century.

Gamal Abdel Nasser of Egypt would prove to be a particular thorn in the side of the Western Allies. Nasser shrewdly played off the West and the Soviets one against the other for his gain. He had a grandiose dream of a high dam across the Nile River at Aswan and counted on American financial support to construct this monstrous engineering feat. He felt he had been assured of such support by Eisenhower's Secretary of State, John Foster Dulles. But when the project seemed to be moving into reality, Dulles withdrew American interest in it. Furious and shamed, Nasser turned to the Russians. They obliged him, putting billions of rubles into the questionable venture.[16] At the same time, they also presented him with thousands of Russian "advisors" to train his army and supplied him

14. Paul Johnson, *Modern Times*, New York, 1991, p.456.

15. His comrades at the Kremlin were so completely in terror of Stalin, that they delayed announcing his death out of fear that he was merely feigning his demise and would yet rise to strike them down for their disloyalty.

16. Many studies have since shown that the Aswan Dam has become an ecological nightmare for Egypt, depriving the farms along the Nile Delta of the silt that provided them free fertilizer. The

with an enormous quantity of Russian arms. Nasser was forced to mortgage the Egyptian cash crop of cotton to Russia in repayment for all of these goodies. The Egyptian economy never recovered from this loss, and Nasser desperately focused on another source of income for his bankrupt government — the revenues from the Suez Canal.

As part of Nasser's ambition of uniting the Arab countries under his rule, he needed a dramatic gesture that would prove to all that he was the leader of the Arab world and not merely of Egypt. To Nasser, British control of the Suez Canal was a particularly galling show of Egyptian weakness. This obvious remnant of colonialism was used by Nasser's rivals in the Arab world to mock his pretensions of grandeur and his promises of an Arab empire. Nasser entered into negotiations with the consortium that controlled and operated the canal under British protection to transfer its assets to Egypt. These negotiations bore no fruitful results and Nasser, with the urging of the Soviets (who wished England out of the Middle East at all costs), became more bellicose about the matter.

All the while, Nasser continued to sponsor terrorist bands that infiltrated Israeli territory, killing and maiming civilian adults and children. A pattern was established at that point that would hold true for the balance of the century. The scenario would run as follows: Initial Arab terrorism; followed by Israeli military reprisals at the terrorist bases or infrastructure; a resulting UN debate on the matter and a final UN resolution (usually from the Security Council) condemning Israel for the violence. Nasser, in cooperation with his Soviet masters, successfully isolated Israel in the international diplomatic arena and almost drove it into the status of a pariah nation. He created a bloc of communist, Arab, Moslem and European nations whose anti-Israel bias was blatant and unashamed. The accepted form of civilized anti-Semitism in the latter half of the twentieth century became anti-Israel bias.

The entire Middle East was becoming increasingly unstable. Anti-Western riots and revolutions, organized by communists and fundamentalist Moslems, plagued Iraq and Iran. England and the United States were involved in putting them down. King Abdullah of Jordan was assassinated in Jerusalem in 1951[17] and after a short interval, his eighteen-year-old grandson, Hussein, became king.[18] The young monarch's govern-

---

dam also created enormous mosquito breeding grounds and malaria, West Nile virus, and bilharziasis (carried by snails from Lake Nasser at the back of the dam) and these diseases still affect Egypt in epidemic proportions. The enormous electric power producing capacity of the dam has yet to be fully exploited by Egypt.

17. He was assassinated by an Egyptian Moslem fanatic who claimed that Abdullah was too moderate in his views on the Jews and was in reality a secret "Zionist agent."

ment was propped up by British aid, officers, civil servants and policy-makers. In an unexpected and bold fashion, Hussein eventually banished England's control. But Jordan's survival remained dependant on a constant flow of foreign aid, now primarily from the United States.

The most dramatic struggle of the Arabs against European domination took place in Algeria. Algeria was not merely a legal colony of France, it was a "department," a province of that country. Theoretically, Algeria was no less French than Alsace or Champagne. But by 1950 the French population of Algeria was less than a third of the total population. Arab nationalists, many of whom had fought in the Mufti's Moslem Brigade with Hitler against the Allies, organized a military organization, FLN, to fight for their independence from France. In one of the worst examples of human cruelty, both sides committed indescribable atrocities in this war that began in 1954. After a decade of fighting, France withdrew completely from the African continent.

This temporary French antagonism to Arab interests opened a window of opportunity for Israel in the days of its diplomatic and military isolation. France soon became Israel's resource of modern weaponry, especially airplanes. Shimon Peres negotiated arms deals with the French on Israel's behalf. Pierre Mendes-France, a Jew, was the premier of France at various times during the 1950's. Whether he helped or hindered the growing Israeli-French relationship is a question that is still the subject of scholarly debate decades later. In any event, Israel was able to modernize and equip its army during this era with the help of the French.[19]

In December 1953, David Ben-Gurion resigned as Israel's prime minister and retired to his kibbutz home in Sde Boker in the Negev. His long-time associate and cabinet foreign minister, Moshe Sharett, became the premier and Pinchas Lavon became Sharett's defense minister. Since 1951, an Israeli intelligence/spy network had operated in Egypt. In 1954, an order was given to this network from "senior governmental sources" to transform itself from a purely intelligence-gathering unit to an active sabotage organization. In July 1954, a series of bombs exploded in the post office of Alexandria, in the American libraries in Cairo and Alexandria and in movie theatres in both cities. The Israeli espionage ring was caught, interrogated, tried and two of them were executed. There

Moshe Sharett

18. Abdullah's son and Hussein's father, Tallah, immediately succeeded his father as king of Jordan and ruled for awhile. However, he was mentally ill and his court soon deposed him in favor of Hussein.

19. France's sale of arms to Israel was carried out over American objections to supplying Israel with weapons. America's position was that Israel's security could rest only on reliance on the United Nations and its peacekeeping machinery. Eisenhower's military assessment was that Israel was too small territorially and in population to stand up to the Arabs, and therefore supplying Israel with arms was useless. Howard M. Sachar, *A History of Israel*, New York, 1996, p.483.

was a mysterious "third man" involved in the matter who transmitted the orders from the "senior official" to the agents in Egypt. As the whole bungled operation became public, Ben-Gurion, who had been chafing at Sharett's handling of foreign and domestic matters, blamed Lavon for the ill-conceived scheme and accused him of being the source of the orders. Lavon heatedly denied the charges. Ben-Gurion tenaciously pursued him and demanded his ouster, eventually succeeding in having him ousted from the powerful Mapai party. In February 1955, Lavon resigned from the government in semi-disgrace. He was rewarded for his years of service to the socialist parties, however, with his appointment as secretary-general of the Histadrut labor union, a prize plum of patronage in Israeli politics. The "third man" was identified as a double agent, arrested and sentenced to ten years in an Israeli prison. To save his government, Sharett appointed Ben-Gurion as defense minister in Lavon's place.

Ben-Gurion was determined not be passive in this role. Throughout 1954 and 1955, Nasser had escalated the attacks of the Arab marauders into Israel. These *fedayeen* ["freedom fighters" or martyrs] exacted a bloody toll on Israeli society. On February 28, 1955, Ben-Gurion ordered a reprisal attack on Egyptian military headquarters in Gaza, which further heightened tensions in the area. The massive inflow of Russian arms to Egypt and Syria[20] and the continuing bombastic rhetoric of Nasser worried Israel greatly. Nasser stepped up the *fedayeen* terrorist raids on Israel throughout 1955 and 1956. After the 1955 elections, Sharett was replaced as premier and Ben-Gurion again became the head of the government in the fall of that year. At that point, there were regular attacks against Israel from Jordanian and Syrian territory as well. Almost no day passed without some sort of incident on Israel's borders. Though Ben-Gurion attempted to practice a policy of restraint, and continually expressed a spirit of understanding for Nasser and the Arabs, he nevertheless realized that the existing situation could not continue indefinitely. Throughout 1955 and 1956, as the Israeli retaliatory attacks on the Egyptians and Jordanians increased in intensity and boldness, so did Israeli casualties incurred in those attacks. The law of diminishing returns exacted its depressing toll on Israeli society. The Middle East was again at the edge of all-out conflict.[21]

---

20. The arms agreement was technically between Egypt and Czechoslovakia, with Russia feigning innocence in the matter. However, Czechoslovakia was firmly in the Soviet grip and completely under its control.

21. Shimon Peres wrote of the situation: "The escalation of sabotage and reprisal brought the Middle East — so it seemed to the Israelis — to the edge of full-scale war, and the question seemed to be not if, but when. Nasser strengthened this impression by a succession of inflammatory speeches, his tone of confidence much buoyed by heavy supplies of modern Soviet weapons which had already reached Egypt." Martin Gilbert, *Israel - A History*, New York, 1998, p.313.

In April 1956, Egyptian artillery shelled many Jewish settlements in the Negev. At the end of July, Nasser announced that Egypt was nationalizing the Suez Canal. England, outraged at Egypt's unilateral and illegal action, consulted with France. The two nations began to plan a military operation to restore the canal to their control. In June 1956, Golda Meir became the Israeli foreign minister, replacing Moshe Sharett. Meir was a much more forceful, outspoken and dominant personality than her predecessor.[22] Her mettle would be tested by the Egyptian ruler shortly.

In the third week of October, Nasser moved a large part of the Egyptian army, with its new heavy equipment, into the Gaza Strip. He also sent a large strike force into the Sinai desert, hard by the Israeli Negev border. It was clear to Israel that Nasser was committed to a new war, and that in his own words, it was to be "a war of annihilation." On the eastern front, King Hussein of Jordan invoked his alliance with Britain, and British aircraft and advisers arrived in Jordan to help "defend" the country. In response to Israel's deep retaliatory raid at Kalakilya against terrorists from Jordan, Hussein invited Iraq to send troops into Jordan to help fight Israel. More than 70 Jordanian soldiers had been killed in that raid, and Israel had also suffered considerable casualties, including eighteen dead. Meir warned Hussein and Iraq not to move. Nasser had closed the Straits of Tiran (at the entrance of the Red Sea and the Gulf of Aqaba) to Israeli and Israel-bound shipping. The tinderbox was about to explode.

After protracted negotiations with the British and French, an Israeli plan was adopted whereby Israel would launch a major attack against Egyptian forces in the Gaza Strip and Sinai.[23] This Israeli incursion would then become the justification for British and French military intervention to "separate the warring parties" and retake control and operation of the Suez Canal. France also undertook to provide Israel with air and sea cover for the Israeli homeland. Ben-Gurion's objectives in this action were clear and limited. He wanted a destruction of the *fedayeen* bases in the Gaza Strip and guarantees that such terrorist raids would cease. He also wanted freedom of navigation in the Red Sea and the Gulf of Aqaba and the removal of Nasser or, failing that, at least a fundamental change in his policies and attitude towards Israel. Israel began its attack on October 29, landing a paratroop brigade near the Mitla Pass in central Sinai and invading the Gaza Strip.

---

22. Regarding Golda Meir, Ben-Gurion was fond of saying, "She was the only man in my cabinet."
23. Moshe Dayan, the Israeli Army Chief of Staff, characterized the Sinai campaign as being "more than a raid and less than a war."

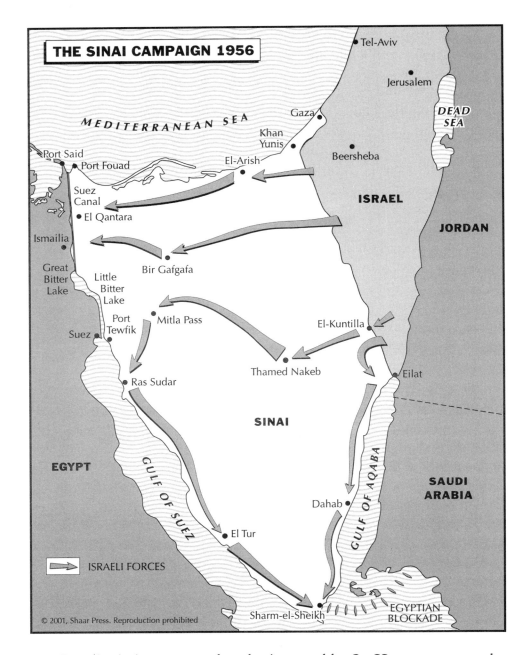

THE SINAI CAMPAIGN 1956

Tel-Aviv

Jerusalem

MEDITERRANEAN SEA

Gaza

Khan
Yunis

DEAD
SEA

Port Said

Port Fouad

El-Arish

Beersheba

ISRAEL

Suez
Canal

El Qantara

JORDAN

Ismailia

Bir Gafgafa

Great
Bitter
Lake

Little
Bitter
Lake

Port
Tewfik

Mitla Pass

El-Kuntilla

Suez

Thamed Nakeb

Eilat

Ras Sudar

SINAI

EGYPT

GULF OF SUEZ

SAUDI
ARABIA

GULF OF AQABA

Dahab

ISRAELI FORCES

El Tur

Sharm-el-Sheikh

EGYPTIAN
BLOCKADE

© 2001, Shaar Press. Reproduction prohibited

Israel's timing appeared to be impeccable. In Hungary, a popular revolution against communist rule and Soviet domination was in full bloom. Russia moved to crush the rebellion, against American warnings, by sending its army into Hungary in overwhelming strength. The United Nations and all of the major governments of the world were seemingly embroiled in this Hungarian crisis and Ben-Gurion hoped that the Sinai action would be effective before the rest of the world mobilized opinion and diplomatic action against Israel. Within six days, Israeli forces had captured most of the Sinai, the Gaza Strip and Sharm-el-Sheikh, the fortress controlling access to the Red Sea and the Gulf of Aqaba. Israel's casualties were 172 killed and 817 wounded. Egyptian casualties numbered in the thousands.

On November 5, 1956, the Anglo-French invasion of the Suez Canal area began. Though militarily successful, it provoked the wrath of both the Soviet Union and the United States. President Eisenhower was in the midst of an election campaign. His legendary temper flared because he had not been privy to the Anglo-French plans for military intervention in Egypt and thus felt betrayed by his allies. America pointedly joined Russia in demanding the withdrawal of the English and French forces. Eisenhower also sent a blunt note to Ben-Gurion, demanding full Israeli withdrawal from Sinai and the Gaza Strip. But even more ominous was the message sent by Russian premier Nikolai Bulganin to Ben-Gurion. In it, the Soviets demanded immediate and full Israeli withdrawal from all Egyptian territory. Bulganin forcefully reminded Israel that Russia possessed ballistic missiles that could reach "any point on the globe." Israel agreed to withdraw, as did France and England.[24]

How to Lose a War After Winning It

THE UNITED NATIONS BROKERED AN AGREEMENT WHEREBY ITS peacekeeping troops were to be stationed on the Israeli-Egyptian border to prevent any further *fedayeen* raids from Egyptian territory and to guarantee freedom of navigation to the southern Israeli port of Eilat. By the end of March 1957, all Israeli troops were back on Israeli soil and the United Nations forces were in place. Contrary to the agreements, Nasser continued to block all Israeli or Israel-bound shipping from using the Suez Canal. Inexplicably, the United Nations allowed Egypt to regain administrative control over the Gaza Strip, though the Egyptian army deployment there was on a much smaller scale than before. Nevertheless, Ben-Gurion felt satisfied that the Sinai campaign had achieved at least two of its main objectives — the opening of free navigation to Eilat and the halt to the *fedayeen* raids from Egypt. Nasser, nevertheless, claimed victory, since he still controlled the Suez Canal and the Gaza Strip. It also became clear to him that the Soviet Union would not allow Israel to topple him, and thus he confidently continued to foment aggression and unrest.

The Sinai Campaign created a new image of Israel. No longer was Israel seen as a weak and submissive country, dependant on foreign

---

24. I remember hearing Edward R. Murrow's CBS News radio broadcast from Tel Aviv on the night that the Israeli withdrawal was announced by Ben-Gurion. Murrow said: "I have seen the look on the faces of the citizens of Tel Aviv tonight before – in Prague in 1938, at the end of the Munich Conference."

benevolence for its existence. This came as a rude awakening to many Jews, especially to those who hoped Israel would have become a "light unto the nations" and a role model for the implementation of pacific prophesies of the Bible. The Jewish intellectual elite, both inside and outside Israel, shuddered at the thought that the Jewish state should somehow be Sparta and not Athens. More practical voices responded that it was better to be a live Sparta than a dead Athens.

Because of Israel's collusion with Britain and France, the Sinai Campaign painted Israel as a "colonialist and imperialist power" in the eyes of many. This characterization was the death knell for any Israeli hopes of garnering support among the Third World countries of Asia and Africa. These countries now would consistently take a strong pro-Arab line on all issues regarding the Middle East. Years later, many Israeli leaders[25] who had planned and participated in the Sinai Campaign expressed their retrospective reservations about the ultimate wisdom and success of the venture. It would color their thinking on all Israeli policy in the future.

The diplomatic fallout after the Sinai Campaign was particularly painful to Israel. The world of the new emerging nations that arose out of the wreckage of colonialism was controlled by a leftist elite group of autocrats and diplomats. As Paul Johnson wrote: *The former colonies thus became superlative prey for the great human scourge of the twentieth century: the professional politician.*[26] *...Reforms [introduced by the colonial powers themselves] created an alien system of representation. A class of men, mainly lawyers, organized themselves to manipulate it. In due course, the governing power was handed over to them. The dialogue was entirely between the old [colonial rulers] and new elites. The ordinary people did not come into the play, except as a gigantic walk-on crowd in the background. The process was to be repeated all over Asia and Africa. [The] new ruling groups were men who had never engaged in any other occupation except politics and had devoted their lives to the exploitation of a flexible concept called "democracy."*[27] Nasser of Egypt, Nehru of India, Sukarno of Indonesia, Nkrumah of Ghana and other newly emerging leaders of Asia and Africa met in April 1955 in Bandung, Indonesia. There they formed a "Third World" that in reality was a mouthpiece for the Left and a supporter of Soviet policies.

Hoping to be of help to them in technology, economics and government administration, Israel had invested a great deal of effort in cultivating emerging countries. (In fact, during the 1950's and 1960's, Israel

---

25. Among them were Abba Eban, Shimon Peres, Yitzchak Rabin and Moshe Dayan.
26. Johnson, *Modern Times*, New York, 1992, p.510.
27. Ibid. p.47

was responsible for the training of six African armies.) Israeli "peace-corps" teams were to be found throughout the underdeveloped world. Despite this record, after the Sinai Campaign, Nasser succeeded in turning this "nonaligned Third World" into an anti-Israel lobby. There was no letup in the calls throughout the Arab world to destroy the "Zionist entity." Nasser continued to pursue his dream of pan-Arabism under his control and leadership. The United Nations General Assembly became a sounding board for vicious propaganda and calumnies against Israel. The Soviet bloc, the Moslem states and the "nonaligned" nations made Israel their whipping boy and a pariah at all UN sessions. Israel found itself increasingly isolated diplomatically, even in the West. Israel would be almost alone in the world for the balance of the century, dependent on the United States to prevent UN actions against it. This left Israel particularly vulnerable to United States' diplomatic pressures, a pressure that it would be unable to resist many times in the future.

A WAVE OF JEWISH IMMIGRATION BROUGHT 125,000 JEWS FROM EGYPT and North Africa to Israel in late 1956 and throughout 1957. As mentioned previously, the 1956 upheaval in Hungary sent 40,000 Jews to Israel and more than 40,000 Rumanian Jews arrived in the late 1950's (added to the 90,000 who had come earlier in the decade), fleeing revived vicious anti-Semitism. Despite the European immigration, the balance of Jewish population in Israel began to reflect the Sephardic majority. However, the government and all official and unofficial economic power still were controlled by the old-time Ashkenazic, socialist-oriented parties. Voluntary power sharing was unthinkable.

The kibbutz movement, which in many respects was the backbone of Israeli military elite and governmental leadership, reached its zenith in the 1950's. (Eventually, by the 1980's, there would be a population of close to 200,000 in the 565 collective farming settlements that comprised the different kibbutz and moshav organizations.[28]) But the strict doctrine of socialism was waning among the younger generation of the kibbutz population. Russian Premier Nikita Khruschev's revelations about the failure of Stalin's socialist paradise had sapped much of the belief in Marxism. The lure of the cities and the wealthy lifestyle of the Western capitalist and moderate socialist societies proved very tempting. The decline of the kibbutz would symbolize a slow, but steady, general decline in the idealistic spirit that had built the state.

Absorption Woes: Who Is a Jew?

---

28. Sachar, p.518.

The large immigration to Israel in the 1950's placed enormous strains on its fledgling economy. The country suffered from the difficulties resulting from the prodigous attempt to absorb more than four times its original population in one decade. Massive help came from Jews around the world through organized fund drives such as the United Jewish Appeal/Keren Hayesod, Jewish National Fund and Israel Bonds, and no less from an outpouring of private Jewish philanthropy. The reparations from Germany were also of invaluable aid in the effort to create a viable economic infrastructure for the young state. But Israel was a poor country. Food was available, but not in wide varieties or bountiful quantities. The agricultural sector of the economy struggled mightily to provide the basic food needs of the population. Many foods, especially grain, were imported in substantial quantities.

There were few, if any, private automobiles in the country; taxis, diplomatic vehicles and government cars made up most of the auto traffic. The road system was in poor repair. Buses were the main mode of transportation. The bus lines were controlled by two cooperatives of drivers — Egged and Dan. Like all monopolies, this created both benefits and problems. But in the early years of the state, being a member of these cooperatives gave one a highly valued place in the society, as well as a fairly high income.

Israel had one of the most regressive tax systems in the world. Individual income was taxed at an exorbitant rate (50-80%), there was a high sales tax and the customs duties on most imported goods were prohibitive. The needs of the country were so great that the government had little choice but to institute such a draconian tax system. A thriving tax-avoidance industry sprang up. Yet Socialist government doctrines provided for generous benefits for immigrants and a large amount of welfare, health care, child support and other benefits.

Because of budget restraints and social conditions, the school day in Israel was (and still is) relatively short — from 8:30 AM to 1:00 PM. All schools met six days a week and the religious school systems provided extra hours of instruction, which were not subsidized by the government. There were also clubs and community centers throughout the country that conducted afternoon programs for students, while many children simply helped their parents by working for a living. As can be expected, there were wide variations in the quality of the schools in various locations, with the lower economic class — mostly Sephardim residing in development towns — receiving a minimal education while the large urban schools, both public and private, provided a higher quality of educational opportunities for their Ashkenazic counterparts.

In 1958, a government coalition crisis occurred in Israel over Ben-Gurion's attempt to revise the rules of the Interior Ministry regarding the registration of citizens and immigrants as "Jewish" on their Israeli identification certificates. Ben-Gurion's leftist Minister of the Interior, Israel Bar Yehuda, wanted to institute procedures by which anyone who in good faith would attest to his or her being "identified" with the Jewish people and claim Jewish nationality would be registered as "Jewish" on official identity papers. This proposal provoked a worldwide storm of protest from many quarters, especially from the religious parties which were then part of Ben-Gurion's coalition government. They objected to handing over a religious and halachic issue to the whims of a changing, secular government. They argued that all matters of family lineage would now come into doubt and the ability of one Jew to marry another without halachic problems would be severely impaired. These parties threatened to resign and topple the government over this issue. Ben-Gurion then sent a letter to many leading Jewish scholars, professors, leaders, rabbis and professional executives all over the world, asking them to respond to this proposal and thus indirectly define "who is a Jew." This question of "who is a Jew," which never arose throughout Jewish history during thousands of years of dispersion and exile, would bedevil Israeli political life for the balance of the century. The overwhelming majority of the 43 responses that Ben-Gurion received stated the traditional equation that a Jew is anyone who is born from a Jewish mother or who has undergone conversion in accordance with Jewish law.[29] This answer was given by secular professors, leaders of the Conservative movement and lay leaders in addition to the Orthodox rabbis queried. Ben-Gurion realized that his proposal had little backing in the Jewish world and quietly let the initiative expire. More than theological faith, it was the unwillingness to divide the Jewish people that truly carried the day. In later years, when those who would seek to promote their own agendas over the unity of the people of Israel would arise periodically, the thorny issue of "who is a Jew" would be resurrected.

An Intangible Strength of Spirit

As the decade concluded, one of the most dramatic events in modern Jewish history began to unfold. On May 23, 1960, Ben Gurion laconically informed the Israeli Knesset that "The Israeli Security Services captured one of the greatest Nazi criminals, Adolf Eichmann, who together with the Nazi leaders was responsible for ... the destruction of six million European Jews. Eichmann is already in detention in Israel

---

29. This includes circumcision for a male, immersion in a *mikvah* (ritual bath) and a declared acceptance of the divinity of Torah and the observance of its commandments. These steps are all to be taken under the supervision of a qualified, recognized rabbinical court/*bais din*.

and will soon be put on trial here..." Eichmann was captured in Argentina, a favorite hiding place for escaped Nazis. The Argentine government protested his capture and "kidnapping." Argentina called for a UN Security Council meeting to condemn Israel's illegal acts. The liberal Western press and many outstanding jurists throughout the world also scolded Israel for flouting the norms of international law. The Arab countries, hardly notorious for enforcing civil rights in their own nations, were especially vociferous in denouncing Israel's "nefarious and brazen criminal behavior." After recriminations and considerable negotiation between Israel and Argentina ensued, the two countries agreed to a joint statement in August 1960 that was — or was not — an apology for infringing Argentine territory, depending on the reader's viewpoint and nationality. The initial furor over this statement died down over the next few months. The world apparently was finally willing to allow Israel to put Eichmann on trial for his crimes. That trial would rivet world attention back again to the horrors of the Holocaust during the early years of the next decade.

Despite its myriad problems, Israel looked back at its first decade with pride and wonder at its achievements. Israel had begun its life besieged, at war, poor, outnumbered by its sworn enemies dedicated to its destruction. It had not only had survived this dangerous decade, but it had actually prospered. There were enormous unsolved problems within Israeli society and Israel was isolated in its world standing. Yet, within the country and the Jewish world there was a feeling of accomplishment and determination, of a focused commitment to realizing the dream of a free, prosperous, secure Jewish state in the Land of Israel. This strength of spirit, intangible but mighty, was perhaps the greatest asset that the small state had as it ended the 1950's.

Jewish Pride Emerges in the Diaspora

AFTER THE DEATH OF STALIN AND A PERIOD OF INFIGHTING, jockeying for position and ruthless killings among the Soviet leadership, Nikita Khruschev emerged as the leader of Russia. A shrewd Ukrainian peasant who reached high office by his cunning and intuitive survival skills, Khruschev unmasked Stalin for the murderer he was at a secret session of the Communist Party's twentieth congress. From then on "the cult of personality" which Stalin personified was denounced in the Soviet Union. Yet Khruschev himself was not in any way a liberal reformer. Though the fear of governmental persecution of Jews abated in the 1950's after Stalin's death, no Jewish schools were ever reopened and the remaining organizations of Jewish culture or religion were infiltrated by the secret police and strongly restrained. Nevertheless, due to outside diplomatic pressure, a yeshivah of sorts, Kol Yaakov, was allowed to open in early 1957. Its ostensible purpose was to train rabbis for Soviet Jewry. The first Jewish calendar published in decades appeared in 1957 as well. But anti-Semitism in the Soviet Union was still widespread and intense.

In that same year, the Iron Curtain parted slightly. Polish Jews living in the Soviet Union were allowed to return to Poland: they then clandestinely left Poland for Israel. Khruschev himself denied that any Soviet Jew would wish to leave the Russian paradise to live in Israel. He said: "There are no files at our Ministry of the Interior with applications from persons of Jewish nationality or other nationalities who wish to emigrate to Israel. On the contrary, we have many letters from Jews in Israel, applying to us with the request to permit them to return from Israel to their homeland, the Soviet Union."[30]

Denying anti-Semitism in the Soviet Union during an interview in 1956, Khruschev said: *At the beginning of the revolution we had many Jews in leading party and government organs. Jews were perhaps more educated, more revolutionary, than the average Russian. After that, we formed new cadres ... our own intelligentsia. If Jews were now to occupy the leading posts in our republics, this would of course arouse unhappiness among the indigenous population. ... But we are not anti-Semites ... we fight against anti-Semitism.*[31] Interviewed two years later, Khruschev offered this opinion: *They do not like collective work, group discipline ... They are individualists ... Jews are essentially intellectuals ... As soon as they are in a position to, they want to go to university ... Their interests are too diverse ... The Jews are interested in everything, study everything deeply, discuss everything and finish by having profound cultural differences.*[32]

In the late 1950's, Jewish consciousness slowly seeped back into mainstream Soviet Jewry. Jewish scientists were in the forefront of Soviet nuclear and space research, but most Jews felt that they were not full citizens of the Soviet Union. Their internal security identification cards listed them as being Jewish and this carried with it a vulnerability to discrimination and isolation, if not worse. Visits by Jews from the West and from Israel, though they were few and were closely monitored by Soviet officials, nevertheless served to strengthen Jewish identity among the masses of Soviet Jews. Though during this time some members of the Israeli Leftist parties were convicted and jailed in Israel for spying against Israel on behalf of the Soviet Union, Jews in Russia were slowly building an emotional bond with Israel and the rest of the Jewish world. The Soviet government was unable to snuff out this newfound longing to identify with other Jews.

---

30. Quoted by Zvi Gitelman, *A Century of Ambivalence*, New York, 1988, p.263.
31. Ibid. p.265.
32. Ibid. p.264.

A slow, but steady, shift took place within American Jewry during the 1950's. The European survivors of the Holocaust asserted themselves, giving new vigor and direction to American Orthodoxy. For many decades, Orthodoxy had seen itself as a poor and aging stepsister of its Conservative and Reform brethren. On almost all major issues that confronted American Jewry it had been obliged to seek the representation and protection of its more affluent, influential non-Orthodox counterparts.[33] Thus, when the Synagogue Council of America was proposed in 1926, to be composed of the national clerical and congregational organs of the Reform, Conservative and Orthodox movements in America, Orthodox groups participated. They were represented by the Union of Orthodox Jewish Congregations of America, later joined by the Rabbinical Council of America.[34] There was no initial controversy regarding Orthodox participation in an organization of "mixed" denominations. The purpose of the organization was to promote a religious Jewish voice in American life, as opposed to the then current exclusively secular representation of American Jewry in American culture and politics by the already established national Jewish organizations. The Synagogue Council never achieved strong prominence or influence and was never a leading force in American Jewish life.[35]

The creation of the Synagogue Council raised the issue of whether Orthodox rabbis should participate in communal boards of rabbis that include non-Orthodox clergy. Leading heads of the American yeshivos, led by Rabbi Aharon Kotler, issued a proclamation in 1954 demanding that the two Orthodox bodies — the Union of Orthodox Jewish Congregations of America and the Rabbinical Council of America — withdraw their affiliations from the Synagogue Council of America. The proclamation also stipulated that Orthodox rabbis anywhere in America should not belong to communal boards of rabbis which included non-Orthodox clergy in their memberships. This proclamation evoked a firestorm of controversy within the Orthodox community, echoes of which would be heard throughout the following decades. This debate led to a continuing struggle within the Orthodox camp over policy, attitudes and the place of Orthodoxy in the modern, American world. The outlook and societal attitude of the "Modern/Centrist" Orthodox faction came

---

33. The major exceptions to this being the work of the Vaad Hatzala and Zeirei Agudath Israel — totally Orthodox organizations that battled to save Jews from Europe at any cost and by any means — during the years of World War II.

34. The Union of Orthodox Rabbis of the United States and Canada — the Agudas HaRabanim — also considered joining the Synagogue Council, but decided against it.

35. The organization finally closed its doors without a whimper in the 1990's.

under increasing criticism and attack by European survivors and their new generation of American students and Torah scholars. This tension within Orthodoxy would continue to grow over the years with bitter words exchanged between the different factions.

The influence of the "right" over Orthodox religious and social practice which began in the 1950's would continue throughout the remaining decades of the century. Orthodoxy would become more independent and assertive in its relationship to non-Orthodox Jewish groups, and less accommodating and subservient than it had been in earlier decades. This new assertiveness of Orthodoxy would open it to charges of being divisive. But this was a price for its newly found inner strength and confidence of purpose that it was apparently prepared to pay.

The decade of the '50's also saw Mizrachi in America begin its precipitous decline[36] while Agudath Israel began its ascent to eventually becoming the mainstream organization of American Orthodox Jewry.

"Mike" Tress, President of Agudath Israel, distributing Chanukah gifts to refugee children in Vienna in 1956

---

36. One of the reasons for the almost complete demise of Mizrachi in America was that its best and brightest leaders and young personalities immigrated to Israel in the 1950's, leaving the organization without the necessary leadership to strengthen itself and its appeal to American Jews. It was a victim of its own ideological success. It did not receive revitilization from the Holocaust survivors who immigrated to America, as most of them were not ideologically associated with Mizrachi. Not

The day school movement grew and prospered in the 1950's with enormous investments of individual idealism and personal sacrifice compensating for its chronic economic shortfall. The established yeshivos all experienced remarkable increases in enrollment and the educational standards were raised, while new yeshivos began to sprout. The Chasidic courts attracted American-born adherents, while Chasidic lifestyle and behavior influenced all American Orthodox groups. The beginnings of the *kollel* system also were noticeable during this decade.[37] In some ways, the 1950's may have represented the nadir of Orthodox Jewish life in America, but it was also the decade when Orthodoxy began its painful comeback from the cusp of assimilated oblivion.

Summer campers in Camp Agudah in Ferndale, New York are visited by Rabbi Yaakov Kamenetsky

The 1950's also saw the rise to greater public notice of outstanding personalities in the American Orthodox world. Rabbi Aharon Kotler, Rabbi Yitzchok Hutner, Rabbi Yaakov Yitzchok Ruderman, Rabbi Eliyahu Meir Bloch, Rabbi Yaakov Kamenetsky and Rabbi Gedaliah Schorr, among others, rose to prominence and influence as their yeshivos (described in earlier chapters) flourished. Rabbi Joseph B. Soloveitchik became the solid and respected spokesman for Modern Orthodoxy.[38]

Rabbi Yoel Teitelbaum, the *Satmar Rav*, created a bastion of Chasidic strength in the Williamsburg section of Brooklyn, New York. He and his followers were known for their great devotion to their customs and traditions, their wide-ranging acts of charity and kindness and for their fierce and vehe-

so the non-Zionist Agudath Israel, which benefited from extraordinary organizational command under Rabbi Moshe Sherer and enlisted hundreds of dynamic yeshivah students and graduates into its leadership roles. Agudath Israel received an enormous tranfusion of vitality, ideology and leadership from the Eastern European rabbis who came to America before, during and after World War II, almost all of whom joined the ranks of the American Agudath Israel.

37. The *kollel* was a postgraduate school of Talmudic studies where young men, already married and with families, were supported financially while they continued their Torah studies. The length of time spent in *kollel* varied from a few years to being a permanent way of life. The *kollel* would become a very popular institution in the Orthodox world for the balance of the century, involving within its system thousands of students. Its popularity was of such a nature that by the end of the century even the non-Orthodox seminaries in America and Israel called their postgraduate studies "*kollel*" as well.

38. Anyone who had the personal honor of knowing Rabbi Soloveitchik personally, as I did, realizes that he was far too multi-faceted and sophisticated a personality to be identified as being himself "Modern" Orthodox or "yeshivah" Orthodox, etc. Though it was the Modern Orthodox camp that claimed him as their spiritual leader and guide, his influence was far wider than that.

ment anti-Zionism. They also became influential in city and state politics in a manner that no other Chasidic group ever before achieved in America.

Rabbi Menachem Mendel Schneerson became the seventh *Lubavitcher Rebbe* at the beginning of the decade, after the death of his father-in-law, Rabbi Yosef Yitzchok Schneerson. Even though Chabad was known in Europe for its zeal, intellectual outlook, sacrifice for its principles and efforts on behalf of other Jews, it was under Rabbi Menachem Mendel Schneerson's gifted leadership that Chabad became a world-wide force. An esteemed Torah scholar who also attended university classes in Paris, he was a man of unbounded energy, vision and innovation. Chabad was a completely independent organization, unlike other Orthodox groups, which always had to contend with the opinions of others in the Orthodox camp. Chabad considered itself answerable to no one but itself and thus was able to undertake controversial projects and stands on issues not dared by other Orthodox groups. Unquestioning personal loyalty to the Rebbe and his dictates marked Chabad and its

Rabbi Menachem Mendel Schneerson

adherents. It was this personal loyalty that built Chabad into an international organization that reached out to millions of Jews around the world. It was also this unquestioning loyalty to a person, almost to the point of deification, which made Chabad a source of continuing controversy and friction in the Orthodox world throughout the century. It would lead to major problems for the movement itself at the end of the century.

The 1950's demonstrated the heroic courage of the Jewish people to raise itself from the ashes of the Holocaust and rebuild a new Jewish life. Whether in the fledgling and beleaguered State of Israel or in the United States and other major centers of the Diaspora, the spirit of purpose and tenacity dominated. Thus, it is no exaggeration to say that this decade represented the finest example of collective Jewish efforts and inner strength exhibited at any time during the twentieth century. It was a time of terrible testing for the Jewish world, but it was also a time of major accomplishments and undaunted will.

Chapter Eight

Danger, Victory and Opportunity

1961-1970

T HE TURBULENCE THAT BUFFETED THE JEWISH PEOPLE THROUGHOUT the twentieth century ebbed and flowed, though it never abated. The decade of the 1960's was one of the more difficult periods in the century, yet it also proved to be most inspirational and hopeful. This decade was a revolutionary and dangerous period in world history as well. John F. Kennedy was elected President of the United States in 1960 and was assassinated three years later. America attempted to crush communist Cuba in the ill-fated Bay of Pigs invasion, and in turn was faced with the introduction of Russian nuclear missiles into Cuba. The superpowers, the United States and Russia, gingerly stepped back from the brink of nuclear self-destruction. When Nikita Khruschev was later deposed from power, his poor performance during the missile crisis debacle was a strong factor.

Lyndon B. Johnson became President of the United States after Kennedy was killed and America continued its slow and fatal drift into the Vietnamese War. The social revolution of the "beatniks" and "hippies" and of the resultant breakdown of the traditional values of patriotism and sexual morality changed American society. Public obscenity and provocative dress, sexual licentiousness and open defiance of authority figures and institutions became acceptable behavior, first on college campuses, and later in other strata of American society.

Because Jews were disproportionately numerous on American college campuses, they were also disproportionately represented in the protest and social change movements that sprung up in the United States and Western Europe, especially in France. The "generation gap" between children and their parents became a characteristic of the '60's and the cliché has endured since that era.[1]

President John F. Kennedy watches the flight of astronaut Alan Shepard on television. Left to right: McGeorge Bundy; Vice President Johnson; Arthur Schlesinger; Admiral Arleigh Burke; President Kennedy; Mrs. Kennedy May 5, 1961

---

1. This "generation gap" was less pronounced in Orthodox and traditional families. Generally, Orthodox families did not send their children away to distant college campuses where the likelihood of succumbing to the new rebellious social behavior was greatest. In addition, the observances of the same religious ritual among family generations solidified the relationship between the young and the old. Nevertheless, the great social revolutions of the 1960's certainly affected and penetrated Orthodox Jewish life in America. The home, the day school and the yeshivah all struggled to meet the new challenges that this social revolution presented, with varying results of success.

The early 1960's marked the coming of age of the "civil rights" movement in American life. The drive to end discrimination, segregation and persecution of Blacks in America, particularly in the southern states, was led by Dr. Martin Luther King and a number of other charismatic African-American personalities. Although Dr. King preached the doctrine of non-violent protest, a great deal of violence accompanied this wrenching attempt to right this great wrong in American society. The American Jewish community rallied to the civil rights cause, supplying money and numerous volunteers, as well as political and moral support.[2] American Jews felt that the cause was not only morally correct on its own merits, but that the destruction of all discriminatory barriers in American life would guarantee Jews the freedom and full equality that they desired as well. The assassination of Dr. King in 1964 sparked severe race riots in many of the major cities of the United States; thereafter, Jewish and African-American interests no longer coincided in some economic, social, housing and neighborhood areas. The Black community also resented what they viewed as Jewish paternalism

---

2. Three young Jews from New York were murdered in Mississippi while working on a Black voter registration drive. Many Jewish leaders openly espoused the cause of the "civil rights" movement. One of the most famous photographs of the era shows Dr. Abraham Joshua Heschel marching arm in arm with Dr. Martin Luther King across the bridge at Selma, Alabama, in a famous protest march against segregation.

towards their cause. Openly anti-Semitic rhetoric began to emerge in the statements of many of the militant leaders, particularly vilifying "Jewish landlords" and "Jewish merchants." Some groups, such as the Black Muslims and the Nation of Islam, openly preached anti-Jewish canards and insults.[3] Despite the mounting Black backlash, the American Jewish community's commitment to equal rights for all survived the many tensions between the two communities for the balance of the century.

LBJ signs the Civil Rights Act of 1964

World attention was riveted on the trial of Adolf Eichmann in Jerusalem during 1961. The trial lasted fourteen weeks and the entire terrible ordeal of the Holocaust was publicly exposed and, in a sense, relived. Holocaust survivors testified at the trial about their unbelievable experiences. In heartrending courtroom scenes, many of the witnesses fainted — and some suffered heart attacks — as they dredged their memories to record the awful facts of Nazi inhumanity. Eichmann's defense was that he was only a spoke in the wheel, a bureaucrat shuffling papers and obeying directives, a mere transportation coordinator.[4] The fact that those papers and directives were the means by which six million Jews were destroyed did not seem to impress him or his conscience. The prosecution, led by Gideon Hausner, proved conclusively that Eichmann was much more than a low level functionary. Thousands of documents of evidence were introduced into the court record: The Germans, after all, were methodical record keepers. As the trial wore on, a synopsis of the day's evidence was provided in the daily newspapers and on world television every night. The published transcript of the trial was over 6,000 pages long.[5] At last, the Holocaust became somewhat more real to those who had not been there. Eichmann was found guilty and all appeals of his death sentence were

---

3. Elijah Muhammed, Malcolm X, Stokely Carmichael and later Louis Farrakhan, among others, were outspoken anti-Semites.

4. Eichmann was a perfect example of what Hannah Arendt termed "the banality of evil." Her book, *Eichmann in Jerusalem*, was widely reviled as an attempt to shift blame from the killers to the victims.

5. The best book on the Eichmann trial, in my opinion, is Gideon Hausner's work, *Justice in Jerusalem*. It is also an excellent history of the Holocaust itself.

rejected. He was hanged at midnight, May 31, 1962, his body cremated and the ashes scattered over the Mediterranean Sea, lest his grave become a shrine for anti-Semites. It was the only death sentence ever executed in the history of the State of Israel.

The Flowering of the Jewish State

IN THE OFFICIAL CENSUS OF 1961, THE ISRAELI GOVERNMENT REPORTED that the Jewish population of Israel numbered 1,932,400. The Jewish population had almost doubled since the earlier 1950 census and was three and a half times larger than what it was in 1948 when the state was created. There were also approximately 250,000 non-Jews living in the country. The economy of Israel had grown commensurately.

A maturing pride in Jewish Israel was reflected in its cultural developments. The beautiful Knesset building in Jerusalem was dedicated and put into use at the beginning of the decade. It was built through the philanthropy of the Rothschild family as a testimony to that family's share in the rebirth of the Jewish state in the Land of Israel. In 1966, on the hill facing the Knesset building, the Israel Museum was dedicated and opened. It joined the Yad Vashem Holocaust Museum, established in 1953, as a public place of remembrance in Jewish Jerusalem.[6] In 1966, Shmuel Yosef Agnon, a famed Hebrew writer, was awarded the Nobel Prize for literature. In his acceptance speech before the King of Sweden, Agnon, an Orthodox Jew, said: "Through a historical catastrophe — the destruction of Jerusalem by the emperor of Rome — I was born in one of the cities of the Diaspora. But I have always deemed myself a child of Jerusalem — one who was really a native of Jerusalem." Agnon's likeness appeared on the Israeli 50 shekel currency bill throughout the last third of the century.

The Mizrachi movement in Israel was undergoing a transformation that became increasingly evident in the 1960's. During the 1940's and 1950's, a number of yeshivos had been established by its Bnei Akiva youth movement and by other rabbis ideologically affiliated with the Mafdal. These yeshivos, of which Kerem B'Yavne was the flagship,[7] created a "*hesder*" system of yeshivah studies combined with military service.

---

6. The Diaspora Museum, opened on the campus of Tel Aviv University in north Tel Aviv in 1978, recorded the story of Jewish life in the world of exile that they inhabited for so many difficult centuries. Towards the last decade of the century, the Museum of the Bible Lands, putting Israel in the context of ancient cultures and events, opened near the Israel Museum.

7. Rabbi Chaim Yaakov Goldvicht, a student of the *Brisker Rav* (Rabbi Yitzchak Zev Soloveitchik), was the founding *rosh yeshivah* of the *hesder* yeshivah Kerem B'Yavne and served as its leader for many decades. Rabbi Moshe Zvi Neriyah, a student of Rabbi Kook, headed the yeshivah in Kfar Haroeh, which became the prototype for many other Bnei Akiva yeshivos. Rabbi Goldvicht actively encouraged his students to do volunteer duties in the army that were dangerous or distateful. Because of this spirit, casualties among the *hesder* soldiers often were disproportionately high.

Under its five year program, instead of the 30-36 month stint for others, the yeshivah student spent a number of years alternating army service and his Talmudic studies.

A new cadre of knowledgeable and committed young leaders entered the Israeli Orthodox scene. Their *kippot srugot* (knitted head covering) became the symbol of the new generation of Mafdal, the successor to the Mizrachi-Hapoel HaMizrachi parties. Due to the influence of their yeshivos, the party membership became more scholarly and punctiliously observant of ritual than its predecessors in the movement. The 1960's were the golden years of Mafdal as it reached its height of political power and national influence. It saw itself as the bridge between the Orthodox world and the secular leaders of Israel and as the protector of the Jewish character of the state. It also gained a new measure of self-confidence and assertiveness in its relations with both the secular and the non-Zionist Orthodox populations in Israel due to the rising number and strength of its own excellent yeshivos.

Political events signaled a change as well. After intense and bitter inner party squabbling, David Ben-Gurion once more resigned as prime minister in 1963 and was succeeded by Levi Eshkol. A man of droll wit and frequent resort to Yiddish aphorisms and jokes, Eshkol was a shrewd politician: His formidable leadership qualities were belied by his unimpressive appearance and bantering style of speech. Ben-Gurion and his former Labor Party colleagues, led by Levi Eshkol and Golda Meir, had a bitter falling out over the Lavon affair (detailed in chapter seven) and other political and personal issues. In 1965 Ben-Gurion, Shimon Peres and Moshe Dayan formed a new political party, Rafi, promising to revolutionize the existing Israeli political and electoral system and to bring young,

An honor guard of Etzel and Lechi underground members beside the coffins of Zev and Johanna Jabotinsky on the Tel Aviv shore. At left, Yitzchak Shamir. July 1964.

dynamic leadership to the fore, replacing the "old Mapai dead wood." But in the Knesset election in 1965, Eshkol and Labor gained 45 seats; Begin and the Right took 26 seats, while Rafi only won ten seats. Mizrachi — now Mafdal — won eleven seats (losing three) and Agudah four seats, while Mapam was reduced to eight. The coalition of Labor, Mapam and Mafdal governed the country while Rafi remained in the opposition. This election was Ben-

Gurion's swan song in politics, a humiliating way for the old lion to leave the political scene that he had dominated for so many decades. After the Six Day War and Ben-Gurion's permanent retirement in Sde Boker, Rafi would disband and its members would rejoin the Labor Party.

The Arab Nations Agree on One Goal

WITH ALL OF ITS POSITIVE STRIDES, THE THREAT OF WAR WAS NEVER distant from Israeli minds. Continuing Arab terrorist raids and bloody incidents marked the early 1960's. Nevertheless, the country continued to develop and stood resolute in the face of its enemies. The surrounding Arab countries, under the fear and influence of Egyptian President Nasser's demagogic pan-Arab oratory, continued their open opposition to Israel's right to exist. Egypt and Syria were now well armed with Russian weapons and military advisers. In April 1963, Egypt, Syria and Iraq signed a treaty of alliance placing their military under a joint, unified command. The stated purpose of the alliance was "the destruction of the Jewish State by the liberation of Palestine." Despite Nasser's blustering, his army of 60,000 men was bogged down in a bitter civil war in Yemen between pro-Egyptian and pro-Saudi Arabian factions. The Egyptian economy was in tatters and Nasser's diplomatic standing had also lessened. In 1961, he created the United Arab Republic by absorbing Syria into the Egyptian orbit. This marriage was of short duration, however, and Syria withdrew from the United Arab Republic in 1962. Yet even after Syria had shed its legal connection to Nasser's rule, it remained Israel's most aggressive and bellicose enemy.

In 1959 Israel had constructed a water pumping station at the northwestern corner of the Sea of Galilee, and in the early '60's Israel continued developing its national water carrier project. The Syrians objected to the project and brought the matter to the United Nations, which uncharacteristically did nothing about the complaint. The Arab League, meeting in Cairo at the end of 1963, recommended joint Arab action to divert the headwaters of the Jordan River from flowing into the Jordan and the Sea of Galilee.[8] Lebanese and Syrian engineers began to work on diverting those water sources. Israel responded with tank, artillery and aircraft fire. The strong Israeli response stopped the work of diversion.

The Syrian army on the Golan Heights began to fire daily on Jewish farmers working their fields in the Chuleh Valley below. This persistent sniping sparked long artillery duels — and even aerial combat —

---

8. The Chatzbani stream and the Banias spring were two sources of the Jordan River, then in Arab hands. The Dan River, which is the third source of the Jordan River, was in Israel.

between Israeli forces and the Syrians. The Syrian government, weak and dictatorial, used the "liberation of Palestine" as a unifying sentiment for its populace, and thus had no interest in lowering the level of violence directed against Israel. For the residents of the kibbutzim and settlements of the northeastern Galilee, the first six years of the decade meant years of sleeping in underground shelters and working with armored tractors under sporadic but frequent Syrian gunfire. All Israeli complaints to the United Nations met with a stolid Russian veto of any condemnation of the continuing Arab violence.

In a sinister and far-reaching development, the Arab League now determined to use the hapless Arab refugees, kept by the Arab host countries and the United Nations in squalid refugee camps for a decade and a half, as the vehicle to undermine Israel's existence and growth. In 1964, The Palestine Liberation Organization was created with the express purpose of attaining "the objective of liquidating Israel." The PLO operated under Egyptian sanction and control from the Gaza Strip. In Syria, another Palestinian organization, the Arab Liberation Movement, commonly called Fatah, was formed. Its leadership consisted of followers of the former Grand Mufti of Jerusalem. This organization later became the base of Yassir Arafat's power. Terror raids and continuous ambushes were mounted against Israeli soldiers and civilians from Syria. Though the Fatah and PLO were then rivals to each other,[9] as were Egypt and Syria, their determination to bring destruction to Israel united them in purpose, if not always in tactics. From 1963 onward, Israel maintained clandestine contacts with King Hussein of Jordan, searching for a way out of the terrorist impasse. Hussein even met secretly with Golda Meir during this time and Jordan did attempt to control terrorist incursions into Israel from its territory, but only with sporadic success. Syria and Egypt, both with strong Soviet military and diplomatic backing, continued to take a very hard and threatening stance against Israel.

UNDER SOVIET AND ARAB ORCHESTRATION, THE UNITED NATIONS became a sounding board for anti-Israel propaganda. The Soviet Union positioned itself as not only the protector of Egypt and Syria, but as the implacable foe of Israel. In 1966, putting a Soviet propaganda spin on Israel's retaliatory raids against Arab terrorism, UN Soviet Ambassador Jakob Malik warned Israeli diplomat Abba Eban that "Israel's aggressive policies endanger Israel's very existence as a state."

Sounds of War Echo in UN Chambers and Beyond

---

9. Ahmed Shukeiry, the head of the PLO until the end of 1967, was wounded in an assassination attempt carried out by his Arab rivals.

More dangerously, the General Assembly of the UN began its decades-long practice of passing one-sided, viciously anti-Israel resolutions. Israel came to rely on the United States for protection in the UN Security Council, a relationship that would seriously hamper Israeli diplomatic independence and influence its policies.

France remained a sometime ally of Israel until the 1967 war. President Charles DeGaulle, who eventually revealed his anti-Jewish prejudices,[10] sought closer ties with the Arab world after he abandoned Algeria. Nevertheless, at the end of 1966 France delivered 50 state-of-the-art fighter-bomber warplanes to Israel, making possible Israel's air victory in the impending, but as yet unforeseen, Six Day War. France also agreed to supply Israel with other modern weapons, including a number of custom-built gunboats that could serve as Israel's battleships. But it was clear that the warmth of the Israeli-French relationship definitely had cooled under DeGaulle's presidency. (It is obvious that all nations have their own self-interests. There are times when that self-interest may come into conflict with the desires, even the well-being, of Israel or of individual Jews. That self-interest cannot always be ascribed to anti-Semitism. The enormous influence of Arab oil on the economic welfare of the West and Japan, for instance, makes unmitigated support for Israel a contradiction to the natural self-interests of those countries. Nevertheless, the behavior of DeGaulle and his attitude toward the Jewish people in labelling them "elitist and arrogant" clearly smacks of anti-Semitism. Similarly, the policies of the Soviet Union towards Israel and its own Jewish population during the long, dark decades of the Cold War reveal their anti-Semitic origins.)

Under Lyndon Johnson's administration, the United States had become more and more involved in the Vietnamese war. There was considerable social and political protest brewing in America over this involvement, with the "Woodstock generation"[11] on college campuses creating hotbeds of dissent. By 1967, it was obvious that America was not winning the war in Vietnam. Social upheavals were tearing society apart, and American leadership was preoccupied with national problems as well as with the failing American involvement in Vietnam. Noting these factors, the Soviet Union believed that a crisis in the Middle East would bring no swift or determined American response. It therefore embarked on a provocative adventure — born of anti-Semitism and an attempt to humble America by

10. Howard M. Sachar, *A History of Israel*, New York 1996, p. 692.

11. The name derived from a raucous rock-music festival held in Woodstock, New York, attended by tens of thousands of college students and other young adults. The festival was noted for its widespread drug abuse, sexual promiscuity and radical rejection of authority and the norms of traditional American life. It became known as the expression and symbol of the cultural and social revolution in America in the 1960's.

proxy — that threatened the very existence of the Jewish state.

Throughout 1966 and 1967, enormous amounts of Soviet weaponry had streamed into Syria and Egypt. As the internal economic and social problems of these countries increased, Nasser and the Syrian leadership deflected local energy and discontent into public preparation for the forthcoming war against Israel. In 1966, Nasser spoke openly about his aim of erasing Israel from the map of the Middle East.

Nasser (left) confers with Aleksei Kosygin, Chairman of Soviet Ministers of the USSR

Confident of Russian support and aware that the West and the United States would not risk war with Russia by intervening in the Middle East, Nasser intensified the border war with Israel and the Gaza Strip with terrorist attacks almost daily. In cooperation with the Egyptian move, Syria moved heavy weapons into the northern border area with Israel and increased its firing from the Golan Heights. Israel warned Syria that it would be forced to take deterrent measures if the Syrian aggression did not abate. At the United Nations, Russia placed the full blame for the tension in the Middle East at Israel's doorstep, accusing Israel of moving heavy troop concentrations to the Syrian border. Prime Minister Eshkol offered to take the Russian ambassador to the Syrian-Israeli border to see for himself that there was no Israeli military buildup. The ambassador never took the offer seriously, for he was under instructions from Moscow to foment trouble, not to ascertain facts.

The Soviet Union next demanded that Nasser take action to protect their Syrian client state. On May 15, 1967, Nasser paraded two large armored divisions of the Egyptian army through the streets of Cairo and moved them across the Suez Canal into the Sinai Peninsula, thereby threatening the Israeli border with Egypt. Israel originally regarded Nasser's war-like statements and military move into the Sinai as dangerously provocative, but more bluff than reality. Self-intoxicated with the fantasy of defeating and destroying Israel, Nasser ordered the UN peacekeeping troops stationed in the Sinai, the Gaza Strip and at the entrance to the Red Sea at Sharm-el-Shiekh to leave his sovereign Egyptian territory. This request, made on May 17, was immediately and cravenly complied with by U Thant, the Burmese Secretary General of the United Nations. The removal of UN troops ended the arrangements for stability which Israel had achieved at the conclusion of the Sinai Campaign a little more than ten years earlier. Emboldened by his cheap victories at the expense of the United Nations and aware that the West would not halt his aggression, Nasser now openly proclaimed his intent to destroy the "Zionist Jewish state."

"Entirely on Our Own..."

BLOODCURDLING STATEMENTS PREDICTING ISRAEL'S DESTRUCTION emanated from surrounding Arab countries. The Arab world was caught up in a frenzy of euphoria and hate. Nasser was now the hero of the Arab street and the bane of all of the other leaders of the Arab countries who now had no choice but to follow his demagogic and warlike lead. On May 21, Nasser announced a blockade of the Straits of Tiran and the Gulf of Eilat by Egypt. He announced that no Israeli shipping whatsoever, or non-Israeli shipping headed for Eilat, would be allowed to pass. Nasser now found himself hoisted on his own petard, unable to stop the momentum towards war that he had himself unleashed. He would have to go to war against Israel, even if his better judgement said otherwise.

Nasser's speech to his air force pilots, made the day after the blockade was announced, virtually declared war on Israel. In his words:

> We are face to face with Israel. Henceforth the situation is in your hands. Our armed forces have occupied Sharm-el-Sheikh ... We shall on no account allow the Israeli flag to pass through the Gulf of Aqaba. The Jews threaten to make war. I reply: Ahlan wa sahlan — Welcome! We are ready for war ... The water is ours.[12]

French defense officials continued shipping war materiel to Israel during the weeks of the crisis. There was a great deal of sympathy for little Israel and its struggle against the Arabs in the French military, still smarting from its defeats at Suez and in Algeria. At the end of May, however, French President Charles DeGaulle warned Abba Eban about Israel going to war against Egypt. "Do not make war! Do not make war! In any event, do not be the first to fire!" An intimidated Abba Eban thanked DeGaulle for his suggestions and flew on to London and Washington. DeGaulle was convinced that Israel would not dare ignore the wisdom of his advice. President Lyndon B. Johnson, in Washington, also warned Eban against Israel "jumping the gun." He assured Eban that "you will not be alone unless you decide to go it alone."[13] He also promised that America would organize an international effort to break the Egyptian blockade of the Straits of Tiran. However, the American involvement in Vietnam was so massive, frustrating and controversial that it soon became clear that the United States would not embark on any new foreign policy

---

12. Quoted by Gilbert, p.368.
13. Howard M. Sachar, *A History of Israel*, New York 1996, pp.629-630.

venture in the Middle East that might involve the use of its armed forces. In addition, there was little support for an international or Western European effort to break Nasser's blockade of the Straits of Tiran. The Israeli Ambassador to Washington, Avraham Harman, realistically advised his government that Israel was all alone in this matter.

In Israel itself, stolid preparations for war were being readied. Golda Meir wrote in her memoir of those days of late May and early June 1967:

> There were also the grim preparations that had to be kept secret: The parks in each city had been consecrated for possible use as mass cemeteries; the hotels cleared of guests so that they could be turned into huge emergency first-aid stations; ...rations stockpiled against the time when the population might have to be fed from some central source; the bandages, drugs, and stretchers obtained and distributed.
>
> And, of course, above all, there were the military preparations, because even though we had by now absorbed the fact that we were entirely on our own, there wasn't a single person in Israel, as far as I know, who had any illusions about the fact that there was no alternative whatsoever to winning the war that was being thrust upon us.
>
> When I think back to those days, what stands out in my mind is the miraculous sense of unity and purpose that transformed us within only a week or two from a small, rather claustrophobic community, coping — and not always well — with all sorts of economic, political and social discontents into two and a half million Jews, each and every one of whom felt personally responsible for the survival of the State of Israel, and each and every one knew that the enemy we faced was committed to our annihilation.[14]

To the consternation of Israel, King Hussein now made a fateful choice and a strategic error that would dominate the Arab-Israeli conflict for the rest of the century. He entered into an alliance with Nasser and placed the Jordanian troops under nominal Egyptian control. Hussein was apparently responding to the fervor of the Arab street masses whipped into an anti-Israel frenzy by Nasser's belligerence and rhetoric. Israel thus was facing a three-front war against Egypt, Syria and Jordan simultaneously. Israel hoped that Hussein was only bluffing and would not actually participate in hostilities, should they break out. Israel had decided to postpone any preemptive strike against Egypt and to wait for developments.

Engulfed by a palpable tension, the entire country — and with it the entire Jewish world — held its breath for a full week, and prayed for

---

14. Quoted from Golda Meir's *My Life,* London, 1975.

deliverance. General Chaim Herzog, a son of the late Chief Rabbi of Israel and a future president of Israel, broadcast daily military and intelligence assessments that had a wondrously soothing effect on the Israeli population. His calm voice, intelligent and truthful analyses of the situation and inherent optimism greatly encouraged morale at this terribly depressing moment. There were also a number of popular songs — "Jerusalem of Gold," "Rabin is Waiting for Nasser," among others — that also lifted the spirits of the people.

But on paper, the statistics of war looked very grim indeed. Egypt had an army of 100,000 men in the Sinai and the Gaza Strip, with 900 tanks and 400 planes poised for action. Syria had mobilized close to 100,000 men, 400 tanks and 150 aircraft. The Jordanians had 32,000 men in the West Bank, with 300 tanks and over 100 warplanes. Egypt maintained a reserve army of an additional 140,000 men and 300 tanks that it could move into the Sinai, if necessary. Ten thousand Iraqi troops, with 150 tanks, were traveling to Jordan to take up positions in the fight against Israel. Against this powerful array, Israel, with full mobilization of its civilian reservists, had an army of 264,000 men, 800 tanks and 300 planes.

Prime Minister/Minister of Defense Levi Eshkol made a public address on radio and television to the Israeli public to clarify the situation and strengthen public morale. The speech had the opposite result, for Eshkol's bumbling and stuttering delivery was uninspired and further depressed the populace. The speech had the effect of raising a national cry for a unity government; Eshkol had no choice but to consent to bringing Menachem Begin into the cabinet as Minister without Portfolio, and to allow Moshe Dayan to assume the post of Minister of Defense. Dayan's appointment heartened the Israeli public who remembered his victories against the Arabs in the 1948 and 1956 wars. The tactical plans for the conduct of the war were already in place well before Dayan came to power and he merely approved the work of the General Staff, which was then under the direction of General Yitzchak Rabin. But Dayan's appointment was a terrific psychological boost for Israel, for he was a person of decision and action.

Gambling on a Surprise Attack

DAYAN, ESHKOL AND THE CABINET DECIDED THAT ISRAEL HAD TO strike the first blow in order to win the war and secretly chose June 5 as the date of the Israeli lightning attack. As a ruse, the army granted Shabbat leave to many of its officers for the weekend of June 3. The following Monday, at 7:45 AM, the Israeli Air Force, commanded by General Mordechai Hod, attacked Egyptian, Jordanian and Syrian air bases. Israel gambled everything in this maneuver, holding back only twelve fighter planes to protect its own airspace. Despite their warlike boasts, the Arabs were caught by surprise — as the Israeli planes flew so low that they could not be detected by Egyptian radar. Most of the Arab planes were destroyed while still on the ground. By the end of the first day of fighting, over 400 Arab aircraft had been destroyed, while Israel had lost seventeen planes. Rabin later said that the destruction of the Arab air forces on the first day of the war "in essence, decided the fate of the war." The military and psychological blow to the Arab armies was a crushing and fatal one. Even though days of bitter fighting and bloody sacrifice still lay ahead, the report of Israel's amazing feat of air warfare fortified the Israeli armed forces and the public.

In an attempt to redress the developing negative military situation, Nasser called Hussein, urging him to attack Israel in Jerusalem and across the Israeli-Jordanian border on the West Bank. To strengthen Hussein's resolve, Nasser informed Hussein that "Haifa and Tel Aviv are in flames" and that the Israeli Air Force had been smashed. Israeli intelligence monitored and recorded the telephone conversation between the two Arab leaders. Foolishly believing Nasser's lies, Hussein ignored the Israeli offer communicated to him through the UN that his forces would not be attacked if he refrained from attacking Israel. Instead, his artillery shelled Jewish Jerusalem, including the Knesset building where the legislative session then adjourned to the safety of the building's underground bomb shelter. Jordanian troops also moved to capture the UN headquarters at Government House in Jerusalem's East Talpiot neighborhood. Once Jordan was involved in the war, Nasser phoned Hussein again and admitted that the Egyptian Air Force had been destroyed, though he blamed American and British fighter planes. This explanation of their air defeat was broadcast worldwide by the Arabs, at the behest of Nasser and Hussein, both of whom knew it to be a lie. Of course, both England and the United States truthfully denied any participation in the hostilities. Hussein's attack on Jerusalem brought a swift and punishing Israeli response, as the Israeli army went on the offensive and began its campaign to reunite the city under Israeli sovereignty.

On the western front, Israeli tank and ground forces attacked the Gaza Strip and effectively cut it off from Egypt by capturing the Egyptian army's road and communications center in Sinai at El Arish. The Israeli army then humbled the Egyptian forces in a three-pronged tank and infantry attack across the Sinai. At Mitla Pass in the center of Sinai, Israeli warplanes and tank gunners destroyed the bulk of the Egyptian armored forces in Sinai. Five thousand Egyptian soldiers were taken prisoner and thousands more were killed and wounded in the first days of the war. The Egyptian and terrorist bases in the Gaza Strip were overrun and

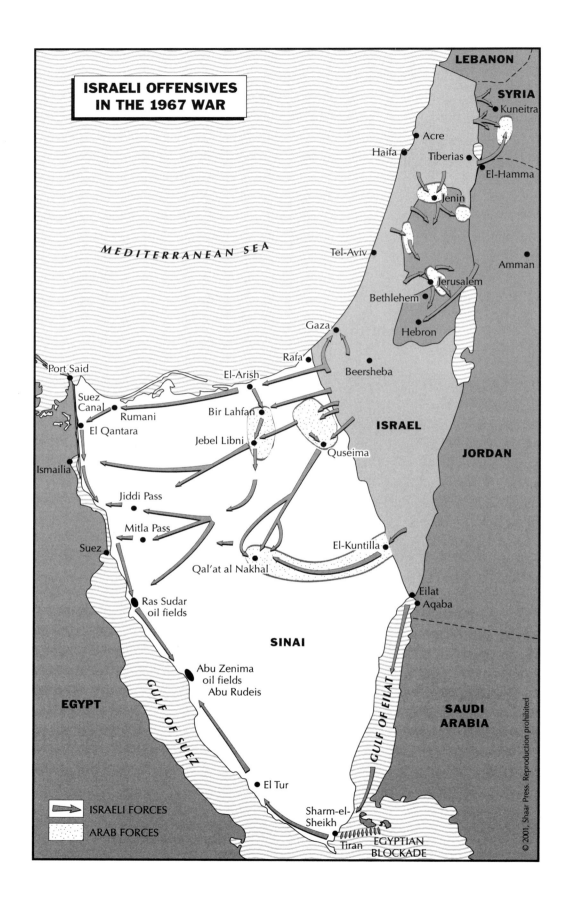

ISRAELI OFFENSIVES IN THE 1967 WAR

LEBANON

SYRIA

Kuneitra

Acre

Haifa

Tiberias

El-Hamma

MEDITERRANEAN SEA

Jenin

Tel-Aviv

Amman

Jerusalem

Bethlehem

Gaza

Hebron

Rafa

Beersheba

Port Said

El-Arish

Suez Canal

Bir Lahfan

ISRAEL

Rumani

El Qantara

Jebel Libni

JORDAN

Quseima

Ismailia

Jiddi Pass

Mitla Pass

El-Kuntilla

Suez

Qal'at al Nakhal

Eilat

Aqaba

Ras Sudar
oil fields

SINAI

Abu Zenima
oil fields
Abu Rudeis

EGYPT

GULF OF SUEZ

SAUDI
ARABIA

GULF OF EILAT

El Tur

Sharm-el-
Sheikh

Tiran

EGYPTIAN
BLOCKADE

→ ISRAELI FORCES

⬚ ARAB FORCES

© 2001, Shaar Press. Reproduction prohibited

Uri Zohar performs for Israeli troops of the Southern front. Mr. Zohar later became a ba'al teshuvah and a strong influence in Israeli religious outreach efforts.

destroyed. By the end of the second day of the war, it was obvious that Egypt had suffered a major defeat. Israeli ground and naval forces were hurrying towards Sharm-el-Shiekh to lift the proclaimed Egyptian blockade of the Straits of Tiran. When the Israelis arrived at Sharm-el-Shiekh, they found the Egyptian gun emplacements abandoned and deserted. The Israeli army reached the Suez Canal on the third day of the war and this marked, for all practical purposes, the end of the war in the Sinai. Nasser's boasts and threats of annihilation of Israel now lay strewn on the sands of Sinai along with thousands of his soldiers' corpses.[15]

In panic, Nasser appealed to his Russian handlers for salvation. But Russia, despite its tough talk and bellicose rhetoric, was not about to become militarily involved in a Mideast war. Nevertheless, the possibility of such intervention by the Soviet Union weighed heavily on the minds of the Israeli government and of the United States as well. On the diplomatic front, the Soviets pressed heavily at the United Nations for a cease-fire resolution that would save the remnants of Nasser's army. Such a cease-fire resolution was adopted on June 7, but Egypt refused to agree to it since it did not demand immediate Israeli withdrawal to the prewar lines. Nasser's refusal to agree to a cease-fire gave Israel the time necessary to pursue victory on the Jordanian and Syrian fronts as well.

---

15. The Egyptian army in the Sinai and the Gaza Strip suffered more than 15,000 dead and a greater number wounded. Tens of thousands of Egyptian soldiers simply fled barefoot across the sands of the Sinai to reach their homes west of the Suez Canal. After disarming all of the Egyptian prisoners that it held, except for officers, the Israeli army released them and sent them back, streaming westward as well across the Sinai. The officers were later repatriated after a cease-fire agreement between Egypt and Israel.

On that same day of June 7, the American warship *Liberty* — an intelligence-gathering vessel with considerable electronic monitoring equipment on board — sailing in the war zone off of Sinai, was attacked and severely damaged by Israeli planes and ships that mistook it for an Egyptian warship. The United States had ordered all of its ships out of the war area, but the order had never reached the *Liberty*. Israel, originally believing the vessel was Egyptian, now mistakenly believed it was a Soviet spy vessel known to be in Mediterranean waters. Appalled at the danger involved in Israel attacking a Soviet ship, Israel was therefore relieved to learn that an American ship had been the target of its guns. The United States also mistook the facts, originally believing that a Soviet plane had attacked the ship. While the United States was searching for an appropriate response to this apparent Russian act of war, it was determined that the attacking planes were, in fact, Israeli. Ironically, the United States was also relieved that the incident was only a matter between itself and Israel. For decades ever since, those who love conspiracy theories have claimed that Israel intentionally attacked the *Liberty* in full knowledge that it was an American ship in order to prevent it from obtaining information about Israeli military moves.

"Jerusalem Is in Our Hands!"

WHILE THIS DIPLOMATIC CRISIS UNFOLDED, THE BATTLE FOR Jerusalem was under way. In response to continuing Jordanian shelling of Jewish Jerusalem, Israeli paratroop brigades, under the command of Colonel Motta Gur, captured Ammunition Hill and large parts of East Jerusalem outside the walled city. The Israelis then attacked and captured the Old City of Jerusalem after a bitter hand-to-hand battle. It

The famed "Ammunition Hill" overlooking Jerusalem

was an electrifying moment in the Jewish story: The Western Wall was restored to Jewish control for the first time in nineteen centuries. Battle-toughened soldiers wept; "secular" Jews placed prayers and wishes on paper and inserted them into the crevices between the stones of the Wall. A sense of divinity and destiny passed through the Jewish world.[16]

The Israeli army also broke through the Jordanian positions on the armistice lines border, thereby surrounding Jerusalem and outflanking the Jordanian army stationed in the West Bank. The Jordanian army withdrew eastward under a withering air attack from the Israeli Air Force. The Israelis now stood at the Jordan River. King Hussein appeared on Jordanian television and made a tearful admission of the defeat suffered by his vaunted Arab Legion. As they had planned to liquidate the Jews had they triumphed, many Arabs apparently were convinced that this fate would now befall them. More than 75,000 Arabs fled the West Bank before the arrival of the Israeli army, adding to the total already being held in woeful conditions in the Jordanian refugee camps: Hence, the panic and flight of so many tens of thousands of Arabs from the Land of Israel during the last days of the Six Day War.

On the northern front, facing the entrenched Syrian positions on the Golan Heights, General Elazar chafed at the inactivity of his forces. The Syrians had shelled Israeli farms and settlements throughout the first days of the war, but had not attempted to advance their ground forces into the Galilee proper. The Syrian army on the Golan was commanded by a young officer, Hafez el-Assad, who was soon to become the dictator over Syria for the next 33 years. General Moshe Dayan was convinced that the Soviet Union would not allow Syria to suffer defeat at the hands of Israel and would retaliate against Israel militarily if Israel attacked Syria. He therefore refused all of Elazar's entreaties to capture the Golan Heights. But the Syrians themselves provided Dayan with the motivation to change his mind. On June 8, reports reached him that elements of the Syrian army were withdrawing, some in disarray, from the Golan Heights. Apparently, the news of Israel's defeat of Egypt and Jordan was causing panic among the Syrian troops. Elazar finally received permission to advance. In a fierce struggle with the remaining Syrian defenders, lasting

---

16. I remember the moment well. I was then the rabbi of Beth Israel Congregation in Miami Beach, Florida. All during the early days of the war, Jews kept streaming into the synagogue, simply to sit in silence or pray for the welfare of Israel. All kinds of Jews came: old, young, religious and much less so, synagogue regulars and people I had never before seen in the building or even on the street. When the news of the capture of the Old City and the redemption of the Western Wall was broadcast on the radio, traffic stopped, people jumped from cars and embraced each other and everyone then in the synagogue wept a sea of tears. There are defining historical moments that people are sometimes privileged to witness: June 7, 1967, was such a moment for all Jews alive on that day.

two days and nights, the Israeli army ousted the Syrians from the Golan Heights, ending the threat to the Galilee.[17] On June 10, the United Nations cease-fire resolution, finally accepted by all parties to the war, took hold. Israel would later take from Syria the military positions at the top of Mount Hermon, overlooking Damascus, after the cease-fire was already supposed to be in force. Other than this and a few sporadic firing incidents in Sinai, the guns fell silent. The Six Day War that changed the dynamics of all future Middle East relationships was over.

The Blueprints for Endless Strife are Drawn

THE DUKE OF WELLINGTON, WHO TRIUMPHED OVER NAPOLEON, once said that victory brings with it far more problems than defeat. Israel certainly had no choice but to win the war or be destroyed. But even this necessary — and in many ways, miraculous — victory brought with it many problems. Israel wanted a permanent peace agreement with its Arab neighbors to emerge from the victory. Minister of Defense Moshe Dayan's words, "I am waiting for the telephone call [from Hussein and Nasser, etc.]" represented the high hopes of the Israeli government and public for a dialogue with Arab leadership. He had offered the Arabs return of much, if not all, of the territory taken by Israel in the Six Day War in exchange for a true peace treaty. Unfortunately, that telephone call from the Arab leaders never came. The matters of borders, Jerusalem, refugees and so much more, would have been considerably easier to resolve at that juncture of history than in later years. In light of all the upheavals and suffering between the Jews and the Arabs for the balance of the century, one can only deeply regret this failure of Arab vision and courage.

Due to the unwillingness of the Arab governments to negotiate a peace settlement,[18] Israel was now laden with the problem of what to do with the West Bank and Gaza, both in the short run and long term. An additional one million Arabs were now under Israeli control and the problems of occupation, administration and developing the infrastructure of the captured territories now became a chief concern.

---

17. Eli Cohen, an Israeli spy who infiltrated the top echelon of the Syrian General Staff, contributed greatly to the Israeli victory. He passed on valuable military information and also successfully identified the Syrian strong points on the Golan. He even convinced Syrian officers to plant shade trees outside their otherwise hidden bunkers, ostensibly for the comfort of their troops. These trees served as markers for Israeli artillery and planes during the struggle for the Golan Heights. Cohen was discovered by Syrian intelligence and hanged publicly in the main square of Damascus, some years before the Six Day War.

18. The leaders of the Arab world, under the leadership of Nasser, met later in 1967 in Khartoum, Sudan, and pronounced their doctrine of "Three Nos" regarding Israel: No war, No peace, No negotiations.

From the outset of its rule over Gaza and the West Bank, the Israeli authorities and the Israeli public were of two minds. One opinion was not to alter the *status quo* of Arab life in those territories and to leave it devoid of Jewish presence. The land and its inhabitants would be returned in toto to Jordan and Egypt, it was believed, once an agreement would be reached with those countries. The other opinion, strongly influenced by the partially messianic belief that this war had been a major step in the process of the final redemption of the Land and People of Israel, emphasized the establishment of full Jewish sovereignty over the entire Land of Israel and the establishment of Jewish presence throughout.

Though not the prime minister, Dayan's clout in the cabinet was the strongest. With an ambivalence which would characterize all Israeli governments throughout the balance of the century, he struck a compromise between these two divergent views; allowing for continued local Arab self-rule throughout the West Bank and Gaza, but under certain security restrictions of the Israeli occupational military authorities. The infrastructure of the West Bank and Gaza — including electricity, water, telephone service and banking — was connected to the Israeli grids and systems. An economic relationship of mutual dependence was created between the Arabs in the territories and the Jews of Israel.

Prime Minister Levi Eshkol (right), Defense Minister Moshe Dayan (left) and General Chaim Bar-Lev visit the West Bank

The city of Jerusalem, divided in 1948, was reunited and placed under complete Israeli control and administrative rule. The Western Wall plaza, which had been narrow and dirty under Jordanian sovereignty, was widened, cleansed and established as the chief synagogue of Israel (and world Jewry). A Jewish settlement outside of Hebron was allowed to begin operation. Originally housed in the Israeli military headquarters near Hebron, the settlement moved to one of the hills adjoining Hebron and grew into the sizeable community of Kiryat Arba.[19] The children and grandchildren of the Jewish farmers of Gush Etzion, located between Hebron and Bethlehem, that was captured and destroyed by the Arabs in 1948, returned to the fields their parents and grandparents had died defending, reestablishing their homes there.[20] Other than these isolated instances, no large scale Israeli settlement or presence was introduced into the territories in the years immediately following the Six Day War. Unfortunately, yet almost predictably, Dayan's compromise would not stand the test of time and of opposing national fervors.

An idea proposed by Yigal Allon, a former general and the Minister of Absorption in Eshkol's cabinet, gained popularity. This idea, forever after called the Allon Plan, envisioned Israeli control over the Jordan Valley and the ridge of mountains just west of it; the annexation of Kiryat Arba and Gush Etzion by Israel; the retention by Israel of the Latrun bulge, and the return of all other territory to Egypt and Jordan. The Gaza Strip and the West Bank would be connected by an extra-territorial highway. This plan was agreed to in principle by the Israeli government in 1969, over the objections of Moshe Dayan. Dayan was in favor of greater Jewish settlement in the territories and the integration of the autonomously governed Arab population into a Greater Israel type of scheme.

But there was still no willingness on the part of the Arabs to talk to Israel about any sort of arrangement, and thus Israel found itself negotiating — with itself! This strange and dispiriting phenomenon of Israeli politicians negotiating with other Israeli politicians publicly and in the media over the fate of the territories would become a hallmark of Israeli political life throughout the balance of the century.

In the aftermath of the Six Day War, the Arab economy on the West Bank became integrated into the Israeli economy. Prior to 1967, the West Bank was the supplier of vegetables and other agricultural products to Jordan, Saudi Arabia and other Arab states. Its imports were exclusively from Arab and European countries. Its laborers and artisans were

---

19. The driving force behind the Kiryat Arba settlement was Rabbi Moshe Levinger.
20. The "new" settlements on the lands of Gush Etzion were Kfar Etzion, Alon Shvut and Rosh Zurim.

employed exclusively by Arab countries and companies. In fact, from 1948 to 1967 there had been a considerable emigration of Arabs living in the West Bank under Jordanian rule to other Arab countries, in search of employment and a better quality of life. Thousands of them made their way to the Gulf states as well as to Europe and America.

The Six Day War changed all of this. Many Arabs now found their way back into the West Bank, for under Israeli rule the area promised a better economic situation for its inhabitants than did the surrounding Arab countries. Israel became a major importer of food and light industrial products on the West Bank, while Jordan still retained a primary import role. However, almost all goods flowing into the West Bank now came from Israel, with the trade balance between Israel and the West Bank tilting heavily in Israel's favor. Tens of thousands — eventually hundreds of thousands — of West Bank Arabs began to work regularly in Israel and/or for Israeli employers and firms. This was especially true in the construction industry. Israel began to depend upon an inexhaustible supply of relatively cheap Arab labor coming from the West Bank. Many unskilled laborers, mostly Sephardic, lost their jobs to West Bank Arabs who undercut their wages. This situation caused violent social reactions within Israeli society itself. But this integration of the economies of the West Bank and Israel, on the surface, promised hope for accommodation and peaceful relations between the Jews and the Arabs. Sadly, the economic intertwining of the two groups eventually provoked unforeseen problems of security, envy, exploitation and bitterness that exacerbated the Arab-Israeli struggle.

The policy of creating "facts on the ground" emerged due to the continued absence of Arab willingness to negotiate.[21] Israel unilaterally straightened its borders to make them more convenient and defensible. Thus the Latrun bulge that had cut off direct access to Tel Aviv from Jerusalem was absorbed into Israel, and work was begun on a new Tel Aviv-Jerusalem highway through Latrun, thus shortening the travel time by car by at least 30 minutes. Though Israel was creating "facts," it was doing so very selectively. Only regarding the reunification of Jerusalem and the granting of Israeli rights to its Arab population was the Israeli position firm, enjoying wide public support. The Israeli government still hoped that negotiations with the Arabs would bring about a settlement of the dispute.

In November 1967, the United Nations Security Council passed Resolution 242, which outlined its attempt to resolve the Arab-Israeli conflict. The operative clauses of that resolution called for: "Withdrawal

---

21. Moshe Dayan said: "If the Arabs refuse to make peace, we cannot stand still. If we are denied their cooperation, let us act on our own." Sachar, p.680.

of Israeli armed forces from territories occupied in the recent conflict; termination of all claims or states of belligerency and respect for and acknowledgement of the sovereignty, territorial integrity and political independence of every State in the area and their right to live in peace within secure and recognized boundaries, free from threats or acts of force." The language used in the resolution had been painstakingly negotiated so as to remain ambiguous until further discussion. Thus Israel was bidden to withdraw from "territories," not "the territories."

The resolution satisfied neither the Arabs nor the Israelis. Yet it was artfully constructed in a manner that allowed each side to place its demands within the ambiguous language. Israel hoped that the resolution would serve as the basis of a negotiated settlement with the Arabs. But the Arabs, again led by Nasser, were not prepared for negotiation.

The War of Attrition Gains Momentum

EGYPT IMMEDIATELY BEGAN REARMING FOR THE CONTINUED MILITARY struggle against Israel. By the end of 1967, the Soviet Union had made good to Egypt and Syria all of their losses in planes, tanks and artillery. Israel had spoken optimistically of a respite of a decade or two from war after its complete and stunning victory in the Six Day War. But by 1968, Israel was involved in a vicious and costly war of attrition. The Egyptian army initiated daily shelling and raids across the Suez Canal. The Israelis responded with air strikes, artillery fire and daring commando raids on Egyptian territory. The Soviet Union supplied Egypt with SAM missiles to interdict and shoot down the Israeli planes. Israel, in turn, developed countermeasures that largely neutralized this model of Soviet anti-aircraft missiles. The Israelis had constructed a series of defensive fortresses and bunkers — known as the the Bar-Lev Line[22] — on the eastern side of the Suez Canal. But these fortifications were not impervious to artillery fire and it fell to the Israeli Air Force to silence the Egyptian batteries. In a sustained aerial offensive of over three months in 1969, the Israeli air force effectively destroyed Egypt's capability of inflicting heavy casualties within the Bar-Lev Line. It also conducted a bombing campaign deep into Egypt that truly alarmed Nasser. It has been estimated that at least 10,000 Egyptian soldiers died in the "War of Attrition" on the banks of the Suez Canal. Israel suffered hundreds of casualties of its own.

Levi Eshkol died in February of 1969. His last great contribution to the security of Israel was an agreement he forged in November 1968 with Lyndon Johnson, making the United States the supplier of advanced

---

22. Named after the Israeli Army Chief of Staff of the time, General Chaim Bar-Lev.

armaments, especially warplanes, to Israel. In effect, the Soviet Union and the United States entered into a Middle East arms race. While the supply of American arms became a necessary ingredient for the survival of Israel, this relationship placed Israel in a position of subservience to American aims and diplomacy in the Middle East. Israel never really became an American client state, but it was hereafter close to becoming one. If Israel had been armed with American planes and tanks in 1967, instead of French planes and British tanks, it is questionable if it would have dared to deliver the preemptive strike that won the Six Day War. Lyndon Johnson's warning not to go it alone would have carried far greater weight if the United States had been Israel's arms supplier.

Charles DeGaulle openly turned against Israel after the Six Day War. He was personally slighted that Israel had ignored his advice not to strike first and said nasty things about Israel and about the Jewish people as well. He forbade the transfer of 50 advanced fighter planes ordered by Israel and for which it had paid; and he also embargoed the gunboats that were built for Israel in French shipyards. France did not even offer to return the money to Israel for the undelivered goods. In a daring but diplomatically questionable feat, Israel succeeded in smuggling the gunboats out of a French harbor and delivering them to the Israeli navy. The French, in turn, then sold 100 advanced warplanes to Libya, and these planes eventually found themselves in the use of the Egyptian Air Force. Israel thus lost France as an ally and a supporter. Throughout its later successive governments in the century, France retained a decidedly pro-Arab tilt in its Middle Eastern foreign policy.

The new U.S. Nixon administration in 1969 also attempted to settle the Middle Eastern problem. Secretary of State William Rogers advanced a plan to end all the hostilities. The Rogers Plan, made public in 1969, proposed that Israel withdraw from all territories conquered in the 1967 war; that Palestinian refugees would be allowed to choose either repatriation to their original homes or compensation; that the matter of Jerusalem would be negotiated between Jordan and Israel directly, and that of Sharm-el-Sheikh and Gaza between Egypt and Israel directly. In return, Israel would be guaranteed freedom of movement through the Suez Canal and the Straits of Tiran and binding final peace treaties with the Arab countries surrounding her. Rogers urged the "Big Four Powers" (United States, Soviet Union, France and Britain) to practically impose this settlement on the Middle East. Nasser refused the plan and the Soviet Union therefore opposed it. Israel was relieved, but at the same time was alarmed, that the Arabs and the Soviet Union would not even consider a settlement that gave the Arabs so much and asked from them so little.

Golda Meir succeeded Levi Eshkol as Prime Minister of Israel in 1969. She was a woman of fixed views and strong personality. When Egypt and Syria again intensified the War of Attrition, Israel responded massively and decisively. Hundreds of Egyptian and Syrian aircraft were downed in the period between 1968 and 1970. Israel, however, lost 593 soldiers and 127 civilians during that time. Meir pressed hard for a cease-fire to stop the bloodletting, offering to travel to Cairo to meet Nasser. He rebuffed her, saying that war was the only possible course for the Arabs to pursue. Nevertheless, the Israeli air offensive against Egypt was so punishing that Nasser and the Soviets begrudgingly accepted an American-brokered cease-fire arrangement. Egypt immediately violated the agreement by moving newly received advanced Russian SAM missiles to the shores of the Suez Canal. Israel, under American pressure, made no response outside of a diplomatic protest.

Terrorism Becomes a Fixed Reality

Meir's attitude towards the Palestine Liberation Organization and towards the Palestinians generally was summed up in her public denial that the Palestinians were an independent nationality or entitled to a separate state. "Who are the Palestinians? Jordan is the Palestinian State!" was her slogan and policy.

Within two years after the Six Day War, there were already some quiet misgivings in the Jewish world about Israeli policy regarding the West Bank. Rabbi Immanuel Jakobovits, the Chief Rabbi of the United Kingdom, a man of thought, vision and courage — and an outspoken critic of the secular and military nature of the government of Israel — wrote: *I had my opinions on Israeli policies and was startled by the manifest ambivalence — subscribing to UN Resolution 242 but opposing the Rogers Plan to implement it; constantly offering the Arabs negotiations without any preconditions — on condition that Israel kept what it had; denouncing the incipient menace of PLO terrorism — whilst asking, in Golda Meir's fateful words, "Who are the Palestinians?"; and bitterly decrying the world's growing isolation of Israel — whilst telling the nations with disdain it could not care less about world opinion.*[23]

The Palestine Liberation Organization was now headed by a relative of the former Grand Mufti of Jerusalem, Yassir Arafat.[24] As men-

---

23. Immanuel Jakobovits, *If Only My People...Zionism in My Life*, London, 1984, p.27.

24. Arafat's full name was Abd al-Rahman abd al-Rauf Arafat al-Qud al-Husseini. His shortened name allowed him to escape identification with the murderous Grand Mufti, whose family name was also al-Husseini.

tioned above, he was one of the founders of the Fatah movement in Syria in the late 1950's. After the Six Day War, Arafat took over the PLO and created an infrastructure of terrorism and guerilla warfare among the Arabs living on the West Bank and in Gaza. Fatah remained the main component of the larger PLO organization. The number of terrorist incidents in Israel in 1968 began to average one per day. The Israeli army retaliated strongly to these incidents, blowing up the houses of Arabs who were suspected of cooperation with the terrorists. By 1969, Israel had broken the PLO infrastructure on the West Bank, and the terrorist group withdrew to the Arab refugee camps, mainly in Jordan. Arafat and the PLO acted to destabilize King Hussein's government in Jordan and create their own state within a state. After a PLO attempt to assassinate him in September of 1970, Hussein moved against the PLO with his army. Thousands of PLO fighters were killed in the action and the rest were driven into Syria and Lebanon. This action, known as "Black September," was abetted by Israel, which moved its tanks up to the Syrian border, thereby warning Syria and Iraq not to intervene against Jordan. In the shifting sands of the Middle East, it is not always easy to identify who is one's friend or foe.

After broadcasting taunting insults to Nasser, the PLO was expelled from Egypt as well. By the end of 1970, it seemed that the PLO was no longer a force to be reckoned with and that Golda Meir was correct in her dismissal of the Palestinian "national movement" as only a marginal force in the Arab-Israeli conflict. Time and evolving circumstances would eventually prove her assessment wrong.

In 1968, the Palestinian terrorist groups embarked on a number of attention-grabbing hijackings of airlines flying to Israel. When the hijackers were captured, foreign governments succumbed to terrorist blackmail and the hijackers generally received light sentences, eventually going free. The terrorists attempted to plant bombs on planes enroute to and from Israel as well. When Israel retaliated by blowing up fourteen empty Arab airliners in a Beirut airport at the end of 1968, it was condemned by the UN Security Council. Security became the watchword of airlines the world over, and El Al's rigorous security measures became the industry standard.

Despite all security precautions, in September 1970 four planes (belonging to TWA, PanAm, BOAC and Swissair) were hijacked simultaneously and parked in the Jordanian desert. Eventually all of the passengers were released[25] and the planes were destroyed. But the incident shook

---

25. One of the victims of this hijacking was Rabbi Yitzchok Hutner and his family. Rabbi Hutner, the *rosh yeshivah* of Yeshiva Chaim Berlin in New York, had established residence in Israel and was active in establishing a number of Torah institutions there.

the Jewish world. Jews, wherever they were, felt vulnerable and threatened. Anti-Israel activities were now decidedly regarded as anti-Jewish.

Palestinian terrorists forged connections with numerous other terrorist organizations throughout the world. The IRA in Ireland, the Japanese Red Army in Japan, the Turkish Liberation Army and even the Uruguayan Tupamoro guerrillas aided the PLO and its affiliates in their terrorist war against Israel. The "New Left," under Soviet and communist influence, also intensified the propaganda war against Israel on college campuses and in radical forums throughout the United States and Western Europe. Many of the student leaders of the "New Left" were themselves Jewish, and this self-hatred only intensified the vitriol of their attacks against Israel.

On September 28, 1970, Gamal Abdel Nasser died of a heart attack.[26] Though mourned as a hero by millions, he was in reality a failure, having brought to Egypt and the Arab world military defeat, economic impoverishment and Soviet dependence, resulting in enormous frustration and rage. He was succeeded by Anwar Sadat, a man whom many inside and outside of Egypt regarded as a lightweight politician, lacking in leadership qualities. Sadat had been a supporter of the Mufti and the Germans during World War II and had bitterly resented British rule in Egypt and its control of the Suez Canal. He had been a loyal "yes" man to Nasser and had never before indicated a penchant for bold or risky action. Israel, along with the rest of the world, underestimated his talents, shrewdness and sense of purpose. Unlike Nasser who was a talker, Sadat was a doer. He turned out to be far more successful than his predecessor in war, peace and in restructuring the Egyptian economy and society.

Jewish Euphoria Spreads Worldwide

THE EFFECT OF ISRAEL'S VICTORY IN THE SIX DAY WAR ON THE JEWISH world was electric. The war effort itself proved to be a unifying force among a normally fractured Jewish people. It inspired a new sense of Jewish pride and identity in most Jews everywhere, contributing to a revival of interest in Judaism and Jewish practice. Although religious outreach had met with some limited success prior to the war, now a much larger number of Jews raised in non-observant homes came to study Torah and became more observant of Jewish ritual and tradition. The new group became known as *ba'alei teshuvah* in the Diaspora, *chozrim*

---

26. I was meeting with Yitzchak Rabin in the Israeli Embassy in Washington, D.C. on what, in retrospect, was a rather trivial matter concerning a plan by a Florida industrialist for American Jewish investment in Israel industry, when a secretary brought in a note stating that Nasser had died. Rabin communicated the news to me impassively and ended the meeting then and there.

b'teshuvah in Israel — but the meaning was essentially the same: these Jews were "returnees," coming home to a way of life which had always been part of their heritage but which they had never known. The thrust of this new movement, both in Israel and in the Diaspora, would gain momentum in the next decades of the century, but the catalyst for this reassessment of Jewish life by many previously indifferent Jews was the Six Day War.

In Israel especially, there was a general acknowledgement that something extraordinary — if not supernatural — had occurred in Israel's victory. The automatic rejection of Jewish tradition by the secular Jew abated, if only temporarily. The historical and emotional significance of regaining Jerusalem, the Temple Mount, the Western Wall, Rachel's Tomb, the Cave of Machpelah and other Jewish holy sites, from which Jews had been barred entry (contrary to the Israeli-Jordanian agreement) for nineteen years, impressed itself on the Israeli mind. All of this would mark the beginning of a slow but steady return of many in Israel to traditional Jewish life and values, even among those who would still insist on calling themselves secular Jews.

Nowhere was the impact of the Israeli triumph more dramatic than among the Jews of the Soviet Union. Jews there had been subjected to increasing official anti-Semitism during the 1960's. Jewish children in Soviet schools were subjected to humiliation, insults and beatings. The Soviet government's campaign in the 1960's against "rootless cosmopolitans" was a thinly-veiled attack against Jews. The Soviet media's bitter and vitriolic attacks on Israel, its unwavering support of the Arabs and its open threats against Israel's continued existence, served to heighten Soviet Jewry's consciousness about Israel and become more Zionistic than ever. In the 1960's, Soviet Jews gathered in front of Moscow's great "Choral Synagogue" on the holiday of Simchas Torah. It was not so much an act of prayer and religion, for they were in the main ignorant of Judaism,[27] but one of Jewish solidarity, nationalism and identity. Jews also gathered to conduct memorial services at mass graves, such as Babi Yar in Kiev, where thousands of Jews had been slaughtered and buried during World War II. The Soviet government actively discouraged such displays of Jewish pride, but the spontaneous Simchas Torah assemblages and the Holocaust memorial gatherings continued nonetheless. Increasingly numerous visits from Western and Israeli Jews to the Soviet Union also strength-

---

27. The exception to this rule were the Jews of Georgia, of the Caucausus and the Chabad Chasidim of Russia who were able to maintain their Jewish identity, synagogues and traditions even under Stalin, often at great personal and communal risk.

ened the feeling of hope among the Soviet Jews and helped lessen their feeling of isolation and abandonment.[28]

Throughout the late 1950's and early 1960's, the Soviet Union allowed for a small immigration of between 1,500-2,000 Soviet Jews annually to Israel. The government refused to allow professionals or young people to leave, though exceptions were made in certain cases. This trickle of immigration from behind the Iron Curtain never was publicized so as not to jeopardize the already strained Israeli-Soviet diplomatic relations. However, a public movement was growing all over the Jewish world, and within Russia itself, for increased, and in fact, unlimited Jewish immigration from the Soviet Union to Israel. As this movement grew and became more vocal, Moscow reacted by clamping down harder on Jewish emigration from Russia. When the scope of the Israeli victory and the Arab and Russian humiliation in the Six Day War became known, there was a tremendous surge of Jewish pride within Soviet Jewry. Zionism was reawakened as an option in the hearts and minds of millions of Soviet Jews. The government's reaction to this was an intensification of anti-Semitic propaganda and anti-Jewish behavior. This, in turn, only strengthened the determination of younger, activist Russian Jews to leave for Israel despite government barriers.

In early 1970, eleven Russian Jews were arrested for planning to hijack a plane to fly them to the West. They were tried in Leningrad and the Jewish underground distributed transcripts of the trial to the Jews of Russia and to the West.[29] The show trial backfired badly on the Soviet government, for it hardened Western public opinion on behalf of Soviet Jewry and inspired the Jews inside Russia to fight on for their right to immigrate to Israel. Tens of thousands of applications from Soviet Jews for emigration permits now flooded the offices of the Soviet bureaucracy. The genie was out of the bottle.

But there were grave risks in applying for immigration to Israel. Loss of job, exclusion from school or university, hazings and beatings by former classmates and/or co-workers were all part of the experience. Extortion of money, housing and goods from the applicants also came to be expected as part of the routine procedure. Yet the applications for emigration from Russia continued to pour in. After a break in diplomatic relations with Israel was initiated by the Soviet Union after the Six Day

---

28. Two books by visitors from outside Russia that capture the beginnings of the Jewish awakening in the Soviet Union in the 1960's are *Jews of Silence* by Elie Wiesel and *Between Hammer and Sickle* by Arieh Eliav (Ben Ami).

29. Yosef Mendelevitch was one of the eleven defendants in the Leningrad trial. He was sentenced to twelve years of "strict regime." He wrote his story in a wonderful book in Hebrew called *Mivtza Chatunah* (*Operation Wedding*). He now teaches Torah in Jerusalem.

War, the Israeli government became considerably more vocal in its demands that Jews from Russia be allowed to come to Israel. The Arab countries desperately petitioned their Soviet patron not to allow such immigration, fearing the demographic and economic consequences that would favor Israel by such a massive *aliyah*. Only 4,675 Jews were allowed to leave Russia for Israel between 1967 and 1970. This paltry number reflected that there was no significant change in Soviet policy towards Israel or towards its Jews at that point. Nevertheless, the plight of Russian Jewry now became a matter of international concern. In all negotiations with Russia after 1970, the United States and Western European countries continued to raise the issue of Soviet Jewry with their Russian counterparts. This diplomatic pressure would help undermine the Soviet stance regarding Soviet Jewry and eventually weaken the dictatorial rule of the communist regime in Russia itself. It is no exaggeration to state that the campaign of the Jews to leave the Soviet Union and immigrate to the West and Israel helped bring down the "evil empire," as President Reagan was later to call the Soviet Union.

The effect of the Six Day War on American Jewry was also important, though certainly not on the same scale as its impact on Russian Jewry. The opposition of segments of the American Reform movement to Zionism ended with the Six Day War. The fund raising efforts of the United Jewish Appeal in America during and after the Six Day War were herculean. The Israel Bonds sales in the United States in 1967 soared to $175,000,000, a figure unimagined fifteen years earlier when Israel Bonds sales began. But perhaps even more significant was the large increase in the number of Americans, most of them young and traditional, who moved to Israel. By the end of 1970, more than 10,000 Americans had arrived in Israel since the Six Day War.

In addition, the practice of graduates from yeshivos and Jewish high schools coming to Israel for a year or more of intensive Torah study came into vogue. As a result of their experience in Israel, many of these students forged stronger ties with their Jewish homeland and considered *aliyah* as a realistic option. Tourism to Israel also took a sharp rise after the Six Day War, though incredibly, the trend seems to have been short-lived. By the end of the century, statistics indicated that the vast majority of American Jews had yet to make even one journey to the Land of Israel.

The Six Day War also erased the last vestiges of anti-Israel policies among the leading official organizations of American Jewry. The Reform movement completed its 180 degree turn from its bitterly anti-Zionist pre-World War stance to becoming one of the leading sources of aid, support and influence for the Jewish state. It opened a branch of Hebrew Union College in Jerusalem under the direction of noted archeologist Dr.

Nelson Gleuck, then president of Hebrew Union College in Cincinnati, Ohio. The application for the construction of the HUC building in Jerusalem was first submitted in the 1950's, but met with a storm of Orthodox and traditional opposition that blocked its approval. Eventually, however, the permit was granted and Reform made its entry into the Israeli scene, albeit on a low-key and minimal level. Even the American Jewish Congress and American Jewish Committee, both of which initially had very little involvement in Zionist affairs and were sometimes seen as hostile to Zionist policies and aims, became strong supporters of Israel. Organized Jewish lobbying in Washington, D.C., became continuous, serious and effective. The Six Day War can be seen as the end of any meaningful debate within American Jewry as to its loyalty to the existence and well-being of the State of Israel.

Israel, as a cause, was now confirmed as the primary "Judaism" of American Jewry. Leading Jewish thinkers from the entire spectrum of American Jewish life warned against overemphasizing this trend at the expense of Jewish education and Jewish commitment. Unfortunately, their warnings went unheeded by leaders of the American Jewish establishment. The euphoria engendered by the victory of Israeli arms unfortunately masked the serious underlying problems that both American and Israeli Jewish societies still faced. The intermarriage rate among American Jews was slowly rising and gaining momentum, as Jews marrying non-Jews became more and more socially acceptable in American society. No feat of Israeli valor could make those underlying problems disappear.

Most Orthodox Jews — of all stripes — considered the triumphs of the Six Day War to be miraculous manifestations of Divine favor, though some divergent views surfaced. The anti-Zionist, anti-state policies of Satmar were not changed by the war. Satmar Chasidim refused to pray at the Western Wall because its liberation was secured by Zionist forces. Nevertheless, Satmar invested large sums of money in Jerusalem; building schools, yeshivos, nurseries and apartments. Hundreds of Satmar Chasidic families moved to Jerusalem and other communities in Israel, decrying the government and state, yet living in the Land of Israel.[30]

---

30. This apparent inconsistency was explained by Rabbi Joseph B. Soloveitchik in his memorable eulogy of his uncle, Rabbi Yitzchak Zev Soloveitchik, the *Brisker Rav*, an avowed anti-Zionist. Rabbi Soloveitchik stated regarding his uncle: "...[If] Love of Zion is expressed by living in the Holy Land, striking roots there, loving its soil and desiring its stones, sharing in the burdens of the community under siege, and being totally committed to the destiny of the Holy City of Jerusalem, then my uncle was a true Lover of Zion. He refused to leave the Holy City even when the enemy besieged its gates. He totally rejected all proposals to emigrate to safe cities outside the Land of Israel. This true Love of Zion found its total fulfillment and realization in a 'Man of Halachah' who was in theological opposition to the State of Israel and separated himself from its ideology." Quoted by Aaron Rakeffet-Rothkoff in *The Rav – The World of Rabbi Joseph B. Soloveitchik*, New York, 1999, Volume Two, p.115.

Rabbi Yoel Teitelbaum, the Grand Rabbi of Satmar and the titular head of the anti-Zionist Eidah HaChareidis community of Jerusalem, published a book regarding the Six Day War and its results.[31] In it, he debunked the idea that the war had anything to do with Jewish, redemption and reiterated the unyielding anti-Zionist sentiments that had existed within parts of the Orthodox establishment for 70 years.

On the other side of the traditional Jewish spectrum, there was a wave of near Messianism. The reunification of Jerusalem and the newly-won Jewish control over almost all of the biblical borders of the Land of Israel were seen as heralding the coming of the Messianic Age. The Six Day War and its results on the ground were deemed nothing short of miraculous. To a certain extent, this feeling helped spark the trend of *aliyah* to Israel from North America, South America, South Africa and other countries of Jewish comfort and affluence. The whole Land of Israel now seemed to be there, just waiting for Jewish settlement and development. The Jewish people could now, so to speak, anticipate the advent of the Messiah and the full redemption of Israel. The redemption of Israel was seen as the dawn — slow, but irreversible. This fantastic feeling would give rise to new forces in Jewish and Israeli life in the next decade that would have profound influence over all later developments in Arab-Israeli relations until the end of the century.

Between these two extremes of ideology and belief lay the vast majority of Jews who did not quite know what to make of the events of the decade. Thrilled by the Israeli victory that delivered the state from the threat of annihilation, Jews the world over were committed to the cause of Israel, but not necessarily to their own personal involvement with it and certainly not to *aliyah*. The increasing comfort and prosperity of American Jewry — and paradoxically, the very strength and growth of Torah institutions in North America — on one hand, and the rapidly rising rate of assimilation on the other hand, strongly lessened the chances of North American Jews emigrating en masse to Israel. Conflicting opinions voiced by great rabbinic and intellectual leaders inside and outside of Israel about the meaning of the Jewish state only served to heighten the confusion of the average Jew. The Jewish world had been transformed by the momentous events of the decade. How these changes would reflect themselves in Jewish national and religious life would be the focus of Jewish concern for the next three decades.

---

31. *Al Hageulah V'al Hatmurah*, New York, 1967.

Chapter Nine

Uncertainty and Profound Changes

1971-1980

THE DECADE OF THE SEVENTIES BEGAN QUIETLY AND INAUSPICIOUSLY. There was, to be sure, continuing Arab terror by the PLO, but Israel and the rest of the world had begun to develop security and counterterrorism measures. Nevertheless, though the dangers were reduced, nothing ever completely eliminated the terrorist threat. There was increased *aliyah* from the West, especially from the United States, in the early 1970's. The Six Day War had given a messianic push to the drive for *aliyah*, especially among young Modern Orthodox Jews. The old Zionist dream that alone had not resonated easily among American Jews was now enhanced by the conviction that the State of Israel and its triumphs were part of the prophetic redemption of Israel and the coming of the Messianic Era. They now felt impelled to be active participants in this final culminating act of Jewish drama and history. In addition, many non-Zionist Jews flocked to Israel, especially to study in its yeshivos and women's seminaries, which increasingly became recognized as the world's pacesetters for Torah study.

The secular Zionists in control of the Jewish Agency and the Israeli government had more earthly reasons for encouraging this *aliyah*. Minister of Defense Moshe Dayan was determined to increase Jewish settlement throughout the West Bank, Gaza and Sinai. He encouraged the purchase of Arab land throughout the West Bank by private Jewish citizens, stating: "I do think that Israel should stay forever and ever and ever and ever in the West Bank, because this is Judea and Samaria. This is our homeland."[1] In addition, he approved the building of the port city of Yamit in the northern Sinai, thereby attempting to permanently separate the Gaza Strip from Egypt.

His interest in expanded Jewish settlement was demonstrated by the development of Kiryat Arba, adjoining Hebron. The Gush Etzion ("Etzion Bloc") area blossomed into substantial villages. Settlements were established in the Jordan Valley and near the Gaza Strip. For Dayan's plans to be realized, a substantial rise in Jewish immigration would have to occur. People were needed to populate the new settlements. As a spur to this goal, the 27th Zionist Congress, meeting in Jerusalem in the winter of 1971, passed an aggressive resolution obligating the leaders of the major Zionist organizations to immigrate to Israel. This resolution loosed a firestorm of controversy and threatened to split the Zionist structure. The resolution was never enforced, but the message that it sent was abundantly clear. Israel needed Jews to move to Israel in order to reclaim and settle its ancient biblical homeland. Since Jewish immigration from Russia was then a bare trickle, only the West could provide those necessary new Israeli Jews. In a few short years, it became apparent that, despite the initial euphoria, massive *aliyah* from the West would not materialize, and Israel shifted its interest to freeing the Jews of the Soviet Union.

International Focus on Soviet Jews

IN THE UNITED STATES, RICHARD NIXON, WHO WAS ELECTED PRESIDENT in 1968 on the promise to end the war in Vietnam, had removed most American troops from that ravaged land, but the war raged on. In 1972, Nixon was reelected by a large margin over the Leftist democratic candidate, George McGovern. Nixon promoted Henry Kissinger from National Security Advisor to Secretary of State. Kissinger, a German-born Jew raised in an Orthodox home, had enjoyed highly successful career as a professor at Harvard University and was a well-regarded expert on diplomacy and international affairs. He had long ago abandoned Jewish observance and had married a non-Jew in his second marriage. Nevertheless, he identified himself as a Jew and a supporter of Israel, and was so viewed by both Jews and non-Jews. Despite his personal leanings, Kissinger was a cold practitioner of "realpolitik" and showed Israel precious little practical favoritism in his dealings with the Middle East. He

---

1. Martin Gilbert, *Israel - A History*, p.422.

arranged for President Nixon to visit China and created a rapprochement between the United States and China after a quarter century of estrangement and conflict. Kissinger was a recipient of the Nobel Peace Prize for ending the Vietnam War (through American abandonment of the South Vietnamese government). He was a larger-than-life figure in international affairs for the first part of the 70's decade.

One of Henry Kissinger's contributions to Jewish freedom was that he proceeded to press Russia on issues of Jewish emigration and religious rights. The campaign to allow Jews from Russia to emigrate from the Soviet Union gathered momentum in the 1970's. In the United States, the campaign became much more vocal, open and confrontational than it

had been in previous years. Rabbi Meir Kahane, the founder of the paramilitary Jewish Defense League and a militant, outspoken anti-Establishment figure in Jewish life, was among the numerous Jewish leaders who raised the issue of Soviet Jewry to the forefront of the American Jewish organizational agenda. Eventually, the movement entered mainstream consciousness and the slogan "Let my people go!" reverberated across Jewish communities in America and Western Europe. The United States Congress passed a law making trade benefits for the Soviet Union contingent upon a relaxation of its opposition to Jewish emigration from the country.

A protest march in New York City on behalf of Soviet Jews

The Israeli government under Golda Meir made Jewish immigration from the Soviet Union one of its primary goals. Israel needed the immigration to help stem the tide of demographic disaster that was running against it. The Arab birthrate was high; the Jewish birthrate was low.[2] Israel needed *aliyah* — mass Jewish *aliyah*. By this time, it was obvious to all that a large *aliyah* from the West was not to be, and that the substantial numbers of Jews needed could come from only one place on the globe — the Soviet Union. The pressure on Moscow began to bear minimal fruit. In 1971, 13,000 Jews left Russia for Israel,[3] traveling via Vienna, where a way station was set up for them. In 1972, 31,000 Russian Jews

2. The Orthodox birthrate in Israel was close to five per family, while the secular birthrate was barely two. The Arab birthrate was more than four.

3. Zvi Gitelman, *A Century of Ambivalence*, p. 280, puts the figure at 14,310.

arrived in Israel and in 1973, 32,000 Jews came.[4] A large proportion of these Russian immigrants were from Georgia, where Jewish ethnicity and religious observance somehow had survived the dark Stalinist years. Unlike most Russian Jews, however, these Jews were relatively unskilled and not part of the technological and professional class. A trickle of Russian Jews also began to arrive in the United States, admitted under special immigration provisions as refugees from communist tyranny.

The Soviet Union was embarrassed by this immigration. How could anyone in his right mind want to leave the "worker's paradise" to live in "fascist Zionist" Israel? To stem the swelling tide of applicants, the Soviet authorities instituted draconian procedures for exit visa applications. The applicant lost his or her job and was subjected to intensive and threatening interviews by the security police. The application had to be accompanied by: a letter of request from a relative abroad asking for family reunion; a declaration of intent to leave; an autobiography; character references from one's place of employment; permission from one's parents to leave, no matter the age of the applicant; permission of a former spouse, in cases of divorce; a certification of good character from the house committee of one's residence; copies of all important official documents (birth certificates, death certificates of relatives, marriage certifi-

A prayer assembly of Orthodox Jews for Soviet Jewry held at Manhattan Center (New York City), January 1971

4. Howard Sachar, *A History of Israel*, p.738.

cates, educational transcripts, etc.) and photographs.[5] Despite all of these bureaucratic obstacles, the number of applications from Russian Jews for exit visas continued to rise throughout the decade.

Though Western and Israeli Jews agreed on the necessity of helping Soviet Jewry, there were sharp differences of opinion regarding the methods, and even the goals, of this help. Many, especially in the Orthodox camp, wanted a more muted, less confrontational campaign mounted against the Soviet government. They feared that the public protests and harsh denunciations of Soviet policy would only exacerbate the difficulties of Soviet Jews. They were undoubtedly influenced by their memory of how the anti-Hitler protests and boycotts of the 1930's resulted in even more cruel treatment of Germany's Jews. Important rabbinic figures, such as Rabbis Joseph B. Soloveitchik, Moshe Feinstein, Yaakov Kamenetsky, Immanuel Jakobovits, Pinchas Teitz, and the leaders of the American Agudath Israel stated that the emphasis regarding Russian Jewry should not be "Let my people go!" as much as "Let my people live." They argued for a campaign to revive Jewish religious and cultural life in the Soviet Union as a parallel drive to the attempts to force the Soviet government to relax its opposition to Jewish emigration from Russia.[6] The call was echoed by Dr. Nachum Goldmann of the World Jewish Congress as well as other secular Jewish leaders. Israeli government prodding, however, insured that the vast bulk of the effort remained concentrated solely in securing the right of Jews to leave Russia and immigrate to Israel.

Alienated Jews Begin a Return to Jewish Heritage

THE EARLY 1970'S ALSO SAW THE FORMALIZATION OF THE *BA'AL teshuvah* (return to religious observance) movement, which had begun a few years earlier. In 1967, Rabbi Shlomo Freifeld of Far Rockaway, New York, had founded Yeshivah Sh'or Yoshuv, the first independent school for *ba'alei teshuvah* in America. In Israel, the first yeshivah geared to returnees, Mevaseret Yerushalayim, had been founded in 1966 by Rabbis Nota Schiller and Noach Weinberg. Closed due to the Six Day War, the yeshivah later reopened as Yeshivah Shema Yisrael, eventually spinning off other institutions with the same ideals.

By 1972, Ohr Sameach College was founded in Jerusalem again by Rabbis Schiller and Weinberg, joined by Rabbi Carl Rosenberg and Mendel Weinbach. Rabbi Weinberg went on to later found and direct Aish Hatorah

---

5. Gitelman, p.280.

6. See Rabbi Immanuel Jakobovits' exposition on this policy in his book, *If Only My People ... Zionism in My Life*, London, 1984, pp.43-48.

College, located in the Old City of Jerusalem, and Rabbi Rosenberg eventually became the founder and head of Machon Shlomo. These institutions, together with Neve Yerushalayim College for Women, founded by Rabbi Dovid Refson, became the prototypes for tens of other such schools catering to the needs of young Jews searching for their roots and heritage. Though there were and are differences of outlook and methods between the many differing institutions that cater to those "returning" to Judaism, all of them set as their goal the promulgation of Torah study and ritual observance among previously alienated or indifferent Jews. Such institutions sprung up worldwide and had an enormous effect upon the Jewish world. Many Jewish communities were revitalized in their commitment and fervor by the influx of idealistic and enthusiastic *ba'alei teshuvah.*

Chabad/Lubavitch, of course, had been engaged in such outreach work for decades. The *Lubavitcher Rebbe,* Rabbi Menachem Mendel Schneerson, sent *shlichim* (agents/messengers) throughout the world to service lonely and far-flung Jewish communities. These dedicated young people created Jewish schools, opened synagogues and tended to the religious needs of Jews. They engaged all types of Jews in Torah study, as well as the study of Chabad *Chasidus,* and led many Jews to become observant of some or all of the Torah commandments.

The "return movement" almost became a victim of its own success, for a startled secular Jewish world, both in Israel and in the United States, contested the legitimacy of the yeshivos, and charged them with creating "cults." This attitude was reinforced by the proliferation of true cults in American and western society, prevalent at the time, which attracted a disproportionate number of young Jews to their ranks. In general, the young, alienated Jew was searching for identity, meaning in life and spirituality. Over the years, however, these *ba'al teshuvah* institutions grew in number and influence and became more accepted in the secular Jewish world, where they made a significant impact and met with major outreach accomplishments.

Discovering a lost Jewish heritage

T HE DECADE ALSO SAW THE STRENGTHENING OF THE FEMINIST movement throughout the world and especially in the United States. The role of women in society had become radically different in the twentieth century because of many different forces: economic, cultural, military, social and technological. The proportion of women engaged in full-time, out-of-the-home employment had increased dramatically and the presence of women in all sectors of the economy was noticeable and increasing. The feminist movement pushed for equality with men in pay scale, social and employment opportunities, military service and all other areas of social life.

New Trends Make Inroads

An amendment to the United States Constitution was introduced in Congress in 1972 to guarantee the equality of women in all areas of public and educational life.[7] The American Jewish establishment, through its official organizations, in the main backed passage of the amendment. The Orthodox Jewish community strongly opposed it, claiming that it would force traditional Jewish norms in schools and social life to be discarded, as separation of the sexes in schools and institutions etc., could be seen as unconstitutional. The amendment was passed by Congress, but eventually failed to achieve the backing necessary of three-quarters of the state legislatures. Nevertheless, it marked the growth of a new challenge to the traditional, centuries-old Jewish worldview of societal matters.

Within Orthodoxy itself, there arose groups espousing a greater role for women in Torah scholarship, prayer service and organizational leadership. Especially sensitive was the issue of women's rights in matters relating to Jewish divorce, in the absence of universally recognized rabbinical courts with the authority to enforce rulings. This issue was disproportionately publicized, mainly due to the steep rise in the incidence of divorce in the Jewish and general communities. The struggle regarding all of these topics remained contentious and emotional throughout the balance of the century and "women's issues" came to dominate a large segment of the Jewish social agenda in the United States and Israel.

Israel Exercises Sovereignty over New Territories

ISRAEL WAS CONVINCED THAT THE SURROUNDING ARAB NATIONS WERE not ready for peace, no matter what territorial concessions were offered. In fact, Israel privately had assured Egypt, Syria and Jordan of the return of nearly all of the territories taken in the Six Day War, all to no avail. There was no response. Dayan, therefore, advocated a policy of allowing the Arab residents of the West Bank and Gaza a great deal of self-rule, including their own elections and educational system and continued economic and social ties to Jordan. Israel provided immense improvements in roads, health care and jobs — raising the living standard of the West Bank Arabs to a higher level than that enjoyed by their fellow Arabs in neighboring countries. By 1972, 40,000 West Bank Arabs were employed within the Israeli economy, earning far higher wages than they did before. Israeli army troops were conspicuously absent in most Arab towns and villages in the West Bank. Dayan envisioned that this benign occupation would continue indefinitely, with Jews and Arabs mingling in a cordial atmosphere. He believed that the

---

7. The amendment was popularly known as the E.R.A. — Equal Rights Amendment.

obvious economic and social benefits of this benevolent arrangement would sway Arab opinion to accept the Israeli presence in the West Bank and Gaza, even on a permanent basis.

Dayan's policies were opposed by Finance Minister Pinchas Sapir and Deputy Premier Yigal Allon. They did not believe that any occupation of the West Bank and Gaza, no matter how beneficial and benign, could be permanent. They argued that Israel could not indefinitely rule over the additional one million Arabs then living in those areas and maintain the demographic and cultural goal of being a Jewish state. The political balance in the country would be severely altered if the Arabs on the West Bank would become part of Israel's democracy. On the other hand, if the Arabs were excluded from participation in Israeli public and political life, democratic principles would be compromised and a festering resentment among the Arabs would be certain. Prime Minister Golda Meir leaned towards Dayan's view of the situation. (His push for the expansion of Jewish settlement in the West Bank was given priority in August of 1973, when the Labor Party government approved plans for an additional 30 settlements.[8] Even Sapir approved an allocation of $300,000,000 for these new settlements.)

Further defining its sovereignty over captured lands, the Israeli government annexed the environs of Jerusalem to the city and began building large new housing projects on previously empty land. There was consensus among the Israeli public and politicians that Jerusalem should be expanded and settled and that the city should be reunified and governed as one municipality. Thus Ramot (Allon), French Hill, Ramot Eshkol, Arzei Habirah, Maalot Dafna and Sanhedria Hamurchevet, among other new neighborhoods in Jerusalem, were quickly built and immediately populated with thousands of Jewish families. Jewish control of the city was viewed as a permanent fact, not open to discussion or negotiation. The Jewish Quarter of the Old City, from which the Jews had been expelled in 1948, began massive reconstruction, and Jewish families once again took up residence there. The dynamic and politically astute mayor of the city, Teddy Kollek, developed a private foundation that raised funds to beautify the city and enhance its services. He also extended all city services to the Arab population of previously Jordanian East Jerusalem, who now found themselves citizens of a united, Jewish-ruled city.

However, in a fateful decision — little noticed by the Jewish world at the time — administrative control of the Temple Mount was given to the Moslem Waqf authorities, while the Western Wall plaza was expand-

---

8. From the then existing 46 settlements to 76.

ed and refurbished under rabbinic control. Kollek, like Dayan, was also confident that the Arabs and Jews of Jerusalem would be able to live together in harmony and cooperation because of their mutual economic, social and governmental interests. A miniscule minority felt that East Jerusalem and the Temple Mount should never be annexed by Israel.

Israel Is Taken by Surprise!

THE LEADERS OF ISRAEL WERE CONVINCED THAT THE ARABS WOULD eventually come around to accepting the results of the 1967 Six Day War. The repeated warnings of Anwar Sadat that Egypt would go to war to regain the Sinai were largely ignored, and even ridiculed. Sadat had said that 1972 would be the "year of decision." When nothing happened in 1972, Israel tended to treat Sadat as no more than a bluffer and a bully, paying no heed to his threats to fight for the Sinai.

But Sadat had squeezed out of the Soviet Union enormous quantities of arms, many of them the most sophisticated in the Russian war arsenal. Russian military advisors swarmed throughout the Egyptian army, training the soldiers in the use and tactics of these new and powerful weapons. Israel remained sanguine in the face of this arms build-up, confident that it retained a margin of military superiority that alone would deter Sadat from attacking.

General Moshe Dayan smugly stated that if the Egyptians attempted to cross the Suez Canal and enter the Sinai Peninsula, "We'll step on them. I will crush them. Let them come … We aren't going to have any war this year. The overall balance of forces is in our favor, and this is what decides the question, and rules out the immediate renewal of the war."[9]

Late in 1972, Anwar Sadat sought to break the creeping Soviet stranglehold on his country, fearing that Soviet influence threatened his rule and any vestige of Egyptian independence. Not wanting Egypt to suffer the fate of the Eastern European satellite states, he ordered the Soviet military advisors out of his country. This amazing development led Israel to assess the possibility of a war with Egypt as practically negligible. Nevertheless, when the Egyptian army went on high alert in May 1973, Israeli Chief of Staff David Elazar called up the reserves of the Israel Defense Forces in a partial mobilization. When the Egyptian threat dissipated and nothing happened, Elazar was roundly criticized for squandering public funds and inconveniencing thousands of Israelis for no good reason.

In September of 1973, an air battle between Israel and Syria took place off of the Syrian port of Latakia. Thirteen Syrian jets were downed

---

9. Gilbert, pp. 423-4.

while Israel lost one plane. Since these Syrian planes were the newest and most sophisticated Soviet models, Israel's air superiority was again proven. Syrian troop movements towards the Israeli line on the Golan Heights were discounted as being only a reaction to the Syrian air defeat.

Unbeknownst to Israel, Egypt's Sadat and Syria's Assad had coordinated their plans to strike at Israel simultaneously in Sinai and on the Golan. Israeli intelligence fact gathering was almost flawless; but interpretation of those facts was abysmally faulty. On Yom Kippur, 1973, corresponding to October 6, Israel received intelligence reports that it would be attacked that very afternoon by Syria and Egypt. At 2:00 PM the sirens sounded in Israel, signifying the outbreak of war. Exceeding his authority, and bravely ignoring the criticism he had suffered for mobilizing the reserves in May, Elazar immediately mobilized the Israeli army. The fact that it was Yom Kippur and that the men could easily be found in synagogues or in their homes, and that the roads were empty, facilitated this speedy and lifesaving mobilization.

The Israeli army was woefully unprepared for war. The sixteen fortifications on the eastern shore of the Suez that comprised the Bar-Lev Line housed only 436 soldiers, almost all of them reservists who had never before experienced combat conditions. There were only three Israeli tanks on the shoreline of the Suez. The Egyptian army burst into the Sinai, capturing or bypassing the Bar-Lev fortifications.[10] The Egyptians were able to ambush a large Israeli tank column rushing westward to the defense of the Canal line. Out of 100 Israeli tanks in this force, 77 were knocked out by Egyptian fire.

The news from the Golan on that first day of the war was even more dreadful. The Syrian forces, led by 1,400 tanks, had driven through the Israeli defense lines and were near the Sea of Galilee in the south, advancing rapidly on the Tapline road[11] that runs through the center of the Golan, and pressing towards the pre-1967 Israel border in the north. The Israeli outpost atop Mount Hermon, with its sensitive secret intelligence-gathering equipment, was captured by a Syrian helicopter force. Israel had only 57 tanks in position to oppose this massive onslaught. Nevertheless, by unbelievable individual personal bravery and ingenuity on the part of a few Israeli soldiers, the Syrian attack was blunted and the Syrian forces advanced no farther in the ensuing fighting of the next days of the war. The Israeli Air Force, which had suffered grievous losses to

10. One of these fortifications held out for the entire period of the war. Another remained under Israeli control and harassed the Egyptian invaders for a week. Most of the fortifications fell on the first day of the war.

11. This road ran alongside the buried oil pipeline that the British used in the days of its mandate to bring crude oil from Iraq to Haifa for refining.

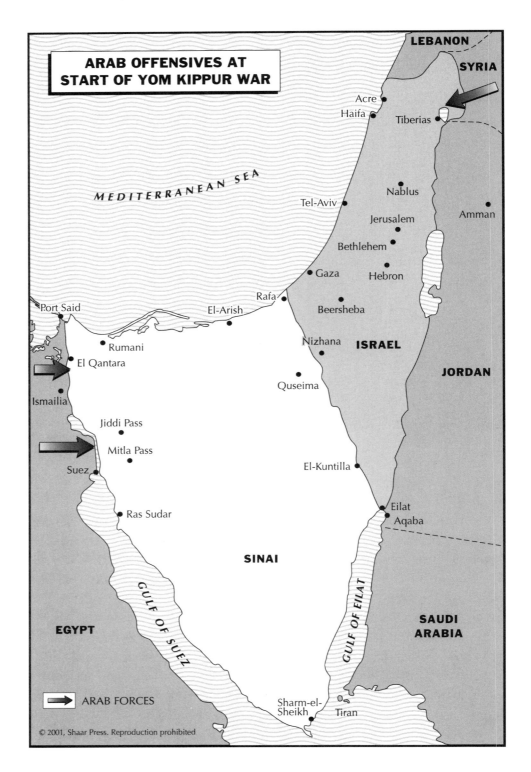

ARAB OFFENSIVES AT
START OF YOM KIPPUR WAR

LEBANON

SYRIA

Acre

Haifa

Tiberias

MEDITERRANEAN SEA

Nablus

Tel-Aviv

Jerusalem

Amman

Bethlehem

Gaza

Hebron

Rafa

Beersheba

Port Said

El-Arish

Nizhana

ISRAEL

Rumani

JORDAN

El Qantara

Ismailia

Quseima

Jiddi Pass

Mitla Pass

El-Kuntilla

Suez

Ras Sudar

Eilat
Aqaba

SINAI

SAUDI
ARABIA

GULF OF SUEZ

GULF OF EILAT

EGYPT

ARAB FORCES

Sharm-el-
Sheikh

Tiran

© 2001, Shaar Press. Reproduction prohibited

Soviet-built SAM anti-aircraft batteries over the Suez and Damascus, found its range and attacked the Syrian tanks. The relatively few Israeli tanks on the scene were utilized with daring skill, and by the end of the second day of the war, upwards of 500 Syrian tanks had been destroyed.

Israeli infantry air cover moves into the battle zone on the Golan Heights

With the Syrian momentum broken, Israel prepared to counterattack on the Golan Heights and drive the Syrian forces back towards Damascus.

The Israeli public was shocked by the outbreak of war and the early Arab military successes. A mood of apprehension and depression swept the country and the entire Jewish world. This was not to be a stunning six-day Israeli victory. Hundreds of Israeli soldiers had been killed on the first day of the war and many more were wounded and maimed. The entire future of the survival of the State of Israel hung in the balance. Dayan himself was crushed by the events and in a panic told Golda Meir, "The Third Temple is being destroyed." Dayan's pessimism was so palpably apparent that Golda Meir did not allow him to conduct a televised news conference on October 8th. The briefing was given instead by General Aharon Yariv, the head of Army Intelligence. He reported that an Israeli counterattack in the Sinai had failed that day and Israel had sustained heavy losses in men and tanks. Yet, the good news was that on that same day Israel had, in fact, established a firm defense line some 30 miles east of the Suez Canal and the Egyptian army was shifting from an offensive posture to a defensive one.

The commanding general of the Southern Front was replaced. General Ariel Sharon, who had just recently retired from the army to enter political life, was recalled and given command of an armored division and General Chaim Bar-Lev was called out of retirement to head the Sinai campaign. In Sinai, Egyptian efforts failed to break through the Israeli lines west of the Mitla Pass. On October 13, one of the greatest tank battles in history took place in Sinai with over 2,000 tanks involved in the fighting. On that day alone, 264 Egyptian tanks were destroyed while Israel lost ten tanks. The Israeli commander of the battle, General Albert Mandler, was killed by an anti-tank shell.

Egyptian losses were severe, both militarily and psychologically. The tide of war was beginning to turn against the Arabs. Jordan sent two brigades of troops to help Syria protect Damascus, but otherwise refused to intervene, thus sparing Israel the necessity of fighting on a third front. Russia encouraged the Arab countries to join Syria and Egypt in the war. Russian tanks were sent to Algeria for units that were to bolster the Egyptian troops in the Sinai. Morocco supplied troops to fight on the Syrian front, as did Iraq,[12] but they did not alter the situation on the Golan, which was now definitely in Israel's favor. An entire Iraqi tank brigade was caught in an Israeli ambush and all 80 of its tanks were destroyed.

During the Yom Kippur War, the United States government was embroiled in a corruption scandal involving Vice President Spiro T. Agnew. He was forced to resign his high office in disgrace. President Nixon was disturbed by the bellicose pronouncements of the Soviet Union, but did not want to be dragged into a great power confrontation, especially in a time of political weakness and scandal. He was aware that the great disgrace of the Watergate break-in[13] and subsequent illegal cover-up, of which he was guilty, was beginning to bubble just below the surface of public recognition.

President Nixon and Henry Kissinger were engaged in trying to manage a very dangerous situation. America had moved its Sixth Fleet naval force into the eastern Mediterranean as a warning to Russia not to intervene. Yet Israel had exhausted its military supplies in the first week of the war and stood in precarious danger, now that Russia had fully re-supplied Egypt and Syria. The Israeli request for American assistance was greeted at first by hesitation on the part of the American administration. It was alleged that Kissinger wanted the US to stand aside so that Israel would be forced to compromise for peace. However, on October 14, under the specific orders of President Nixon, American C-5 cargo planes began flying to Israel with the necessary supplies of war materiel for Israel's survival. England, in a shameful display of bias, refused to allow the American planes to use any of its bases to refuel the cargo planes and embargoed the shipment of spare parts to Israel for its British-made

---

12. As many as 15,000 Iraqi troops were sent to Syria to aid in the effort to overrun the Golan Heights.

13. The offices of the Democratic National Committee in the Watergate Apartment Complex in Washington, D.C. were broken into by operatives of the Committee to Re-elect President Nixon. Their criminal break-in and the subsequent attempted cover-up of its connection with the Nixon campaign eventually caused Nixon to resign from the presidency.

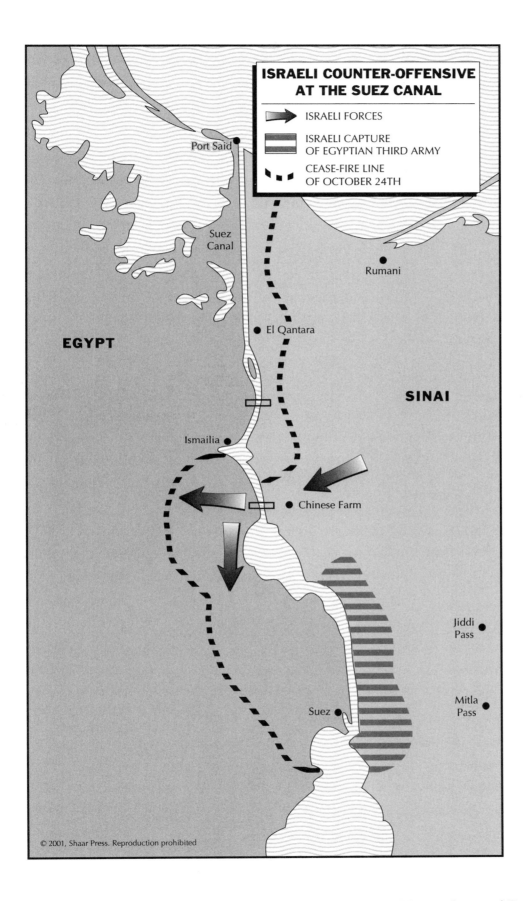

Centurion tanks. Nonetheless, the American airlift continued and Israel was able to use the much-needed supplies for new offensives.

From the beginning of the war, General Ariel Sharon had proposed an Israeli counterstrike at the Suez Canal. He drew up plans for an Israeli crossing of the Canal to its western side, thereby enabling the destruction of the SAM anti-aircraft batteries that were severely hampering the efforts of the Israeli Air Force in the Sinai battle. Large forces could not yet be brought across because the Egyptians still controlled the access roads to the Canal on its eastern side. On the evening of October 14, 30 Israeli tanks and one battalion of soldiers crossed the Canal on barges and rafts. Any concentrated Egyptian attack that night would have easily overcome their precarious beachhead. The Egyptians, however, were oblivious to the true nature of Sharon's attack, thinking it only a diversionary raid, and instead concentrated their efforts on defending their lines east of the Canal. In a terribly fierce and costly battle,[14] the Israelis cleared a section of the east bank of the Canal and brought forth makeshift bridging equipment and pontoons. On the next day, large numbers of Israeli soldiers and arms, under constant Egyptian artillery fire, began crossing to the west side of the Canal. Fanning out from the original beachhead, they began to methodically destroy the SAM sites that had been so instrumental in Egypt's early military success. The Egyptian army had only one armored division and a paratroop brigade left on the west side of the Canal, having committed almost its entire force to the Sinai invasion.

The road to Cairo was open. The Israeli air force, freed from the danger of the SAM batteries, was now heavily punishing the Egyptian troops on both sides of the Canal. The Egyptians were forced to withdraw large numbers of tanks from Sinai and bring them west of the Canal in order to defend their capital. The Egyptian Third Army was now surrounded by Israeli forces on both sides of the Canal. Sharon's bold move had brought the Egyptian army to the edge of defeat.

On the Northern Front, the Israeli army began to drive the Syrians back to their original positions. Avigdor Kahalani commanded a tank brigade that wiped out over 300 Syrian tanks in the "Valley of Tears." An

---

14. The heaviest fighting took place at an agricultural experimentation station mistakenly called the "Chinese Farm." (It had been established by Japanese researchers.) The battle there lasted all night of the 14th and most of the next day. The carnage on that battlefield was awful to behold, for tanks fought tanks from a range of barely ten meters. Because of this struggle and heavy Egyptian fire, Israeli traffic to the beachhead crossing was hopelessly snarled and the pre-constructed bridge could not be brought forward. It would be another two days before proper bridges across the Canal could be put into place. By then, the battle had already been decided in Israel's favor by the troops and tanks floated across the Canal on the makeshift barges, pontoons and tank bridging equipment brought to the water's edge earlier.

Israeli tank patrol penetrated deep into Syrian territory and prevented an Iraqi tank force from reaching the battlefront. However, the Soviet Union, which had armed the Arabs before the war, continued to do so during the war. All of the Syrian tank and artillery losses were replaced immediately by the Soviet Union. Israel, wary of Russian intervention and not ready to increase its already long and bloody casualty list, had no intention of attacking Damascus directly and contented itself with occasionally lobbing shells into the military installation in the suburbs of the city from its defensive "box"[15] some eighteen miles south and west of the city. Russia warned the United States that its airborne troops were on their way to protect Damascus. Israel destroyed a number of Soviet cargo planes on the ground at the Damascus airport, but prudently avoided shooting down any of the Russian supply planes while they were flying towards Syria.

By October 15, the Syrian troops had been driven off of the Golan Heights completely and the Syrian part of the war was for all practical strategic purposes ended, though the blood-letting continued for months. The Soviet Union branded Israel as the aggressor in the war,

Destroyed Syrian tanks and engineering equipment left behind by the retreating Syrian army on the Golan Heights

---

15. This defensive "box" consisted of a large rectangular position, based on natural defensive geographic features, stacked with Israeli armor and artillary that threatened Damascus.

mobilizing Soviet-bloc countries and "nonaligned third world" countries in a harsh diplomatic offensive against Israel. Once again the Jewish state was dramatically and visibly isolated in its struggle for survival.

The prospect of the imminent military defeat of both Egypt and Syria galvanized the Soviet Union into a frenzy of diplomatic activity. Soviet Prime Minister Aleksei Kosygin flew to Cairo to assess the military situation firsthand. He was appalled to discover that Israel had crossed the Suez Canal and was now threatening the destruction of the Egyptian army (as well as the very existence of the Sadat government). Kosygin immediately invited Henry Kissinger to Moscow to work out terms of a cease-fire that would then be presented for United Nations approval. Kissinger flew to Moscow and met with Leonid Brezhnev, chairman of the Soviet politboro.

Despite Soviet blustering and warlike talk, Kissinger and Brezhnev agreed to a cease-fire and for direct negotiations between Egypt and Israel. The UN Security Council Resolution 338, which embodied the terms of this cease-fire, called upon Israel and Egypt to begin immediate negotiations under "appropriate auspices to achieve a just and durable peace." The resolution also made reference to UN Security Council Resolution 242 passed after the 1967 war, which made ambiguous reference to Israeli withdrawal from "territories." Egypt and Israel immediately accepted the cease-fire, though severe fighting between the two armies still continued for the next few days. The failed Israeli attempt to capture the city of Suez before the cease-fire time resulted in heavy casualties to its forces. By the night of October 27, the cease-fire began to take hold and only sporadic firing continued thereafter.

Chief of Staff David Elazar landing near frontline positions on the Golan Heights

Although the cease-fire had been signed between Israel and Egypt, and had already taken hold, Syria attempted a number of strong counter-attacks to break into the Israeli "box" protecting the Golan Heights and threatening Damascus. With Iraqi, Jordanian and Moroccan forces supporting its troops, Syria attacked again towards the Golan. The Syrian attack failed, and Israel's military success forced Syria into accepting the UN cease-fire. In a last-minute attempt to fortify itself further, Israel recaptured its lookout outpost atop Mount Hermon, which Syrian para-troopers had overrun on the first day of the war. Israeli casualties were heavy in this encounter, the last major military action of the Yom Kippur War.[16] Syria nevertheless continued a war of attrition against Israeli troops on the Golan until a final disengagement of forces agreement was signed in the late spring of 1974.

ON OCTOBER 27, ISRAELI AND EGYPTIAN OFFICERS MET AT KILOMETER 101 on the Suez-Cairo Highway. There they agreed that Israel would allow non-military supplies to reach the besieged and isolated Third Army. The discussions at kilometer 101 regarding the disengagement of the armies did not go well. The Egyptians demanded an extensive Israeli withdrawal deep into the Sinai Peninsula. Israel countered by demanding that the Egyptians withdraw to the west bank of the Canal, while Israel would withdraw its forces to the east bank. The Israeli proposal would leave Egypt in the same geographical position that it occupied before the war. This was patently unacceptable to Sadat and the talks between the generals failed to break the impasse. By the middle of November, however, with intensive American mediation, Egypt and Israel agreed to establish a safe corridor to supply the trapped Egyptian Third Army, to scrupulously observe the cease-fire and to exchange the prisoners of war in their hands. On November 15, the prisoner exchange of over 8,000 Egyptian soldiers for 238 Israeli prisoners took place under the auspices of the International Red Cross. The matter of troop disengagement and a new arrangement of forces in Sinai remained yet unresolved between the parties.

Henry Kissinger then undertook a long, torturous, but eventually successful series of "shuttle" negotiations between the parties. His purpose was to convene a peace conference at Geneva where the parties, under the mediation of the United States, the Soviet Union and the United Nations, could meet face to face and hopefully arrive at a solu-

Painstaking Negotiations and Postwar Upheaval

---

16. For an excellent review of the war and a detailed account of all aspects of the struggle, see Chaim Herzog's two books, *The War of Atonement* and *The Arab-Israeli Wars*.

tion to the Arab-Israeli conflict. Israel did not trust the proposal, fearing the pressure of the UN and Russia at the conference. Kissinger assured Israel that the negotiating would be between Israel and the Arabs directly, that the PLO and Yassir Arafat would be excluded from the conference, and that the participation of the other parties was merely a formality. Egypt agreed to attend, as did Jordan, but Syria stated that it would not talk directly with Israel unless it first had a commitment from Israel to withdraw fully from the Golan Heights. Syria also refused to discuss a disengagement of forces agreement with Israel and would give no information regarding Israeli prisoners of war that it held. Kissinger put Syria aside and concentrated on Egypt. On December 22, the Geneva Conference opened. The talks were less than cordial, with the Arabs refusing even to sit next to their Israeli counterparts. After one day, the conference adjourned and the negotiations between Israel and Egypt returned to kilometer 101. But there, too, little progress was made.

Kissinger then boldly volunteered himself to be a negotiator for both sides. He shuttled back and forth from Israel to Egypt, prodding both sides to be flexible and to turn away from continued armed conflict. Both Israel and Egypt had been on the verge of defeat in the war just ended — Israel at the beginning of the war and Egypt at its end. Having stared into the abyss of military disaster, both countries were anxious to reach an agreement. Kissinger hammered out the details of the agreement, applying strong pressure on Israel for major concessions, and it was signed on January 18, 1974. Israel withdrew completely from the west and east banks of Sinai, and a military buffer zone, patrolled by UN troops, was created. Egyptian forces were thinned out in the Suez Canal zone, as were Israeli forces in the Sinai. The Suez Canal was to be reopened and shipping headed for Israel (though not under an Israeli flag) would be allowed passage. The oil fields Israel had developed near the Canal were given to Egypt, with Israel guaranteed the right to purchase that oil at fixed and reasonable prices. The agreement was welcomed by both sides and was carefully observed by them throughout the balance of the decade.

The negotiations with Syria were much more complex than those with Egypt, as Syria obstinately conducted a continuing war of attrition against Israel throughout the spring of 1974. Kissinger struggled mightily to come to a disengagement of forces agreement between the two countries. Beginning in April, Kissinger conducted a non-stop shuttle negotiation lasting 32 days that finally resulted in a disengagement of forces and permanent cease-fire agreement. Israel withdrew from the "box" that threatened Damascus, returned the city of Kuneitra to Syria and established a buffer zone to be patrolled by UN observers. Both sides also agreed to thin out their troop and tank deployments facing each other on the Golan Heights. Israel retained its listening post on Mount Hermon, as well as three strategic hill positions in the eastern Golan. Prisoners of war finally were exchanged. Many of the Israeli prisoners came back from their Syrian captivity emotionally and physically ruined. By the end of May 1974, the Golan was finally at peace. Both Israel and Syria observed the terms of this disengagement agreement on the Golan for the remaining quarter of the century.

Elections for the Israeli Knesset were held on the last day of 1973. The Labor Party Alignment emerged again as the largest party, winning 51 seats.[17] Seventy-five-year-old Mrs. Meir again became prime minister and she was once more able to form a government, primarily with the backing of the National Religious Party's ten seats. General Ariel Sharon, the hero of the Suez crossing that turned the tide of war in Sinai, resigned from the army and helped form a right-wing alignment, under the leadership of Menachem Begin, that gained 39 seats in the new Knesset. This alignment included Sharon's party, Begin's party and other right-wing groups that became the Likud political grouping.

Disturbed by the country's lack of preparedness for war and its heavy losses, the government had appointed a special commission of inquiry into the handling of the war. This commission was headed by Justice Shlomo Agranat and its findings, made public in April 1974, shattered the old guard. The military and civilian leaders of the government were directly or indirectly condemned for the failures of intelligence, preparedness and strategy that had cost Israel so dearly. Golda Meir and Moshe Dayan both resigned. Yitzchak Rabin became the new prime minister and Shimon Peres took over as minister of defense. Rabin clashed with the National Religious Party almost immediately on matters of religious conversions and also on the question of new settlements in Judea and Samaria. The disagreement was downplayed after a few months, but it marked the beginning of the end of the historic coalition between the Religious Zionists and Labor that had ruled Israel for its first 30 years.

I N THE HAZE OF SMOKE OF A WAR JUST ENDING, AN ARAB SUMMIT MEETING in Morocco on October 25, 1973 proclaimed the PLO as the sole representative of the Palestinian people, thus undercutting any Jordanian hopes for returning the West Bank to its control. Terrible terrorist attacks rocked Israel in the aftermath of the war. In April 1974, eighteen Jews

The PLO Reveals its True Agenda

---

17. This was a loss of five seats from the previous election, four years earlier.

were murdered in Kiryat Shmonah, Israel's northernmost city. On May 14, 22 sleeping students from a religious school in Safed were murdered in cold blood in Maalot in northern Israel. The terrorists also murdered a Jewish couple and their child sleeping in an apartment nearby. One of the countless factions that made up the PLO took "credit" for these exploits. In June, three Jewish women were murdered at Kibbutz Shamir in the northern Galilee. There were also terrorist attacks in Naharia and Beit Shean, which cost many more lives.

Because of the Arab oil boycott that accompanied the Yom Kippur War, the industrialized nations of the world were intimidated by the Arabs and the PLO. Anti-Semitic statements, placards and acts threatened Jewish communities the world over. In the United States, there was a dramatic increase in anti-Jewish behavior. The Jews were blamed for the long lines at the gasoline pumps, for the steep rise in oil prices and the disruption of the comfort that gas-guzzling automobiles brought to American life. The Arabs finally ended their oil boycott of the West in 1974, but they hiked the price of oil dramatically. This sparked a worldwide inflationary trend that would wreak havoc with the stability of the world's economies over the next decade.

In November 1974, Yassir Arafat, armed with a pistol that he placed on the lectern as he spoke at the UN, stated: "We have entered the world through its widest gate. Now Zionism will get out of this world — and from Palestine in particular — under the blow of the people's struggle. We shall never stop until we can go back home and Israel is destroyed. The goal of our struggle is the end of Israel, and there can be no compromise or mediations. We don't want peace, we want victory. Peace for us means Israel's destruction, and nothing else."[18] The PLO was granted official observer status at the UN. With the aid of Soviet, Arab and nonaligned nations, the PLO succeeded in ousting Israel from a number of international agencies and Zionism was officially condemned by these bodies. The climax came in a resolution passed by the UN General Assembly in November 1975, condemning Zionism as "racism." The Israeli UN delegate, Chaim Herzog, mounted the podium and tore up a copy of the resolution in the delegates' faces.

The PLO cooperated with other terrorist groups throughout the 1970's, especially those with Marxist ideologies. The Japanese Red Army, the German Baader-Meinhof gang, the Irish Republican Army, the Red Brigade of Italy, the Basque separatists in Spain, as well as other revolu-

---

18. Quoted by Gilbert, p.467.

tionary terrorist groups in Africa, Asia and South America were all bene-ficiaries of the PLO's training facilities and funding.[19]

Terrorist attacks against Israel and Jewish targets worldwide would continue unabated throughout the next decades. Bombs in Jerusalem, amphibious raids on the coast of Israel, hijacked buses and kidnapped Israelis held for hostage were all too common in 1974 and 1975. Israel retaliated by attacking the PLO bases in southern Lebanon,[20] the staging area for its terrorist attacks against Israel. Israel was severely censured for these retaliatory raids by the UN and many Western governments, while the Soviet Union kept up the drumbeat of anti-Semitism and threats to Israel's existence.

Trouble in Soviet Paradise: Refuseniks Rock the Boat

THE UNITED STATES, SHOCKED BY THE SCANDAL OF NIXON'S RESIGNA-tion and the weakness of President Gerald Ford's caretaker government,[21] seemed paralyzed in the face of the economic and terrorist dangers undermining world stability. On the other hand, the Soviet Union under Leonid Brezhnev seemed to be on the ascendancy — aggressive, confident and brutal in pursuing its policies of expansion and forced conformity. In addition, the Soviet KGB played a sinister role in supporting and protecting terrorist activities and their perpetrators.

Under the surface of Brezhnev's Soviet empire, however, the seeds of its self-destruction began to sprout. The Soviet Union invaded Czechoslovakia in 1968 to stop the liberalization movement of the local communist leader, Alexander Dubcek, and end the "Prague Spring." The truth was that all of the Soviet satellite nations in Eastern Europe were restive under the Soviet boot. In Russia itself, intellectuals such as Alexander Solzhynitsin and Andrei Sakharov exposed the oppressive Soviet system and demanded basic human rights for the Russian people. In 1977, Brezhnev responded harshly to this agitation by stating: *In our country it is not forbidden to think differently from the majority ... It is quite another matter if a few individuals who have ... actively come out against the social-ist system, embark on the road of anti-Soviet activity, violate laws and, find-ing no support inside their own country, turn for support abroad, to imperi-*

---

19. Most of the PLO's money came from the Arab oil states. It was a classic case of extortion and protection money. Much of the money found its way into the private accounts of PLO leaders, establishing a pattern of organized corruption that would accompany the PLO throughout the balance of the century.

20. Commonly known in Israel as "Fatahland," after the name of Arafat's own armed wing of the PLO.

21. After Spiro Agnew resigned as vice-president in 1973, Gerald Ford, the House Republican leader, was appointed to the position. When President Nixon resigned from the presidency, Ford succeeded him and Nelson Rockefeller was chosen as vice-president.

alist subversive centers ... Our citizens demand that such ... activists be treated as opponents of socialism, as persons acting against their own motherland, as accomplices if not actual agents of imperialism ... We have taken and will continue to take against them measures envisaged by our law.[22]

The Brezhnev regime was troubled by the phenomenon of the Jewish "refuseniks," Jews who refused to cease their agitation for religious freedom and the right to emigrate. The 1970's saw a rising clamor within Russia by these young Jews who, with clandestine help from abroad, taught themselves Hebrew and Jewish tradition and demanded their right to leave Russia for Israel. Jews from the free world began visiting Russia, and though constantly harassed by the KGB and the police, made contact with the refuseniks, smuggling in religious necessities, books, audiotapes, kosher food and other physical necessities of Jewish life. The pressure on the Soviets to allow Russian Jews to emigrate was now not just from outside world Jewry, but also from within the Soviet Union itself. The circle of refuseniks expanded and their cause gained wide attention in the Soviet Union and worldwide. Even though many of them were arrested and sentenced to long prison terms, their cause gained momentum as they individually attained international heroic stature. New names — Mendelevitch, Grilius, Nudel, Sharansky, Essas and many others — now entered the ages-old list of Jewish heroes and martyrs. Jews in Israel and in the Diaspora vowed not to forget these "Prisoners of Zion" and continued pressing for their release from prison and their right to immigrate to Israel. It is not an exaggeration to say that the agitation of the Jewish refuseniks in the 1970's was one of the causes of destabilization and the implosion of the Soviet Union a little more than a decade later.[23]

The cause of Soviet Jewry, originally muted in American Jewish life, now became one of the community's major concerns. The various Jewish organizations lobbied Congress and the administration to raise the cause of Soviet Jewry in all bilateral negotiations with the Soviets. The famed "Jackson-Vanik Amendment"[24] to the United States Trade Act of 1979 demanded that the Soviets allow Jewish immigration to Israel as a prerequisite to the Soviet Union's receiving favorable trade and monetary considerations from the United States. Though the Soviets loudly protested this interference in their internal affairs, they were not immune to the pressures brought upon them. A small but steady stream of Soviet Jews began to arrive in Israel at the end of the

---

22. Quoted by Paul Johnson, in *Modern Times*, p.682.

23. See Natan Sharansky's article "From Helsinki to Oslo" in the *Journal of International Security Affairs*, Vol.1, No.1, June 2001.

24. Senator Robert M. Jackson of Washington was the prime spokesman in Congress for the cause of Soviet Jewry.

decade and their presence in Israel portended the forthcoming flood of Soviet Jewish immigrants to Israel in the late 1980's and 1990's. An entire "underground railway" system, which operated with the knowledge of the Soviets (though officially it was still illegal for Soviet citizens to leave for Israel), was established with stopping-off points in Austria and Italy. Austria, under the chancellorship of Bruno Kreisky, capitulated to PLO terror and eventually closed its facilities that temporarily housed Russian Jews. Yet the exodus of Soviet Jewry was well under way. The miracle of Russian Jews, after 60 years of communism, atheism and oppression, reuniting with their people, their land and their history, was one of the major events of twentieth century Jewish life.

A Sudden Burst of Glory

ON JUNE 27, 1976, ARAB HIJACKERS DIVERTED AN AIR FRANCE JETLINER to Libya. The non-Jewish passengers on the plane were released there, but the plane with 98 Jews on board was flown to Entebbe, Uganda. The country was then ruled by the megalomaniacal, murderous Idi Amin, an ally of terrorism, a Soviet puppet and a cruel, corrupt dictator. Amin fit the profile of many of Africa's post-colonial rulers of the time. For a week, the Jewish hostages were held prisoner while outrageous demands were submitted to Israel to effect their release. In a brilliantly planned, executed and God-blessed action, Israeli commandos landed at Entebbe airport, thousands of miles from Tel Aviv, killed the terrorists and engaged the Ugandan troops guarding the plane. Three hostages were killed in the crossfire. Another hostage, who was in an Entebbe hospital at the time, was murdered there in cold blood to avenge Idi Amin's loss of face. Yonatan Netanyahu, the commander of the mission, was the only Israeli fatality in the daring action. The world was electrified by the successful Israeli raid, and the spirits of the people of Israel and Jews the world over were raised. As Shimon Peres stated: "In one short hour, the stature of the Jewish people was enhanced — as was the stature of free and responsible people throughout the world."[25] Not long after, however, the UN Security Council debated the violation of Ugandan sovereignty and most countries, even Europeans, typically criticized Israel!

Ideologies Align on the Question of Settlements

IN ISRAEL, A GROUP KNOWN AS GUSH EMUNIM (THE BLOC OF THE Faithful) gained adherents and legitimacy. The avowed purpose of this organization was to build Jewish settlements, towns and cities throughout

---

25. Quoted by Gilbert, p.473.

the Land of Israel. The absence of Arab willingness to negotiate peace with Israel, coupled with the ideological motive of reclaiming and rebuilding all of the Land of Israel (especially land conquered in 1967), created a climate of governmental and public approval of Gush Emunim's goals. Rabbi Zvi Yehuda Kook, the son of the former Chief Rabbi Avraham Yitzchak Kook and the head of the Mercaz HaRav yeshivah in Jerusalem, became the spiritual mentor of Gush Emunim. Like his father, Rabbi Kook saw the redemption of the Land of Israel by Jewish settlement as part of the redemption of the Jewish people from exile and the eventual Messianic process of universal human redemption. He encouraged his students to head groups of young people and found new Jewish communities throughout Judea, Samaria and the Gaza area. Under Yitzchak Rabin, the Israeli government was ambivalent in its attitude towards these proposed new settlements. In December 1975, Gush Emunim was given "temporary" permission to build a settlement, Eilon Moreh, north of the Arab-populated city of Nablus. The temporary permission became permanent and Eilon Moreh became the forerunner of many more such settlements throughout Israel. Gush Emunim became the ideological engine of the Israeli right wing parties. Ironically, its initial growth and much later support came under the rule of a left wing Labor government.

Because of their ideological basis, the new settlements attracted highly motivated and dedicated young people to populate them. Later, there were "suburban" settlements near the densely populated greater Tel Aviv and Jerusalem areas. They were built within a few miles, or even a few meters, of the 1949 borders of Israel. These new towns and cities had less of an ideological base than the earlier and far-flung settlements. But in the eyes of the Arabs, as well as much of the world, they were part and parcel of the settlements created on "Arab lands." The drawback to the ideological settlements, aside from the political and diplomatic problems that they posed, was that they absorbed the best of the idealistic young Israelis, especially of the religious camp, moving them far away from the centers of Israeli life and culture where they could have acted as a counterweight to the growing post-Zionist culture of the secular Left. Thus, as post-Zionism gained strength, Gush Emunim slowly lost the influence and respect of Israeli society — respect that it would so sorely need in order to maintain its settlements and land redemption program in later years.

The opponents of Gush Emunim were on the opposite end of the political and ideological spectrum. This group, nameless, but with great and growing intellectual influence, opposed all Jewish settlement in areas located over the "green line" of the 1967 borders of Israel. Eventually this group would become the "peace camp" in Israeli society, and would dominate Israeli policy in the 1990's. Composed of professors, intellectuals and a younger generation of Leftist politicians, the assessment of the group was that the Palestinians were entitled to their own state and that Israel should evacuate all territory acquired in the Six Day War to accommodate that state. In their view, the settlement of the Arab-Israeli dispute was dependent on far-reaching Israeli concessions to the Arabs, and these concessions were worth the price, as they were the only way Israel would gain peace. The peace group was hardly known outside of its own circle in the 1970's, but its tenacity and unwavering belief in the sole validity of its position would help it grow in numbers and political influence.[26]

At the end of 1976, Rabin ousted the religious parties from his coalition over their complaints about a reception for three new American fighter jets that impinged on, but did not actually violate, the Sabbath.[27] A gruff and straightforward person, Rabin ruffled the sensitivities of many political leaders, even in his own party. Lacking in knowledge of Judaism, his relationship with the religious parties was especially prickly. Under pressure from Gush Emunim, and in response to the increasingly anti-religious nature and policies of the Israeli Left, the Religious Zionists looked to the Right — to Menachem Begin and his party — as an ally. This realignment of Israeli politics would have important repercussions throughout the remainder of the century.

Political Rebellion Destroys the Old Guard

DUE TO THE OUSTER OF THE RELIGIOUS PARTIES FROM RABIN'S coalition, Rabin opted for new elections. Shimon Peres, whose relations with Rabin were extremely negative, challenged Rabin for leadership of the Labor Party. Peres criticized Rabin over the handling of the plane ceremony affair, calling Rabin's decision to sever the Labor alliance with the religious parties "a tragic mistake." In the elections for leadership of the Labor Party, Rabin nosed out Peres with 1,445 votes to 1,404 votes, with sixteen abstentions. Rabin and Peres remained bitter personal and political foes until they overcame their differences in the 1990's and joined forces in an attempt to reach a peace agreement with the PLO.

The struggle between Peres and Rabin, and its razor-thin decision, resulted in bitterness between the candidates' partisans, greatly weakening the Labor Party for the forthcoming election. The accumulated mistakes and corruption of a party too long in power finally caught up with it. The suicide of the Labor government's housing minister in early 1977

---

26. For an excellent review of the growth of the "peace camp" and a penetrating analysis of post-Zionism, see Yoram Hazoni, *The Jewish State – The Struggle for Israel's Soul*, New York, 2000.
27. The ceremony ended seventeen minutes before sunset.

only seemed to confirm the public's growing distrust of the entrenched Labor establishment, and after nearly 30 years of Labor rule, the Israeli public tired of its leadership.

An unexpected scandal hit Yitzchak Rabin at the beginning of the election campaign. His wife had maintained a private bank account in the United States during his tenure there as the Israeli ambassador. This was perfectly legal for Israelis living abroad. But when they returned to Israel, they neglected to close the account. At that time, it was illegal for Israelis residing in Israel to have a foreign bank account. Leah Rabin was tried, found guilty and fined for maintaining the American bank account. Rabin, embarrassed by the scandal and weakened by Shimon Peres' challenge to his leadership, resigned as prime minister and was replaced by Peres as the caretaker leader of the government until the election.

But Peres was unable to lead Labor to victory in the elections of May 1977. A political earthquake overtook Israel as the bulk of the Sephardic vote — which Labor had always taken for granted — rebelled against what it perceived as Ashkenazic discrimination and protest voted instead for Likud and Menachem Begin. Labor won only 32 seats, while a new centrist party, Dash (*Democratya v'Shinuy*, i.e. Democratic Movement for Change), headed by Yigael Yadin, gained fifteen seats. The major winner was Menachem Begin and his Likud party, which captured 43 seats. With the religious parties supplying him with seventeen votes, Ariel Sharon's party adding two more votes, and the defection of Moshe Dayan from Labor to Likud, Begin formed his government without Dash or Labor. Ezer Weizman was Begin's defense minister and Begin appointed Moshe Dayan as his foreign minister. Eventually Dash also joined Begin's government coalition, giving him a comfortable majority of 78 of 120 seats.

Menachem Begin's electoral victory sent shock waves through the ranks of the American Jewish organizations. Accustomed for half a century to dealing only with the Left in Israel, American leadership had adopted the bias against Begin that the Left had so assiduously fostered. Begin was viewed as irresponsible, a terrorist, a demagogue, a danger to American-Israeli relations. Alexander Schindler, as head of the Conference of Presidents of Major Jewish Organizations, as well as the leading executive of Reform Jewry, publicly extended an olive branch to Begin. Yet his true attitudes were thinly veiled. According to a later obituary of Schindler in *The Jerusalem Post*, "No more than ten months into Begin's term, Schindler's own deputy in the Reform movement, Albert Vorspan, joined the thirty-seven 'prominent' American Jews in a page one *New York Times* publicity blitz against Begin and in support of Peace Now. Encouraged by Israel's Labor Party — by 1978 Peres was using the United States media to call for a partial West Bank pullout — the elected

Prime Minister Begin in conversation with Rabbi Moshe Feinstein in the latter's Lower East Side apartment in New York in 1977

government of Israel [under Begin's leadership] could no longer count on the US Jewish leadership for unconditional political support."[28]

American President Jimmy Carter had publicly expressed his support for the old Rogers Plan (renamed for President Reagan's first secretary of state), which basically demanded the return of Israel to its 1949 borders. Yet both Israel and the United States refused to recognize the PLO as anything but a terrorist organization, envisioning any settlement of the dispute over the West Bank to be an Israeli-Jordanian matter. Begin attempted to draw King Hussein of Jordan into negotiations regarding the West Bank, but the king refused, stating that he would not serve as the representative of Palestinian interests in light of the Arab League decision in 1974 which designated the PLO as the exclusive representative of the Palestinians. President Carter also publicly objected to the continuation of Jewish settlement on the West Bank, contending that constructing such settlements was illegal. Despite this strong American objection, Begin continued his policy of expanding Jewish settlement throughout Judea, Samaria and Gaza.

B EGIN'S PRIMARY FOREIGN AFFAIRS FOCUS WAS NOT ON JORDAN, BUT ON Egypt. Anwar Sadat of Egypt had sent feelers to Israel regarding a possible meeting with Begin — and a peace treaty between Egypt and Israel that would restore the Sinai to Egypt. Secret meetings held in Morocco between Moshe Dayan and Egyptian Deputy Prime Minister Hassan

A Flicker of Peace Brightens the Horizon

---

28. From an obituary on Alexander Schindler printed in *The Jerusalem Post*, December 8, 2000.

Tuhami cleared the way for direct peace negotiations between Israel and Egypt. While President Carter pushed for the reconvening of the long dormant 1974 Geneva peace conference, both Israel and Egypt were looking for a way to outflank Russia and America and arrive at a deal on their own.

At this point, the PLO, driven from Jordan, was attempting to gain control over much of Lebanon. A bitter civil war broke out in Lebanon. Christian militias fought with various Moslem groups, and especially against the PLO. Israel rashly intervened on the side of the Christian militias, particularly in southern Lebanon near the Israeli border. Carter strongly warned Israel not to intervene in Lebanon, and Begin withdrew. Nevertheless, the PLO kept up the pressure against Israel from inside Lebanon, firing katyusha rockets at the city of Nahariya with resultant deaths and damage. Begin ordered a retaliatory air raid against PLO positions in Lebanon.

Begin had been chastened by Carter's strong position and unfriendly attitude, but he attempted to placate the American president, distracting him from the continuing construction of new Jewish settlements on the West Bank. The only effort that Begin saw as effective for the advancement of joint Israeli and American interests was pursuing peace with Egypt. He therefore signaled Sadat that he would be a welcome guest in Israel and that an agreement that would satisfy Egypt was more than likely to result from such a visit.

In November 1977, Sadat gave a speech in the Egyptian parliament, offering to come to Israel and speak in the Knesset in an effort to forge a peace arrangement. Begin responded by extending an official invitation to Sadat to come to Jerusalem and address the Knesset. Most Israeli officials viewed Sadat's offer as pure grandstanding and were deeply suspicious of his motives and intent. But on November 19, Anwar Sadat did, in fact, come to Israel and address the Knesset. He made a hard-line speech, emphasizing the rights of the Palestinians to a state and the necessity for full Israeli withdrawal to the pre-1967 borders.

But few Israelis paid attention to his words. Instead, they were fixated by the very fact that he came to Jerusalem and spoke to the Knesset. Cheering crowds lined his motorcade route in Jerusalem and he was seen not only as a celebrity, but as a hero. So strong was the desire and hope of Israelis for peace that all of Sadat's past sins — support of Hitler in World War II, complicity in all of Nasser's pan-Arab adventures, organized terrorism and wars, initiating the bloody Yom Kippur War — were completely overlooked. His state visit had broken through a psychological barrier. He had sensed what no other Arab leader, except perhaps King Hussein of Jordan, understood — that Israel would be willing to make enormous concessions to any Arab leader who would publicly acknowledge that Israel has a legitimate right to exist and that violent means of

confronting Israel would now be foresworn. Peace requires a sense of trust and not merely signatures on a piece of paper. Sadat's dramatic visit to Jerusalem created the possibility of such human trust.

The Egyptians and Israelis entered into serious negotiations over a peace treaty. But after eight months of hard and often acrimonious bargaining, the entire peace effort seemed to have faltered. Begin despairingly reported that the terms agreed upon thus far were "nothing for nothing." Egypt's adamant insistence upon the return of the complete Sinai Peninsula to her sovereignty and her demand for recognition of Palestinian statehood were the main stumbling blocks to agreement. From his personal viewpoint, Sadat had risked so much that he despaired of success in the negotiations. He alternatively threatened to resign, to renew the war or to let the UN decide all outstanding issues. Within Israel itself, the growing Peace Now movement demanded that Begin make all necessary concessions to Egypt to bring about an agreement. Though Begin publicly refused to be influenced by the call of Peace Now for concessions, the appearance of a strong and vocal peace camp within Israeli society undoubtedly affected all Israeli foreign and military policy for the remaining decades of the century. President Carter, in a last-ditch effort to salvage the peace talks, invited Sadat, Begin and their staffs to his presidential retreat at Camp David in the Maryland hills. Carter promised that he would take an active personal role in the negotiations, confident that neither the President of Egypt nor the Prime Minister of Israel could afford to say no to the President of the United States.

In August 1978, both Egypt and Israel accepted Carter's invitation to negotiate at Camp David. The conference began on September 5 and

President Sadat and Prime Minister Begin after their first conference at Sadat's residence in Ismailia

came to an impasse almost immediately. Begin was unwilling to give up all of the Sinai, especially the Israeli air bases there that represented Israel's front line of security on the southern front. Sadat not only insisted on all of the Sinai, but also on Israel's withdrawal from all territories gained after the 1967 war, the return of Jerusalem to Arab sovereignty, and the right of Arab refugees to return to their homes in Israel proper. Both Begin and Sadat threatened to leave and return home. Though the two leaders did not relate well on a personal basis, Moshe Dayan, and to a greater extent, Ezer Weizman, did develop a warmer and friendlier rapport with the Egyptian leader.[29]

Under strong pressure from the Americans and intensive negotiations conducted through Dayan and Weizman, the outlines of a deal eventually emerged. Israel would return all of Sinai to Egypt and the area left under dispute, the resort area of Tabah, which each claimed was on its side of the border, would be subject to international arbitration.[30] Israel and Egypt also agreed on a vague formula for Palestinian "autonomy" within five years, in cooperation with Jordan. Israel also agreed to respect "the legitimate rights of the Palestinian people." Egypt agreed to a full peace treaty with Israel with the exchange of ambassadors and embassies. It also agreed to drop its request for linkage of the Palestinian issues to the Egyptian treaty, and to provide oil to Israel from the Sinai oil fields, even in the face of another Arab oil boycott. In a side letter, Israel made vague promises to Sadat and Egypt to make progress on the Palestinian autonomy issue. For its part, the United States agreed to rebuild the Egyptian armed forces and provide massive annual aid and grants to the Egyptian economy. It also promised to build two air force bases for Israel in the Negev, at its own expense, to replace the two air bases that Israel was now surrendering in the Sinai. A package of continuing military and economic aid to Israel was also part of the American commitment.

In announcing the signing of the peace agreement with Egypt to the Israeli public on worldwide television, Begin donned a *kippah* and recited the traditional Jewish blessing *Shehechiyanu*, "that He has kept us alive, preserved us and enabled us to reach this day." Though not legally bound to do so according to the opinion of the attorney general of Israel, Begin submitted the Camp David accords to the Knesset for its approval. On September 27, 1978, the Knesset approved those accords by a vote of

---

29. For a wonderfully human and incisive eyewitness report on the Camp David conference, as well as a sympathetic analysis of the complex character of Moshe Dayan, see Naftali Lavie's book, *Balaam's Prophecy*. Lavie served as Israeli Consul-General in New York and as Dayan's trusted executive secretary and confidant.

30. The international arbitrator decided in favor of Egypt in the 1980's.

84-19 with seventeen abstentions.[31] Yitzchak Shamir, a veteran of Lechi and a future prime minister, was one of those who abstained, as did many members of the National Religious Party. Likud stalwarts Moshe Arens and Yigal Allon voted against the accords. There were bitter recriminations within Likud itself over Begin's concessions to Sadat, but the treaty enjoyed vast support among the general Israeli public, and Begin's popularity was at an all time high. Both Begin and Sadat were recipients of the Nobel Peace Prize in recognition of their efforts at ending the 30-year-old Egyptian-Israeli hostilities.

A Dangerous Precedent Takes Root

THE TREATY, HOWEVER, SET CERTAIN PRECEDENTS THAT ISRAEL WISH-fully ignored at the time of its negotiation and signing. These guidelines would influence all future negotiations with the Arabs, at least as far as the Arabs were concerned. Sadat regained every inch of lost Egyptian territory, Israel dismantled its settlements in Sinai and forcibly moved its own citizens back behind "the green line" of the pre-1967 borders. Israel accepted a "side letter" from Sadat in which he repeated all of the maximalist Arab demands regarding a Palestinian state, pre-1967 borders, dismantling of all settlements, an Arab Jerusalem and the right of return to Israel of all Arab refugees. Begin explained to the Israeli public that the country could be generous in ceding the Sinai Desert since it was not within the Biblically ordained borders of Israel, and it was bereft of any sizeable population. He discounted the significance of Sadat's "side letter," saying that it was only a protective "fig leaf" to placate the Arab masses over the peace treaty with Israel itself. He deeply regretted the necessity of evacuating the Sinai town of Yamit, but maintained that it was that particular, painful concession that enabled Egyptian agreement to the overall peace treaty.

Though there certainly was merit in Begin's position and explanation, every future negotiation with Arab countries and/or the Palestinians met with the same Arab demands regarding every inch of territory, the return to the 1967 borders, an Arab Jerusalem, the right of refugees to return to Israel and the dismantling of all Jewish settlements. Whether Begin truly contemplated the precedent set by the Israeli-Egyptian treaty is a matter of debate.

Begin and Sharon initiated and supported intensified Jewish settlement throughout the West Bank and Gaza over the next four years. In 1980 alone, the Begin government established 38 new settlements

---

31. The final ratification of the fully completed and detailed Egyptian-Israeli peace treaty by the Knesset took place in March 1979 by a vote of 95-18.

throughout the West Bank and Gaza. A Jewish presence was reestablished in the heart of Hebron in 1979, when a number of Jewish families moved into Beit Hadassah, which had been a center of Jewish life in Hebron before the pogrom of 1929. This Jewish enclave, located in the midst of a very hostile Arab population, required substantial military protection. It eventually expanded and an apartment bloc was built for new Jewish families arriving in the city. Begin also succeeded in passing a Basic Law in the Knesset declaring Jerusalem the eternal capital of Israel and not subject to division.[32] This action was greeted by international criticism; and numerous foreign governments, which until then had established embassies in Jerusalem, moved them to Tel Aviv. The law received wide support in the Knesset, even from the Labor Party. Begin's hard-line policies eventually alienated both Moshe Dayan and Ezer Weizman and they resigned from their cabinet posts and ministries. But Begin remained unshaken in his support of new settlements throughout the boundaries of the Biblical Land of Israel.

Like the Labor governments before him, Begin hoped to attract major immigration to Israel from the Western countries, especially the United States. Many of the new settlements that were founded on the West Bank were populated by new American immigrants. They arrived in Israel with a sense of idealism and a willingness to sacrifice in order to settle the entire Biblical Land of Israel. The Israeli government encouraged this immigration and helped facilitate it by providing housing and infrastructure for the new settlements. Larger towns were also planned and American Jewish communities were recruited to move en masse to these proposed urban developments. The most famous example of this group *aliyah* was the establishment of the town of Efrata (popularly known as Efrat) near Bethlehem, by Rabbi Shlomo Riskin and members of his Lincoln Square Congregation in New York City.[33] Chasidic communities from Boston and Pittsburgh also developed new communities in Israel, though they were mainly concentrated within already existing Israeli urban areas. Though approximately only 10,000 American Jews settled in Israel permanently, their influence was pronounced in Israeli life. They were viewed askance by the Israeli Left which resented the influx of johnny-come-lately religious and nationalist "extremists."

32. Israel has no written constitution. Its framework of government and society is therefore determined by special "Basic Laws" passed by the Knesset. The interpretation of these "Basic Laws" was left to the decisions of the Supreme Court of Israel.

33. The first residents of Efrata moved into their homes in 1982.

The Changing Face of American Jewry

Rabbi Shlomo Zalman Auerbach

The Steipler

I N THE JEWISH COMMUNITY IN THE UNITED STATES, TRENDS THAT HAD begun in the '60's continued to develop at a rapid rate. Like Israeli society, it began going in two directions at one and the same time. Within the Orthodox community, which was growing in numbers and self-confidence,[34] a pronounced turn towards a more rigorous standard of religious observance developed, a product of the yeshivah generation educated by the surviving Eastern European *roshei yeshivah* and Chasidic leaders. The *kollel* system of learning, which had relatively few adherents in the previous decades of American Jewish life, now became popular and accepted. Young men continued to study in yeshivah long after their marriage, and some remained permanently in the lifelong study of Torah. Their efforts were supported by their wives working outside of their homes, in itself a revolutionary development in Orthodox family life, as well as by their parents and in-laws. Liberal government welfare programs, put in place by Lyndon Johnson's "Great Society" 1960's anti-poverty programs, and retained and expanded throughout the 1970's by succeeding administrations, indirectly helped finance the emerging *kollel* system. The sleepy town of Lakewood, New Jersey, grew into a bastion of Orthodox yeshivah life with the Beth Medrash Govoha, now headed by Rabbi Shneur Kotler, the son of the founder, Rabbi Aharon Kotler, growing into a student body of thousands. Lakewood's yeshivah established branches in other communities that grew into established and popular yeshivos in their own right.[35] Lakewood itself became a very large Jewish community, as many of the yeshivah students and other Orthodox Jews settled there. Rabbi Moshe Feinstein continued to be recognized as the prime decisor of halachic matters in the world of the Diaspora, while Rabbi Yaakov Kamenetsky, retiring from active leadership of Yeshivah Torah Vodaath, filled the role of sage and counselor par excellence. (Rabbi Shlomo Zalman Auerbach of Jerusalem and Rabbi Yaakov Kanievsky — known as the "Steipler" — of Bnei Brak filled similar roles respectively in Israel.) The great Chasidic dynasties of Lubavitch, Gur, Belz, Vizhnitz, Skver, Stolin and others continued to grow. Their leaders were enormously influential in Orthodox Jewish life and in Israeli political life as well.

---

34. For the first time, Orthodoxy represented itself in the halls of Congress and state capitals independent of the usual Jewish lobbying groups. Rabbi Moshe Sherer established strong lobbying offices in Washington and Albany on behalf of Agudath Israel. Other organizations followed suit in later years. The Orthodox viewpoint on many contentious issues oftentimes clashed with the opinion put forth by the national Jewish organizations that previously were the sole representatives of American Jewry to the government. These independent government-lobbying offices were another indication of the newfound confidence that infused American Orthodoxy in this decade.

35. Yeshivos in Philadelphia and Scranton, Pennsylvania and Long Beach, New York were some of the early "Lakewood-type" yeshivos then founded. These yeshivos included a high school program with full secular studies and a "Torah-only" approach after high school graduation.

The 1970's saw the extensive development of another trend begun in the late 1960's: Large numbers of American Orthodox youth went to Israel for a year or two of intensive Torah study after high school graduation. Many programs for Torah study were established in a large number of Israeli institutions. The older, traditional yeshivos benefited from an influx of American students, though they did not provide any special programs for the newcomers. The *hesder* yeshivos often did create special divisions and programs for their non-Israeli students. New yeshivos and women's seminaries, catering to the American, and to a lesser degree to the English, South African and Australian post-high school student were established. By the end of the decade, the number of young, non-Israeli, Orthodox students studying in Israeli institutions numbered in the thousands.

The face of American Orthodoxy also began to change in a literal sense. The clean-shaven, fashionably dressed Modern Orthodox rabbi of the previous four decades slowly began to give way to his bearded, more traditionally dressed, black-hatted successor. Mixed seating — i.e. without a *mechitzah* — in "traditional" synagogues was bitterly denounced in Orthodox circles. Synagogues tolerating this practice, and their Orthodox rabbis, came under increasing pressure to conform to standard Orthodox practice. Because of this demand, a few synagogues returned to separate seating, but others severed their ties with Orthodoxy completely and joined the Conservative movement. Mixed seating at banquets, weddings and other social affairs also declined in popularity. Mixed dancing, a practice that was accepted by some segments of American Orthodox society earlier in the century, disappeared completely from the Orthodox scene. Chasidic dress and behavior also became more popular, many times making inroads even in German, Lithuanian and yeshivah communities. The widespread presence of Chabad Chasidim, and their public pride in Jewish heritage and practice, also contributed to the new Orthodox self-confidence.

Kosher food supervision in the United States and throughout the world expanded greatly in the 1970's. The Kashrus division of the Union of Orthodox Jewish Congregations of America — the OU — certified thousands of different food items and provided the basic infrastructure for all *kashrus* supervision in America. There were also quite a number of other private *kashrus*-certifying agencies and organizations that flourished in this decade. The exclusive use of *cholov Yisrael* dairy products[36] and *glatt kosher*

---

36. Literally, the term means "Jewish milk." Its requirement is that a Jew supervise the milking process to make certain that milk from non-kosher animals is not introduced into the product. Although there is strong halachic opinion that governmental supervision of milk may also be sufficient, numerous kosher Jewish milk dairies arose and the strong public demand for Jewish milk grew.

meat[37] now became normative standards of *kashrus* for much of the Orthodox world.

The youth division of the Orthodox Union — NCSY — also experienced impressive growth during this decade. It attracted thousands of Jewish teenagers with minimal or no Jewish education and gave them an informal educational and social milieu that eventually strengthened their ties to Judaism and Jewish observance. Other youth movements — Pirchai Agudath Israel, Bnei Akiva and the Conservative movement's United Synagogue Youth — also flourished during this period.

Numerous social and welfare organizations were created by American Orthodox Jewry, especially by the Chasidic/yeshivah societies during this

---

37. The Yiddish term *glatt,* or in Hebrew *chalak,* signifies "smoothness," or the absence of any *kashrus* problems whatsoever regarding the animal that has been slaughtered. In its popular usage, the term signifies a higher and more rigorous standard of *kashrus* inspection of food and is no longer restricted to meat.

decade. Such organizations as Hatzolah,[38] Ohel Children's Services, numerous free loan societies, Bikur Cholim organizations,[39] independent Orthodox Jewish funeral homes and senior citizen facilities flourished.

Torah education and outreach were strengthened enormously by the development of Jewish publishing companies, particularly Mesorah Publications. This company originated the famed ArtScroll Series of books on Jewish subjects and Torah topics. It would be no exaggeration to say that by the end of the century, Mesorah had developed from its small beginnings in 1976 into the largest "teacher" in the Jewish world. Its excellent renditions of the Jewish classical books — the Bible, the Mishnah and eventually the Talmud — in elegant but simple English, taught and influenced thousands of Jews. Eventually the ArtScroll *Chumash* and prayer books became staples of synagogues and homes. The ArtScroll books also were blessed with excellent graphics and were marketed efficiently to a Jewish public hungry for Jewish study aids and literature.

Jewish music also grew in popularity and commercial use during the 1970's.[40] Until the 1960's and 1970's, Jewish music throughout the century had consisted mainly of cantorial renditions, Yiddish folk songs and Israeli folk tunes. The new troubadour of Jewish song was Shlomo Carlebach. A former student of the Lakewood yeshivah and a member of a famous rabbinic family, Carlebach and his guitar incessantly traveled the Jewish world. His mix of storytelling, nostalgia, original melodies and personal charisma attracted a large following. Though his association with anti-Establishment forces during the 1960's "hippie" revolution earned him severe criticism in many Orthodox circles, his music nevertheless penetrated into almost all synagogues and Jewish gatherings. Many an alienated Jew was attracted by Carlebach to reexamine his relationship to Judaism, and a number of his original melodies became the accepted music for prayer and celebration in the Jewish world. Other musical performers and groups followed in his footsteps as Jewish music emerged in numerous genres — rock, classical, ballad and sacred. The Jewish music world began to produce its own popular heroes, usually frowned upon by the older generation but

---

38. An Orthodox ambulance service that conformed to all halachic rules and operated not only during the week but, more importantly, on Sabbath and holidays as well. Beginning in New York, the organization soon had independent branches in most major Jewish communities in the United States and Canada. It became famous for its immediate response time and for the compassionate care administered to the patient.

39. Organizations for visiting the sick. Among other services, these groups often provided Sabbath homes near the hospital for the patient's family; visited the hospitals regularly; and provided kosher meals, as well as material and psychological help, to the sick person and his or her family.

40. I will not enter into the scholarly debate as to what truly constitutes Jewish music. The tunes used in the synagogue prayers, the music at Jewish weddings, concerts and on recordings produced for the Jewish market are currently referred to as Jewish music. So be it.

embraced by the young, performing their music worldwide. This musical renaissance within Jewish life — particularly and perhaps unexpectedly from within Orthodoxy — was another confirmation of the vitality and creativity of traditional Jewish life in the modern era.

There was a changing of the guard in the leadership of long-standing Jewish organizations and institutions as well. Rabbi Dr. Samuel Belkin, the head of Yeshiva University, passed away and was succeeded by Rabbi Dr. Norman Lamm. Rabbi Lamm was a successful pulpit rabbi, a scholar of note and an articulate spokesman for Centrist (née Modern) Orthodoxy. Rabbi Lamm inherited a school with an enormous financial debt that threatened the very existence of this oldest of American yeshivos. His herculean efforts at fundraising, coupled with the restructuring of tens of millions of dollars in bank loans, steered Yeshiva University through the shoals of potential bankruptcy to a secure solvency.

Within the rabbinic faculty of Yeshiva University, the tendency towards a more rigorous interpretation of Orthodoxy began to prevail. There were also a number of Yeshiva University graduates who found their way into Lakewood and other such yeshivos. Most importantly, Yeshiva University itself established a *kollel* program of its own and strengthened the scholarship requirements for its rabbinic ordination. Rabbi Joseph B. Soloveitchik's public lectures drew immense audiences and were widely anticipated. His writings were also published and made a profound impact

Rabbi Joseph B. Soloveitchik meets with Israeli Prime Minister Menachem Begin at the Waldorf Astoria Hotel (NYC) in 1977. Note the cluster of photographers visible in the mirror behind the Rav.

in the world of Jewish scholarship and thought. A new type of committed and scholarly Jew was emerging in Modern Orthodoxy.[41] Very few students from Orthodox families or schools would henceforth be found transferring to non-Orthodox institutions of Jewish studies.

The graduates of the American yeshivos, both Centrist and right wing, could be found in every profession and enterprise in commercial American life. Orthodox scholars began to appear as professors in Judaic Studies programs, as well as other disciplines, on college campuses throughout the country.[42] The *kippah*-wearing, sometimes bearded, completely traditional — yet fully American — Jew was becoming an accepted part of American life. Even though the caricatured Orthodox Jew — quaint, nostalgic, but hopelessly out of touch with the modern world — was still portrayed widely in Hollywood movies and in much of the print media, the caricature was no longer even close to being accurate.

There was a new sense of confidence in Orthodox circles, as the dire predictions regarding the death of Orthodoxy of just a few decades before had been proven wrong. But though the statistics regarding the growth of observant Judasim seemed to confirm a renaissance, this optimism was tempered by the overwhelming majority of American Jews who remained non-Orthodox and who had lost interest in any kind of Jewish affiliation.

Reform and Conservative Movements Grapple with New Demands

WHEN DR. NELSON GLEUCK LEFT THE PRESIDENCY OF THE REFORM movement's Hebrew Union College, he was succeeded by Dr. Alfred Gottschalk. Even under Gleuck's tenure, certain more traditional forms of Jewish life had been introduced at the college, initiated by the students themselves. Kosher food became available, optional morning prayer services in Hebrew began and some students wore a *kippah*. Gleuck did not encourage any of these changes, but they occurred nevertheless.

In the early 1970's, the college began admitting women to its rabbinic program and female rabbis now served in Reform temples throughout the country. However, the major change in Reform came not from the faculty of Hebrew Union College, but rather from the aggressively adventurous executive head of the Union of American Hebrew Congregations, Alexander Schindler. In December 1978, Schindler called on Reform to "reach out" to intermarried couples and to bring the non-Jewish spouse into the Reform temple, even without any form of conversion to Judaism. He

---

41. In a conversation that I had in 1977 with Rabbi Joseph B. Soloveitchik at Yeshiva University, he told me that he had never before had such a high caliber of Talmudic students overall as he did then.
42. Rabbi Dr. Isadore Twersky, Rabbi Joseph Soloveitchik's son-in-law, was a leader in his field at Harvard University.

stated that it was Reform's duty to attempt to bring into its fold the non-Jewish spouses of interfaith marriages and to reach out to the "unchurched" non-Jew and welcome them into Reform. In short, Schindler advocated proselytism that would swell the ranks of Reform, albeit with people that neither the Orthodox nor Conservative movements recognized as Jewish. Schindler called these additions to the Reform movement "Jews by choice." By the 1990's, these "Jews by choice" made up a large segment of the membership of many Reform temples in America.

The Reform movement made determined efforts to establish itself in Israel. As the Hebrew Union College branch in Jerusalem grew, Reform spokesmen in Israel demanded recognition and governmental support. Reform decried the monopoly of the Orthodox Chief Rabbinate over religious matters in Israel. Though Reform made very little practical headway in Israel during these years, it constantly kept the political pot boiling. Reform in Israel was much more traditional in behavior and practice than its parent in America. Despite its more devout appearance, it met a hostile reception from the Orthodox establishment and also from the traditionally minded, if not fully observant, Israeli man or woman on the street.

The Reform problem remained, so to speak, its inability to solve the Talmudic riddle of how to break the barrel and yet not spill a drop of the wine therein. In an article by a leading Reform spokesman of the time, W. Gunther Plaut, this problem was succinctly addressed:

> *The weakness of Sabbath worship [in Reform temples] is only in part due to the weakness of worship feeling in our time. It is due also, and in greater measure than usually recognized, to the erosion of Shabbat Kodesh (the holy Sabbath). It is the Sabbath which keeps communal worship alive as much as worship keeps the Sabbath alive. The attenuation of Sabbath observance is due to the popular confusion of Reform Judaism with extreme permissiveness, which is in turn caused by our failure to formulate a Reform halachah. What is true in general is true for the Sabbath.[43]*

In 1972, Gerson Cohen succeeded Louis Finkelstein as head of the Jewish Theological Seminary of America. The Seminary, which was the leading school of the Conservative movement,[44] still retained a faculty of well-accepted, traditionally observant scholars. In addition to Professor Saul Lieberman in the Talmud department, the Seminary procured the

---

43. W. Gunther Plaut as quoted in *Reform Judaism – A Historical Perspective*, edited by Joseph L. Blau, New York, 1973, p.245.

44. The Seminary also maintained a branch in Los Angeles, California known as the University of Judaism, which eventually was empowered to ordain rabbis for the Conservative movement over the initial objections of the Seminary in New York. It operated a school in Israel, as described later in the text of this book.

services of Dr. David Weiss-Halivni, a young scholar who had studied in Orthodox yeshivos.

The issue of the role of women in the synagogue and the rabbinate plagued the Conservative movement throughout the 1970's. Women began to be called to the Torah in public prayer in many Conservative congregations. Though under pressure from Reform innovation and the demands of many of its own lay leaders, Gerson Cohen as chancellor of the Seminary nevertheless took a hard stance in 1973 when the issue of female Conservative rabbis was first raised:

"Let me make plain that I will resist admitting women [to the Seminary's rabbinical program] ... To institute a change with respect to the place of women in official religious capacities within a community, without careful reflection on the effects of such a change on the pattern of law, custom and social posture of the whole complex of its tradition, is to be swayed by the private ambitions of some or what is more likely the case, by current feminist fads, which in reality are part of a much wider movement of social revolt and upheaval."[45]

By 1979, Cohen reversed course and changed his position to support the admission of women to the Conservative rabbinate. However, he met intense opposition from the traditionalists on the faculty of the Seminary led by Lieberman and Weiss-Halivni. At the end of 1979, a motion to table any further discussion of the issue was approved by the Seminary's faculty.[46] But the issue of female rabbis in the Conservative movement would not go away; it was only a matter of time and attrition of the older faculty members before the Conservative movement would follow the lead of Reform on this matter.

Dr. Simon Greenberg, also a former student at an Orthodox yeshiva, developed the Seminary's Israel programs, Neve Schechter and Midreshet Jerusalem. Though the original classes in the 1970's numbered only 20 students, these institutions grew in size and scope and a permanent presence was was established in Jerusalem headquarters under the direction of Reuven Hammer. As with the introduction of Reform to Israel, the arrival of the Conservative movement also provoked an outcry from Orthodox circles. The Conservative movement found wider acceptance in Israel than did Reform, especially among American immigrant families who came from a Conservative background in the United States. These people were, by definition of their *aliyah* to Israel, idealistic and Jewishly committed. Conservative synagogues were founded in many Israeli cities and towns, and rabbis for these congregations came from Seminary graduates living in

---

45. *Tradition Revisited*, edited by Jack Wertheimer, New York, 1997, Volume 1, p.257.
46. The vote was 25 to 19.

Israel and a few rabbis previously serving in Modern Orthodox Israeli communities. Israeli Jews who joined the Conservative movement, renamed "Masorti" in Israel,[47] were on the whole more committed to the ideals and goals of the Conservative movement, and more religiously observant than their American counterparts. The Conservative movement unsuccessfully demanded governmental recognition for its rabbis and acceptance of Conservative marriages, divorces and conversions by the Israeli Chief Rabbinate and the Ministry of Interior.

In response to an aggressive campaign of the Reform and Masorti movements to attract High Holy Days worshippers in 1979, the Israeli Chief Rabbinate issued a ruling, publicized widely, declaring the unacceptability of Conservative and Reform as any form of Judaism, and stating that hearing the shofar sounded in a Conservative or Reform house of worship on Rosh Hashanah was tantamount to not hearing the shofar sounded at all. (This ruling had been propounded by Rabbi J. B. Soloveitchik in the United States years before.) The publicizing of this ruling brought a bitter response from Conservative and Reform leaders and laity, especially in the United States. Gerson Cohen bitterly responded, saying that, "Orthodoxy has not been the preserver of Judaism."

The Chief Rabbinate's ruling also had the perhaps unforeseen and undesired effect of uniting the Conservative and Reform movements politically in Israel, though in matters of doctrine, ritual and religious observance they remained widely separated. The campaign for "pluralism" — i.e. the acceptance of Reform and Conservative as expressions of Judaism equal to Orthodoxy — became a political football in Israel (as did almost any issue of lasting importance) and would only intensify in vitriol and divisiveness during the coming decades.

The 1970's was a decade of momentous changes in Jewish society. The myth of Israeli military invincibility was shattered, as was the long rule of the Labor Party in Israel. These changes would give rise to different approaches to settling the Israeli-Arab struggle in coming years. American Jewry assimilated and diminished in large numbers, at a rate never before experienced in the Diaspora history of the Jews, while at the same time Orthodox learning, observance and numbers increased at an unprecedented pace. Unforeseen innovations were introduced in all sectors of Jewish life, and old problems and divisions continued to fester in new environments. Change is always unsettling: For Jews worldwide, the decade ended on an uncertain and troubling note.

---

47. The Conservative movement in Israel adopted the name "Masorti." The translation of the word Conservative in Hebrew — *Shamrani* — would not resonate at all with the general Israeli public. The term *shamrani* in Hebrew usually implies right wing conservatism, as opposed to a liberal, progressive movement: The name *Masorti*, on the other hand, signifies tradition and continuity in Hebrew.

Chapter Ten

New Realities

1981-1990

THE DECADE OF THE 1980'S GAVE RISE TO NEW LEADERS AND NEW policies in much of the world. But Israel and the Jewish people still faced lingering problems, many of them well over a century old. Nevertheless, the changes in leadership and policies in the world had an impact on Israel as well, both directly and indirectly. England's prime minister was now Margaret Thatcher, the leader of the Conservative Party. A very strong and principled person, she preached old values of morality, thrift, industry, loyalty and patriotism. Early on in her tenure, she became known as the "Iron Lady." She faced down the trade unions in England, especially the miners' and printers' unions, whose corrupt power grabs had crippled the British economy for decades. She successfully went to war with Argentina to restore the Falkland Islands to British rule after the Argentineans unilaterally invaded and annexed them. She stood strong against Russian bluff and thunder, unlike other Western European leaders, in supporting the deployment of United States missiles on European soil. She changed the tone of public discourse and political governing not only in Great Britain, but in much of the Western world as well. She strengthened the spine of the democratic group of nations at a time when it was most sorely needed. An excellent politician and campaigner, she performed the miracle in

British politics of winning three consecutive elections, ruling the United Kingdom for over a decade.

One of her most respected confidants was Rabbi Immanuel Jakobovits, the Chief Rabbi of Great Britain. She admired Rabbi Jakobovits' outspoken defense of faith and tradition, of public and private morality and his spiritual vision of a better society for all. She honored Rabbi Jakobovits, and through him all of Anglo-Jewry, by appointing him as a member of the House of Lords — a most singular and unprecedented honor for a devout, Orthodox Jew and rabbi.

In the 1980 election for President of the United States, Ronald Reagan, the former governor of California, unseated the incumbent Jimmy Carter. Carter's most notable foreign policy achievement in office was the brokering of the Camp David peace accords between Israel and Egypt. In contrast to Carter's generally poor political skills, Ronald Reagan was known as the "great communicator." He was able to clearly articulate a vision of a strong and self-sufficient America. A conservative politically and economically, he spoke against the ills of big government, too powerful labor unions and overregulation of the economy and industries.[1]

President Reagan and staff in the cabinet room in 1981. Left to right: Secretary of State Alexander Haig, National Security Advisor Richard Allen, President Reagan, Deputy Secretary of State William Clark, Chief of Staff James Baker III and Secretary of Defense Casper Weinberger

1. As a former Hollywood actor he was a master debater as well. He simply outclassed Carter — not in substance, but in style — in the presidential election debates of the 1980 campaign. Reagan had honed his political skills as president of the Screen Actors Guild and as governor of California.

In the main, American Jewry continued its usual tradition of supporting the Democratic candidate for President, but Reagan was successful in attracting a larger Jewish vote, certainly among Orthodox Jews, than did previous Republican candidates for the office. He and General Alexander M. Haig, his first secretary of state, were more sympathetic to Israel than their predecessors (perhaps due to the Soviet Union's support of the Arabs against Israel), though Reagan and Prime Minister Begin did not get along well personally. Early on, Haig warned Israel that it was losing the battle for world public opinion, saying that, "the sympathy that the world once had for Israel is now steadily being transferred to the Palestinians."

At the beginning of Reagan's term, the American government proposed selling a number of AWACS early warning radar planes to Saudi Arabia. Israel protested bitterly, claiming that this would change the balance of military power in the region and put Israel in jeopardy. Israel maintained that in the event of any military conflict between the Arabs and Israel, even if the Saudis were not directly involved, the planes would be used to support the Arab cause. When Israel made no headway in its complaints to the administration itself, Begin leapfrogged Reagan by personally appearing in Congress to urge cancellation of the proposed sale. Infuriated by Begin's direct appeal to Congress, Reagan did everything in his power to have the sale approved. The sale went through, and Begin was now in the awkward position of having publicly bucked the American president and lost. Support for Israel in Congress and the allocation of American military and economic aid to Israel also suffered because of the bruising public dispute. This lesson was not lost on subsequent Israeli prime ministers. For the balance of the century, no Israeli prime minister publicly argued with a sitting U.S. president.

The Soviet Union was also undergoing change. As before, its internal problems were masked behind the secretive suppression of truth by the aging communist leadership. Yet rumblings of discontent were becoming more pronounced in the satellite Warsaw Pact nations, especially in Poland. Visits to Poland by Pope John Paul II, himself a Pole, occasioned enormous public gatherings that sparked deep emotions. Intentionally or not, the papal visits destabilized the communist government of the country and created a decade of strife. Lech Walensa, a shipyard electrician from Gdansk, created the Solidarity movement, which eventually succeeded in toppling the communist government in Poland. Though the Soviet leader Leonid Brezhnev took a very hard public line against all dissent, the USSR was becoming increasingly impotent in confronting such uprisings. The Jewish refuseniks and "Prisoners of Zion," demanding their right of emigration from the Soviet Union, were yet another annoyance. Anatoly (Natan) Sharansky was transformed into an international Jewish hero when he was tried, convicted and sentenced to serve many years at hard labor by a Soviet court for his attempt to immigrate to Israel. His speech to the court, declaring the Jewish longing for the Land of Israel and Jerusalem, was distributed by the refusenik underground and publicized worldwide, inspiring new efforts on behalf of the cause of Soviet Jewry.

Russian economic resources were strained to the limit trying to counter President Reagan's bluntly threatening deployment of missiles in Western Europe and by a conspicuously expensive modernization and expansion of American military capability. Russia wavered between the choices presented by Reagan: a serious mutual disarmament or an arms race. As new American weapons systems continued to develop, despite Western European and American congressional criticism, the Soviet economy began to collapse under the burden of the arms race. Crippled by the central planning and social engineering dogmas of Lenin and Stalin, the Soviet economy was increasingly unable to provide sufficient products for its own civilian population.

When Brezhnev died in 1982, he was succeeded by Yuri Andropov, who had headed the Soviet KGB Secret Police for fifteen years. Andropov died a few months later and was succeeded by an old party hack, Konstantin Chernenko. In 1985, Chernenko died and Mikhael Gorbachev became the new chairman of the Communist Party. The final collapse of the Soviet Union was not far off.

Embarking on an adventure that would hasten its demise a little more than a decade later, the Soviet Union supported a revolution in Afghanistan that brought a Marxist government to power. The new regime had great social-engineering plans for that backward country. "But the experience of the twentieth century shows emphatically that Utopianism is never far from gangsterism."[2] The Moslem population of the country was not prepared for Marxism and a fundamentalist Moslem militia, backed by the new regime in neighboring Iran, mounted a guerilla war against the Marxist dictator. The Soviet Union sent in military "advisors" to help prop up the regime, eventually supplying over 120,000 troops in a futile effort to save its Marxist puppet. The United States clandestinely helped the Moslem rebels. Both sides committed terrible atrocities. By the end of the decade, the Soviet Union withdrew its troops and the Afghans were left under the rule of a brutal and severe Moslem terrorist dictatorship. Afghanistan became a terrorist training base and sanctuary throughout the balance of the century. It specialized in anti-Israel

2. I owe this most felicitous phrase and devastatingly accurate assessment to Paul Johnson, *Modern Times*, 1991 edition, p.718.

and anti-United States acts of terrorism, as well as promoting a flourishing drug trade. The United States has come to rue its role in helping an enemy come to power.

Another major change in the stability of the world's powers occurred when the Shah of Iran was deposed in 1979 and an Islamic Shiite fundamentalist group of clerics, led by Ayatollah Ruhollah Khomeini, took power in Teheran. The Shah's regime had been marked by endemic corruption and brutal repression in its final years of power. Khomeini, in exile in France, rallied the masses in Teheran against the Shah. Sick with the cancer that would kill him, the Shah lost his will to fight them, and even his American allies could no longer help him sustain his hold. He fled the country and Khomeini returned in triumph to rule.

Ayatollah Khomeini

Khomeini instituted an even more brutal regime than his predecessor's. Shiite Islamic laws were enforced literally and all visible signs of Western culture were eliminated from the country. Thousands of former supporters of the Shah were summarily tried by religious courts and executed. All other religions were persecuted. Bahai followers suffered particularly destructive acts. Synagogues and churches were destroyed. Many Iranian Jews escaped through various underground channels and settled in Israel and the West. However, a substantial number of Jews – approximately 35,000 — remained under Khomeini's iron rule. The American Embassy in Teheran was sacked and its inhabitants held hostage for about a year, being released only on the day that Jimmy Carter left office. America was dubbed "the Great Satan" by Khomeini and he also pledged to eliminate the "Zionist Entity" from the Middle East.

The Shiite clerics who now ruled Iran purged the Iranian army of its officer ranks, particularly those who were deemed to have been loyal to the Shah. This naturally weakened Iran's fighting capabilities, albeit only temporarily. Next door to Iran was Iraq, ruled by a megalomaniacal dictator and reckless adventurer, Saddam Hussein. Iraq had long harbored a desire to "correct" its border situation with Iran, the subject of a decades-long running feud between the two countries. Iraq particularly coveted control over the Shat-al-Arab waterway entrance to the Persian Gulf and the rich oil fields nearby. Sensing Iran's temporary weakness, Saddam attacked Iran in 1980 to gain his objectives. He hoped for a quick victory, but instead the Iraq-Iran war deteriorated into a horrendous eight-year-long war of attrition.[3] In spite of Saddam's use of chemical weapons and long range Scud missile attacks against Teheran, the war ended with no material gain whatsoever for Iraq.

---

3. Over one million soldiers died in this most futile and unnecessary of wars. Millions more were maimed and wounded. Children from eight to twelve years old fought in both armies as "martyrs" for the cause of Islam.

In the Shadow of Camp David

At the onset of the decade, Israel was beginning to exhibit signs of postpartum depression. The baby – the Egyptian-Israeli peace accord — was born, but the euphoria that it had engendered at the time of its signing had rapidly dissipated. The country was suffering through an economic recession in 1980 and 1981; none of its internal divisions had healed; its politics were as vicious and contentious as ever and the movement towards peace with the Arabs had slowed. Emigration from Russia slowed as many of the Russian Jews waiting in Western European transit camps opted to settle in the West rather than continue their journey to Israel. The limited immigration to Israel in the early 1980's included mainly Ethiopians and young Orthodox Jews from America, most of the latter fired by the dream of Gush Emunim. Begin's coalition government was weakened by the resignations from his cabinet of the more dovish Moshe Dayan and Ezer Weizman.

Egyptian-Israeli negotiations regarding the "autonomy" arrangement for the Palestinians, envisioned in the Camp David peace treaty between the two countries, continued in a desultory fashion throughout 1980 and most of 1981. The Egyptians, to the surprise of the Israelis, showed no flexibility in their demands on behalf of the Palestinians. They insisted on maximum terms for the Arab cause — return of the Arab refugees to Israel, control over Jerusalem, full Israeli withdrawal to the 1967 borders and the recognition of a Palestinian state. Menachem Begin was not prepared to grant any one of these demands, let alone all of them. Begin defined Palestinian "autonomy" in personal, individual and local terms, but not in national terms. As far as Begin was concerned, the Palestinians would be free to live their own lives as they wished, without Israeli interference other than the usual requirements of government, but there would be no sovereign Palestinian entity allowed in the West Bank. Begin also insisted that the Israelis would have the right to continue building new settlements on land purchased from the Arabs or on vacant property throughout the West Bank. As these two widely divergent views hardened during the drawn out negotiations, Sadat despaired of arriving at an agreement regarding Palestinian "autonomy." The Israeli-Egyptian peace treaty now turned into a very chilly relationship between the two countries and the optimistic hopes for lasting friendship and cooperation for mutual benefit spawned by Camp David rapidly evaporated.

Despite this disappointing outcome, Begin fulfilled the terms of the Camp David treaty to the letter, even using force to remove some of the diehard settlers of Yamit in the Sinai Desert from their homes in 1982. But the hostility of the Egyptian media towards Israel and the absence of any meaningful Egyptian tourist or commercial cooperation from Egypt worried him. Both Begin and Sadat had unrealistic hopes and expectations of one another. What Begin had considered a "fig leaf" letter attached by Sadat to the Camp David accords — requiring full Palestinian statehood and all West Bank territory — Sadat considered sacrosanct. And to Begin's demands — total peace and the full gamut of normal friendly relations between two neighboring countries – Sadat offered only an absence of war, a glorified cease-fire. In order to bridge this gaping misunderstanding, President Carter planned to host a second Camp David conference after the November 1980 elections. After Carter's defeat at the polls, however, this meeting never took place. Begin and Sadat would continue to meet on their own throughout 1980 and 1981, but no substantial progress on any Arab-Israeli issues was achieved.

Begin continued to pursue a vigorous policy of expanding Jewish settlement throughout the West Bank and Gaza. He was aided by Minister of National Infrastructure Ariel Sharon and by the growing numbers and influence of Gush Emunim. The National Religious Party — Mafdal — became completely identified with the settlers and abandoned its traditional role of religious moderation and cooperation with the Labor Party. The Peace Now camp decried this settlement policy, claiming that it would cause irreparable harm to Israel in the future. Between these two poles of opinion, most Israelis were of two minds on the subject. There was an emotional, almost religious tug towards helping Jews settle the entire Biblical Land of Israel. Nevertheless, there was also a nagging realization that the growing number of West Bank settlements could pose an obstacle to peace with the Arabs. Thus there arose a contest for the minds and hearts of the general Israeli public regarding the settlements and the settlers — a contest in which the peace groups would prove more adept than the settlers at shaping public opinion over the next two decades. Begin proved to be a true believer in his settlement policy and implemented it against domestic and foreign opposition.

In the spring of 1981, American intelligence photographs revealed that Saddam Hussein was building an atomic reactor at a site not far from Baghdad and that it was rapidly nearing completion. At the time, France was supplying Iraq with technical know-how and fissionable material, just as it had for Israel's atomic program decades earlier. Francois Mitterand became president of France in 1981 and, professing his personal sympathy towards Israel, promised to change France's anti-Israel diplomatic and economic stance instituted by DeGaulle at the end of the 1960's and continued by his successors throughout the 1970's. He promised to regulate France's shipments of uranium rods to Iraq so that there would never be sufficient fissionable material present at one time to use in the construction of a bomb.

But Israel was alarmed by Saddam's threat. Iraq had never signed even a cease-fire agreement with Israel and it had participated with troops and weapons on the Arab side in the 1948 and 1973 wars. The one thing that Iraq and Iran agreed on, even in the midst of their murderous war against each other, was their common goal of destroying the Jewish state. Israel had attempted to abort Iraq's atomic project through clandestine operations within France itself.[4]

Begin decided to take a bold gamble. On June 7, 1981, in a remarkable exhibition of pinpoint bombing, Israeli fighter-bombers destroyed the atomic reactor site in Iraq. In so doing, Israeli planes had to violate the airspace of Saudi Arabia and Jordan in order to reach their target. A howl of hypocritical diplomatic protest enveloped the world. President Ronald Reagan at first approved of the bombing; but the State Department soon changed his mind and America led the charge at the UN, where a resolution was passed condemning Israel for an "aggressive act against a fellow member of the United Nations." As a sign of its displeasure, America postponed the delivery of planes and other military goods to Israel, while the Arab nations, many of which were secretly delighted with Saddam's comeuppance, orchestrated a shrill, hostile chorus against Israel. Anwar Sadat declared himself to be heartsick at the Israeli air raid. Begin stood by his decision; and a decade later, during the Gulf War, it was proven to have been a wise and fortuitous one.

President Ronald Reagan was joined by former Presidents Gerald R. Ford, Jimmy Carter and Richard M. Nixon at the funeral of Anwar Sadat

4. The assassination of the leading atomic scientist working for Iraq and the destruction of uranium rods scheduled to be shipped to Iraq were some of the actions taken by the Mossad to prevent Iraqi-French progress on the atomic project.

While reviewing a military parade on October 6, 1981, Egyptian President Anwar Sadat was assassinated. The Islamic fundamentalists responsible for his murder said that he was killed because he had dared to make peace with Israel. Sadat was succeeded by Hosni Mubarak, Egypt's vice-president. Mubarak, who had none of the personal charm of Sadat, nevertheless kept the lid on Egypt during the balance of the century. A ruthless dictator and autocrat, Mubarak filled Egypt's prisons with his political opponents.

The future of Egyptian-Israeli relations was altered completely. Mubarak's relations with Israel were never warm and oftentimes were absolutely frigid. He allowed the Egyptian media to engage in a continuous anti-Israel and anti-Jewish publicity campaign that poisoned any attempts for regional cooperation between Israel and Egypt. He withdrew his ambassador to Israel a number of times over the ensuing decades as a protest against Israeli policies and actions that he did not favor.

Hosni Mubarak

Chareidim and Sephardim Take On Political Clout

O N JUNE 30, 1981, THE ELECTION RESULTS FOR THE TENTH KNESSET maintained Menachem Begin in power. His Likud party won 48 seats, an increase of five over the previous election. The Labor party regained the fifteen seats it had lost in the last election to the now defunct Dash party and had 47 seats in the Knesset. The religious parties won fourteen seats, and it was with their support that Begin formed his new, narrow-majority government. Begin met many of the long-standing demands of the religious parties: Greater funding was given to religious schools, El Al Israel Airlines stopped flying on Shabbos and the status quo regarding the recognition of only Orthodox conversions to Judaism was continued. The religious parties had now confirmed their shift from continuing accommodation with the Labor party to full alliance with the Likud party. The continuing gung-ho policies of Mafdal regarding settlements on the West Bank alienated some of its more moderate traditional constituency and led to a steady decline in the number of seats the party would gain in the ensuing elections.

There was also a growing trend among former Mafdal voters to identify themselves with a more rigorous and strict observance of Orthodox stricture and attitudes. The 1980's saw the birth of the term "Chareidi" in the Jewish world, a term that Mafdal invented in order to separate itself from the non-Zionist, Chasidic and yeshivah segments of Orthodoxy. It was later adopted by "Chareidim" themselves, to describe their society as one that is literally "in awe" of God and scrupulous in avoiding modern influences and behavior. (It was the Israeli version of the unfortunate term "ultra-Orthodox" used in the English-speaking world.)

*Archeologists at work
in the Old City
of Jerusalem*

Over the years, however, there was a growing attraction among the children of Mafdal towards that Chareidi world.

In 1981, a major dispute arose between the Chareidi community and the Israeli archeological commission, then planning excavations at the Southern Wall area of the Temple Mount. The archeological project involved digging the site of a cemetery, which may have been Jewish. (In general, the archeologists in Israel showed little sensitivity to the halachic — and deeply emotional — issues of disturbing ancient Jewish gravesites.) Demonstrations, arrests, violent clashes with the police and disagreements between the rabbis themselves over the propriety of the dig marked the progress of this archeological site. The confrontations continued for almost four years, but the dig was completed, revealing much: a southern staircase to the Temple; many of the stones — some still in place, some fallen, with many yet in excellent condition — of the retaining walls of the Temple; ritual baths and store stalls of the Second Temple period; and the original pavement of the streets that surrounded the Temple. The site eventually became a very popular, accepted tourist and educational area in Jerusalem, viewed by Chareidim and by religious and secular visitors alike. But the scars of the battle over its excavation remained, increasing the distrust between the Chareidim and other segments of Israeli society.

A new leader of the "Lithuanian yeshivah" element[5] of the Chareidi world emerged by the beginning of the 1980's. Rabbi Eliezer Menachem Mann Shach was the *rosh yeshivah* of the famed Ponovezh Yeshivah in Bnei Brak. A person of strongly-held opinions, decisiveness, courage and straight talk, he objected to the makeup of the political structure of the Chareidi community at that time. Agudath Israel had been the main Chareidi political party since the founding of the state. Agudath Israel was comprised of three main factions: the original Jerusalem-based founding

5. This group was Ashkenazic and non-Chasidic. Its power and numbers were concentrated in the students, graduates and ongoing *kollel* members of the major yeshivos in Israel. Though it was small in number compared to the other factions of Agudath Israel, it was a group that commanded great prestige due to the outstanding Torah scholarship of its leaders and adherents.

families of the party, dating back to the beginning of the century; the large, but loosely-connected, Chasidic community headed by the dynasties of Gur, Vizhnitz, Belz and others; and the Lithuanian yeshivah faction, led by the heads of the Lithuanian yeshivos in Israel. As the movement in Israel was dominated by its Chasidic element, the yeshivah grouping felt itself shunted aside in practical and ideological terms. Rabbi Shach would move to correct that situation by forming new political parties that would strengthen the political power of the Chareidim, though it also intensified internal divisions between the different groupings of that community. He formed a political party, called Shas, that represented the Sephardic community, long restive under the discrimination and condescension of the politically dominant Ashkenazic establishment. This party had Ashkenazic backing and leadership at its outset, but it soon stood on its own, with its own Sephardic rabbinic and political leadership, as Rabbi Shach himself sent it off on its own way.[6] It would steadily gain strength and political clout during the next decades of its existence. Rabbi Ovadiah Yosef, a former Sephardic Chief Rabbi of Israel and a recognized scholar and authority in the world of Torah, became its spiritual mentor and religious leader. Rabbi Yosef would prove himself no stranger to controversy, but his ability to rally the Sephardic community in Israel to the Shas banner gave the party unexpected success.

Rabbi Shach also formed another political party, separate from Agudath Israel, to represent the interests and policies of the Lithuanian yeshivah world. This party was named Degel HaTorah. Although Degel HaTorah and Agudath Israel ran as one party under the banner of United Torah Judaism in national elections for the Knesset, Degel HaTorah saw itself as independent of the directions and policies of Agudath Israel.[7] Rabbi Shach's iron will and decisiveness made Degel HaTorah a force far greater in influence than its mere numbers would perhaps warrant. Degel also began publishing a newspaper, *Yated Neeman*, in Israel and in the United States, differing from the traditional Agudah newspaper, *Hamodia*, in editorial content and emphasis.

Rabbi Shach openly criticized the secularism of the ruling elite of the Israeli state, directing special criticism at the leftist kibbutzim for their

Rabbi Shach

---

6. It organized its own separate Sephardic "Council of Torah Sages" to determine religious and political policy for the party.

7. In the United States, Agudath Israel did not splinter and divide, as did its Israeli counterpart. Its rabbinic leadership had the benefit of the gifted organizational leadership of Rabbi Moshe Sherer. Rabbi Sherer's talents and astuteness, and the natural tendency of Americans to be more inclusive than exclusive, were the governing factors in maintaining Chareidi unity in the United States. Of course, the cause of unity was greatly helped in the American Agudah by the absence of the problems present in Israel: political patronage, government power and competing school systems fighting for government allocations.

anti-religious behavior and attitudes. Though he sparked controversy with his pronouncements, he never moderated his stance. Opposed to Jewish settlement in the West Bank, he was a staunch supporter of peace efforts and working towards an accommodation with the Arabs. He cautioned his followers not to be caught up in the idealistic, near-messianic fervor of Gush Emunim and objected to any Chareidi settlements outside of the pre-1967 borders of Israel. (The original plans for Kiryat Sefer, for instance, were within the Green Line.)

He was especially critical of the nascent messianism that marked Chabad/Lubavitch in the 1980's. He objected to the call for "forcing" the Messiah's appearance, an idea advocated by Rabbi Menachem Mendel Schneerson, the *Lubavitcher Rebbe*. And when certain elements in Chabad actually identified Rabbi Schneerson as the possible Messiah, Rabbi Shach advocated a complete boycott of Chabad, its institutions and projects by his constituents. His outspokenness was disturbing to many, but he saw himself as bearing a great responsibility for dealing with ideas and movements that, in his opinion, could eventually prove damaging to the cause of Torah.[8] He never shirked from discharging his duty as he saw that duty to be.

Israel Wades into the Quicksand of Lebanon

THE EGYPTIAN-ISRAELI PEACE AGREEMENT HAD UNINTENDED SIDE effects. Lebanon, which had been under French mandate until the end of World War II, flourished as a financial and tourist center, with its capital of Beirut described as "the Paris of the Middle East." It was a country of many different religious communities — Maronite Christians, Sunni and Shiite Moslems, Druze and Jews. Under a very complicated and fragile system of shared government powers, the country prospered. However, after the 1948 Israeli War of Independence in which Lebanon participated, over 100,000 Arab refugees entered the country, while almost all of the Lebanese Jews left. The Arab refugees were never assimilated into the general population. Instead, were intentionally kept in refugee camps near Beirut. After the 1967 Six Day War, an added number of Arab refugees made their way into the squalor of those refugee camps. In 1970, after Black September, King Hussein expelled the Palestine Liberation Organization from Jordan and they now made their headquarters in Lebanon. From its bases in southern Lebanon, the PLO

---

8. In a conversation that he had with an American rabbi in the 1980's, to which I was privy, Rav Shach stated: "The Americans think that I am too controversial and divisive. But in a time when no one else is willing to speak up on behalf of our true tradition, I feel myself impelled to do so."

continued its murderous raids into Israel. It also developed a political infrastructure in Lebanon that threatened the stability of the country. In a power grab that was to alter the delicate balance of groups within the Lebanese government, the Shiite Moslems began an armed struggle for supremacy. The PLO supported the Shiites. Each of the groups, Christian, Sunni and Shiite Moslems and Druze — had its own private militia and used it liberally. The Lebanese civil war raged for almost two decades. Tens of thousands were killed, Beirut was destroyed and the country plunged into complete anarchy.

On June 3, 1982, the Israeli ambassador to England, Shlomo Argov, was shot and paralyzed permanently by a Palestinian gunman. The PLO also began intensified shelling on Israeli cities, settlements and kibbutzim in the Galilee from southern Lebanon, which was now under its complete control. The Israeli military reacted quickly. On June 6, 1982, the Israeli army crossed the Lebanese frontier with the publicly stated aim of driving the PLO out of southern Lebanon. Minister of Defense Ariel Sharon assured the Israeli Cabinet that this incursion into Lebanon was only a limited military action that would end, in all probability, in three to four days. Begin dubbed the war "The War for the Peace of Galilee." His opponents had harsher names for it. Sharon pursued the war all of the way into Beirut. The war lasted for weeks, not days. Israel fought Syrian troops and planes in the Beka Valley and near Beirut. The Phalangist Christian militia fought against the PLO as well. Israel intended to install Bashir Jemayel, the Phalange leader, as the new president of Lebanon and to conclude a peace treaty

Israeli paratrooper with a new friend in Beirut

with him that would settle the Lebanese border and drive the PLO out of Lebanon, just as it had been driven out of Jordan in the previous decade. On June 11, a UN cease-fire came into effect, but it did not hold. Beirut was placed under siege by the Israeli army and was cut off from all supplies, including water. The city came under constant Israeli bombardment, especially the PLO strongholds in the refugee camps around the area. The American government negotiated a deal by which the PLO would leave Beirut for its new headquarters in Tunisia. An international force, including American Marines, was to safeguard the PLO's departure by sea for Tunis. On August 30, 12,000 PLO members, led by Yassir Arafat himself, departed from Beirut.[9]

A brief two weeks later, on September 14, Bashir Jemayel, the Christian president-elect of Lebanon, was assassinated by the PLO. Assuming responsibility for maintaining law and order in Beirut, the Israeli army moved into West Beirut to prevent the Phalangists from wreaking revenge on the Palestinians residing in the Sabra and Chatilla refugee camps in that area. However, the Israelis allowed Phalangist militiamen to enter the camp in order to arrest the PLO operatives who remained there. In a monumental blunder, Israel sealed off the camps from the outside world and allowed the Phalangists entry to the camps without any Israeli army supervision. In a fury of revenge over the assassination of their leader, the Lebanese Christian fighters indiscriminately massacred more than 2,300 men, women and children. Israel and the world were shocked. World opinion turned forcefully against Israel for permitting the atrocity.[10] The whole Lebanon War operation now came tumbling down on the Israeli government's head.

From the beginning of the Lebanon War, there had been strong opposition voiced within Israel against its pursuit and purpose. When the costs of the war were revealed,[11] public outcry against the continued Israeli occupation in Lebanon increased. Peace Now organized a demonstration in Tel Aviv that drew a huge attendance: It demanded Israeli withdrawal from Lebanon and the appointment of a commission to study the entire war, making punitive recommendations, if necessary. Begin had no choice but to appoint such a commission of inquiry, putting Supreme Court Justice Yitzchak Kahan at its head.

The report of the Kahan Commission would rock Israel and eventually bring down the Begin government. On February 7, 1983, the report was made public. It placed blame, albeit indirectly, on Chief of Staff General Rafael Eitan, Director of Israel Military Intelligence Yehoshua Saguy and Minister of Defense Ariel Sharon for the occurrence of the Sabra and Chatilla massacres. Sharon was chastised "for disregarding the danger of acts of revenge and bloodshed by the Phalange against the population in

---

9. An Israeli sniper had Arafat in his sights as he left his bunker to depart Beirut. But fearing the repercussions of this assassination, the Israeli government had ordered its troops not to kill him, even if there were an easy opportunity to do so.

10. Begin's comment that "Christians kill Moslems and the Jews are blamed," was quite accurate, but not at all diplomatically helpful at the time.

11. Israeli casualties eventually amounted to over 600 dead and close to 4,000 wounded. The PLO sustained losses of 6,000 dead with many more wounded, and the Syrians lost 600 troops. Hundreds of Lebanese civilians and militiamen from all factions also were killed in the fighting. Three Israeli soldiers were reported missing in action and as of this date of writing, their fate has never been discovered, despite an intensive campaign by their families to gain closure on this tragedy.

the refugee camps ... for not taking this danger into consideration when he decided to let the Phalange into the camps ... for not taking appropriate measures to prevent or limit this danger." Eitan and Saguy left their posts in the wake of the Commission's findings. Sharon, deemed unfit to be minister of defense due to his "indirect responsibility" cited in the report, was removed from his position, though he remained in the Cabinet as minister without portfolio.[12] Prime Minister Begin was flooded by letters of protest from the general public and from bereaved parents who had lost their sons in the Lebanon War; and many of these letters were publicized in the press. Begin himself was criticized by the Kahan Commission for "unjustified indifference" regarding the actions of the Phalangists.

Israeli public opinion was split as never before in its history.[13] A terrible example of this polarization of Israeli society occurred when a hand grenade was thrown by a Jew into a crowd of Peace Now protesters outside Begin's Jerusalem office. A Jew was killed, and suddenly the frightening specter of civil violence — Jew upon Jew — was raised. Begin attempted to calm the atmosphere, but he himself was a shaken, almost shattered person. He searched for a way to extricate Israel from Lebanon honorably and quickly. The situation in Lebanon had deteriorated rapidly, with Syria sending in tens of thousands of troops, virtually annexing the country. Neither Israel nor Syria wanted a war with each other: An uneasy *status quo* of shared occupation of Lebanon continued.

President Reagan's new secretary of state was George W. Schultz. As former head of the prosperous Bechtel Corporation, he had wide acquaintance in the Arab world where this corporation had built many major projects. Because of this previous involvement, Schultz's appointment was greeted very warily by the American Jewish community and by Israel. However, Schultz would prove himself to be pragmatic, fair and restrained regarding Israel and its Arab neighbors. In May 1983, he succeeded in negotiating a settlement between Lebanon, represented by its new President Amin Jemayel, Bashir's brother, and Israel. All foreign armies were to be withdrawn; Lebanon would not be used as a staging area for attacks against Israel; monetary

---

12. In a related development, Sharon was accused in *Time* magazine of having actually encouraged the Phalangists to kill the Palestinian Moslems in the refugee camps. Sharon sued the magazine for libel and won the case, though he received no monetary compensation for his verdict since the jury felt that he had not proven *Time* guilty of malice, as required by American libel law, in printing the false accusation. His victory in court was Sharon's first step on his long road of public rehabilitation and return to political influence and power after the Lebanon War debacle.

13. Rabbi Immanuel Jakobovits was particularly vociferous in his criticism of the Lebanon War and Israeli policy in its aftermath. See his *"If Only My People...,"* 1984, pp.112-117. His comments were disseminated by the "peace camp" in Israel to further its agenda.

A casket exchange ceremony of fallen and missing IDF soldiers from the Yom Kippur and the Lebanon Wars, on the Syrian border of the Golan Heights

compensation would flow to Lebanon to rebuild the shattered country and a "state of non-belligerence" would now exist between the two countries. This excellent diplomatic achievement by Schultz proved useless: President Assad of Syria refused to agree to it and, in fact, intensified Syrian troop occupation of Lebanon. Assad's dream of "Greater Syria," which included Lebanon in its parameters, governed all of his behavior towards his Arab neighbor. He would ignore all UN and U.S. orders, resolutions and inducements to leave the country. At the end of the century, Lebanon still remained a puppet of Syria, forced to house thousands of Syrian occupation troops within its borders.

Israel began to withdraw from northern Lebanon in September 1983, establishing a Lebanese militia of Maronite Christians under Major Saad Hadad to help it police the areas of southern Lebanon where the PLO had previously encamped. This surrogate Israeli army eventually developed into the Southern Lebanese Army and was an Israeli ally until it was unceremoniously abandoned in the final Israeli evacuation of Lebanon in July 2000. In March 1984, under intense Syrian pressure, Amin Jemayel canceled the agreement with Israel that he had signed ten months earlier. The PLO slowly infiltrated back into Lebanon and a new, Iranian-supported terrorist organization, Hezbollah, organized itself in the Shiite villages in Lebanon. Though the war in Lebanon had given Israel certain short-range gains and freed the Galilee from regular daily shelling by the PLO, its overall consequences for Israel were far from positive. Israel lost stature and sympathy, its society was riven with hostile dispute, Syria became the dominant force in Lebanon and the PLO was not destroyed. On balance, the Lebanon War was a failure, and it proved to be a watershed in Israeli political life as well. Even though Likud would provide leadership for later Israeli governments in the 1980's and 1990's, its actions would always be subject to bitter suspicion and venomous criticism by its political opponents. The ghost of the Lebanon War would haunt Likud for the rest of the century.

I N JULY 1983, CRUSHED BY THE DEATH OF HIS BELOVED WIFE AND THE burden of the fallout from the Lebanon War, Menachem Begin resigned from his office as prime minister and from leadership of Likud. He went into a reclusive retirement, a tragic end for one of the most dynamic and courageous Jewish leaders of the century. He lived to see some of his dreams realized, while others were utterly destroyed.

Begin's place was taken by Yitzchak Shamir, a tough veteran of Lechi and a hard-line opponent of concessions or accommodation with the PLO. Shamir had none of Begin's charm or charisma, but he was a person of organizational talent, experience and tenacity. He had served as Begin's foreign minister after Dayan's resignation and was successful in his assigned tasks. As the new prime minister, he faced two major, almost monumental, problems. The first was how to withdraw the Israeli army from Lebanon. The second problem concerned an economic crisis caused by the collapse of share prices in Israel's leading banks.

Shamir had little new to say about Lebanon. (It would not be until July 2000 that the last Israeli soldier would leave the soil of Lebanon, and even then the Lebanese problem would not yet be completely resolved.) The economic crisis regarding Israel's bank share prices became his top priority. The inflation rate in Israel had climbed out of control during 1983 and it approached 400% annually. The war in Lebanon, the building of settlements and the granting of subsidies and grants to large sections of the Israeli population had bankrupted the treasury. The only solution was to print more money, and Israeli currency became valueless. People withdrew their money from the Israeli stock market, savings plans and pension funds, attempting to buy hard goods and/or real estate as a defense against the raging, ruinous inflation. The greatest run in the market was in Israeli bank shares. These shares, which were dollar-linked, had been run up by reckless speculation and the banks' own manipulation of their value to an unsustainable and unrealistic share price.

In a January 19, 2001 article in the newspaper *Haaretz*, a leading Israeli journalist, Amnon Dankner, compared the Oslo "peace process" to the bank share price debacle of 1983:

> *The phenomenon [of the elite's denial of reality] reminds us more than anything of the last time that the elite in politics, economics, academia and media united to stir a rotten machine, even though it was clear that it would shatter at the end. I mean the scandal of the*

A "Fiscal Cult" Wreaks Havoc

bank stocks that came to a bitter end in 1983. Then, too, these elites carried out in action, agreement and silence an unrealistic process that pretended to create, against the laws of nature and economics, a policy through which profits would constantly be generated and there would never be losses. They burst the bubble, and while they slowly diverted the process, they revealed that it was too late to stop it, crossed their hands and prayed that it would continue like this forever, something which obviously cannot happen.

And even though everything was clear, no one made a sound, no one wrote in a newspaper, no one cried out loud, and the bank stocks became a central fiscal cult, an economic belief system that swept away the entire country until everything was smashed with the loud thunder of giant losses.

New elections for the Knesset were set for July 1984. A new factor in the Israeli political scene was the appearance of Rabbi Meir Kahane as a candidate for Knesset. Kahane, one of the founders of the militant Jewish Defense League in the United States, immigrated to Israel in the 1970's. He founded the Kach party in Israel, a militant, right wing, openly anti-Arab party that advocated settling the entire Biblical Land of Israel and the expropriation of Arab land for that purpose. In the two elections for the Knesset prior to 1984, Kach was unable to cross the minimum threshold of receiving one percent of the total votes cast in the election. But in the 1984 elections, Kahane was elected to the Knesset. There, he would be a never-ending source of controversy and rancor. The Knesset finally passed legislation that, in effect, banned Kahane and Kach from campaigning again for election to the Knesset. Nevertheless, Kahane and his vociferous followers would not be muzzled in their advocacy of their absolutist approach to the Arab-Israeli struggle. While delivering a lecture in New York City in November 1990, Kahane was murdered by an Arab. In an ironic twist of fate, his son and daughter-in-law were murdered by Arab terrorists ten years later, while driving along a road in the West Bank.

The results of the 1984 Knesset elections revealed a deadlock in Israeli society. The Labor Alignment, led by Shimon Peres, won 46 seats. Likud declined to 41 seats, but the seats gained by other right wing parties more than balanced Labor's total. The deadlock on the formation of a new government went on for a few months. Finally, a national unity government was formed on the basis of the rotation of the portfolios of prime minister and foreign minister. For the first 25 months of the life of the government, Shimon Peres would serve as prime minister and Yitzchak Shamir as foreign minister. They would exchange positions for the last 25 months of the life of the government. It was also agreed that Yitzchak Rabin would remain as defense minister throughout the duration of the coalition. As unlikely as it first appeared, this arrangement brought stability to the country and suggested solutions to Israel's major problems.

SHIMON PERES WAS AN ABLE PRIME MINISTER AND A TIRELESS WORKER. He created a coalition of national interest groups that tackled the problem of inflation. His first task was to rein in the Histadrut labor union whose wage demands fueled the inflationary cycle. The Histadrut was a prime example of a labor union grown too fat, too powerful and too self-centered for its own good, or that of the country. Though Peres was no Margaret Thatcher when it came to dealing with the labor unions, he did gain their cooperation for his forthcoming measures to end the inflationary spiral. Together with his Finance Minister Yitzchak Modai, Peres created an Economic Stabilization Plan which highlighted severe cuts in government operating and defense budgets; a restrictive monetary policy; a dramatic devaluation of the shekel, coupled with a guarantee that there would be no near-term further devaluation; and the removal of government subsidies on many products, including food staples. In June 1984, the inflation rate was 240% annually. In July, it climbed to 336% annually. In August, after the Economic Stabilization Plan was put into force, the inflation rate declined to 30% annually, and at the end of 1984 it stood at 18%. It would continue to decline and become manageable as more power was transferred to the National Bank of Israel to regulate interest rates and initiate sound monetary policy. By the year 2000, the annual inflation rate in Israel was 0% annually! Peres had accomplished the economic miracle that saved Israel from economic ruin.

He also dealt with the problem in Lebanon. Amin Jemayel was overthrown in August 1984 in a coup led by a fellow officer of the Phalange militia.[14] The new leaders in Lebanon made a pact with Syria, allowing it to send in 35,000 troops to pacify the country and granting effective rule in the country to the Moslem majority. Lebanon now became a vassal state of Syria, which controlled its foreign and defense policies. Syria ruthlessly put down all Christian and Moslem opposition to its rule, and allowed the PLO and Hezbollah terrorist groups to continue their operations against Israel from southern Lebanon. Peres withdrew the Israeli army from Lebanon and established a "security zone" near the Lebanese-Israeli border. This narrow swath of Lebanese territory was patrolled and governed by the Southern Lebanese Army, the Israel-backed and financed

Peres Tackles the Runaway Shekel

---

14. The officer was Elie Hobeika, who had been in charge of the Phalange group responsible for the Sabra and Chatilla massacre. The Middle East is a strange place.

Christian militia described above. The Israeli army supplied backup and "advisors" to the SLA, but the Lebanese border never remained quiet for any extended period of time, as the PLO and Hezbollah continued to operate freely in the area. Israel opened "The Good Fence," near Metullah on its border with Lebanon. This crossing allowed Lebanese Arabs, mainly Christian, to cross into Israel for work and shopping. It also became a well-known tourist site. Peres had succeeded in disengaging Israel from Lebanon, but not in solving the problem of Arab terrorism emanating from that country.

Sporadic Arab terrorism continued within Israel and worldwide in the 1980's. Peres was convinced that only a permanent solution to the Palestinian problem could eventually bring peace and security to the Middle East. He courted King Hussein of Jordan all through 1984 and 1985, suggesting various arrangements with Jordan that would restore parts of the West Bank to Jordanian sovereignty and help resettle the Arabs then living in the refugee camps in Jordan and the West Bank. Though Hussein was receptive to Peres' ideas, he told the prime minister bluntly that he did not wish to be assassinated as was Anwar Sadat and his grandfather, King Abdullah, for attempting to make peace with Israel. Peres nevertheless persisted and, in fact, met clandestinely with Hussein in London to try and strike a deal. American Secretary of State George Schultz also attempted to facilitate a Jordanian-Israeli arrangement, but nothing concrete was agreed upon between the parties at that time.

The immigration of Ethiopian Jews to Israel had begun secretly in the 1970's. The president of Sudan, Jaafal el Numeiri, was bribed by Israel to allow the immigrants to cross from Ethiopia into Sudan, from where they would be flown to Israel.[15] In 1981, after Sadat's assassination, Numeiri, fearing for his own life, closed the border. In 1984, however, he relented and Operation Moses, the task of bringing 8,000 Ethiopian Jews to Israel, began. The secret of the Ethiopian immigration to Israel was discovered, however, and concentrated Arab pressure on Ethiopia and Sudan temporarily ended the operation in January 1985. (The rest of the Ethiopian Jewish community was airlifted in May of 1991 to Israel in Operation Solomon. Due to an emergency situation caused by extreme persecution of the Jews during an Ethiopian civil war, 14,200 Jews had to be flown out of Ethiopia in a matter of 36 hours. The task was accomplished by 40 flights of the Israel Air Force and El Al Airlines.)

---

15. Howard M. Sachar, *A History of Israel*, 1996, p.940.

A young Ethiopian immigrant carries his mother from the plane at the Israeli airport in Lod

For many Jews worldwide, this mass immigration was the first they heard of the existence of an Ethiopian Jewish population, despite sporadic tales related about them from time to time. Jewish tradition ascribes the origins of Ethiopian Jewry to the time of King Solomon and the Queen of Sheba. The Ethiopian Jews were also reputed to be connected to the tribe of Dan. Their existence is recorded in rabbinic responsa of the sixteenth century and contact was made with them by Western Jews in the nineteenth century. Their language and holy books, however, were written in Amharic, not Hebrew, and they were unaware of much of the ritual and laws of rabbinic Judaism, as they had been isolated from the rest of the Jewish world for millennia.

Once in Israel, there were halachic questions regarding the true Jewish status of the Ethiopian immigrants. The Chief Rabbinate worked out practical solutions to the problem and Ethiopians were eventually accepted as Jews into Israeli society. In contrast to the spiritually devastating absorption of the previous Yemenite *aliyah*, many, if not most, Ethiopian children were permitted to attend religious schools. They would have the same economic and social difficulties common to all immigrant generations, especially since they came from a culture that had never modernized. By the end of the century, the situation of the Ethiopians had improved dramatically, though there were still substantial pockets of hard-core unemployment and deep social problems within the group. In addition, the Ethiopians harbored strong resentments against

Photo: Zion Ozeri

the religious establishment for not initially accepting them as Jews. They also complained of racial discrimination against them in general Israeli society. It would take time for the painful process of absorption to be truly successful.

While it is tempting to view *aliyah* as a one-way street, it must be remembered that there was also a *yeridah* — an emigration of Jews from Israel to the Diaspora — throughout the years of the state, and even earlier. Individual Jews often found it difficult to adjust to life in Israel, no matter how idealistic and good-intentioned they were. Many were unable to earn a living in Israel and others could not bear the tension of the continuing state of Arab war and terrorism. And the attractions of the Western world — the schools, financial opportunities, quality of life and opportunities for career and personal advancement — were irresistible. The state itself, as well as educational and commercial institutions, sent many Israelis abroad for advanced training and education, or for national service to Jewish communities in the Diaspora. It became almost *de rigeur* for young Israelis to travel abroad after army service. After visiting awhile, the comforts and security of life in Western countries, particularly in the United States and Canada, proved too difficult to leave. Most Israelis who emigrated told their relatives, friends and themselves that they were only leaving Israel for a short time, to make their fortunes and then return home. But 90% of the *yordim* never returned to live in Israel again.

There are conflicting figures as to the numbers of *yordim* who left Israel since the formation of the state: They range from a low estimate of 250,000 people to a high estimate of over 750,000. The majority of *yordim* went to the United States. While many found their way to leading educational and financial positions, others continued in their original occupations in the food industry or as hairdressers, taxi drivers and laborers. Israelis also settled in every Western country in Europe, in North and South America, as well as in Asia and Australia.

Upon arrival in their new home countries, most Israelis had very little to do with organized Jewish life. The synagogue, which for centuries had been the familiar center of Jewish life to immigrants in the Diaspora, was a strange and foreboding place to most of them. They had been raised in the secular culture unfortunately common to many Israelis, and they generally saw no need to identify with religious institutions. As time wore on, however, some *yordim* became part of the fabric of their Jewish communities and enrolled their children in local Jewish schools. Overall, however, Israeli immigrants dropped their connection to Jewish life in droves and assimilated very rapidly. Their impulse to ignore their Jewishness in favor of identification with the world at large was a repeat of the earlier "immigration generation syndrome" that had so ravaged the Jewish lifestyles of Eastern Europeans at the beginning of the century.

In February 1986, Natan Sharansky was released from Soviet prison as part of an arrangement between the Soviet Union and the United States. When he arrived in Israel, he immediately threw himself into the task of freeing the other "Prisoners of Zion" languishing in Soviet prisons and labor camps, and opening the gates of emigration for Soviet Jewry. In 1987, his presence at an enormous rally on behalf of Soviet Jewry in Washington, D.C. coincided with a Reagan-Gorbachev summit meeting and helped increase pressure on the USSR to increase the flow of Soviet Jews to Israel.[16] Sharansky's dramatic story helped skyrocket him to political power in Israel.

Avital and Anatoly Sharansky (left), riding with Prime Minister Shimon Peres and Vice-Premier Yitzchak Shamir to the terminal building in Ben-Gurion Airport

He eventually headed a Russian immigrants' political party, Yisrael B'Aliyah, serving as a minister in a number of Israeli government cabinets in the next decade.

---

16. In 1986, only 914 Soviet Jews reached Israel. In 1987, the number rose to 6,000. In 1988, 17,000 Soviet Jews arrived in Israel and in 1989, close to 60,000 came. In 1990, the number permitted to leave Russia rose to 200,000! Of these, 90% settled in Israel. This would prove to be only the beginning of the mass immigration of three-quarters of a million Russian Jews to Israel in the early 1990's.

The Soviet Union is Dismembered and Disgraced

THE SOVIET UNION ITSELF WAS UNDERGOING GREAT CHANGE. PREMIER Gorbachev's power as head of state was eroding and the state of the Soviet economy was appalling. Gorbachev attempted to introduce a market economy, freeing 5% of Russian agricultural land for private farming. This 5% soon was producing almost half of all Russian produce, highlighting the glaring inefficiency of centralized collective farming. Subsidies to Soviet manufacturing were cut because of the worsening economic situation, and soon production in all areas of Russian industry fell. Gorbachev's idea of *perestroika* (remodeling) included a drive against alcoholism, which long had been a scourge of Russian society. But a great deal of the government's money came from its control over the liquor industry and this reform, like most of Gorbachev's proposals, was never fully implemented.

Gorbachev withdrew the Soviet army from Afghanistan in 1987, admitting the failure of strategy and tactics that had cost his country so dearly. He now proclaimed a period of *glasnost* (reconciliation) with the West and sought to come to an accommodation with Reagan and Thatcher on disarmament and other key issues. The USSR had by now clearly fallen behind the West in technology, economic strength and armed might. Food shortages and long pent-up dissatisfaction with the communist regime began to surface. Gorbachev hoped to use the Western leaders' approval of himself and his policies to prop himself up in the eyes of the Russian people. But it was a losing struggle. The "evil empire," as President Reagan called it, was beginning to melt and ooze away into the mud of failed history. By the end of 1989, Hungary and Poland had defected from the Warsaw Pact of Soviet satellite nations and established non-communist governments. Czechoslovakia broke away from Soviet control with its "velvet revolution" and became allied with the West. Gorbachev was no longer able or willing to invoke the "Brezhnev Doctrine" of Soviet troops restoring communist government in the Eastern Union. The communist government of East Germany collapsed under the pressure of enormous street demonstrations. The Berlin Wall was dismantled. The Baltic states[17] and the Ukraine declared their independence of the USSR. Georgia and other ethnic states in the Caucasus and Asiatic Russia also broke away from Moscow's rule. These changes affected millions of people in numerous ways, the Jews no less than anyone. The turmoil would soon release Soviet Jewry from its confinement of 70 years.

---

17. Lithuania, Latvia and Estonia.

T RUE TO HIS WORD AND TO THE TERMS OF THE COALITION AGREEMENT between Labor and Likud, Shimon Peres relinquished his premiership in favor of Yitzchak Shamir in October of 1986. Now the foreign minister, Peres was determined to break the deadlock in negotiations between the Arabs and Israel. In April 1987, he reached a secret agreement with King Hussein of Jordan over the parameters of an Israeli-Jordanian peace treaty, which would include the settlement of the Palestinian Arab problem under the leadership of Jordan. However, Peres had done this secretly, without even Shamir's previous knowledge. Angry at Peres, Shamir and the other Likud members of the cabinet voted against the peace initiative. The entire matter was leaked to the press. King Hussein, furious at the dangerous breach of secrecy, publicly disavowed the plan, proclaiming that only the PLO would henceforth represent the interests of the Palestinian Arabs. In 1988, Hussein formally renounced any Jordanian claims to the West Bank in favor of the PLO. Israel would come to rue the day that this 1987 agreement with Hussein was not approved.

Arab terrorism was continued by Fatah, Yassir Arafat's armed militia, as well as a new organization, Hamas (meaning "pious zeal"). A fundamentalist Moslem group, Hamas espoused an uncompromising hatred of Israel and worked for the complete elimination of the Jewish state. Its leaders disparaged Arafat and the PLO and gained wide popularity among the disaffected Arabs of the refugee camps, especially in the Gaza Strip. Militant to an extreme, it created its own active terrorist cells. Israel quietly allowed Hamas to operate schools, health clinics and social services in the Arab refugee camps, in the hope that it would prove to be a counterweight to the PLO and that it would eventually moderate its extreme anti-Israel stance. Arafat recognized Hamas as a threat to his own hegemony, but did not take any action against it due to Hamas' wide popularity among the Palestinian population.

There was enormously widespread Arab resentment against the continuing building of Jewish settlements in Gaza, Judea and Samaria, as well as in the environs of Jerusalem. Shamir had pursued an expanded settlement policy in the face of increasing United States and UN public disapproval. A large section of Israeli society also came to disagree with the policy of expanding Jewish settlement in the West Bank. Though it may have won major victories "on the ground," the Gush Emunim group became increasingly distant from much of the Israeli public, both in kilometers and in the important struggle for ideas. One of the reasons that the Mafdal party diminished in influence was because it now espoused the Gush Emunim cause as its sole *raison d'etre*, and many moderates in the Israeli religious public left its ranks. A new political party of these reli-

Festering Bitterness Brews the Intifada

gious moderates emerged, called Meimad. It had wide intellectual backing, but little popular support.

Throughout the 1980's, over and above the recurring PLO terrorist acts against Israel, the Palestinian Arabs in Gaza and the West Bank proved restive under Israeli rule. Sporadic incidents of stone throwing and burning tires on the roads of the West Bank were now part of Israeli life. Another militant terrorist group, Islamic Jihad, arose from the slums of Gaza and swore to destroy the Jewish state. At the end of 1987, four Arab workers were accidentally run over and killed by an Israeli truck, and full scale Arab violence in the West Bank and in Gaza broke out. The Arabs were not armed with conventional weapons, but made effective use of stones, fire and knives. Israeli soldiers and civilians were stoned and attacked throughout the country. This was the beginning of the "*intifada*," meaning literally, "shaking off" (of foreign domination, presumably). Its implications were not at first properly understood by Israel.

Minister of Defense Yitzchak Rabin ordered the use of measured force to put down the riots. He advocated beating a rioter with a police baton rather than shooting him. However, the quotation that was attributed to him — "Break their bones" — did little to aid Israel's cause in world opinion. More than 50 Arab demonstrators were killed and hundreds more wounded in the early months of the intifada. The United Nations passed a resolution condemning Israel's use of force, though, as was its wont, it ignored the Arab rioting completely. By the end of the decade, more than 100 Israeli soldiers and civilians were killed by Arab violence and many more hundreds injured. After a period of time, the intifada became an accepted, if unpleasant, fact of daily Israeli life. Tourism, which had stopped at the beginning of the rioting, slowly returned to pre-intifada levels. Bulletproof buses and shatterproof windows and windshields for automobiles became common on Israeli roads.

The Shamir government retaliated for Arab killings of Israeli civilians living in the West Bank by continuing the expansion of existing settlements and founding new ones. Hamas appeared to be much more in charge of the intifada than was the PLO, which had not initiated the action. Much of the violence of the intifada degenerated into Arab on Arab violence, with factions wreaking vengeance on other factions and on suspected "collaborators" with Israel.

Arab labor in Israel also suffered from the uprising, as Hamas declared numerous strike days.[18] In addition, Israel would regularly close

---

18. To maintain its status as the primary organization fighting against Israel, the PLO declared its own separate strike days and disregarded those of Hamas. Most of the Arabs on the West Bank, fearful of offending the sponsor of any of the strike days, observed them all, to their financial near-ruin.

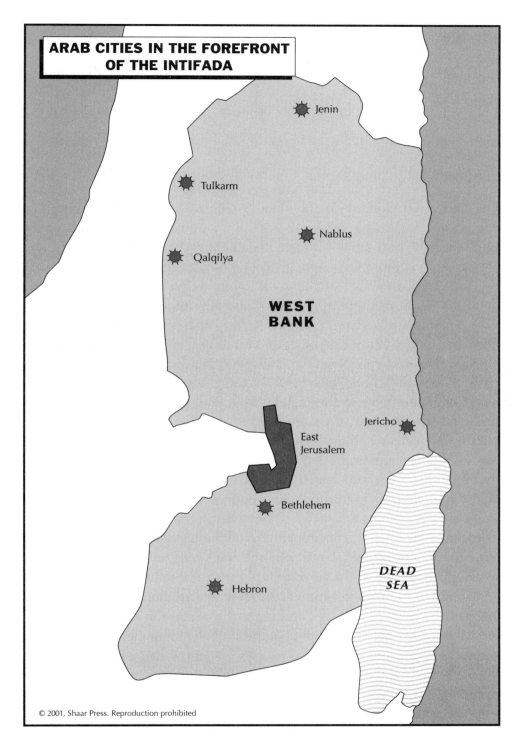

ARAB CITIES IN THE FOREFRONT
OF THE INTIFADA

Jenin

Tulkarm

Nablus

Qalqilya

WEST
BANK

Jericho

East
Jerusalem

Bethlehem

DEAD
SEA

Hebron

roads in the West Bank after terrorist incidents, preventing Arabs from entering Israeli areas. Arab labor became more and more unreliable, and fewer Arabs were hired by Israelis. Foreign labor from Rumania, the Philippines, Thailand and other countries began to pour into Israel. This attempt to solve the problem of a dearth of unskilled labor — primarily for agriculture, construction and tourist/hotel services — raised its own problems. Crime, drugs and prostitution increased. The Arab and Israeli economies were so closely intertwined that the economic fallout of the intifada was a major factor in the waning of enthusiasm for it on the part of the general population, leaving only the hard-core terrorists to continue the fight.

On November 1, 1988, elections for the Knesset were held. Likud was the largest party again, but it won only 40 seats. Labor declined to 39 seats. The new Shas party, led by the young and charismatic Aryeh Deri, gained six seats while Mafdal had five seats, as did Agudath Israel. Meimad failed to gain a seat, though it undoubtedly siphoned off votes from Mafdal. Shamir once again formed a national unity government with Labor, Shas, Mafdal and the other smaller right wing parties. But this time there was to be no rotating of prime ministers. Shamir appointed Shimon Peres as minister of finance and Rabin remained the minister of defense. Aryeh Deri became minister of the interior and Zevulun Hammer of Mafdal was minister of education.

Menachem Porush of Agudath Israel delivering a speech at the Knesset

Prime Minister Shamir remained adamant in opposing any concessions to the Palestinians that would induce them to enter into peace negotiations with Israel. But the intifada destroyed Israeli unity: A large segment of Israeli society regarded the suppression of the intafada as unjustifiably harsh. Believing that the new settlements only inflamed Arab hostility, Finance Minister Peres refused to transfer funds for the establishment of six new settlements, as agreed upon in the national unity government agreement. Shamir demanded Peres' resignation. Soon after, a no-confidence vote against Shamir failed, and the Labor ministers promptly resigned. Shamir then formed a narrow coalition government based on the religious parties, the right wing parties and Likud.

Shamir was vastly encouraged by the growing flood of Russian Jewish immigration. He claimed that this new immigration justified the necessity of "Greater Israel" and continued expansion of Jewish settlement throughout Gaza and the West Bank. The Labor party, Peace Now and other groups objected to Shamir's policies, enlisting the aid of some American Jewish personalities and groups in loud protest. President George Bush and Secretary of State James Baker were known to be lukewarm, at best, towards Israel and its interests, and the personal relationship between Shamir and the American administration was very cold. Baker personally resented the fact that a new West Bank Jewish settlement was founded to coincide with his arrival every time he visited Israel. Though badly frustrated by Shamir's policies and persona, Bush attempted to broker a peace conference between Israel, the Palestinians and the Jordanians. Israel finally agreed to hold elections for Arab representatives in Gaza and the West Bank. The purpose of those elections was to create a public Arab body that would negotiate with Israel, first for Arab autonomous self-rule, and later on for a permanent agreement ending the Israeli-Palestinian struggle. But both Israel and the Palestinians added such onerous conditions to this proposal as to render it unworkable.

As far as Fatah was concerned, the way to stop settlement was to stop immigration to Israel through violence, not peace talks. In an interview given by Yassir Arafat to a Lebanese newspaper in April 1990, he stated:

> *I want to say clearly: open fire on the new Jewish immigrants, be they Soviet, Falasha [Ethiopian] or anything else. It would be disgraceful of us if we were to see herds of immigrants conquering our land and settling our territory and not raise a finger. I want you to shoot on the ground or in the air, at every immigrant who thinks our land is a playground and that immigration to it is a vacation or a picnic. I give you explicit instructions to open fire. Do everything to stop the flow of immigration.[19]*

Terrorist acts continued unabated. In addition to terrorism in Israel, Arab terrorists exploded a bomb in the World Trade Center in New York City, causing panic and death. Libyan terrorists with connections to the Soviet Union and the PLO planted a bomb on a Pan Am jumbo jet flying from London to New York. The resultant explosion over Lockerbie, Scotland, killed all 259 people on board and eleven more when the plane fell on their homes. A high-ranking Libyan intelligence officer was eventually convicted of the crime, though he was only one of the many cogs in that particular wheel of murder.

Peace with the Palestinians seemed to be an elusive dream. Yet the United States kept pressing Israel to come up with a formula that would allow peace negotiations to begin. For his part, Shamir remained adamant that the Palestinians had to evince a desire for peace by discontinuing violence against Israel in order for meaningful discussions to take place.

The Splintering of the American Jewish Community

THE JEWISH COMMUNITY IN THE UNITED STATES ENTERED INTO A form of free fall in the 1980's. The bitter dispute in Israel over settlements spilled over into American Jewish life. Both Peace Now and Gush Emunim conducted extensive campaigns for support and funding among American Jewish communities. This exporting of Israeli divisions, the biased anti-Israel coverage of the intifada in the American media — coupled with the Shamir government's lack of charm — and the contin-

---

19. Quoted by Gilbert, *Israel – A History,* page 544.

uing ravages of the rapidly increasing rates of intermarriage and assimilation (which rendered identification with Jewish causes meaningless) helped to further polarize the American Jewish community.

Other Americans were also influenced by the media's sympathy to the Palestinian cause. Large sections of the African-American community in the United States took up the Palestinian cause. A growing community of Moslems, much of it Palestinian, in many American cities made blatant support for Israel by politicians hazardous to their careers. This shift in American public opinion enabled the Bush administration to punish Israel a number of times for its "intransigence" on the settlements without creating too much of a public or political uproar.

Anti-Semitism was expressed in the political arena in the late 1980's and early 1990's. The "campaign" is against Tom Lantos, who was running for Congress in California.

In addition, Jewish support for Israel and its policies was weakened by Israel's handling of "the Pollard affair." In November 1985, an American named Jonathan Jay Pollard was arrested for transferring American classified information and intelligence documents to Israeli operatives in Washington, D.C. Pollard was a Jewish worker at the United States Naval Intelligence Service who felt that the United States was not living up to its obligations to share vital intelligence information with Israel. Israel at first denied any connection to Pollard and was not forthcoming during the investigation. The judge in the case chose not to honor a plea bargain arrangement, and the defense secretary sent a secret memorandum to the judge, claiming that Pollard had done more damage to the United States than any spy in American history. Bearing the full fury of the American government, Pollard and his wife were sentenced to extraordinarily harsh prison terms. Pollard was put in solitary confinement and received a life sentence. His wife was denied essential medical care and was given a five-year sentence. Compared to other more serious cases of spying in the annals of American history, these sentences were draconian in nature. Eventually, Israel owned up to its responsibility in the affair and even granted Jonathan Pollard citizenship. Later, Israeli governments and many Jewish organizations would rally to help Pollard's efforts to have his sentence reduced, though others criticized the involvement of the Jewish community in the matter. At the conclusion of the century, Pollard still remained in prison.

American Jewry also became more divided along the fault line of the Orthodox/non-Orthodox dispute. Because of intermarriage, the Reform movement increasingly had a constituency of people who were not recognized as Jewish by traditional Jewish Law. The Reform movement therefore adopted a rule allowing either patrilineal or matrilineal descent to determine who is a Jew, thereby increasing manyfold the number of people they considered Jewish. This blatant flouting of *halachah* was rejected by Orthodoxy and by the Conservative movement.

The Reform movement's stand on patrilineal descent must be seen as a watershed in its relations with traditional Judaism, exposing its pattern of disregard for the consequences of its actions, and causing bitter divisiveness in Jewish life. For many millennia the determination of who is Jewish was always based on matrilineal descent exclusively. No group within the Jewish people, including Reform itself for two centuries, had ever challenged this definition and policy. It should be noted that Reform in Israel, as of the date of this book, does not recognize patrilineal descent as a definition of being Jewish. Thus Reform, in essence, established different definitions of Jewishness for different venues, a situation which is highly illogical and is guaranteed to cause future pain and frustration to the very people that Reform attempted to accommodate with its redefinition of Jewishness.

In 1984, the Conservative movement also contributed to the growing divisiveness in American Jewry by accepting women in its rabbinical program at the Jewish Theological Seminary, a reversal of its earlier policy. This move caused a furor at the Seminary, with the more traditional members of the faculty protesting loudly and publicly. Dr. Weiss-Halivni resigned his post in the Talmud department of the Seminary, and he and other professors in the Conservative movement established an alternative rabbinical seminary for the training of Conservative rabbis. They were joined by a number of Conservative rabbis in establishing the Union of Traditional Judaism, an organization promoting a more traditional and ritually observant form of Conservative Judaism. This split within the Conservative movement did not prevent the majority of Conservative rabbis and lay leaders from continuing with their program of changes in Jewish tradition. The traditionalist wing of the Conservative movement, previously in control of the Jewish Theological Seminary, lost its power base there and was unable to influence the steady movement of the Conservative movement towards more liberal policies.

Despite these internal upheavals, the Conservative day school movement experienced considerable growth during this decade, as did Conservative-sponsored summer camp and Israel-based programs. Dr. Ismar Schorsch, the new head of the Seminary, was much less traditional in outlook than his predecessors. He was also very aggressive in highlighting the differences between Conservative and Orthodox practices and beliefs and in attacking the Orthodox establishment, something that many of his predecessors had soft-pedaled.

In Israel, Conservative congregations were founded throughout the country,[20] serving a primarily Anglo population, with little impact either on the established religious community or on the mass of secular Jews in Israel. Many in Israel regarded Conservative Judaism as an American social phenomenon and resented the exportation of the American Conservative vs. Orthodox strife to Israel.

The secular political parties in Israel, constantly warring with the growing political strength of the religious parties, exploited the presence of the Conservative and Reform movements in Israel to further their aim of toppling the Orthodox religious establishment. This alliance only exacerbated the conflict of the non-Orthodox with Orthodox Jews in Israel and in America, polluting the climate of Jewish society everywhere with foul divisiveness.

The Orthodox world, especially in the United States, faced its own controversial issues in this decade. The most contentious issue regarded the changing role of women in Orthodox society. The continuing improvement and intensity of religious education for women created new demands on the Orthodox establishment from some women. Pressure increased throughout the decade for women's prayer groups, women's *hakafos* on Simchas Torah, women's study of the Talmud and female halachic advisors. However, the most emotional and public issue was that of some women being unable to obtain a divorce from recalcitrant hus-

---

20. In accordance with the Conservative movement's political policy on Israel, however, none were created in the Jewish settlements in Gaza, Judea and Samaria.

bands, colloquially known as the *agunah* problem.[21] With an increasing divorce rate in Orthodox society, this issue took on urgency and importance, especially in the United States where the rabbis had no civil powers to enforce the decrees of a religious court. Attempts to remedy the situation by such means as New York's "Get Law" complicated the matter, since there was strong rabbinic opinion opposing the validity of Jewish divorces "forced upon the husband" by civil courts.[22] Organizations were formed to help women in such straits, some with rabbinic backing, others in defiant opposition to halachic authorities, and the problem received wide publicity in the press. In Israel, where the rabbinate does possess punitive powers, the problem also existed, but in a more muted fashion.

A long-cherished goal of raising Holocaust awareness in the public mind was reached when the national Holocaust Museum was established in Washington, D.C. in the 1980's. Allotted a prime location near the Smithsonian Institute by the US government, the museum portrayed the Holocaust with graphically and emotionally powerful impact. The museum became one of the largest tourist attractions in Washington, and the overwhelming majority of its visitors were non-Jews. A "Museum of Tolerance," also dealing with the Holocaust, was built in Los Angeles at the same time under the aegis of the Simon Wiesenthal Foundation. It proved to be a major attraction as well, with millions of visitors annually. Holocaust museums were built in Miami Beach and other American cities, large and small.

Despite these efforts, the Holocaust seemed to be receding into the background of Jewish and general consciousness. When President Reagan attended a memorial service at a cemetery in Bitburg, Germany, where SS troopers are buried, the noted Holocaust survivor and Nobel Peace Prize winner Elie Wiesel publicly protested. But his plea was to no avail. The event caused many to fear that the hold of the Holocaust on the world's conscience was beginning to weaken, as were the lives of many of its survivors as the final decade of the century began.

And yet — while it became evident that Jews and Judaism could not survive and prosper solely on Holocaust projects and memories — the Holocaust occupied a unique position in world history. The sporadic specter of rising anti-Semitism in various places of the world continued to refresh the memory of the Holocaust experience for both Jews and non-Jews.

---

21. This term is somewhat of a misnomer. The classic case of "*agunah,*" as recorded in the Talmud and rabbinic literature throughout the ages, dealt with a woman whose husband has disappeared and evidence of his death or whereabouts is not available. The problem of recalcitrant husbands is also dealt with in the Talmud and rabbinic sources, but it is not described as an *agunah* issue.

22. The first Get Law — barring civil remarriage when there is an unresolved issue regarding a religious divorce from a previous marriage – did have rabbinic consensus. The later strengthened law — providing for monetary punishment if a recalcitrant spouse did not agree to a religious divorce — was opposed by many rabbis.

Chapter Eleven

Hopes, Dreams and Illusions

1991-2000

THE RAGING INTIFADA HAD AN EFFECT ON THE ARAB CITIZENS OF Israel as well as on the Palestinian Arabs in Gaza and the West Bank. Abdel Wahab Darawashe, an Arab member of Knesset, of the Labor Party Alignment, resigned from Labor and formed his own party, the Arab Democratic Party. Other Arab political parties now came into being, as Israeli Arabs began to see themselves less as Israelis and more as Palestinian loyalists. This change in Arab mood within Israel had profound political and social repercussions in this decade of intensified Arab-Israeli hostility. The dream of converting Israel into a miniature "melting pot," like the United States of America, still burned brightly in the minds and hearts of many influential Jewish intellectuals in Israel. Their goal was to make Israel less "Jewish" and more "democratic." As appealing as that idea was intellectually, and as popular as it once may have seemed politically, intensified Arab loyalties would eventually give the lie to such a possibility.

Entering the 1990's, the Soviet Union was on the verge of collapse. Its satellite empire had disappeared, its economy was in a shambles and its army, recalled from comfortable duty in the Eastern European bloc countries to the harsh realities of Russian life, was demoralized. Gorbachev's hold on the country was slipping and he was torn between the demands of the old communist hard-liners to restore the dictatorship on the one hand, and the pressure of liberals to convert the Soviet Union into a full-fledged democracy on the other. The hard-liners made their move by kidnapping Gorbachev and claiming to have taken over the country. The army seemed to be on their side and surrounded the legislative building in Moscow. Boris Yeltsin, a former communist hard-liner himself and the mayor of Moscow, now emerged as the champion of the democratic forces. He faced down the army generals and had Gorbachev released. The ringleaders of the kidnapping coup were arrested and the democratization of Russia was now in full force.

The Cold War that had terrorized the world for over four decades ended, not with a bang, but with a whimper. But even shorn of her empire and her terror, the Soviet Union remained one of the world's formidable powers.[1] Yeltsin faced Gorbachev in a free election for the presidency of the new state and won. Statues of Stalin and Lenin were torn down and vandalized all over Russia. The "great experiment" in social engineering had failed.

Return and Revival

THESE CHANGES BROUGHT ABOUT NEW POSSIBILITIES. THE GATES OF the Soviet Union were finally open for Jews to leave. Hundreds of thousands of them took the opportunity to do so and went to Israel. Among the immigrants were many who were not halachically Jewish or even descended from Jews in any way at all. It was a reprise in a minor key of the Exodus from Egypt when a "mixture of peoples" left bondage with Moses and the Jews. Just as this group created problems for Israel in the desert and thereafter, the Russian immigration would also not be free of difficulties. The Russian Orthodox Church became the fastest growing religious group in Israel. Christmas trees and celebrations became widespread for the first time in the history of the Jewish state. Anti-Semitic graffiti and slurs against "*Zhids*" were expressed on the streets of Israel's cities.

On the whole, however, the Russian immigration was a miraculous gift to Israel and to the Russian immigrants themselves. The Russian Jews acclimated themselves to Israeli life rapidly and successfully. Bereft of Jewish knowledge and experience for over 70 years, they familiarized themselves with Judaism, quickly learned Hebrew, and became more aware of Jewish holidays. Less than 10% of the new immigrants actually affiliated themselves in any way with religious Jewry, however.

---

1. The nineteenth century description of Russia, which Paul Johnson attributes to the French diplomat, Talleyrand — "Russia is never as strong as she appears; Russia is never as weak as she appears" — remained accurate for all of the twentieth century as well.

A classic scene of the Diaspora. Friends and family say good-bye at a train station in Moldavia as Russian Jews depart for Israel.

Unlike populations of earlier mass migrations to Israel, Jews from the Soviet Union immediately entered political life. During the 1990's, there were three Russian immigrant political parties active in Israel, the largest — Yisrael B'Aliyah — headed by Natan Sharansky. Because of the large number of Russian immigrants who had halachic problems establishing their Jewishness, the Russian parties supported a civil system of marriage, divorce and personal status. This placed them in opposition to the religious parties and curtailed the ability of the religious organizations to have greater influence in the Russian sector of the population. Chabad, which had been the main (and possibly, the sole) religious Jewish group operating continuously within the Soviet Union during the years of the communist tyranny, continued to be effective in Israel in its work with the Russian immigrants. A number of Jewish religious organizations opened outreach centers and yeshivos, and offered school programs and home visits to help Russian Jews rediscover their heritage. Prayer books, Bibles and other religious works were translated and printed in Russian and distributed widely. The large Russian Christian population that also immigrated to Israel under the porous "Law of Return" (all claiming some Jewish ancestry) encouraged strong Christian missionary activity among the new *olim* as well. Yet after so many generations of Soviet government-indoctrinated atheism, most Russian Jews in their first generation in Israel remained adamantly, though not militantly, secular.

Not only was there Jewish immigration from the Soviet Union to Israel, there was a rebirth of Jewish life in Russia itself. Free of the restrictions of the communist regime, Jewish schools and synagogues were established in major cities, and numerous new Jewish educational, religious and social organizations arose. The dedicated work of Rabbi Pinchos Goldschmidt and his wife in Moscow, built upon the pioneering work of Rabbi Shayovich, fostered a functioning Jewish community there. Chabad reemerged from its underground operations and organized a network of schools. The Jewish Agency and other Israeli organizations, mainly religious, also established schools, camps and day-care centers, sending their own personnel to teach the Russian Jewish population.

American Jewry also invested in the Jewish revival in Russia. Reform sponsored a number of synagogues and schools there, as did the Conservative movement. However, the main activities in the Former Soviet Union on behalf of the rebirth of Judaism came from various Orthodox organizations and individuals living in Israel and in the U.S. The Union of Orthodox Jewish Congregations of America; Agudath Israel; the famed Chasidic dynasties of Karlin-Stolin, Gur, Skver; the Va'ad L'Hatzolas Nidchei Yisrael ("The Organization to Save Oppressed Jews"); Migdal Ohr Institutions; Rabbi Adin Steinsaltz and others labored mightily to restore Jewish education and Jewish traditional life in Russia, Ukraine, Belarus, Lithuania, Hungary, Poland, Georgia and Uzbekistan, to name just some of the outreach locations. Special note must be taken of the work of the Chief Rabbi of Ukraine Rabbi Yaakov Bleich, a disciple of Karlin-Stolin, who created a complete Jewish infrastructure — religious, educational and social — in Ukraine. In fact, the Ukrainian government included Rabbi Bleich in its delegations to represent it to presidents of the United States and even to the pope in Rome. Though many of the "official" Jewish organizations claimed much of the credit for their work in Eastern Europe, the unsung heroes who truly revolutionized Jewish life there were from the aforementioned groups and individuals.

With global travel now relatively comfortable, another phenomenon surfaced: The fascination of many American Jews with their "roots" in the "Old Home," and the thousands of Western and Israeli Chasidim who went to Eastern Europe to visit the graves of the famous Chasidic masters, led to a significant tourist business in Poland, Ukraine and Lithuania. Ironically, the former concentration camp at Auschwitz became Poland's leading tourist attraction. Jews visiting Poland were struck by the fact that virulent Polish anti-Semitism still remained, even after the country was practically "*judenrein*," i.e. without Jews, in accordance with the Nazi plan.[2] In addition, although there were fewer than 10,000 Jews in Poland toward the end of the century, politicians and commentators still blamed the Jews for Poland's problems. The unforeseen and sudden collapse of communism and Soviet power, and new economic realities, turned the Eastern European world on its head. Having once gotten rid of their Jews in this century, these countries now appealed to Jews worldwide to come and visit, invest and even settle (!) in their former homelands. As of this writing, it will still require time and wisdom to sort out the matter.

A War Endured in Sealed Rooms

ON AUGUST 2, 1990, THE IRAQI DICTATOR SADDAM HUSSEIN ORDERED his army to invade and annex the Persian Gulf state of Kuwait, which bordered on Iraq. Saddam Hussein claimed that Kuwait was rightfully a "province" of Iraq. The Iraqi army easily overran the small country, committing untold atrocities on the civilian population in the wake of its conquest. Thousands of Kuwaitis were slaughtered or disappeared.

At the end of August, Saddam threatened Israel, boasting that his Scud missiles, laden with chemical warheads, could reach the Jewish state. When the United States and Britain, among others, demanded his withdrawal from Kuwait, Saddam countered with an offer to do so if Israel would withdraw from the Golan Heights, Gaza, Lebanon and the West Bank. The Soviet Union backed this outrageous demand, but the United States refused to allow Saddam to convert his aggression into an anti-Israel crusade that would rally the Arab world in his support. As it was, the Arab political leaders in Israel defended Saddam's invasion of Kuwait, as did the PLO. Jordan openly sided with him and aided Iraq during the ensuing Gulf War. However, the United States, with United Nations approval, was able to build a tenuous coalition of other Arab states (Egypt, Saudi Arabia, the Gulf Emirates and Syria) together with England and other NATO countries and threatened to oust Iraq from Kuwait by force. The American-led force was brought to Saudi Arabia for training and preparation, while Saddam continued his blustering diatribes, promising his foes "the mother of all wars."

Saddam Hussein

On January 17, 1991 the Allied air force began subjecting Iraqi military installations, including those in the capital city of Baghdad, to aerial bombardment. This was a "television war," with the raids and destruction appearing on television screens throughout the world. The Allied ground forces invaded Kuwait on February 24, and soon routed the Iraqi

---

2. When I visited Warsaw in 1999, ordinary Poles on the street extended the Nazi salute to me! It is as though they forgot that three million non-Jewish Poles were also killed by the Germans in World War II. Anti-Semitism and alcoholism remain two Polish curses that have survived the century.

army, driving it back, deep into Iraq. It is estimated that Iraq lost over 100,000 men in the war, and most of its armor and air force was destroyed or disabled. The Allied army could have easily reached Baghdad and attempted to depose Saddam, but the political leaders of the United States and England chose not to do so, partly out of deference to their Arab allies who wanted Saddam contained, but not necessarily destroyed. In an ecological nightmare, the Iraqi army put Kuwait's oil wells to the torch before retreating, and it would take months until the fires were extinguished and the black pall of smoke that hung over the Gulf finally dissipated. On Purim 1991, the Gulf War officially ended with Iraq's complete defeat.

Saddam had intended to draw Israel into the war in order to force the Arab countries to withdraw from the UN coalition and support him in his mad aspirations. In order to do so, he began firing Scud missiles against Israel on January 18. The distance from Iraq to Tel Aviv is approximately 400 kilometers (240 miles); it took Scud missiles only seven minutes to reach their targets. Forty such missiles were fired during the next nine weeks of the Gulf War at Israeli targets, aimed primarily at the densely populated Tel Aviv/Ramat Gan area. Despite Saddam's threats, all of the Scuds that bombarded Israel were tipped with conventional weapons and did not carry chemical or biological warheads. Over 25 Scud missiles were also fired at Saudi Arabia, mainly at American and Saudi military installations, though there were attacks on Saudi cities as well. Because of the fear of Saddam's chemical and biological arsenal, all residents and visitors to Israel were issued gas masks and were required to stay in previously prepared "sealed rooms" in their homes during the period of the attacks. The United States supplied Israel with Patriot anti-missile batteries to combat the Scuds. The Patriots were a great boost to Israeli morale, but not very effective against the missiles.

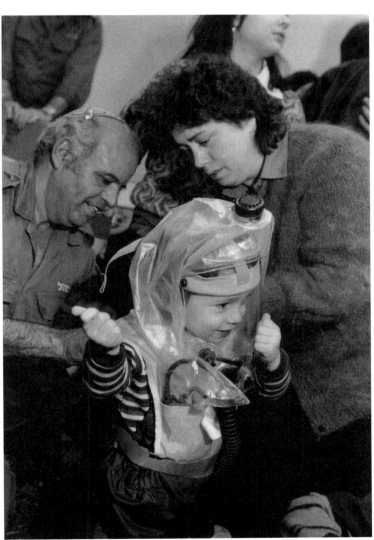

Photo: Zion Ozeri

A new Russian oleh is taught to adjust a gas mask on her child

Miraculously, only one Israeli was killed by a Scud directly and another dozen died of gas mask suffocation or fear-induced heart attacks. Two hundred other civilians were wounded, most suffering from shock and bruises from falling debris. Over 4,000 buildings were damaged, but the main damage was to Israel's psyche.

Israel had proven vulnerable to Iraq's missile attacks. The allied governments strongly indicated to Israel not to respond to Iraq's attacks in order to preserve their fragile coalition, which included Arab states. The Shamir government was hard put to refuse President Bush's request. It was the first time in Israeli history that Israel was attacked and did not respond. The vaunted Israeli armed forces were deemed by the Arabs, and even by some Israelis themselves, as impotent — unable to defend itself and counter missile attacks due to international diplomatic pressure. Israel was also shocked by the depth of hatred shown by the Palestinian Arabs who stood on the rooftops of their homes, cheering Saddam's missiles as they hurtled toward Israeli cities. It gave the Israeli public pause, at least temporarily, as it questioned whether Israel could ever truly arrive at a settlement with the Palestinians.

While Israel had suffered only one direct fatality due to the Scud attacks, U.S. forces in Saudi Arabia suffered a considerable number of fatalities, providing a strong impetus to impose UN inspections of Iraq after the war. The UN inspections proved ineffective, but nothing was done about it.

Poles Apart

THE UNITED STATES AND ITS ALLIES SAW IN THE DEFEAT OF SADDAM Hussein a golden opportunity to reach a comprehensive settlement in the Middle East. The fact that Jordan and the Palestinians had supported Saddam was overlooked, as it would raise complications in this new drive to impose a settlement on the region. Israel, shell-shocked and emotionally bruised from the unanswered Scud missile attacks it had absorbed, was ambivalent towards this rushed initiative. The Peace Now camp claimed that the Gulf War and Saddam Hussein's missiles clearly proved that only a peace settlement with the Palestinians, Syria and Jordan could provide Israel with security. The group received extensive support from wealthy American Jews who were convinced that a possibility for peace existed and that Israel should take the initiative in the matter. Shamir and the Likud were of the opinion that the Arabs had once again clearly demonstrated their enmity towards Israel and were not yet psychologically ready to make the necessary compromises that a lasting peace would require. They felt that any hurried push for peace "now" would only result in unilateral Israeli concessions and eventually even more Arab violence. This point of view also received extensive support from sections of American Jewry, mainly in the form of financial aid to the existing and newly planned settlements, especially in the Jerusalem area. In essence, the debate between these two opposite points of view continued in Israel and in the Jewish world throughout the decade and into the next century as well.

After long and tortuous negotiations, American Secretary of State James Baker arranged a Middle East peace conference that convened in Madrid on October 30, 1991. Israel refused to recognize the PLO as an independent organization, so the Palestinian delegation was considered part of a joint delegation with Jordan. Yitzchak Shamir himself represented Israel at the conference while Syria, Egypt, Jordan and Lebanon were represented by only their foreign ministers. Bitter words directed at Israel were spoken by all of the Arab worthies at that conference, especially by the Palestinian and Syrian delegates. It took all of Shamir's self-control, and intense American diplomatic pressure on him, to prevent him from walking out of the conference after the opening sessions.[3]

The conference agreed to create three separate negotiating teams — those of Jordan/Palestine, Syria and Lebanon — and these negotiations would begin in Washington on December 10, 1991. Because of the collapse of the Soviet Union, the United States was the only major power left in the world that could influence both parties. Other bilateral negotiations between the Israelis and the Arabs on matters of regional development, water, refugee welfare and arms control also took place in different world capitals. However, aside from the notable fact that the adversaries were at last confronting each other across a conference table and that the conferences droned on until the summer of 1993, very little progress on any of the issues of the Israeli-Arab dispute was recorded.

The hard-line right wing parties that were part of Shamir's coalition[4] objected to Shamir even considering peace concessions to the Arabs, especially to the Palestinians. In a typically self-destructive, but ideologically righteous move, these parties withdrew from the government, forcing Shamir to call for Knesset elections to take place in June of 1992. After the usual acrimonious and personal battle between Peres and Rabin for leadership of the Labor Party, Rabin emerged victorious. This time, Peres made a conscious effort to reconcile his relations with Rabin and it was a united Labor Party that went to the elections. The Likud itself was badly splintered and Shamir waged an ineffective campaign, lashing out at the Bush administration as an enemy of Israel.

---

3. Shamir later confessed that after the bitter opening session, his strategy at Madrid was only to stall. He was convinced that the Arabs were not ready for a true peace with Israel.

4. Techiya and Moledet.

He was particularly bitter about a proposal that the United States government guarantee ten billion dollars worth of proposed bank loans to Israel, to help finance the absorption of the Soviet Jews in Israel, which was opposed by the Bush administration unless it was contingent on the halting of Israeli settlement activities on the West Bank. (The loan guarantees were eventually approved after Shamir's electoral defeat.)

Labor won the most seats in the election, 44 mandates. Much of Labor's support had come from the new Soviet immigrants who voted overwhelmingly in its favor. Likud fell to 32 seats and Meretz, a new combination of three militantly leftist parties, won twelve mandates. Rabin cobbled together a very narrow coalition, based partly on the tacit support of the five Arab members of Knesset. He was also able to bring Shas into his coalition.[5] Shas emerged with six seats in the Knesset. Rabbi Eliezer Shach had forbidden any of the Chareidi parties — Agudath Israel, Degel HaTorah and Shas — from joining a Labor-led coalition. However, Aryeh Deri, the leader of Shas, with the backing of Rabbi Ovadiah Yosef, disregarded Rabbi Shach's opinion and Shas joined Rabin's coalition government, giving it some parliamentary stability. Rabin had a reputation in Israel as a security-first leader who would not capitulate to Arab demands or threats. Thus, his actions in promoting peace talks with the Palestinians following his election took the Israeli population by surprise.

Post-Zionism Cripples the State

THE ISRAELI LEFT HAD LONG HAD SECRET CONTACTS WITH THE PLO, attempting to forge a settlement of the Arab-Israeli struggle. One of the leading intellectual lights of the Peace Now movement was a protegé of Shimon Peres, Dr. Yossi Beilin. Peres appointed him assistant foreign minister in 1992. Beilin was a brilliant and innovative person, but he possessed radical ideas about the Jewish people and the State of Israel. He was the chief spokesman of the "post-Zionist" movement and the darling of the intellectual elitist Left who, though small in number, wielded hefty influence in the government and media. According to a policy study of the Institute of the World Jewish Congress, Beilin advocated, among other things, the following tenets:

---

5. Shas empowered the Sephardic population in Israel in numerous ways. Many of its members still nursed bitter memories of discrimination by the ruling Ashkenazic powers during the Sephardic absorption into Israeli society in the 1950's and 1960's. Shas provided not only political power to the Sephardim, it also gave them social standing, an independent Sephardic school system, religious leadership and, above all else, a sense of pride and reconnection to their Sephardic heritage.

"Zionism was not the culmination of 2,000 years of the Jewish dream to return to Zion. It was simply a response to anti-Semitism. In fact, the Land of Israel was only a fallback, even as a haven for Jews in distress.

"[He argues] that his grandfather, a Russian Chovevei Zion activist, was mistaken to have opposed Theodor Herzl's proposal early in the 20th century to adopt Uganda as a Jewish homeland. Indeed, had Herzl succeeded with Uganda, Dr. Beilin maintains that the Jews of Europe might have been saved from the Shoah.

"*Aliyah* does not provide a solution to the Jewish problem. In fact, four times more Israelis emigrate to America than Americans make *aliyah*, and it is more dangerous for a Jew to live in Israel than in the Diaspora. But Israel's future is secure in contrast to the Diaspora.

"Israelis need not be concerned as to whether their children will remain Jews. Many Jews, however, fear that Israel is evolving into a right wing and religious version of the old ghetto. [Dr. Beilin maintains] that the Orthodox stranglehold on Jewish life in Israel must be terminated by religious pluralism.

"Although the era of Jewish communities in distress is over, the era of Jewish population decline is underway. Intermarriage and a low birth rate will reduce the number of Diaspora Jews. To compensate for these losses, we must find creative ways to accept those who are not halachically Jewish, as well as those who do not undergo religious conversion. As Dr. Beilin views the Jewish people as a club, he believes that the simplest way to resolve the problem of affiliation is to provide membership of the Jewish people through a secular conversion. Such a conversion would depend on an applicant's self-definition as a Jew, or possibly on a referral by two members of the Jewish community 'as is customary … when joining a club.'

"The outdated Zionist organizations should be dissolved and replaced with a new international Jewish umbrella group based on a partnership between America and Israel, and would subsequently be expanded to include the remaining 20% of Diaspora Jewry living outside of the United States. The new umbrella group would promote programs such as 'Birthright,' which aims to provide every Jewish youngster with a free visit to Israel.

"Jewish education will be globalized through the Internet. Israelis and Diaspora Jews should jointly launch a 'peace corps' type aid program for the Third World, which will enable the Jewish people in the 21st century to become 'a light unto the nations.'"[6]

---

6. *Policy Study Number 21*, Institute of the World Jewish Congress, authored by Isi Liebler, Jerusalem, 2000, pp.6-7.

Shimon Peres

The Left, as represented by Beilin, saw the achievement of peace with the Palestinians as a means towards a greater end – a new, secular, less Jewish Israel and a new Middle East – and not as an end in itself. And that eventual end was so important to the Left that the means to achieve it — the "peace process" itself — could be justified, no matter what the actual cost. Rabin and Peres, however, saw the achievement of peace with the Arabs as an end in itself. Not every end justifies every cost, so both Rabin and Peres initially were more cautious regarding the "peace process" and its chances for long term success.[7]

Peace Now, Peace Not

THE "PEACE PROCESS" TOOK ON A LIFE OF ITS OWN. THE VISION OF the Left and Peace Now prevailed, and both Rabin and Peres soon succumbed to it. In August 1993, Israel and the PLO agreed on a "Declaration of Principles" — known as the Oslo Accords — that Rabin dutifully brought to the Knesset for approval. With the government coalition of 62 mandates, plus five Arab mandates holding firm, approval was won. The Oslo Accords gave the PLO empowerment in the West Bank and Gaza with a view toward an independent Palestinian state in the Arab-populated areas of Israel in five years. The Gaza Strip and Jericho would be transferred to PLO control. Israel would also transfer tax monies on a regular basis to support the new Palestinian entity and would arm a Palestinian police force of no more than 12,000 people. The right wing parties protested vehemently to the agreements. They warned of greater violence, of the "Palestinization" of Israel's own Arab population, of a Palestinian army that would use Israel's weapons against Israel and of the untrustworthiness of Arafat and the PLO. But it was all to no avail: Israel and most of Diaspora Jewry, encouraged by American President Bill Clinton, were swept away in a mood of euphoria, refusing to see any downside to the Oslo Accords.

Over time, the presumptions upon which the Oslo Accords were based unfortunately were proven inaccurate. Among those presumptions were that Arafat and the PLO truly wanted peace, were willing to recognize Israel's right to exist, and would do what they could to limit Arab violence and terrorism against Israel. Although Arafat never once explicitly articulated these goals, the Israelis were somehow convinced that the Palestinian view of the final settlement would be reasonable and that such delicate issues as the status of Jerusalem, the annexation of Jewish settle-

---

7. Rabin repeatedly told American visitors who expressed to him their concern about handing over territory in exchange for promises that if it did not work out, "we will go back and take it away again." Later events showed the naiveté and wishful thinking of that statement.

ments to Israel, the resettlement of the Palestinian refugees and the final borders of the Palestinian state would all be amenable to reasonable compromise and settlement. On the schedule devised in Oslo, the easy points were to be talked over first, leaving such thorny issues as the right of return and Jerusalem to be discussed later — after the Palestinian Authority would be armed and in possession of territory.

The Israelis viewed the publicly stated maximalist PLO demands regarding the sovereignty of the Arabs over Jerusalem and the full return of Palestinian refugees to their homes only as opening negotiating gambits, not as serious policy positions. This presumption regarding the true nature of the Palestinian demands was badly in error. Israel, through Rabin and Peres, convinced itself that *this* time Arafat could be trusted. They chose to ignore all of Arafat's bloodthirsty diatribes against Israel that he continued to make in his Arabic speeches to his people, believing instead his more soothing, semi-peaceful English rhetoric. Arafat was thereby resurrected as a major player in the Middle East. The PLO, which had declined precipitously in influence, prestige and power, even in the perception of its own Palestinian constituency, was now officially elevated as the recognized and exclusive "government" of the Palestinian people. Arafat and the PLO were saved from political and economic oblivion and isolation by the Oslo Accords. Thus Israel plunged ahead hopefully into the very murky waters of the "peace process," a sequence that was to consume Israeli attention for the remainder of the decade.

The Oslo Accords were officially signed on the lawn of the White House in Washington, D.C. on September 13, 1993, and Rabin and Arafat awkwardly shook hands under Bill Clinton's prodding.[8] In a most moving address, Rabin, the gruff, taciturn soldier, poured out his heart to Arafat and said:

"We are destined to live together, on the same soil in the same land. We, the soldiers who have returned from battle stained with blood, we who have seen our relatives and friends killed before our eyes, we who have attended their funerals and cannot look in the eyes of parents and orphans, we who have come from a land where parents bury their children, we who have fought against you, the Palestinians — We say to you today in a loud and clear voice: Enough of blood and tears. Enough. We harbor no hatred towards you. We have no desire for revenge. We, like you, are people who want to build a home, plant a tree, love, live side by

---

8. At the last moment, Arafat balked at signing and demanded certain revisions to the agreement. The Americans angrily refused this tactic and forced him to go ahead with the signing and the attendant public ceremony. It was a tactic that Arafat would use again in future scheduled agreement-signings with Israel.

side with you — in dignity, in empathy, as human beings, as free men. We are today giving peace a chance and saying to you: Enough. Let us pray that a day will come when we all will say: 'Farewell to arms.'"

It should be noted that Arafat did not make any such speech in return. Nevertheless, the handshake between Rabin and Arafat, though forced on them by the American president, came to symbolize the new "peace process" that would finally bring a century of Arab-Jewish violence to an end.

There were many in the Arab camp and in the Israeli state who opposed the Oslo Accords. There were fundamentalist Islamic organizations such as Hamas and Islamic Jihad who denied the right of the PLO to negotiate with Israel. These organizations continued to demand the complete destruction of the "Zionist entity." Arafat tried various policies of inclusion and exclusion with these organizations. It was always a matter of debate whether Arafat was actually working in collaboration with these organizations or not. In any event, Hamas and Islamic Jihad continued to carry on a terror campaign against Israel throughout the balance of the decade, killing more than 500 Jews. The PLO did not take any effective measures to destroy the terrorist infrastructure and/or curb the violence. Officially, the signing of the Oslo Accords ended the intifada, but Arab violence continued. Within a year, the intifada claimed 1,225 Arab lives. Of these, 528 Arabs were killed by other Arabs to settle personal or political scores. These Arab deaths were officially categorized by the PLO as "justice meted out to collaborators."

Among Israelis, there were also many who opposed the "peace process" and resorted to violence to thwart it. This was not a new idea. In the 1980's, an underground organization of Jews was discovered whose members had killed or maimed a number of leading Arab political figures in the West Bank. The members of this group were arrested, tried and sentenced to substantial prison terms. On February 25, 1994, Dr. Baruch Goldstein, under the impression, it was later claimed, that he believed the Arabs were planning an attack on the Hebron Jewish community, killed 29 Arabs in the mosque of the Cave of Machpelah, before he was killed by the other Arab worshippers.[9] Arafat immediately broke off negotiations with the Israelis. In retaliation to Goldstein's act, two passenger buses in the heart of Israel (in the towns of Afula and Hadera) were attacked by Arab suicide bombers, killing fourteen Jews and wound-

---

9. Dr. Goldstein's act seemed incongruous with his previous behavior and personality. He was a well-known physician whose compassion for his patients, Jews and Arabs alike, was recognized. In retrospect, it is clear that his act of violence tore the fabric of the "peace process" before it could be substantially fashioned.

ing scores more. Rabin, paraphrasing Ben-Gurion's comment on the British White Paper of 1939, stated: "We will pursue the 'peace process' as though there was no terror. We will pursue the eradication of terror as though there was no 'peace process.'" In the wake of the killings in Hebron, United Nations observers were stationed there to help calm the situation. But Hebron remained a flash point of Arab-Israeli violence for the rest of the century.

On May 4, 1994, the agreement that was reached in Washington was finalized by a detailed document and series of maps that were to be signed by both parties in Cairo, Egypt. Once again Arafat haggled to the end, refusing to sign the maps. Rabin would not sign the agreement until Arafat signed the maps. Though Arafat eventually signed, under Egyptian and American pressure, the incident gave the Israeli public some pause as to his true intentions. Just a few days later, speaking in Arabic in South Africa, Arafat gave a fiery address proclaiming a continuing *jihad* (holy war) against Israel to "liberate Jerusalem."

Again, the Peace Now supporters tried to soothe the doubts of the Israeli public, saying that Arafat's rhetoric was meant only for domestic Arab consumption and in no way reflected his true intent to make a final peace with Israel on mutually reasonable terms. But half of Israel did not trust Arafat and opposed the continuation of a "peace process" that gave up hard territory, money and weapons to the Palestinians in exchange for unfulfilled promises of controlling acts of terror. The PLO was also supposed to officially change its charter, which called for Israel's destruction, and to stop all propaganda and incitement against Israel in its media and in its school curriculums. None of these steps were fulfilled by the PLO. Rabin's razor-thin majority in the Knesset was now based on the support of the Arab parties. It marked the first time in Israeli political history that the Knesset disregarded its unwritten rule that no security or national interest issues would be decided by a majority which depended upon Arab votes.

A RAB TERROR CONTINUED UNABATED THROUGHOUT 1994 AND 1995. Israeli soldiers were kidnapped and murdered, while all Israeli and Diaspora Jews mourned. Suicide bombers continued to blow up buses and attack bystanders at bus stops. The Palestinian street cheered each of these atrocities. Rabin halted negotiations with the PLO after every terrorist incident, but always returned dutifully to the bargaining table a short time later. The opposition parties in the Knesset demanded a halt to the entire "peace process," claiming that Arafat was a liar and a murderer and not a fit partner for any meaningful peace agreement. Yet, Rabin and Peres pushed doggedly on with the negotiations, convinced that if a peace

Rabin Enters Dangerous Waters

arrangement with the Palestinians could be made, the Israeli public would accept it no matter how onerous the concessions. Rabin did not help the tenor of public discussion when he called the Gush Emunim camp, which was bitterly opposed to his policies, "crybabies." The violent and vociferous public demonstrations of the opposition increased.

Israeli society was torn apart by the "peace process" issue. The "Women in Black" regularly protested the Israeli presence in the West Bank and in Gaza. The "Women in Green" angrily protested the continuation of the "peace process" itself. The division extended to the entire Jewish world. Raging debates and harsh words were the order of the day among American Jews and throughout the Diaspora over this issue, which both sides perceived as being of life-and-death importance.

Prime Minister Rabin speaking with King Hussein in the Royal Palace in Amman

Parallel to the Palestinian negotiations, talks were held with Jordan regarding a peace treaty between the two countries. King Hussein, suffering from the cancer that would soon cause his demise, was anxious to cap his reign with a final agreement that would leave Jordan at peace. Shimon Peres had negotiated the outline of the agreement with Prince Hassan, the King's brother and the then-heir apparent to the throne. The final details of the agreement were settled between Rabin and Hussein at a marathon meeting in Amman on October 16, 1994. On October 26, 1994 the Israel-Jordan peace treaty was signed at Aqaba, the Jordanian twin port to Eilat, on the Red Sea. Israel gave up territory, water rights and other compensation to Jordan under the terms of the peace treaty. There was also a veiled reference in the document to the recognition of Jordanian rights regarding the Moslem holy places in Jerusalem. Jordan committed itself to peace with Israel, economic cooperation and mutual security arrangements. The peace with Jordan began as a very warm one. President Clinton attended the ceremony and Rabin went for a sail with Hussein on the king's royal yacht.

Peace with Jordan did not guarantee, unfortunately, that all would remain calm on the eastern border of Israel. In March 1997, a deranged Jordanian soldier opened fire and killed seven Israeli schoolgirls on the "Island of Peace" in the Jordan River. Hussein himself traveled to Israel to pay a condolence call to the bereaved families. The visit made a strong impression on all Israelis and helped bolster Hussein's image as a true peacemaker. It also served to outline in Israeli minds the strong difference between Hussein's talk and behavior and that of Yassir Arafat.

With Hussein's death and the accession of his son Abdullah to the throne — instead of his more conciliatory brother, Hassan — in February 1999, the Jordanian peace became a very lukewarm affair. King Abdullah came under strong pressure from the majority Palestinian population living in Jordan and he took a decidedly colder stance towards Israel. As a result, Israeli-Jordanian diplomatic and economic relations deteriorated. There were open calls in Jordan for the abrogation of the peace treaty with Israel only a few short years after it had been signed.

The Turbulent Tide of Bloody Protest

O N SEPTEMBER 28, 1995, RABIN RETURNED TO MEET ARAFAT IN Washington to sign a new interim agreement, dubbed the Oslo II Accords. It gave the PLO control over 96% of the Palestinians living in Gaza and the West Bank. It also transferred all of the major Palestinian towns and cities on the West Bank, as well as considerably more territory, to PLO control. In turn, Israel received much the same promises that had been included in the agreements of Oslo I — a determined effort to uproot the infrastructure of terror, a halt to propaganda incitement against Israel and economic and security cooperation. None of these PLO promises had been fulfilled by them in the first years of the "peace process," but Israel hoped that somehow things would change for the better after the signing of the Oslo II documents. The right wing members of the Knesset howled with rage over the new agreements.[10] President Ezer Weizman, himself a dove on peace issues, stated that the Oslo II agreement had been concluded "too quickly and without sleep."[11]

Rabin and Peres were openly called "traitors" by their political opponents. Automobiles of government ministers were stoned. Large, vociferous street demonstrations against the agreement occurred in Jerusalem and Tel Aviv. Posters showing Rabin wearing Arafat's kafiyah headdress were widely disseminated throughout the country. Even posters of Rabin wearing a Nazi SS uniform were circulated. The "peace process" created

President Ezer Weizman

---

10. Rechavem Zeevi, the head of the Moledet party, said: "This is an insane government that has decided to commit national suicide." Binyamin Netanyahu, the head of Likud, stated: "It is absurd that we are entrusting our security to Yassir Arafat. Gaza has become a safe haven for terrorists."

11. Gilbert, *Israel*, p.585.

a terrible climate of division, distrust and demonization in Israeli society. It would soon breed tragic violence as well.

On October 6, 1995, the Knesset approved the Oslo II agreements by the barest of margins, 61-59. What made this vote particularly galling was that this majority was attained by the votes of the Arab parties and by the defection of a Knesset member of a right wing, anti-peace process party, Alex Goldfarb, to vote with the government coalition in favor of the accords. MK Goldfarb was amply rewarded for his newly found love of peace: He was appointed a deputy minister and received a new government car for his use. Ezer Weizman opined that it was "Goldfarb's Mitsubishi" that passed Oslo II in the Knesset.

Despite the slim margin of approval, Rabin and Peres were now so convinced that the "peace process" would be good for Israel that nothing could deter them from pursuing it, no matter what the moral or human cost. Arab terror attacks had not abated and public pronouncements by Arab leaders urging the destruction of Israel had not been muted. Nevertheless, where the "process" would lead seemed less important than keeping the "process" going at all costs. And the cost would prove to be quite substantial.

In response to the continuing demonstrations against the "process," the government coalition and Peace Now organized a large rally in Tel Aviv in its support. The rally took place on Saturday night, November 4, 1995. Yitzchak Rabin spoke to the gathering:

> This is a course which is fraught with difficulties and pain. For Israel, there is no path without pain. But the path of peace is preferable to the path of war. I say this to you, as one who was a military man, someone who is today minister of defense and sees the pain of the families of the IDF soldiers. For them, for our children, in my case for our grandchildren, I want this government to exhaust every opening, every possibility, to promote and achieve a comprehensive peace. Even with Syria, it will be possible to make peace.[12]

These were to be his last public words. As Rabin was leaving the rally to get into his waiting automobile, a Jew named Yigal Amir shot him at point blank range. Rabin died shortly thereafter and the Jewish world went into traumatic shock.

Rabin's funeral in Jerusalem was attended by King Hussein, President Mubarak of Egypt, the prime minister of Morocco, cabinet ministers from the Gulf States, the queen of the Netherlands, the prince of Wales, and the president of the United States. At the conclusion of his

---

12. Ibid., p.587.

The family of slain Prime Minister Yitzchak Rabin watches as his coffin is carried from the Knesset en route to burial at Mount Herzl in Jerusalem

eulogy, President Clinton uttered two Hebrew words that came to represent the tragedy of Rabin's assassination — *"Shalom, chaver."*

Rabin's assassin was a university law student, a former yeshivah student and an active right wing opponent of the "peace process." He expressed no remorse for his murderous act, believing that Rabin's death would abort the Oslo agreements. Tried and convicted by an Israeli court for murder, he was given a life sentence in prison. Because Amir was a religious Jew, a bitter backlash against all religious Jews ensued, fueled by the anguished acrimony of the Left and Peace Now.[13] Contrary to Amir's warped hopes, the assassination gave greater impetus to the "peace process." Shimon Peres succeeded Rabin as head of the Labor party and as prime minister. He was more determined than ever to push the "peace process" to a speedy conclusion. The acts of both Goldstein and Amir, born out of rage over their perception of the betrayal of Israel's true interests, only strengthened the very policies that they attempted to undermine by their violence.

---

13. Rabin's widow, Leah Rabin, stated that she would prefer that her descendants marry Arabs rather than religious Jews. She refused to acknowledge Binyamin Netanyahu's condolences at the funeral and publicly snubbed his outstretched hand.

Further progress of the "peace process" was decisively endangered by Arab terrorism. In early 1996, a wave of terrorist bombings killed tens of Israelis on crowded city buses in Jerusalem and Tel Aviv. Israel had assassinated the leading bomb maker in the Palestinian territories, Yahiya Ayash, and his cohorts responded with a vengeance. The wave of bombings that swept Israel brought a bitter comment from Shimon Peres himself. Reciting all of the territorial and economic concessions that Israel had made to the PLO thus far in the peace effort, Peres concluded: "Instead of thanks, we got bombs." More than one hundred Jews were killed in this wave of bombings and five hundred more were wounded, many severely and permanently. Peres himself felt the pressure of the Israeli public on him to do something to stop the violence. The words of King David in Psalms 120 seemed to describe the situation exactly — "When I speak of peace, they are still for war."

Another front opened against Israel at the southern Lebanese border. Hezbollah, the Iranian and Syrian backed guerilla army, launched mortar and rocket attacks across the border at Israeli towns and cities in the Galilee. Peres responded harshly and decisively. In what was operationally called "Grapes of Wrath," the Israeli artillery and air force pounded southern Lebanon for seventeen consecutive days. More than 125 Lebanese civilians were killed in the bombardment, as well as an undetermined number of Hezbollah fighters. Under strong pressure and condemnation from the United States and the United Nations, Israel agreed to an understanding that it would limit its retaliatory acts to purely military objectives[14] while Hezbollah would refrain from firing its katyusha rockets at the Galilee. Even with the "Grapes of Wrath" understandings, the border with Lebanon was constantly lit up with the firing of guns and artillery between the sides. Syria, which demanded an agreement by Israel for complete withdrawal from the Golan Heights, was interested in keeping the Lebanese border hot as a means of pressuring Israel to accept its terms.

Netanyahu Raises Hopes

IN MAY 1996, ELECTIONS FOR THE KNESSET TOOK PLACE. COMPLICATING matters, Israel had passed a law mandating the election of the prime minister directly and no longer through parliamentary party agreements. This new law pitted Shimon Peres and Binyamin Netanyahu against each other in the race for prime minister. The hard fought election campaign opened all of the wounds in Israeli society: secular vs. religious, Left vs.

---

14. This soon became an impossible condition to fulfill because Hezbollah located its storage depots and rocket positions in the midst of civilian areas, even next to hospitals and schools.

Right, Gush Emunim vs. Peace Now, Sephardi vs. Ashkenazi. Though exit polls and early vote projections indicated a Peres victory, the final result showed that Netanyahu had received 29,457 more votes than Peres; this out of a total of 2,972,589 ballots cast.

Labor won 34 seats in the Knesset, while Likud won 32 seats. Shas now occupied ten seats, up from six; Mafdal remained at five with United Torah Judaism at four. The new Russian immigrants' party, Yisrael B'Aliyah, gained ten seats. Avigdor Kahlani, a hero of battle on the Golan Heights, led the new Third Way party to four seats on a platform that encouraged peace, but without relinquishing the Golan Heights. The Third Way included Meimad and one of its Knesset members was a leading religious intellectual of Meimad. From these disparate parties, Netanyahu cobbled together a governing coalition. From the outset, his government was beset with both external and internal problems.

Netanyahu was a gifted public speaker, in both Hebrew and English. He had been an excellent UN representative for Israel under Shamir's government and appeared regularly in the American media as an articulate and clever defender of Israel's positions. He was also a skilled campaigner, and these combined talents helped him win the office of prime minister. His victory was not seen in Israel nor the world at large as a repudiation of the Oslo agreements, but rather as a wish for better security arrangements for Israel while the peace talks continued.

Prime Minister Netanyahu meets with Jordan's King Hussein

Netanyahu's finest hour came at the beginning of his administration when he addressed the United States Congress in Washington, D.C. He pointed out that any agreement had to be based on reciprocity, and that Arafat had yet to live up to any part of his side of the bargain. He also reminded the Congress and the public that there was not one Arab nation that operated under a system of democracy and personal and economic freedom. If democratic governments were not forthcoming in the Arab world, the chances for a just and lasting peace with them were minimal. He asked America to be understanding of Israel's position and not be blinded to the realities of the Middle East by the rosy vision of peace. He also promised to phase out American aid, an important pillar of his early popularity. Netanyahu won a standing ovation at the conclusion of his speech. However, he was unable to deliver on his promises of firmness, security, reciprocity and caution. He, too, sank in the quicksand of the "peace process."

One of Netanyahu's major confrontations with Palestinian ire occurred in Jerusalem. For years, Israeli archeologists had worked at uncovering the foundation to the Temple Mount and the Western Wall. They conducted the work in a tunnel running alongside much of the length of the Western Wall, which dated back to the days of the Hasmonean kings, almost 22 centuries earlier. The tunnel excavation was finally completed in the fall of 1996, and an exit from the tunnel into the Moslem Quarter of the Old City of Jerusalem was opened to facilitate tourist traffic in the tunnel. The tunnel opening was done quietly and without prior notice to the Palestinians. As soon as the tunnel was opened, hysterical statements that this was phase one of a Jewish plot to destroy the mosques on the Temple Mount enraged the Arab population, and the Palestinians responded with a renewal of the intifada. In the ensuing Arab riots, fifteen Israeli soldiers were killed, as were 56 Arab rioters. To get the "peace process" back on track, the American government pressed hard on the Netanyahu coalition to conclude an agreement with Arafat regarding the city of Hebron. The so-called "Hebron Treaty" was signed on January 17, 1997. It gave the Palestinians control over the city, except for the Jewish suburb of Kiryat Arba and a small Jewish enclave in the heart of Hebron in which Jews had lived before the Arab pogrom of 1929. Netanyahu also agreed to withdraw from additional parts of the West Bank and to make further withdrawals in mid-1998. These concessions, while in no way satisfying the Arabs, angered the right wing parties in Netanyahu's coalition and his government teetered on the verge of instability.

The new prime minister was also handicapped by a credibility problem. His fellow cabinet members criticized him openly and often for apparent deviousness and a lack of consistency. His administration was also haunted by continued tinges of scandal, real or imagined by political opponents and a very hostile Israeli press. Aryeh Deri, the head of Shas, had been accused of bribery and misuse of public funds. Netanyahu had appointed Roni Bar-On as attorney general. The Israeli media charged that Bar-On's appointment was part of a political deal between

Aryeh Deri (center) in the Knesset

Netanyahu and Shas, whereby Bar-On would dismiss the case against Deri in return for Shas support of the Hebron Agreement. Bar-On resigned after only a few days in office. A police investigation recommended prosecution of Deri, as well as Justice Minister Zachi Hanegbi, Chief of Staff Avigdor Lieberman and Netanyahu himself. The state prosecutor eventually recommended indicting only Deri in this scandal, but the report issued contained a scathing criticism of Netanyahu's behavior in the matter. Though Netanyahu claimed that the whole matter was a conspiracy of the media and the opposition parties to discredit him, his public standing was sorely diminished by the affair.

In June 1997, the Labor party held primary elections for leadership of the party after Peres' defeat in the elections a year earlier. Ehud Barak, a protegé of Yitzchak Rabin, was chosen to head the party and to be its candidate for prime minister in the next election. Barak, a former IDF chief of staff, was Israel's most decorated soldier. He was a man of great intelligence and supreme self-confidence. He had been an opponent of the original Oslo Accords when they were signed, and gave the impression of being more to the right within the ideological spectrum of the Labor party. He defeated Yossi Beilin for the leadership of Labor, promising economic growth, internal and external security for Israel, and a final peace with the Arabs as his platform for the next election campaign. He would soon have an opportunity to deliver on his promises.

The Netanyahu government continued its policy of expanding Jewish housing in the existing Jewish towns and settlements on the West Bank and in Gaza. In Jerusalem, it approved the beginning of construction for new Jewish neighborhoods at Har Choma. This caused a worldwide uproar among opponents of increased Jewish settlement. But Netanyahu stood his ground, despite the intense displeasure of the American State Department. Netanyahu stated in an interview given to *The Times* of London: "Mr. Arafat must tell his people openly and squarely that peace will not be achieved on the 1967 lines. Israel will not reduce itself to a fragile ghetto state on the Mediterranean shores."[15]

Yet Netanyahu was caught in a trap between the Right in his own coalition and the vociferous opposition to him and his policies of the Left in the Knesset. A number of his cabinet ministers and staff — Don Meridor, David Levy, Avigdor Lieberman and others — resigned during his tenure as prime minister because of personal feuds and policy disagreements, or because of the taint of scandal. Ideologues who represented Gush Emunim without compromise or moderation never forgave Netanyahu for the Hebron Agreements. He was finding it increasingly difficult to govern over such a fractious government coalition and a bitterly divided Knesset.

The American secretary of state during President Clinton's second term in office was Madeline Albright, who had served very successfully as the American representative to the United Nations. Although she was descended from Czech Jews who had escaped Hitler's Europe, she was

---

15. Gilbert, p.609.

raised as a Christian and did not acknowledge her Jewish roots until journalists discovered her background after her appointment as secretary of state. Albright enthusiastically endorsed President Clinton's belief that a peace agreement between Israel and the Palestinians was possible under the framework of the Oslo Accords. Employing the skills of three American Middle East specialists, all of whom were Jews — Dennis Ross, Martin Indyk and Aaron Miller — intensive pressure was brought to bear on both Arafat and Netanyahu to meet at the Wye River Plantation in Maryland for negotiations. Israel's foreign minister in 1998 was Ariel Sharon. Under heated coalition squabbling and virulent criticism from the opposition parties, Prime Minister Netanyahu made an agreement at Wye that granted further land to the Palestinians in return for further promises to "fight terror" and live up to the promises that the PLO had made in the previous Oslo agreements.

Israel had suffered from a number of botched Mossad operations against the Palestinians and its failed attempted assassination of a Hamas leader on Jordanian territory was particularly embarrassing and costly. It had also sustained a number of blows to its military image by a disastrous collision of two helicopters, killing 72 men, and by its inability to contain Hezbollah attacks on Israeli troops in southern Lebanon and on civilian settlements in the Galilee. To assuage the wrath of King Hussein for the failed Mossad assassination attempt on Jordanian soil, Israel was forced to release Shiekh Ahmed Yassin, the spiritual head of Hamas, from prison as a quid pro quo for the return of its captured secret agents in Jordan. Israel's vaunted reputation for military deterrents and espionage expertise was slowly eroding.

As before, the American government protested Israeli building in Jerusalem's Har Choma area. Albright openly stated that Israel should stop confiscating Arab land, stop demolishing Palestinian homes and stop building in East Jerusalem and the West Bank. She also piously hoped that the Palestinian Authority would act more vigorously to deter terrorism and arrest those terrorists in its control. Israel denied these charges, pointing out that building was initiated on land that was either ownerless or that had been bought from Arabs.

During the entire period from Oslo to the end of the decade, the Palestinian Authority maintained a "revolving door" policy towards arresting terrorists. It did arrest many of them and imprison some of them, but it then quietly released most of them after a short period of time, allowing them to continue their terrorist activities against Israel. Cooperation between the Palestinian police and the Israeli police regarding anti-terrorism was spotty, Arafat turning it on and off as the situation suited him: This, despite the fact that police cooperation was one of the prime "accomplishments" of the Oslo Accords from the Israeli point of view. It should be noted, however, that despite the poor record of cooperation, the number of terrorist attacks and resulting Israeli casualties during the time of the Netanyahu government was much lower than it had been during the previous Rabin-Peres rule.

THE OLD DIVISIVE ISSUE OF "WHO IS A JEW" REVIVED IN FURY DURING this decade, which saw a flood of non-Jewish immigrants from the Soviet Union into Israel. The Chief Rabbinate, in accordance with *halachah* and traditional practice, required proof that an immigrant's mother was Jewish before allowing that person to be registered as Jewish. This raised serious problems for these immigrants, many of whom were non-Jewish. The Russian immigrant parties clamored to reduce the role of the rabbis in this matter, or to at least lower the bar of proof necessary to be declared a Jew.

Who's Not a Jew

A lighted match was thrown into this tinderbox from an unexpected direction. An ill-advised news conference in New York, called by some members of the Union of Orthodox Rabbis of the United States and Canada,[16] proclaimed the illegitimacy of the Conservative and Reform movements to represent Judaism in light of their public abandonment of *halachah* and tradition. Misled by a misinterpretation of the statement in the *Los Angeles Times*, media worldwide erroneously proclaimed that the rabbis said that Orthodoxy did not recognize Jews who belonged to the Conservative or Reform movements as being Jews. A firestorm of protest raged all over the Jewish world, and no amount of Orthodox explanation could dampen the rage and enmity caused by this event.

In addition, the Israeli Supreme Court had given the Knesset an ultimatum to pass a "Who is a Jew" bill or the Court itself would decide the matter. The extreme activism and patently anti-religious bias of the Court under the leadership of Chief Justice Aharon Barak frightened and embittered the religious public in Israel: There was no doubt which way the Court would rule on "Who is a Jew." The Reform and Conservative movements mounted an intensive campaign to have their conversions and rabbis recognized by the Israeli Chief Rabbinate. They were abetted by the secular parties who saw this as an opportunity to diminish the influence and power of the religious establishment in Israel.

The government appointed a commission to try to deal with this explosive issue, under the threat of some Reform and Conservative leaders to boycott support for Israel unless it granted their demands. This

---

16. By the 1990's, this organization was only a shell of its former self, with most American Orthodox rabbis not affiliated with or participating in it.

commission was headed by Yaakov Neeman, an Orthodox Jew and a well-respected attorney who later would serve as treasury minister. The commission finally advocated a system of conversions whereby "schools for conversion" would include Conservative and Reform teachers, but that the actual conversion procedure would remain in the hands of the Chief Rabbinate. Although there were appeals to the Supreme Court by Orthodox, Conservative and Reform leaders, as well as complaints about the implementation of this system, the Neeman compromise still remains in place at the time of this writing in 2001. The divisive issue of "Who is a Jew"[17] had been again diffused, albeit only temporarily, as in the past.

The entire issue of "pluralism," as the Conservative and Reform thrust for recognition and power now was called, was further exacerbated by the secular parties sponsoring Reform and Conservative representatives to the Religious Councils of many municipalities, including Jerusalem, in place of the secular representation that was there previously. The Orthodox representatives fell into this political trap and attempted to circumvent these appointments by either preventing a quorum to be present for the meetings of the councils or by brazenly defying the law and ignoring the appointments. This issue regarding the Religious Councils was also resolved by pragmatic compromise, but the bitterness engendered by the pluralism struggle in Israel poisoned the atmosphere of inter-Jewish relationships in Jewish communities throughout the world.

Netanyahu's government ended in 1999, his coalition badly fractured. Key members of his cabinet resigned, often publicly and brandishing strong recriminations. The parties on the Right, engaging in the ideologically correct suicidal behavior which they had learned from their compatriots on the Left, withdrew from his coalition because of the Wye Agreement. In the election of May 1999, Ehud Barak of the "One Israel" party was elected prime minister over Netanyahu by a very convincing 12% margin. Netanyahu thereupon retired from the active political scene and resigned from the Knesset. In the concurrent Knesset elections, Barak's One Israel party[18] won 31 seats, Likud nineteen, Shas seventeen, Meretz ten, the Russian parties ten, the Arab parties ten, Shinui[19] six, United Torah Judaism five, Mafdal five, the Center Party[20] four and the right wing

---

17. Rabbi Yisrael Meir Lau, the Ashkenazic Chief Rabbi, made the ironic comment that the issue was not so much "Who is a Jew" as it is "Who is a Rabbi."

18. One Israel was composed of the Labor Party, Gesher and Meimad.

19. A militantly anti-religious party headed by television personality and Holocaust survivor Tommy Lapid.

20. Composed of Likud defectors Ronny Milo, Don Meridor, Yitzchak Mordechai and Rabin's daughter, Dalia Rabin-Philosof.

National Unity Party four seats. Barak formed a coalition government consisting of One Israel, Shas, Yisrael B'Aliyah, Meretz and the Center Party. Mafdal and United Torah Judaism were also part of the government. With the additional support of the ten Arab Knesset members, Barak began with a very large majority in the Knesset. He possessed a mandate from the Israeli public to pursue his campaign promises of obtaining a peace agreement with Syria; withdrawing Israeli forces from Lebanon; completing the "peace process" with Arafat and the Palestinians; slicing Israeli unemployment and creating 300,000 new jobs; solving the yeshivah draft problem and other contentious social issues.

Lightning Hits the Chareidi World

In order for this overly ambitious program to approach reality, Barak needed the continuing cooperation of many differing forces, especially the parliamentary representatives of the Israeli Arabs. This cooperation was not forthcoming. Barak was a loner, a supremely self-confident and precise person. However, he was a babe in the political woods of Israel: As one who took almost no one into his confidence, he did not build the trust needed to cement the support he needed. His coalition of Meretz and Shas, which were at opposite extremes, was an impossibility from the beginning. Yossi Sarid, the head of Meretz, was appointed as minister of education and attempted "affirmative action" policies on behalf of the Arab and secular school systems at the expense of the religious school systems. The religious parties, particularly Shas, complained that it was they who needed "affirmative action," since the religious school systems had been systematically discriminated against from the beginning of the state. The Shas school system, Mayan HaTorah, had a very large deficit and despite repeated government promises, the monies to relieve the pressure of that deficit were doled out only partially and haphazardly. Shas therefore was always halfway out of Barak's coalition, even when it was officially part of his government. The conviction and imprisonment of Aryeh Deri, the former head of Shas, during Barak's tenure also weakened his hold on Shas cooperation.

Barak also advocated what journalists dubbed a "secular revolution" during his time in office. Such a revolution would break the *status quo* in religion-state matters that had been in place for the entire history of Israel. The planned "civil revolution," among other innovations, provided for civil marriage and divorce; "pluralism" (i.e. inclusion of Conservative and Reform) in the Rabbinate; removal of Sabbath restrictions on public travel and business; permission for El Al to fly on the Sabbath; and the full drafting of Israeli yeshivah students.

Earlier, Barak had appointed a commission headed by former Supreme Court Justice Tal, empowering it to arrive at a solution to the contentious and emotional issue of the draft of yeshivah students to the IDF. This commission acted in the shadow of a Supreme Court decision ordering the Knesset to solve the problem by the early part of the year 2000. The Tal Commission presented a compromise solution to the problem: It would allow yeshivah students to study in a yeshivah until their mid-twenties. Each then would have the option of committing himself to a lifetime of Torah study, or to service in the army or national service work for a limited time. This service would allow the former yeshivah student to enter the work force, something which most of them were not able to do legally until age 45, under the total deferment policy that then existed. The Tal Commission's report and recommendations were roundly criticized by both the secular parties and by some of the heads of the yeshivah world. The Tal Commission's recommendation passed its first reading in the legislature.[21] But the bill was never brought up for its final readings because of the erosion of support for Barak and his peace policies, as well as Barak's own fluctuating attitude towards the "secular revolution," which poisoned his relationship with the religious parties and the public.

The question of the role of religion in the State of Israel was as complicated and troublesome as ever, but the lines of secular and religious lifestyles were never as clearly drawn as the extremists on both sides liked to portray them. In 1995, an intensive study of religious life and attitudes in Israel, completed by the Louis Guttman Israel Institute of Applied Social Research, was published. It stated, in part:

"The rhetoric of secular and religious polarization generally used to characterize Israeli society is highly misleading ... Israeli society has a strong traditional bent, and as far as religious practice is concerned ... there is a continuum from the 'strictly observant' to the 'non-observant,' rather than a great divide between a religious minority and a secular majority.

"Israeli Jews are strongly committed to the continuing Jewish character of their society, even while they are selective in the forms of their observance. They believe that public life should respect the tradition but are critical of the '*status quo*' governing state and religion."[22]

---

21. Under Israeli law, a bill proposed in the Knesset requires affirmative votes at each of three readings to take legal effect. Most of the time, the first reading is the crucial test as to whether the bill will eventually pass.

22. *The Jewish Condition* published by the Louis Guttmann Israel Institute of Applied Social Research, New York, 1995, pp.83-84.

Desperate
Concessions
are
Offered...
and
Rebuffed!

Upon taking office, Barak immediately entered into intensive negotiations with both the Syrians and the Palestinians regarding peace treaties. Attempting to play off each against the other, Barak was not successful on either track. President Hafez al-Assad of Syria refused to meet with Barak and sent his dour and insolent foreign minister, Farouk Ashara, to conduct negotiations with Barak and President Clinton. Ashara never shook hands with Barak, nor did he ever dare smile during the long and tough talks. Syria repeated its demand that Israel withdraw from every inch of the Golan and forfeit its early warning station on Mount Hermon. Barak eventually offered Syria everything it demanded, except for a strip of land a few meters wide on the northeastern corner of the Sea of Galilee that Israel needed in order to keep control of the lake itself. He did so out of the deep conviction that a peace treaty with Syria would force the Palestinians to finally make peace with Israel also, ending the Arab-Israeli conflict once and for all. Furthermore, since Syria had always been the most adamant anti-Israel nation among the Arabs, a peace treaty with it would diminish support for Arab terrorism throughout the Moslem world.

Israel was willing to give up the military security that the land buffer of the Golan provided, the water reserves that fed the Jordan and the Sea of Galilee and to dismantle the many Jewish settlements that had been built on the Golan in more than 30 years since the Six Day War. But Syria refused the deal, preferring a state of war to that of peace and normalization. Even a private conference between Assad and Clinton in Geneva failed to soften the Syrian position. The Syrian peace front remained frozen with the death of Hafez al-Assad in early 2000 and the ascent of his son, Bashir, to power.

Rebuffed by Syria, Barak now plunged headlong into negotiations with the Palestinians. But he was rapidly losing control over the government and the Knesset. Foreign Minister David Levy resigned over the negotiations with the Palestinians, charging that Barak's concessions to Arafat were dangerous and counterproductive. In a Knesset election for President of Israel, the Likud candidate, Moshe Katzav, defeated the Labor and government coalition candidate, Shimon Peres.[23] Though there were personal reasons and petty vendettas

Foreign Minister David Levy with Yassir Arafat prior to Levy's resignation from the Barak government

---

23. The previous president, Ezer Weizman, resigned from the office because of a monetary scandal in which he was involved.

involved in this election, the Knesset's message was quite clear: The Nobel Prize-winning architect of the Oslo Accords was no longer viewed as a hero in Israel. Katzav was a religious Jew of Sephardic origin. Although he had served as a minister in previous Likud-led governments, he was not thought to be presidential timber by the media nor by the intellectual elite of the country. His election sent shock waves among the self-proclaimed opinion makers in Israel.

Despite the ongoing Arab violence and Israeli political opposition, Barak and Clinton attempted to forge a conclusive peace settlement. No longer was there discussion of an interim agreement as Oslo had been; the thrust was for nothing less than a final arrangements document that would outline the settlement of all outstanding issues between Israel and the Palestinians. Towards the accomplishment of this goal, Barak and Clinton attempted to enlist the aid of President Mubarak of Egypt and the new King Abdullah of Jordan. Barak's new foreign minister, the dovish Shlomo Ben-Ami, as well as Yossi Beilin, Shimon Peres and Yossi Sarid, supported the dramatic compromises that Barak now, almost recklessly, proposed to the Palestinians.

Dogged by his own personal scandal, President Clinton attempted to leave a presidential legacy of diplomatic achievement: He convened another summit meeting between Arafat and Barak at Camp David in the summer of 2000. Barak there agreed to: relinquish 95% of the West Bank and Gaza; grant the Palestinians control (though not necessarily sovereignty) over East Jerusalem and most of the Old City, including the Temple Mount; exchange Israeli territory in the Negev for the 5% of the West Bank to be annexed to Israel; dismantle one-fifth of the existing Jewish settlements and withdraw from the Jordan Valley. These breathtaking concessions caused consternation even within the Israeli negotiating team at Camp David.

It is possible that Arafat's thinking regarding the negotiations at Camp David were influenced by the hasty and poorly executed total withdrawal of Israel from southern Lebanon some time prior to the talks. Barak had withdrawn the army as per his campaign pledge. The Southern Lebanon Army also was evacuated, though most of its members remained in Lebanon to face charges of collaboration with Israel. The Israeli withdrawal was more like a rout than a redeployment, and fed the impression that Israel had been forced to flee. If Hezbollah could cause this, why not the Palestinian Authority?

Despite this fortuitous event for Arafat, Barak's concessions at Camp David were insufficient to move him. Israel finally began to notice that Arafat had never proposed any counteroffer to Israel's proposals during the entire period of the "peace process." It was as though Israel were only negotiating with itself. After the Camp David summit ended in failure, Barak returned home. In a rare moment of candor, he admitted publicly that there was "no partner for peace."

Barak's desperate willingness to give the Palestinans far more than anticipated exposed him to severely negative political repercussions. Leah Rabin, Yitzchak Rabin's widow who had been the very spirit of the "peace process," stated that "Yitzchak is turning in his grave" at Barak's proposals. Shas, Yisrael B'Aliyah and the Center Party all voiced their objections to Barak's plans and withdrew from the coalition, toppling the Barak government's majority. The Knesset was in an uproar, and motions for new elections filled the air.

Yet, under the influence of Beilin, Ben-Ami and Sarid, Barak almost hypnotically continued negotiations with the Palestinians. President Clinton had originally placed the onus of blame regarding the Camp David debacle on Arafat. Most of the world's press and governments followed that lead. Even in the face of world disapproval, Arafat was not willing to give up on his ultimate goal of destroying the State of Israel, and thus he brooked no compromise on his maximalist demands for the return of the refugees to their pre-1947 homes in Israel, Palestinian sovereignty over Jerusalem and the Temple Mount (including the Western Wall), the dismantling of all Israeli settlements and a return, to the last millimeter, to the 1967 borders. To restore "evenhandedness" in American diplomacy (which had always been an avowed goal), Clinton now followed his initial disparagement of Arafat's behavior with the restoration of Arafat as a worthy partner in the "peace process." Barak and the Peace Now camp dutifully followed suit.

Yet Arafat still faced the loss of diplomatic initiative due to negative world opinion and he resorted to his time-honored tactic — war and terrorism — to regain world sympathy and to unite the Arab world behind him. This time, he planned a renewal of the intifada with live ammunition, not just stones. Arafat sensed that Barak's weak political position

Ariel Sharon at the Western Wall

would enable him to extract even greater concessions, and that the intifada would place great pressure upon an Israel which had grown soft and confused. What was needed was a credible trigger to renewed violence.

In early September 2000, Likud leader Ariel Sharon visited the Temple Mount, a visit which at the time sparked no Arab reaction and, in fact, had been sanctioned by the Moslem Waqf which had religious authority over the Temple Mount. Arafat had found his trigger. Claiming that Israel was out to destroy the mosque on the Temple Mount and that Sharon's visit there was the beginning of the takeover, Arafat called for an "intifada Al-Aksa." On cue, organized armed rioting began in the West Bank and Gaza. When the Israeli army responded in kind, Arafat cruelly sent stone-throwing children into the line of fire. Television cameras recorded the horror of the children being killed, while their parents proclaimed their glory as martyrs. Barak issued threats, ultimatums and warnings to stop the violence, but he was mocked by Arafat, who bluntly told him publicly, "Go to Hell!"

Barak threatened to discontinue negotiations with Arafat as long as the violence persisted. He issued an ultimatum demanding that the violence stop within 48 hours. But the violence did not stop and Barak soon capitulated, returning to the bargaining table to face a newly-triumphant Arafat. Israeli soldiers were lynched by Arab mobs; civilians were killed on the roads. Terrorists who had been held in Palestinian prisons, in a show of cooperation with the Accords, were released by Arafat, and soon buses and cars all over Israel were terrorist targets. The media was filled with bloody scenes of bombings. The Tomb of Joseph in Nablus was captured, its defending Jews murdered. Vandalized by the Arab victors, the tomb was soon turned into a mosque.

Israel was at war with the Palestinians. Nevertheless, the "peace camp" argued with greater intensity that only an agreement would end the violence and that agreement had to be made only with Arafat. The Israeli public, now shocked out of its heartfelt belief in the "peace process," realized that no agreement would be possible with this ruthless leader of the Palestinians. Hundreds of Palestinians had died in the last few months of the century, as had scores of Israelis.

The "peace process," with all of its attached hopes and dreams, was dead to all but the most loyal of its architects. Clinton frantically tried to salvage something from the wreckage, holding conferences in Switzerland and Egypt that produced dramatic cease-fire documents — which were promptly ignored by Arafat. The Palestinian strategy was clear. Arafat wanted to provoke a war that would involve all of the Arab countries against Israel and thus achieve his dream of eliminating the Jewish state entirely. Barak still desperately attempted to negotiate a final status agreement, but his further unbelievable concessions, going far beyond those made at Camp David, were also refused by Arafat. Reeling from constant rebuff and mounting antagonism on the home front, Barak announced in December 2000 that he was resigning as prime minister. He called for a new election for prime minister in 60 days.[24]

---

24. In the election held on February 6, 2001, Barak was defeated by Ariel Sharon by a margin of 25 percentage points, the largest majority ever recorded in an Israeli election.

Even though both Barak and President Clinton were "lame-duck" leaders,[25] they continued to negotiate with Arafat until the last moment of their political tenures. Clinton issued his recommendations — Arab control over East Jerusalem and the Temple Mount, dismantling of settlements, return to practically the 1967 borders, but no right of return to Israel proper of Arab refugees. Israel, through Barak and Ben-Ami, accepted them in principle. The outcry against the "peace camp" in Israel now reached fever pitch. Every day, there were fresh killings and the intifada showed no signs of abatement, despite the planned concessions. The neighborhood of Gilo in southern Jerusalem came under regular fire from the adjoining Arab village of Beit Jallah. Hezbollah kidnapped three Israeli soldiers from the area of the new Lebanese border, as well as an Israeli businessman in Switzerland. Organized groups of Lebanese nationals arrived every day at the border to throw stones at Israeli soldiers and farmers on the other side of the border. Israel was in the worst predicament that it had been in since the Six Day War. Even many of the "peace process" supporters of the Left realized that Oslo had, in fact, been a trap, and that it would take enormous effort, patience and good fortune for Israel to extricate itself from it. Yet hard core leftist ideologues in Israel and the United States persisted in insisting that the "peace process" had to continue with Arafat, no matter what the consequences.

One of the most worrisome fallouts of the "intifada Al-Aksa" was the complete, open identification of Israeli Arabs with the Palestinians. The first days of rioting saw large disturbances in the Arab villages and cities of Israel. Jewish cars were stoned on the roads by Israeli Arabs and many of the roads were closed by Arab roadblocks. When police responded to the disturbances with force, a firestorm of Arab protest and anger was provoked. The Arab members of Knesset openly encouraged the intifada, calling it just and necessary. The Israeli Arabs soon abandoned open calls to violence, but the scars were deep and lasting.[26]

Bitter anti-Israel statements by Egyptian Foreign Minister Amr Moussa, the refusal of Jordan to replace its absent ambassador to Israel and the constant threats of war from Iraq, Iran and Syria combined to restore the siege mentality that had prevailed in Israel for most of its earlier decades. The end of the decade and the century brought grief and sadness to both Jews and Arabs living in the Land of Israel.

---

25. The American presidential election of November 2000 resulted in the victory of George W. Bush over Al Gore.

26. In the election for prime minister in February 2001, the overwhelming majority of Israeli Arabs, following instructions from the Palestinian Authority, refused to vote.

Steps Toward the Future

During the early part of the year 2000, Pope John Paul II visited Israel. Unlike his predecessor, Paul VI, who visited Israel in the early 1960's and was very cold to the Jewish state generally and its officials particularly, John Paul II was a warm visitor. He made positive speeches, visited Yad Vashem and the Western Wall and conducted himself as a friend to Israel. John Paul II apologized for the Catholic Church's past anti-Semitism and pledged that he would turn over a new leaf in Christian-Jewish relations. The diplomatic recognition of the State of Israel by the Vatican during this decade was in itself a noteworthy development, and marked a departure in the Church's long-held anti-Israel bias in world and diplomatic circles. The bitter events of the twentieth century undoubtedly contributed to the Church's reassessment of its policies and attitudes towards the Jewish people.

Pope John Paul II visits Israel's Chief Rabbis Yisrael Meir Lau and Eliyahu Bakshi Doron in Jerusalem

The 1990's marked a changing of the guard in the leadership of Orthodox Jewry. Many of its rabbinic leaders, Chasidic masters, scholars, gifted administrators, dedicated public servants and great educators — all of whom rebuilt the Torah world after the Holocaust — passed away, leaving a younger generation who had not experienced prewar Europe to carry on in their stead. Thus new leadership perforce arose to help Torah life survive and flourish, but people of the high caliber of the previous generation were not easily replaceable. Orthodoxy faced many difficult issues within its own camp — increasing numbers of children who were at risk of leaving Judaism and joining decadent levels of society, issues related to women's rights, schism between Sephardim and Ashkenazim, the temptations of a new affluence in the Jewish world, the necessity for corrections and innovations in its school systems, and the ready access of secular culture through advances in technology and communications were only some of the problems facing Orthodox Jews worldwide. The Jewish people needed leaders of wisdom, compassion, pragmatism and vision for the forthcoming century. History indicates that such leaders would always be found and would help ensure the eternity of Israel.

A notable event in Jewish life took place in 2000 with the nomination of an Orthodox Jew, Senator Joseph I. Lieberman, as the Democratic Party's candidate for vice president of the United States. Even though Lieberman,

The study of a page of Talmud daily — the international "Daf Yomi" program — became increasingly popular in the 1990's. Above, a group of commuters study the Daf Yomi aboard the Long Island Railroad.

Daf Yomi culminates with a "Siyum HaShas," completion of the Talmud, every seven years. Above, the Tenth Siyum HaShas held in 1997 by Agudath Israel at Madison Square Garden in New York City, as well as the Nassau Coliseum and in numerous other cities worldwide. The revival of Torah study in America is apparent.

running with Al Gore as the presidential candidate, lost a very close and disputed election, his nomination itself was a monumental event for American and world Jewry. At the beginning of the twentieth century, it was accepted wisdom in the American Jewish community that the way to success and achievement in American life required being less noticeably Jewish — and

Ehud Barak meets with Senator Joseph I. Lieberman (left), American Vice Presidential candidate.

certainly by casting off observance of Torah ritual and *halachah*. It was therefore ironic and challenging for assimilated American Jews to note, a full century later, that the first Jew ever nominated for the second highest political office in American government observed the Sabbath, ate kosher, prayed regularly in an Orthodox synagogue, sent his daughter to an Orthodox day school and spoke openly and proudly of his faith. Lieberman gained respect in the Senate and in the country because of his moral positions and his personal faith. His candidacy was a testimony to how far Jews had come in America. It was just as importantly a testimony to the maturing of America's vision of equality, fairness and tolerance for all.

The most unpredictable and turbulent of Jewish centuries thus ended with great doubts, profound hopes and enormous physical and spiritual struggles. No one a scant hundred years before could have predicted what the world would look like at the end of the century. The story is too unbelievable to be true, but true it is. The noted historian, Paul Johnson, summed up the twentieth century quite well:

"Certainly by the last decade of the [twentieth] century, some lessons had plainly been learned. But it was not yet clear whether the underlying evils which had made possible its catastrophic failures and tragedies — the rise of moral relativism, the decline of personal responsibility, the repudiation of Judeo-Christian values, not least the arrogant belief that men and women could solve all the mysteries of the universe by their own unaided intellects — were in the process of being eradicated. On that would depend the chances of the twenty-first century becoming, by contrast, an age of hope for mankind."[27]

The "Jewish twentieth century" contained many lessons as well. All of the false gods of the Jewish world of the nineteenth century now lay smashed in the temples of modernity, progressivism, assimilation and social engineering. Even Zionism was under attack, in the very State of Israel itself. Hopefully, Israel would not have to relearn the painful lessons of the twentieth century ever again.

---

27. Paul Johnson, *Modern Times*, New York, 1992, p.784.

Epilogue

A S I STATED IN THE INTRODUCTION TO THIS BOOK, HISTORY DOES not move according to man-made calendars. A century is an arbitrary division of time that provides no clear cutoffs in the unfolding of events. The twentieth century, however, must be seen as the century that disproved the accepted norms and wisdom of the century that preceded it. After the events of the twentieth century, war would no longer be limited and heroic. The barbarism of human beings was fully exposed, yet the story of the Jewish people in that century is a light that illuminates the possibilities for a better world in the twenty-first century and beyond.

The siren call of the idealistic "'isms" that ravaged the Jewish world in the nineteenth century was stilled by the end of the twentieth century. Many nineteenth century Jews estranged from their tradition and faith would be surprised, even shocked, to find that their twentieth century descendants searched for ways to discover Judaism. Though at the start of the century it seemed that poverty and drudgery were the enemies of Jewish continuity, it was apparent as the century ended that affluence and leisure were no less detrimental to Jewish spiritual growth and survival. Many who opposed the ideas of Zionism and the return of the Jewish People to the Land of Israel from the Exile at the beginning of the twentieth century perhaps would now, upon reaction to twentieth century events, alter their opinion. Many who doubted that a halachically-observant, Torah lifestyle could survive the secular nature of Israeli leadership, as well as the pressures of American life and culture, would now look with awe upon the rebirth of tradition, Torah study and observant practice in Israel and the Diaspora. Even though assimilation was as virulent as ever in the Jewish world, the twentieth century proved that the tenacity of a hard core of Jews struggling to succeed in the preservation of Sinai among the Jewish People would always be present.

Though the problems that faced the State of Israel, and with it Jewish people everywhere, at the end of the twentieth century were enormous, the bald fact that the Jewish People had come through the twentieth century at all was comforting and reassuring. By the end of the century, more than five million Jews lived in the State of Israel, American Jewry had acquired power and affluence, and a cadre of loyal Jews undreamt of at the beginning of the century existed worldwide. The enemies of the Jews — as represented by Hitler and Stalin — had failed to destroy the Jewish People and its spirit. All of this stood as a testament to the God of Jewish history and the resilience and soul of Israel. There is no doubt that the events of the twentieth century reconfirmed the words of God's promise in the Torah: "For I shall never forsake you until I fulfill the commitments and goals that I have set before you." May we see the next stage of Jewish history reach these goals.

I wish to express my deep appreciation to my dear friends, Isi and Naomi Liebler of Jerusalem. They possess one of the largest libraries of English Judaica in the world and they allowed me to use their books and premises for some of the research for this work. Their graciousness, cooperation and hospitality made this part of the task of writing this book most pleasurable and rewarding.

Photo Credits

Agudath Israel of America, with thanks to Rabbi Moshe Kolodny:
5, 11, 13, 17 (Seattle and Denver), 89, 90 (Turkel collection), 100, 172, 185, 189 (aid for refugees), 190, 192, 217, 218, 219, 251, 252, 289, 291, 320, 395.

Corbis Images:
175, 181, 183.

Franklin Delano Roosevelt Library:
142, 145, 167, 176, 177, 178 (German surrender).

Israel Government Press Office:
20, 26, 31, 35, 62, 67, 105, 106, 131, 148, 151, 152, 194, 196, 197, 199, 201, 202, 203, 305, 207, 209, 211, 233, 234, 239, 253, 259, 269, 297, 301, 307, 315, 316, 338, 341, 344, 351, 356, 376, 379, 382, 394, 396.

John F. Kennedy Library, Boston, Mass.:
255.

Lyndon Baines Johnson Library:
256, 257.

Museum of the City of New York:
39, 40.

National Archives and Records Administration (NARA), Washington, D.C. and the Simon Wiesenthal Center (see below):
182, 189, 205 (memo, NARA).

Orthodox Union:
322.

Ronald Reagan Library:
330, 336.

Simon Wiesenthal Center Library and Archives, Los Angeles, Calif., with thanks to Fama Mor:
88, 138, 161, 191.

The Jerusalem Post:
153, 164, 263, 333, 337, 339, 366, 372, 377, 381, 389, 391.

United States Holocaust Museum, Washington, D.C.:
178.

Yad Vashem:
97, 133, 136, 139, 171.

Yeshiva University:
155.

YIVO Institute for Jewish Research, with thanks to Erica Blankstein:
9, 17 (Connecticut), 42, 43, 74, 77, 78, 154, 173, 186, 288, 358.

Zion Ozeri, photographer:
349, 350, 364, 367.

Thank you to Rabbi Yaakov Spivak, dean of the Ayshel Avraham Rabbinical Seminary, for the use of the yeshivah's research library.

Index

For ease of use, honorific titles have been omitted.